THE NEW ATLANTIC
CHALLENGE

It is necessary to set up a continuing dialogue between Europe and America, and the first task is to change the climate ... which exists today

JEAN MONNET

The New Atlantic Challenge

Edited by
RICHARD MAYNE

A HALSTED PRESS BOOK

JOHN WILEY & SONS
New York

Published in the U.S.A.
by Halsted Press, a Division of
John Wiley & Sons, Inc., New York

© *1975 British Atlantic Committee*

'A Halsted Press book.'
Papers and comments presented at a Europe/America
conference held in Amsterdam, 26-28 Mar. 1973.
1. America—Foreign relations—Europe. 2. Europe—
Foreign relations—America. I. Mayne, Richard, J., ed.
JX1395.N4 1975   327'.09171'3   74-20105
ISBN 0-470-58035-6

JX 1395
N 4

Printed in Great Britain

Preface

OUR WORLD IS IN CRISIS, and men's minds are paralysed by a sense of drift. The democracies know they must pull together: but they increasingly lack a sense of common purpose. European unity, Atlantic partnership, the cohesion of the West – to many people such phrases have a faded air today. Europe is uniting, certainly; but progress is fitful and scarred. The partnership across the Atlantic once championed by President Kennedy is called in question by the diversion of American attention elsewhere, both abroad and at home, as well as by squabbles with Europe. The cohesion of the West seems more precarious and, to some, less obviously necessary in the age of *détente* and *Ostpolitik*. And even were once familiar concepts still unblemished, they would still be overshadowed by new preoccupations – with Japan and China, with oil and inflation, with the whole great debate about world resources, human purposes, and the structure of society that today seems so much more vivid and urgent than the slogans of ten or twenty years ago. We need to take our bearings in this new country of the mind.

In doing so, we face the inevitable question of whether older landmarks are still valid. Does it still make sense to speak of "Atlantic" problems? Are America and Europe destined to follow divergent courses? Can room be found in a new world system for Japan today and perhaps Brazil tomorrow? Is *détente* real, or is it partly illusion? What new models of world order is it sensible to set ourselves? Should we even aspire to order – or should we resign ourselves to competitive multipolarity, reproducing on a world scale the hazardous muddle of 18th-century Europe? Can we avoid a new 1929? With "interdependence" forced upon us by technology, can we even afford any choice?

These are some of the questions that loom between the lines of euphoric communiqués and speeches on both sides of the Atlantic. Bretton Woods is not the only system that has visibly disintegrated in recent years. The new Atlantic challenge is to rethink our more facile assumptions, to see what links us and where we differ, to test again the validity of Kennedy-era slogans, to rebuild more complicated models of what we can reasonably want.

5

To do so will take time and long discussion; and the present symposium of views from both sides of the Atlantic is a contribution to that debate. Its origin was the Europe/America Conference held in Amsterdam on 26-28 March, 1973, attended by some three hundred citizens of Belgium, Canada, Denmark, France, Germany, Ireland, Italy, Luxembourg, the Netherlands, Norway, the United Kingdom and the United States. These were labour leaders, members of Parliament, former prime ministers, businessmen, bankers, economists, defence experts, private citizens, journalists, commentators, and even a few civil servants heavily disguised. Like most such gatherings, it was wordy, untidy, and argumentative. It had its due share of rhetoric and platitudes, but also a core of hard analysis and common sense. To that end the organising committee commissioned papers and studies by fifteen international authorities on the subjects most relevant to the continuing debate.

These studies form the nucleus of the present book; but I have supplemented them with some of the very pertinent comments made by other participants. In editing the text for the press, partly from transcripts of the discussion, I have taken the liberty of cutting and rephrasing where necessary for the sake of clarity and concision. But I have made no attempt to iron out disagreements or to reach a false, purely verbal synthesis of conflicting views and emphases. This is a debate, not a monolithic thesis; and I believe that attentive readers will find what I have found in reading through the many thousand words of thoughtful and searching comment: that some of the most original insights are contained, not in polished, often-recited phrases, but in the confusion of ideas struggling for expression, sometimes with a sting of impatience in the tail.

My task as part-planner of the conference and as editor of the present book has been made easier by a host of friends and colleagues on both sides of the Atlantic. They will know whom I mean, and to whom I am offering thanks. But a special word of appreciation must go to Joseph Godson and Alan Lee Williams of the British Atlantic Committee, without whose energy and enterprise the whole project would never have begun. I should like also to express my gratitude to the Commission of the European Communities, to whose service I returned after editing this book, for granting permission to publish it. Such permission, of course, in no way implies responsibility for or agreement with any of the views expressed.

Contents

7

Contributors

RAYMOND ARON — Occupies Chair of Sociology of Modern Civilisation, Collège de France; also columnist for *Figaro*

GEORGE BALL — Former U.S. Under-Secretary of State

FRANK BARNETT — President, National Strategy Information Centre, New York

PRINCE BERNHARD OF THE NETHERLANDS

HARVEY BROOKS — Dean of Engineering and Applied Physics, Harvard University; President, American Academy of Arts and Sciences; Chairman, Board of Trustees of the German Marshall Fund of the United States

NEVILLE BROWN — University of Birmingham

ZBIGNIEW BRZEZINSKI — Director, Trilateral Commission, while on leave as Herbert Lehman Professor of Government and Director of the Research Institute on Communist Affairs at Columbia University

SIR BERNARD BURROWS — Director-General, Federal Trust, London

GUIDO COLONNA DI PALIANO — Chairman, La Rinascente, Rome

RICHARD N. COOPER — Yale University

9

PETER C. DOBELL

Director, Parliamentary Centre for Foreign Affairs and Foreign Trade, Ottawa; adviser to Commons Committee on External Affairs and National Defence and to Senate Committee on Foreign Affairs in the Canadian Parliament

SIR DEREK EZRA

Chairman, National Coal Board, London

ANDRÉ FONTAINE

Editor-in-Chief, *Le Monde*, Paris

HENRY H. FOWLER

Secretary of the U.S. Treasury 1965–68; Partner at Goldman, Sachs & Co., New York

ISAIAH FRANK

William L. Clayton Professor of International Economics, Johns Hopkins University, Washington DC; formerly Deputy Assistant Secretary of State for Economic Affairs and Executive Director of President's Commission on International Trade and Investment Policy

WILLIAM S. GAUD

IBRD, Washington DC

WALTER HALLSTEIN

Former President, EEC Commission; past President, International European Movement

PIERRE HASSNER

Senior Research Associate, Centre d'Etude des Relations Internationales, Paris; Professor of Politics, Johns Hopkins University, Bologna

JOHAN HOLST

Director, Norwegian Institute of International Affairs

JEAN HOUSSAY

General (Ret'd); Secretary General, French Atlantic Association; former French representative on the NATO Standing Group

ROY JENKINS	Home Secretary, United Kingdom
LANE KIRKLAND	Secretary Treasurer, AFL-CIO, Washington DC
MAX KOHNSTAMM	Rector, European University Institute; Director, European Community Institute for University Studies, Brussels
JENS OTTO KRAG	Chief Representative, EEC, Worthington; Former Prime Minister, Denmark
WALTER J. LEVY	Petroleum adviser to industry and governments, New York
RODERICK MACFARQUHAR	M.P., Fellow of Royal Institute of International Affairs, London
LAWRENCE MCQUADE	President and Chief Executive Officer, Procon Inc., Illinois; Assistant Secretary of the United States Department of Commerce, 1967–69
SICCO L. MANSHOLT	Former President, EC Commission
S. W. B. MENAUL	Director, Royal United Services Institute, London
DAVID PACKARD	Chairman of the Board, Hewlett-Packard Company, California
GIUSEPPE PETRILLI	Chairman, Institut per la Ricostruzione Industriale, Italy
ROBERT PFALTZGRAFF	Associate Professor of International Politics, Fletcher School of Law and Diplomacy, Tufts University; Director, Foreign Policy Research Institute, Philadelphia
JOHN PINDER	Director, Political and Economic Planning, London

RONALD S. RITCHIE	Chairman, Atlantic Council of Canada; Governor, Atlantic Institute for International Affairs, Paris; Senior Vice-President and Director, Imperial Oil Ltd, Toronto
MARY T. W. ROBINSON	Reid Professor of Law, Trinity College, Dublin; Irish Member of Vedel Committee on powers of European Parliament
NELSON D. ROCKEFELLER	Governor, New York State
EUGENE V. ROSTOW	Professor, Yale University
JEAN ROYER	International Chamber of Commerce, Paris
A. E. SAFARIAN	University of Toronto
CLAUDIO SEGRÉ	Former Director, EEC Commission; former Partner, Lazard Frères & Cie, Paris; President, Compagnie Européenne de Placements, Paris
ARTHUR J. R. SMITH	President of Conference Board, Canada
THEO SOMMER	Editor-in-Chief, *Die Zeit*, Hamburg
PIERRE URI	Atlantic Institute, Paris
CYRUS R. VANCE	Lawyer and former government official, having served in the U.S. Departments of Defense and State during the 1960s
ALBERT WOHLSTETTER	Professor, University of Chicago; Consultant to State Department and to Arms Control and Disarmament Agency

List of Abbreviations and Acronyms

ABM   Anti-ballistic missile
ADELA   Association of major industrials in Latin America
AFL-CIO   American Federation of Labor—Congress of
          Industrial Organizations
ASW   Anti Submarine Warfare
BIS   Bank for International Settlements
CAP   Common Agricultural Policy
CERN   Conseil Européen pour la Recherche Nucléaire
Comecon   Council for Mutual Economic Assistance
CSCE   Conference on Security and Co-operation in Europe
EC   European Communities
EEC   European Economic Community
EURATOM   European Atomic Energy Community
FAO   Food and Agricultural Organisation (of the United
       Nations)
FBS   Forward-based System
GARP   Global Atmospheric Research Programme
GATT   General Agreement on Tariffs and Trade
GDR   German Democratic Republic
GNP   Gross National Product
GSP   Generalized System of Preferences
IAEA   International Atomic Energy Authority
IBP   International Biological Programme
ICBM   Intercontinental Ballistic Missile
IDA   International Development Association
IDOE   International Decade of Ocean Exploration
IMF   International Monetary Fund
IISS   International Institute for Strategic Studies
JOIDES   U.S. consortium for deep sea exploration
LDC   Less developed countries
LMFBR   Liquid Metal Fast Breeder Reactor
MAD   Mutual Assured Destruction
MBFR   Mutual and Balanced Force Reductions
MIT   Massachusetts Institute of Technology
MNC   Multinational Corporation

13

MPT   Multilateral Preparatory Talks
NAL   National Accelerator Laboratory
NATO   North Atlantic Treaty Organisation
NPG   Nuclear Planning Group
OAPEC   Organisation of Arab Petroleum Exporting Countries
OECD   Organisation for Economic Co-operation and Development
OEEC   Organisation for European Economic Co-operation
OPEC   Organisation of Petroleum Exporting Countries
PICA   Association of major industrials in Asia
SAC   Strategic Air Command
SALT   Strategic Arms Limitation Talks
SDR   Special Drawing Rights
SLBM   Submarine-launched Ballistic Missile
UNCTAD   United Nations Conference on Trade and Development
VLA   Very low frequency radio astronomy system
WTO   Warsaw Treaty Organisation

PART ONE

Introductory

Chapter I

The Problem Stated

GEORGE BALL

I AM SOMEWHAT DISTURBED at some of the trends which
I perceive in the evolution of Europe's political and economic
thought and action, but I am equally disturbed at certain trends
that are now visible in my own country, so if these words are
cautionary words they represent a very deep feeling on my part.
Since there is an inevitable interreaction between what is said and
done on each side of the Atlantic, there is a danger it seems to
me that we may by indifference or by carelessness, or simply by
pique and frustration, create a climate in which these dangerous
trends will be encouraged and intensified.

In Europe and America we on each side of the Atlantic, have
been through intense and rewarding years together. We have
much to gain by preserving and building on the habits and
systems of co-operation, and working together that we have
developed ever since the war. Until the last three or four years,
most of us tended, I think foolishly, to take it for granted that
these habits and systems had been permanently established, that
the design for effective co-operation we had worked out would
provide an enduring mechanism which we could improve and
perfect, and that in this way we could develop to a much higher
point the areas of common effort and expand our common
interests.

Today I am not so sure. The most fundamental assumptions
that have supported our post-war co-operation are now in doubt
because of several complex developments that may be worth
briefly considering here.

For more than two decades, Europe has been able to concentrate largely on its own internal affairs because it could rest
its security primarily on the United States guarantee and on the
precarious balance of terror which had resulted from the nuclear
stand-off between Moscow and Washington. At the same time,
with the progressive shedding of its colonial positions, Europe
has been relieved of its most direct world responsibilities. The

17

fruit of this concentration, this ability to look very hard and long at its own affairs, has been the conception and development of the European Economic Community and particularly the creation within the framework of that community of a great mass market. The direct and indirect benefits that have flowed from the European Common Market have, I am confident, been the most important single factor in launching and sustaining an unprecedented era of economic growth. As a result, Europe has developed a new sense of resilience and an increasing conviction that, except perhaps in matters of security, it is now able to stand on its own two feet, and this is good. In fact, even concerns about security have lost much of their urgency as a result of all the new talk about *détente* between East and West.

One might have hoped that by this time Europe's new sense of well-being and self-confidence would have encouraged it to move towards the assumption of a larger role, a role more nearly commensurate with its resources, or in other words with the role that the individual countries of Europe played in pre-war days. But I see very little evidence of such an intention. Instead, it seems to me that Europeans are, if anything, becoming even more preoccupied with their own affairs and less concerned than ever about the problems and dangers of the rest of the world. Although the idea may be painful to many, Europeans have in my view become isolationists so that even conceding a unity that is more metaphysical and metaphorical than real, Europe today exerts little more than a regional influence. At the same time, in the realm of North Atlantic relations, Europeans do not look towards the United States with anything approaching the same recognition of common interests that prevailed some years ago. To be sure, even the most vocally anti-American of my European friends still hope that my country will continue to maintain its troop deployments on European soil, but there is a growing resentment of Americans in Europe.

Yet if Europe is eyeing the United States with a jaundiced eye, the American attitude towards Europe has also deteriorated. For this, a number of factors are to blame. Most important is the painful, frustrating, and profitless ordeal in Vietnam, an experience that has done incalculable harm, not merely to America's prestige but to its internal coherence, its belief in its own national mission and as a result to the spaciousness of its foreign policy. These effects have intensified the unfortunate coincidence of two other developments which, each in its own way, have tended to undermine self-confidence, to put America on the defensive, and to generate an anxious and somewhat surly mood.

The first is the dislocation in our national life created by our belated efforts to rectify a very old injustice. G. K. Chesterton once remarked that progress is the maker of problems, and in the case of America's treatment of its black citizens, that is certainly proved to be true. Together with the distressing state of our cities and the new focus on the dangers to our environment, problems which Europe is only beginning to experience, there is much fashionable talk of what I believe to be a false dilemma — whether America can any longer afford to devote vast resources to the maintenance of a world role or must concentrate all of its resources on the unfinished business on its home front.

The second disturbing development has been the succession of financial crises triggered by America's persistent inability to move towards equilibrium in its balance of external accounts. Because the United States' internal market spreads over the length and breadth of a continent, foreign trade has not in modern times played as significant a role in our national life as in the case of smaller nations. As a result, the concept of a balance of payments on international accounts has never had much reality to the American people. For a country which emerged from the Second World War with huge financial reserves and a disturbingly large annual surplus in its accounts with the rest of the world, the idea that the United States would ever show persistent deficits in its balance of payments and recently deficits in its merchandised trading accounts, has been a very hard one to accept or explain. Americans have always thought of such deficits, if they have thought of them at all, as chronic diseases of weak nations, and they find it difficult to reconcile a burgeoning internal economy with a deepening concern over our inability to balance our international books. Apparent contradictions of this kind, the paradox of visible strength and inexplicable weakness, defy public understanding since they lie outside normal logic and experience. We have had a number of instances of this, including for example the situation right after the war when we emerged as the strongest nation with the only atomic weapon in the world and suddenly found ourselves placed with the Soviet Union similarly armed, and for the first time in our national history we were vulnerable on our home soil. Then, the result was the McCarthy period. Today, we suffer from a simple paradox of simultaneous strength and weakness. The result has been an almost inevitable tendency to frustration and the kind of suspicion that inspires the search for a scapegoat – a reaction stemming from the assumption that because these problems seem to have no rational base, they could have arisen only through the malignancy or at least the unfairness of third persons, which in this context means America's principal trading partners. Unhealthy as may be the effect of these suspicions on internal politics, they would have made only a minimal impact on trans-Atlantic relations had Western Europeans achieved anything like the progress towards full economic integration and political unity that was optimistically predicted in the days of innocence before the famous thunderbolt was hurled from the Elysée just ten years ago.

Until then, a structure had seemed to be taking shape through which Western Europe could organise its powers and then equip itself to play a major and constructive role in world politics. That structure, as it appeared to many Americans in the early days of the Kennedy administration, foreshadowed a Europe moving towards political unity and thus ultimately achieving the ability to speak with a single voice and to act as a single political force. Because of our common heritage of ideas and institutions, and because of our common attitude towards the pre-eminence of the individual and his rights to life and liberty, we Americans took it for granted, as we quite properly should have, that a united Europe and a resolute America could work shoulder to shoulder in the pursuit of their common objective of a peaceful and secure world. Although I know it is now fashionable in some European quarters to regard the concept of an Atlantic partnership with considerable cynicism, as though it were merely a rhetorical device through which America hoped to influence, if not dominate, European policy, this was never in the minds of any American Government with which I was associated. On the contrary, we were all too sadly aware that the United States had no monopoly of wisdom, and we felt confident that a strong independent Europe would not only collaborate effectively in common enterprises but might also help deter us from some unwise moves – and we have made a few. At the end of the day we foresaw the bright prospect that with the common strength that such a partnership could bring, the West could work towards a gradual reduction of tensions and the improvement of relations with the East from a solid position of strength.

It seemed to many of us at that time, and it still seems to me, that this conception was fundamentally sound. No one has proposed anything nearly so attractive to replace it. But unfortunately, though Europe has made notable progress in building a mass market that has benefited not only Europeans but my own country as well, progress towards political unity has been lamentably slow, lamentably meagre.

Were the United States today in a buoyant and optimistic mood, we might accept the disappointing lack of progress without losing our sanguine view of the future; but given our current attitude of uneasiness and general disenchantment, what Europe does or fails to do is viewed with a more than usually critical eye. It is not surprising, therefore, that doubts are increasingly being expressed at high levels of government as to whether the European Community will ever be more than a trading block, basically antipathetic to United States interests. Because our commercial policy is now largely in the hands of the technicians, it is no longer regarded as bad form to speculate that America may have made a major error in encouraging the creation of the Community during the 1960s, or even to suggest that we should shape our policies so as to try to weaken rather than strengthen the fabric of European unity.

Irresponsible chatter of this kind is often attributed to the recrudescence of America's traditional isolationism; but such a diagnosis, it seems to me, is far from the mark. In my view what we are witnessing is not isolationism in anything like its classical form, but the creeping emergence of an American variant of Gaullism. One can see this manifested in the procedural aspects of our political life, in the subordination of the legislative branch to the assertive executive, in the increasing use of theatre, spectacle, summitry and surprise in our international affairs, and in the effort to bend the deliberations of international organisations to serve special national ends. But procedure is only the surface evidence of a significant shift in the direction of American foreign policy of which we should all take careful note: a shift away from an alliance policy, towards the kind of unilateralism so brilliantly practised by General de Gaulle, but this time supported by the weight and resources of a superpower. The direct discussions that former President Nixon conducted at various times with the leaders of China and the Soviet Union were expressions of this. There is other evidence that America's emerging new diplomacy puts a high premium on flexibility of manoeuvre, without the hobbling need to consult alliance partners or I may say even the former Secretary of State. One may regard such flexibility as essential if America seriously sets out to play the role of balancing power among those key world power centres which President Nixon named in his now famous *Time* magazine interview: the United States, the Soviet Union, China, Western Europe, and Japan. Obviously, if such a concept should finally dominate American policy, the implications would be greatly disturbing for Europe because the logic of unilateralism prefers fragmentation to unity, since that would make the balancing role far easier to play.

In today's complex world, where economies and politics are tightly interrelated, the direction chosen by a great nation necessarily cuts across the entire spectrum of policy. Thus, if we are not all very careful, the American trend towards unilateralism and the equal and opposite reactions of Europe could greatly complicate the problems of re-building and modernising our common institutions for guiding economic, monetary, and even political policy. I am not suggesting that the new American Gaullism has been fully incorporated in the United States' policy today, but merely that there are strong pressures in that direction.

Whether or not those pressures prevail will depend in large part on Europe's reactions, for such views would enjoy little response in America if Europe had gone farther towards achieving the vision of political unity, the concept of a Europe able to act with a single will and speak with a single voice. In the absence of such unity, America finds it difficult and exasperating to try to conduct business with Europe. In most matters it must still deal with nine separate governments and even in commercial matters, where the Community purports to act as a collectivity, decisions are delayed and diluted since they emerge only after complex internal negotiations. The result of all this is that the American Government finds it far easier to go it alone with only minimum prior consultation or none at all. An increasing number of Americans both in and out of Government express their disenchantment by dismissing the Community as little more than the instrument for the commercial advantage of a group of self-centred European States that connive to create policies aimed against the longer range economic and commercial interests of the United States. Distorted though this picture is, there is just enough vocal anti-Americanism in Europe to give it a measure of credibility.

On the political front we should be aware of the fact that if American distrust of Europe continues to increase, the United States Government will almost certainly be forced to withdraw American troop deployments from Western Europe. This could well start a chain-reaction leading to a diminished NATO contribution on the part of other Western Powers.

It is an old adage of the political philosophers that in order for a nation to achieve unity there must be a unifying state. Such a state might in theory be a member of a group such as Prussia with the *Zollverein* or alternatively it might be a common enemy which compelled unity by posing a common threat. In any event, the role of unifying state is important; and one might even contend that a certain amount of anti-Americanism would be healthy if it led Europe to unite in order to face the pressures of competition from America. But no matter how strident anti-American sentiments may become, let us not delude ourselves that the United States will play the constructive role of common enemy, for though it may annoy Europeans it will never terrify them. On the contrary, since the resentment of America is being generated far more from pique than from fear, the alienation of the United States from Europe or of Europe from the United States would be far more likely to lead Europe to fragment than to unify.

In this context one may regard West Germany as a special case, to the extent that it would then feel less anchored to the West: its diplomatic adventures with the East could create further strains in the European structure, perhaps leaving Britain and France to re-establish a pale imitation of the *entente cordiale*. Even more dangerous are the probable effects of Western disarray in encouraging the Soviet Union to try to extend its influence, for if the West ceases its efforts to achieve unity and the individual nation states respond to American unilateralism with a unilateralism of their own, a succession of European governments may be tempted to make their own special arrangements with Moscow in what would necessarily be a position of relative weakness.

If, as a result of the interaction of policies being followed on both sides of the Atlantic, America's presence and influence were largely withdrawn from Europe, but at the same time the European nation states resumed their ancient rivalry, the Soviet Union would automatically emerge as the politically dominant power over the whole European land-mass, simply by what has been well called the logic of numbers.

Mankind's capacity for wishful thinking is almost limitless and today there is a rapidly spreading belief that the cold war has ended and a permanent *détente* settled like a blanket over the whole of Europe. It is a pleasant thought, I hope it is true. But it is not yet a sufficiently solid hypothesis to support a major policy. All one can safely say is that the Soviet Union has altered its tactics; but whether it has abandoned its strategic objectives is still a matter of conjecture. Thus in the decade of the '70s the

Soviet threat appears not so much the possible use of naked power as a possible extension of its political influence reinforced by power. This, it seems to me, is the danger that exists for all of us in the weakening of transatlantic understanding particularly if that should lead to policies of unilateralism on both sides of the ocean. And today there are disturbing signs that such understanding may suffer erosion, not merely in respect of political relations or arising from political relations, but even more vividly from our economic, financial and commercial dealings.

In the atmosphere of crisis and confusion that surrounds world monetary policy, America has, but perhaps only for the moment, moved away from the negative posture of unilateralism, the new Gaullism that characterised its attitude and actions in 1972, and for the moment seems to be pursuing a more affirmative policy. If the problems themselves are far from solved, the possibility of a final breakdown and a return to the dog-eat-dog jungle conditions of the 1930s can still not be ruled out, particularly if the politicians remain disengaged and solutions are left solely in the hands of the technicians. Still, it is in commercial rather than monetary policy that the greatest dangers lurk, for on neither side of the Atlantic do I see a very high level of statesmanship. Protectionism is rising in America as a by-product of the anger and frustration that I referred to earlier; and at a time when the legislative and executive branches of the American Government are hardly on speaking terms, the danger that pressure groups may trigger irresponsible actions is uncomfortably high, while Europeans on their part seem more querulous than understanding. 1973 was to be the year of Europe so far as American policy is concerned, but I regard all that with extreme scepticism. The congressional hurdles that must be surmounted in America are very high and the process of equipping the President with adequate negotiating powers is not only time-consuming but by no means certain in outcome. At the same time it requires a large quantum of optimism to assume that the European Community will, within the next few months, have been able to solve the formidable problems of assimilating three new members while at the same time evolving a negotiating posture that reflects more than a tradesman's haggle. Meanwhile the broad directions of American policy remain not yet fully determined. To what extent shall we re-embrace the policy of alliances which has been primarily grounded on Atlantic relations? To what extent shall we be tempted by unilateralism – by the new American Gaullism? The issue is a complex one, affected by many different influences, of which perhaps the most important is the power struggle now taking place between Congress and the President. Yet in the final analysis a great deal will depend on what happens in Europe, on the actions and reactions of Europeans. Will they continue down their present narrowly focused course, paying scant attention to events that occur outside their immediate neighbourhood and rejecting responsibility for events that are taking place farther afield? In that case, America's own introspectiveness is likely to increase.

Some years ago I was asked at an international meeting, whether America would continue to stay interested in Europe. I replied that that depended on whether Europe continued to do anything very interesting. Well, it has done something interesting in this past year. The enlargement of the European Community has lifted all our hearts, for it has made it possible for Europe to regain something of the hope and idealism, the spacious vision, that led to the creation of the Community more than two decades ago. Yet a structural change of this kind is not enough unless it reveals its meanings in a new attitude, a broader comprehension, a firmer will, a real desire to get on.

We have much to do on both sides of the Atlantic, and what each of us does leaves its imprint on the policies of the other. As can be seen in the chapters that follow, the list of problems that can be effectively solved only through common action is a long and increasingly important one. Shall we have the will and wisdom to try to find common solutions, or will each of us become so absorbed in the narrow short-range advantage that the only durable solutions are lost to us for ever? That is the question we should each of us ponder in the weeks and months ahead.

Chapter II

The Need for Vision

WALTER HALLSTEIN

ONE CAN APPROACH THE PRESENT European–American relations and their future in two different, even opposite ways. The optimist may ask why we should discuss those relations at all. Many objectives of European post-war policy and American post-war policy towards Europe have been achieved. The ravaged economies of Europe have been restored to a point beyond the wildest dreams of the late '40s; an intra-European Western conflict is unthinkable, and Franco–German relations, the cause of two world wars, are close and exclude any basic conflict. The unity of Europe, for long years the central theme of American foreign policy, is progressing, so the optimist continues. It may be too slow, but it is progressing irrevocably. The entry of the United Kingdom, Denmark and the Irish Republic into the process of European integration is an event of tremendous importance and has removed long and frustrating obstacles to the further development of the Community. In the field of security, NATO has achieved its objective – to preserve freedom for Western Europe and a process of *détente* with our Eastern European neighbours and in particular with the Soviet Union is slowly emerging. The presence of substantial American forces in Europe is of vital importance, and this presence today is still a reality. The United States has basically terminated the conflict in South-East Asia which both for its domestic political life and for its external relations has for long years been a very heavy burden. And all this leads the optimist to ask "What is wrong with relations between Europe and the United States?"

The pessimist has a totally different story. He argues that since the beginning of the '60s, relations between the United States and Europe have steadily deteriorated. The dream of 1962, the Atlantic partnership between two equals, is in danger of turning into an Atlantic rivalry between the United States, on the one hand, and a group of loosely connected European countries on the other. This is most evident in the economic field. The days when

27

the United States gave absolute priority to its political objective of support for European integration over all possible economic disadvantages are definitely over. This is partly because of the relative weakening of the United States economy, partly because of the failure to obtain a unity in Europe going beyond the strictly economic minimum. The result is not partnership but rivalry in the vital fields of monetary and trade matters. And as to security, the pessimist continues, it is simply unhistorical to suppose that an American military commitment of the present size could go on indefinitely, the more so because domestic problems in the U.S. are gaining priority over its foreign affairs. The same process exists in many European countries – which makes it highly improbable that an equal sharing of the defence burdens which could satisfy American desires, could be achieved. Gradual American withdrawal from Europe, together with rivalry in monetary and trade matters, so the pessimist continues, will expose the Western system to pressures from the East without the formidable barrier of the cohesive and consistent policy of the Atlantic countries. It will lead to the fragmentation of the old Atlantic system and escalate to a point where both security and economic relations with the Atlantic world will collapse. In other words the dream of the '50s and the beginning of the '60s has proved to be an illusion, and the nightmare of fragmentation is nearer than ever, nearer than we ever could have imagined.

It is a platitude – although platitudes quite often happen to be true – that the truth probably lies somewhere between these extreme points of view. Unfortunately I cannot align myself with the optimist's approach, but fortunately I do not share the pessimist's gloom. It is undoubtedly true that what may be called the simple days of American–European relations are over. In the late '40s, in the '50s, and the beginning of the '60s, there were of course problems between the two sides of the ocean, but they were marginal in relation to the basic element of the relationship. The U.S. was the undisputed leader of the Western system. It exerted its leadership most in the economic, political and military fields, as a matter of utmost priority, and in a cohesive conceptual framework. It guided the economic order of the free world: its leadership was based on its economic strength and its monetary reserves, both far greater than those of any of its trading partners. It supported European unification, without any reservation or hesitation. Its immense military capability shielded Western Europe against any possibility of military or political pressure from our adversaries. Now we are living in a different period. I should like to make it clear here that for me there is no question of blaming one side or the other for what I, with great concern, see as a deterioration of our relationship. If there is a question of blame, then I think a sharing of the blame is more obvious than a sharing of the burden.

Let me just mention a few very broad general tendencies which have led to the predicament in which we find ourselves today. First, the growing prosperity and sense of common European identity are transforming European attitudes towards the U.S. Even before its enlargement, the European Community was already a major economic power, the world's largest trading entity, with influence in international and economic affairs second, if not equal, to that of the United States. But the gross disparity and the extreme one-way dependence characteristic of transatlantic economic relationships in the post-war period, have been replaced by more equal economic capabilities and a more moderate economic interdependence. Second, although economically and technologically not debarred from acquiring an independent defence capability, the West European countries are unwilling to divert from higher priority non-military domestic roles the resources needed to achieve that objective. Their resulting dependence on the United States nuclear guarantee generates two reactions. The first is anxiety regarding their safety, since they have doubts about the reliability of the United States commitment and about the assurance that the U.S. would not reach a *détente* with the Soviet Union over their heads. The second is the desire to have a role in NATO policy-making commensurate with their growing economic power and with the importance of the interest they have at stake. Most West Europeans are aware of the fact that only if their economic integration is matched by political and military unification, would they be likely to achieve a sufficient defence capability and end their total dependence on the U.S. And yet they are unwilling to merge sovereignty in the integrated political and economic institutions necessary for this desired role in world politics as an *interlocuteur valable* of the United States. So long as these and other dilemmas are unresolved the attitude of most West Europeans will continue to be more or less ambivalent. Fearful that the withdrawal of American conventional forces will make the United States nuclear guarantee no longer credible, they are at the same time increasingly resentful of their dependence on the United States, and many of them refuse to consider what a real sharing of the burden means. There is also a third point. Compared with the post-war period the United States in world politics is now bound to be more selective in the finding of central interests; it is bound to be more insistent on limiting costs, both absolutely and relative to those borne by prosperous allies, and less intent on trying to have the determining voice in situations in which it becomes involved. Finally, it is less willing to forgo possible direct and immediate benefits for the sake of foreign nations or long-term gains. Moreover, the economic and monetary problems and conflicts in U.S. relations with Western Europe will influence the United States' willingness and ability to participate in mutual defence agreements and arrangements to a far greater extent than during the post-war period.

In other words, while in Europe there is a tendency to deal with monetary and trade problems separately from security arrangements, in the United States there is a desire to link economic and political/military relationships. These rather recent phenomena are only examples of a situation which is fluid and in which most problems are not really solved between the two sides of the ocean.

And this leads to a rather delicate phase in our relations – delicate in the sense that on the solution of the main existing problems depends the question whether we will live in a cohesive Western system or in a fragmented world of competing Atlantic countries and a beggar-my-neighbour atmosphere. I am convinced that what is now required of political leadership in the United States and Europe is vision and courage and willingness to act in harmony with the over-arching political and social challenges of our times. Narrow interests must not be allowed to hack away at great Atlantic purposes. Prompt and constructive measures are essential not only in the interests of the Atlantic area but also for the peace of the world. No real problem can be solved without the closest possible co-operation between the two sides of the ocean and, in many fields, together with Japan. As an example of the last I would like to mention the energy problem, on which Mr Walter Levy has written such a brilliant and convincing chapter.

Let me conclude by emphasising the need for policy-makers and their advisers to have a broader and more open-minded conceptual approach to all these questions, much more so than was the case in recent years. In doing so I do hope that their efforts will be based on the probable realities of a changing future rather than on nostalgia for the hopes and fears of periods that are now past.

Chapter III

The Atlantic Nucleus

PRINCE BERNHARD OF THE NETHERLANDS

THE UNITY of the North Atlantic area and its peoples is a fact of life and we are concerned about this unity. When we have unity things go well, and when there has not been unity in the past things have gone badly. Much and great things have united us in a permanent fashion, and our unity has very deep roots: a common, Western culture, a Western civilisation which is visible in Christianity and in Humanism – in our common ethic. North America speaks one of the great languages of Western Europe. Geography links America with Europe by the Atlantic and the Mediterranean; in terms of strategic and political constraints this means that we do have a common destiny which is also an economic one. Europe and America have a common political philosophy, common constitutional concepts because the Atlantic people for centuries have given a common soul and a common purpose to their society, modern democracy. The American War of Independence and the great French Revolution led to a great impetus for freedom which has changed a society of the privileged into a society of common law, into a society in which equality of life and equality of opportunity is part and parcel of our very philosophy. We have a system of government, of society, and a constitutional concept which is common, and we have a sharing of power. Power has to be subordinate to law; laws have to be voted unanimously or by a majority of the citizens voting freely. Each government is called upon to vacate the seat of power at regular intervals and this emancipation of society has an enormous significance which cannot be exactly gauged, which goes far beyond the purely economic facts of life.

In the 19th century in the Atlantic area we had a system of economics and a system of society which belonged to the highest peaks of civilisation. In the 20th century, it resisted the onslaught of two world wars. This philosophy of freedom was also able to resist the negation of the purposes of human society which are symbolised by Communism. The Havana Charter and the Charter of the United Nations symbolised a new beginning. It was not so much a renaissance as a new affirmation. The anatomical substance of the 19th century, on the basis of the sovereign nation-state, underwent a process of change and indeed of erosion in terms of the developments which emerged from the war and the concept of supra-nationalism, indeed of supra-continentalism, emerged. Instead of sovereignty and dependence we now have inter-dependence. This is something new: and it is something which has to be organised. Its organisation followed three ways.

First of all, we had intercontinental regionalism. The OEEC was the first organisation which led to European co-operation and the most successful and the most political expression of this particular fact of interdependence. It was given whole-hearted support by the United States of America. This was a new, original conception of democratic organisation, of co-operation between economies and societies. The concept of federalism, which the United States symbolises, gives political and economic functions to common institutions, which have of course an impact primarily in economic and social terms, but which lead to unity and this unity is something which is bound to emerge on that very basis. This has been the general evolution that we have seen in the Western-world.

The second path which has been followed has been particularly significant – monetary co-operation in the form of the International Monetary Fund set up at Bretton Woods and also, in trade and commercial matters, the setting-up of the General Agreement on Tariffs and Trade, GATT. Here we had the opportunity to overcome the difficulties and problems which had been the legacy of two world wars: bilateralism, protectionism, preferential treatment, unilateral advantages for the powerful states. Equality of treatment was the postulate, except that for the United States there were exceptions when it came for example, to planning certain discriminatory agreements and certain rules concerning the balance of payments. These were conducted in the interest of others in order to attenuate the effects of the dollar crisis. We also had other ways and means of co-operation in terms of the United Nations and this particularly as far as the developing countries are concerned.

Perhaps the most significant event, however, has been the expansive world evolutionary tendency of Communism, and the defensive alliance of NATO set up in order to provide security for the democratic countries of the Atlantic area. The European

Economic Community has been a spectacular example of a supra-national solution on a continental scale, but we should not forget that NATO itself is not only a military alliance but an alliance which has an active interest in all the problems of the free world, and which therefore can have an enormous positive influence provided that this influence is accepted.

In the same quarter of a century during which these successes on various levels and various scales have been achieved, there have been profound changes in the conditions in which history has been progressing. There has been a greater *détente* as far as the dangers of war are concerned, we have had the Vietnam imbroglio in the Far East and many other very heated disputations and arguments in various corners of the world, and we have had also problems in various countries. As far as the construction of a common system is concerned, there has been much vehement discussion and disputation, so that in commercial arrangements within the GATT framework there have been continental part-ners willing to protect their own interests, particularly in agricultural policies. But in terms of growth and the political unity of the EEC there has been a growing bilateral development which has led to great sensitivity and feeling of rivalry between the Atlantic partners, and the end result of all this has been a great tendency towards protectionism, and in respect of standards and of principles has been retrogressive. Within GATT we have had many exceptions as far as preferential customs regulations are concerned to the advantage of the EEC, and this has been of course interpreted widely in various quarters as being a tendency towards greater autonomy and less interdependence. As far as the developing countries are concerned this has led to a very general definition of a commercial policy which is a policy of conflict: certainly if we look at the Japanese example this is the case. The authors of GATT looked at the problem primarily in terms of the balance of payments of the Western countries and in particular the problem of the American balance of pay-ments, and we may well ask ourselves to what extent discrimin-ation is possible and indeed permissible in the world of trade if we look at all the various aspects of the GATT charter, which are founded on monetary bases.

So reform and renovation is necessary, and this leads to the necessary solution of material problems. The present organis-ations appear to fulfil their purpose in terms of present conditions, but this does lead to problems. We are concerned here with the relationship between the European Community and the United

States of America and Canada; however the field of application of supra-national and supra-continental organisations goes beyond this limited framework. We have to look at what we can do and what we can recommend for the Europe/America relationship; but what will the effects be for other countries and peoples? We have to have complete clarity on a world-wide level and we have to assume responsibility for problems at world level. It may well be that the nucleus of a Europe/America relationship could be a solution, an embryonic solution, to a more general system which would have a greater political impact as time goes by.

These various topics, I think, all boil down to a great inter-relationship of problems which we have to consider *in extenso*. Independently from these questions, there is of course the problem not only of organisation but of the dangers of disorganisation. A permanent Atlantic dialogue should be organised to ensure proper mutual co-operation on the basis of the communication to avoid surprises which are often nasty surprises. As far as the contents of such reforms is concerned any forecast at this stage would be premature, but we are convinced of the value of the Atlantic relationship; the Atlantic partnership is indivisible. This partnership has not only ensured freedom and peace in the past. To us Europeans over many years this has led to an enormously powerful political support in progress towards greater unity, and it is fitting that we should address a word of thanks to those who have helped us in this way. In order to reinforce this partnership, we should endeavour to establish close co-operation without dreaming of an Atlantic Community on the basis of the European Community because we do not want to be Utopian, we want to be realistic. As President of the European Movement, I can say that we ought to give greater importance to the concept of European unity, because this can lead to the solution of Atlantic problems. The European Community is a foundation stone of the Atlantic building. It is not an alternative to an Atlantic relationship: it is an integral part of it. We are not thinking in terms of satisfying purely egoistic interests on both sides of the Atlantic; we are not looking at it in terms of European national-ism which is something which should be differentiated from what we are trying to achieve. We have no national or supra-national aims which are identifiable with the old nationalism of the past. We are conscious of our European heritage and our European vocation and this is a vocation which gives us duties and responsi-bilities towards the world. We have to have wide-reaching co-operation which goes beyond trade and which goes beyond the organisation of industry and market economies; we have to look at it in a much wider framework of political co-operation which will lead from regionalism to universalism via the nucleus of the Atlantic area. And we should not forget that in so doing, in defending our interests and defending the interests of the Western world and the developing world, we should also think about our security. We should not endeavour to dramatise our problems. Far from it, we should always keep a due sense of proportion and as far as Atlantic unity is concerned we have here large, broad problems which are far more important than the small, detailed problems which we may have to face in our everyday lives. Whatever the name we may like to apply to this partnership, it is a question of trust and confidence. It was, after all, an American statesman who said that the United States is a European power.

Chapter IV

Allies and Rivals

RAYMOND ARON

TWENTY-SIX YEARS HAVE ELAPSED since The Hague Conference presided over by Winston Churchill, which gave rise to the Council of Europe, I belong to those who participated in that Conference, older but not necessarily wiser by 26 years. The comparison between the hopes of yesterday and our experiences today would lead us to meditate on the irony of history; on the failures which sanction success; the unforeseen success which compensates for failure. Those who on the morrow of the war were following America's policy hoped for the recovery of Western Europe, and these were satisfied. They imagined a political future for the nations who were due to have a common future together; and these were disappointed An extraordinary economic success; a political community which has failed – this is the unanimous judgment which can be expressed on the outcome of the undertaking the initial point of which, at least symbolically, was situated in The Hague.

I wonder as to the feelings of the generations which will come after my own: those who are now 40 and are taking on important functions, and those who are 20 years of age. Do they share our concern, do they share our hopes? What does the North Atlantic Alliance mean for them? To my mind, this alliance created a framework within which the European nations were able to recover, to live together and build up their prosperity. This political and economic success, whether they are aware of it or not, young Europeans live this as a daily reality. They cross the frontiers without realising it and Europe is their mother country as much as their own. The United States appears as a rival and a protector, a rival in the economic field, and a protector from the military standpoint.

In fact, the two enterprises of European unity and Atlantic co-operation have never been without some difficulties and without misunderstandings on both sides. At a time when we considered this as the two sides of a bridge which would cover the

Atlantic, it was considered that non-proliferation was an important element. The United States preserved nuclear energy and nuclear arms for themselves, for supreme recourse, calling for a restriction of the Europeans to conventional weapons – a sharing of responsibility on defence, which from Washington's standpoint is rational and may indeed be so, but which implies a double drawback. Politically it imposes on the United States the permanent responsibility for European security; and on the other hand, psychologically, it weakens and disguises the will of the Europeans to take on the responsibility for their own defence. And thus we have reached one of the topics of the transatlantic debate which I will sum up as follows: the dis-proportion between economic prosperity and the political/ military powerlessness of Western Europe. This, with six countries and even more so with nine, represents one of the big powers in the world, certainly one of the largest in the trade field – while it is a dwarf in the inter-state system, or it doesn't even exist as an actor in that system. Can it discuss on an equal footing with regard to customs duties? Yes, but it is threatened by the blackmail of the withdrawal of American troops.

Young Europeans might object, and wonder why we should fear the withdrawal of American troops. Why should we imagine this as a possibility, that Soviet tyrants should come to the West? I think I should withdraw these objections and eliminate any misunderstanding. If most of us believe in the advisability of a military presence of the United States in Europe, it is not because we consider that the Soviet Union may have aggressive intentions in the classical or military sense of the term: nor is it that we would prefer confrontation rather than *détente* and a Cold War rather than peaceful co-existence. If these expressions have a precise meaning, which is something I very much doubt, it is rather that the Soviet Union today is one of the two main military powers in the world, and this power is ruled according to methods which are substantially and essentially different from the Western methods. Why therefore should it not be tempted to extend its influence, if not its rule, if it does not come up against any form of resistance on the part of a power comparable to its own? This very simple reason, based on historical experience, can explain the fact that we are so very much attached to the Atlantic Alliance. Besides the technical or military or diplomatic controversy we should never lose sight of the paradoxical nature of our present situation. Warsaw and Budapest are part of historical Europe, of European culture, as are London, Paris and Rome. This is maybe

not the case for New York or San Francisco; but notwithstanding
its geographical proximity and its past, Eastern Europe belongs
neither to the same economic market nor to the same political
unity as Western Europe. In the full sense of the term there is
no Atlantic Community: nevertheless it is true today that our
political and economic universe comprises the United States
and Western Europe up to the borderline traced at the time of
the last war, and notwithstanding the *détente* it does not include
Prague, Budapest or Warsaw. So there is a temporary contradiction between geographical proximity and political differences;
and the political differences contradict the spiritual and cultural
affinity between the two parts of Europe. There will remain an
element of confrontation even during a period of *détente* so long
as certain constitutional freedoms of our civilisation have not
been re-established so close, and so far away from us.

This economic and political environment to which we belong,
we Americans and Europeans, is it threatened by a disruption?

The planetary economy, to speak in Marxist terms, is divided
into two world markets: the political allies are at the same time
and by definition, rivals. There is no longer any true economic
conflict if not between allies or quasi-allies. Is it necessary to add
that there is no economic solidarity if not between allies? The
French, for their own prosperity, need German prosperity, and
similarly the French and Germans together need American
prosperity. In details, however, there is competition, rivalry and
opposition of interests between one and the others.

When I was young, we jokingly spoke of that tradesman who
was losing when selling individual objects but was able to make
a profit on the whole of his business. We may say that the Atlantic
community today offers an example of this apparent contradiction; an overall solidarity at macro-economic level which
hides on various occasions differences of interests. Are these
oppositions likely to compromise overall solidarity? Have we
returned to the savage devaluations or the shifts of manpower
from one country to another for monetary reasons? I don't think
so. For the time being we are in a situation without precedent
and for the first time that currency which in a certain manner
has been a trans-national currency, has ceased to inspire trust.
American investments abroad during the previous period were
financed, partially at least, not by a surplus in the U.S. balance
of payments, but by deficits, by credits from the foreign central
banks. The monetary crisis obviously questions this system: the

rates of exchange, the GATT rules, tariff barriers, non-tariff barriers, and so on.

European and American economies are so much integrated into each other that it is difficult to see what the consequence of a dissociation might be. On the other hand, so long as the dollar plays the role it does, the people responsible in Washington will have to measure both the privileges and the servitudes of a trans-national currency. A devaluation of 15% of the dollar in 1960 would probably have avoided part of the difficulties in which we find ourselves today; but nevertheless how can we fail to fear that having invested pride and prestige in maintaining the rate of exchange between the dollar and gold and the dollar and the other currencies, the Americans will turn to another extreme doctrine and rely on the variations of rate, and the variations of rate alone, in order to re-establish balances between commercial exchanges and payments? The terrible effects of devaluation, in view of the structure of American exports, could continue for a period which is difficult to foresee. I also think we have other reasons for concern. According to the statements of official personalities, the purpose would not only be that of establishing an American payments balance, but the surplus necessary in order to finance investments abroad. Why this objective? Because the assets of outside investments have for a long time enabled Great Britain, for example, to accept a commercial deficit. The problem is the cost of a foreign policy, and particularly the cost of American troops stationed in Europe. I think that it would be better once and for all to have a dialogue which is very frank and I think it is right for the Europeans, if they wish for the presence of American troops in Europe, to pay the price in currency. I think it is regrettable for maintaining a friendship to mix up, or to give the feeling that one is mixing up, protection and trade, the stationing of troops, and the reimbursement of the Value Added Tax.

I am not among those who criticise President Nixon's diplomacy: I admired it as a very realistic approach and a very realistic exercise of power. It enabled the United States to withdraw from Vietnam in conditions which were very close to the conditions the President had established at the beginning of his mandate. He had the courage to transform the old relationship with China. The Crusade period is over. Americans have all too often preached this wisdom and modesty, and they should not blame it today. Nevertheless, I wish to be excused if I raise the question aloud which so many others murmur. According to a formula of Monte-

squieu's, even in wisdom there can be excess. We should not mix
up the opponent with the devil, but we should not confuse him
with a friend. Perhaps one should consider one's opponent of today
as if tomorrow he might be a friend, but in any case one should not
consider him as a friend before he has actually become so. With
Nixon's visit to Peking, with the devaluation of the dollar, and
with the end of the Vietnam war, a period of history came
to an end – the period, which started in 1947 with the Truman
doctrine, or in 1949 with the North Atlantic Treaty. Now
President Ford has entered the White House and a new order
of our Atlantic relations should develop. We should meet
together, Americans and Europeans, not in order to recall the past,
but rather in order to negotiate new commitments; to become
aware of economic problems which we can analyse but maybe
not solve without the participation of others, at least the Japanese.
And finally and especially in order to overcome, thanks to the
awareness of what is essential, the daily contradictions which are
the life and the weakness of democracies.

Chapter V

Europe Must Act

ROY JENKINS

ONE OF THE GREAT CONCEITS of politics is to believe that we are always standing at a crossroads of history. Therefore a certain healthy scepticism is reasonable. Nevertheless I think there is a certain truth in the cliché at the moment. A truth in the sense that the 25 years through which we have until recently lived will I believe form a recognisable unity, and that any period within that 25 years will be more like any other than are the decades which are about to come.

What are the main differences between this period through which we have lived and the period we are now entering?

The first is the qualitative change in the position of the United States. Over the past quarter of a century the West, to its great benefit, has lived under the clear captaincy of America; and none of us in Europe should underestimate what this has meant and the benefits that we have derived from it, particularly in the early days.

When last spring I was honoured by the city of Aachen and looked back at the list of those who over 25 years or more had received the Charlemagne Prize, they were all Europeans – with one exception. The one exception was General George Marshall. And yet, for a prize commemorating the unity and the recovery of Europe, one could almost argue that Secretary Marshall's name was the most appropriate of the lot, because it was undoubtedly behind the American shield and through American generosity that Europe picked itself up off the floor of its despair in 1946 and '47.

But I do not think that we should deceive ourselves that the old pre-eminence is or can or should be there today. I do not myself think that the change has been primarily due to the United States' involvement in Vietnam. That has exacerbated and accelerated the change, but I believe that it would have taken place, no doubt more slowly, for more fundamental reasons in any event.

The nature of the change is perhaps most vividly illustrated

43

in the monetary field. The Bretton Woods system, inaugurated in 1954, served the world remarkably well. It facilitated the greatest expansion of international trade and national incomes which have ever been seen in any comparable period. There is no reason at all to be critical of its achievement; but there is no reason either to pretend that in its original form at least it is not now dead. We do not at the present time have an international monetary system; we have a chicken running around with its head cut off, but that is a process which I believe cannot continue indefinitely.

The essence of Bretton Woods was clearly the paramountcy of the dollar; it was the currency, not merely quantitatively more powerful but qualitatively different from every other. Without a doubt it was a deliberately asymmetrical system. For other governments there was the obligation to maintain the value of their currency within narrow margins against the dollar; to use their own reserves for the purpose; to exercise their drawing rights with the International Monetary Fund if reserves ran short; and to devalue only if there was a fundamental disequilibrium. The United States was free of these particular obligations. She has not been responsible in the past for maintaining the parity of the dollar in the foreign exchange markets of the world. When it was weak, other countries have had to bear the brunt. She has not in the past used her own reserves for day-to-day dealing. She has never borrowed from the IMF despite her massive recent deficits. But of course from 1944 to 1971 she accepted a wider responsibility, and a heavier responsibility: that of being the only currency directly linked to gold; that of being willing to pay out the metal on demand (although this willingness became substantially modified after 1968); that of maintaining a reserve currency throughout nearly the whole world; that of being pivotal to the system; that of not being able to devalue; that of trying only occasionally to encourage other countries to revalue against her – during the period when the system worked fully up to 1968 the score was 59 devaluations and 2 revaluations.

This was not, as a matter of history, a role thrust upon a reluctant United States. Maynard Keynes had proposed an alternative and much more international system, with more or less equal obligations and privileges attached to all currencies. But in 1944 the United States chose otherwise, and in those circumstances, and those which prevailed for two decades thereafter, it was probably right, both for the United States and the world. Two decades of foresight, in personal or political affairs, is something which we can all on the whole be very pleased if we achieve.

But once the apparently impregnable American competitive position, and the massive trade surpluses which went with it, began to disappear, the writing was on the wall. The essence of a fully acceptable reserve asset is that it should be desirable and sought after. Those who have it should want to hold it and even get more. But once the spell of desirability has been broken, it is very difficult to recreate. Therefore the dollar standard, at least in its fully acceptable and theoretically consistent Bretton Woods form, has collapsed. We may have to struggle on for some time with it in an attenuated form, but the search for a new system should be urgent, perhaps more urgent than it has been in the past two years.

There should, I think, ideally be five qualifications to be fulfilled in looking for such a new system.

First, the new reserve asset must be fully international. I do not believe that it can be based now upon a single country or even upon a single block of countries. At one stage it appeared to me that two reserve currencies, one based upon the United States, and the other upon the European economies – including of course the United Kingdom – as a whole would make sense. I think we have now passed that stage. Even the strength of the United States economy could not sustain the burden of carrying the dollar as a world reserve currency. I do not believe that any of the rest of us would be able to do it or should attempt to do it apart from on a fully international basis.

The second qualification is that the new asset should lubricate world trade as successfully as the dollar has done. And of course the dollar did it very successfully. In a sense we all benefited very greatly from the American deficit for a very substantial period. But eventually it illustrated the truth by which even the best things can become too good, and after lubricating us success-fully for a very long time, the dollar eventually drowned us in oil and that became a little more than the world system could sustain.

Thirdly, we must pay adequate regard in creating the new system to the vastly important role that the dollar, as by far the most important single currency in the world, will still have to play in the world trading system. The old asymmetry has gone, but the new system must be created in a form as acceptable to the United States as possible. Otherwise there will be great dangers in Europe's using our new monetary strength in a way that could damage our fundamental defence and political and indeed trading interests.

Fourthly, the world reserve currency should be responsive to the needs of the third world. We should not let ourselves think that our problems are the only ones which exist in the world, and that if we solve them, nothing else greatly matters. The challenge of the grindingly poor parts of the world will I think become an increasingly major one as the remaining decades of this century wear on. And such prosperity and security as we are able to create will inevitably be endangered if we live surrounded by the rest of a world which is poor, embittered and therefore menacing. And if, as I think one must reluctantly accept to be the case, the United States believes that she has done a lot in the past, and is not greatly attracted by doing a great deal in the third world in the near future, then this becomes a part of the burden which it is the more urgent for Europe, with its new strength, to pick up.

Fifthly, the new world monetary system should be able, so far as is possible, to deal with the position, which if the energy forecasts bear even the remotest relationship to the truth, will place in the hands of a few low-consumption and high oil-producing countries, reserves, masses of currency manoeuvre, on a scale which will make what we have seen on the Euro-dollar market recently look puny.

I would regard these five issues as important in the urgent search for replacing what is now the crippled world currency system, though working tolerably in the short run, by a new one.

The second major change which has occurred is that the European Community has in a sense come of age, both because of enlargement and because of the search for new directions and political purpose. By enlargement, and by an increasing concentration upon political aims within the Community, a major and sustained objective of United States policy for several decades past has thus been achieved – though at the time of its achievement there is some disenchantment in the United States with the Community. So far the Community has been economic rather than political; and this indeed has been an essential foundation of its progress so far. It was the genius of Jean Monnet that he turned in the economic direction at precisely the right moment, when the attempt at military advance had been frustrated in 1954. But now the emphasis should in my view be much more political than economic; now the stress should be upon the term European Community rather than Common Market.

But as the Community becomes, as I hope and think it may,

more political, there will be some additional strains for the United States, the greater because they come at a time of some trading and competitive difficulty. A relationship of greater equality, desired by both sides, will nonetheless in a way be a more difficult one to move towards and sustain.

A moderate change in the balance of any human relationship is always psychologically difficult to achieve. It is easy either to stay as you have been, or to over-react. But the first is in present circumstances impossible, and the second is highly undesirable.

And the difficulties of carrying through this change in the balance of the relationship between the two sides of the Atlantic Ocean is not made easier by the fact that fear, which was the great cement of the late '40s and the '50s, and even to some extent the '60s, is now lower than ever before. It is extremely difficult, in these circumstances, to arouse enthusiasm for defence, yet a moderate but sufficient Western effort is clearly an essential basis of the degree of *détente* which has been achieved. It is highly desirable that a moderate, yet sufficient effort should continue on an Atlantic basis, rather than on a purely European basis. No doubt there will inevitably and desirably be some shift in the balance, particularly of conventional contributions, but so far as the nuclear deterrent is concerned, it seems to me that this must remain overwhelmingly American for a substantial time to come, if only because to attempt to make it otherwise would for some years ahead at any rate be deeply divisive within the European Community itself.

Therefore what we now hope for, and expect with confidence on the basis of what has been done in the past by the United States, is in my view one of the most difficult things in the world: to step down. To remain *primus inter pares*, but no longer a sun with planets, and yet at the same time to remain outward-looking, responsible, committed.

What about the future of the Community, of the European side of the Alliance? What has the Community achieved so far? Broadly and crudely, I would say two successes. First, it has buried the Franco–German quarrel, which so bedevilled Europe for generations, and buried it so completely that we now almost forget that it could be otherwise. And yet, could this have been done earlier, 25 or 50 or 70 years earlier, what a difference it would have made to the lives of everybody in Europe, and indeed in America and much of the rest of the world! Secondly, it has made Europe, or helped to make Europe, rich. The Common Market has brought a high degree of common material prosperity, beyond the bounds of our hopes, over a 20-year period since the movement towards unity effectively began.

But the new Europe has not yet matched her wealth by her inspiration or her influence in the world. In part, this is because we have all of us, inside and outside the old Community of the Six, grown used to being a somewhat ill-coordinated group of junior partners within the Western Alliance. We want that Alliance to continue, we want it to have a new balance, but to achieve this we have to get a political coherence which Europe has so far lacked and get it quickly. We have to recognise that the United States cannot perform quite her old role, but that she is still crucially necessary to all of us. We have to recognise, too, that she may well not perform that new role unless we show understanding and response to her new problems. And we have to remember, finally, that even if we can solve all the problems of the North Atlantic area we are still less than a quarter of the world, and that the future of none of us can be secure if we live too cosily in the rich West and shut our eyes to what is happening outside.

Chapter VI

Time for Change

GIUSEPPE PETRILLI

THERE IS INDEED NO NEED TO INSIST once again on the complementary nature of the countries looking out on to the North Atlantic, both regarding their monetary relations and their security. On the morrow of the Second World War this complementary nature was expressed by the considerable contribution given by the Marshall Plan to the reconstruction of Europe which had suffered so greatly from an economic standpoint. And the Atlantic Alliance strengthened it from an economic as well as from a political and military standpoint. No one could forget the important role played by the Americans in setting up the common European institutions, over and beyond the linguistic, historical and cultural links which have always related so closely the peoples of Europe and North America. Atlantic co-operation was the obvious expression of the common destiny linking our countries as a direct result of the international balance which derived from the war. Very obviously, this complementary nature has not disappeared since then. It remains a fundamental element, and all policy on both sides should necessarily take this into account.

This should not lead us, however, to underestimate the importance of the evolution which has taken place over the past decades on the two sides of the ocean, and which has so deeply modified the general framework of our relations.

The European partners of the United States, which had been so seriously affected by the consequences of a fratricidal war, recovered rapidly, and have enjoyed economic development without any precedent, benefiting from a series of favourable circumstances, among which one can never fail to underline the progress accomplished in integrating the economies within the framework of the European Community. Through the implementation of a common agricultural policy and a Common Market, the European Community has known a new evolution thanks to its geographical enlargement, and by the development of its economic and monetary unity.

At the same time, within the framework of a vast world balance, a new situation was developing progressively. Alongside the United States and the Soviet Union, considered so far as the two pivots of this balance, other poles of attraction were developing from various standpoints. China and Japan in the Far East, and at least potentially the countries of our own Community. President Nixon himself recognised this new situation when he spoke of the birth of a new multi-polar balance. It was perfectly natural that a development of this kind, so encouraged from the start by American aid, should lead to tensions over long periods of time which were not perceived initially. An instance of this is the concern expressed by the United States on several occasions, which has increased considerably since the participation of the British, about the discriminatory consequences of our union, not only from an agricultural standpoint, but also with regard to trade in industrial products. This concern, which the recent difficulties of the international monetary system have only enhanced, is justified to a considerable extent by the legitimate desire to avoid a protectionist deterioration of the conditions of world trade.

On their side, the Europeans are especially concerned with the phase of structural instability which monetary relations are going through at present, and would hope to see their American partners adopt measures which would not only bring pressure to bear on their commercial balance but might also favour capital currency. While not isolationist, a new attitude is developing in certain parts of public opinion across the Atlantic: many fear that the new American strategy, turning on an overall negotiation with the Soviet Union and China, might in the long run weaken, though indirectly, the solidarity of the United States with regard to its traditional allies. These reciprocal attitudes are all the more worrying in that we have entered a phase of important negotiations, both from a monetary and from a commercial standpoint. From a political point of view the Conference on Security and Co-operation in Europe will soon force us to reconsider the whole of these problems, and within this context it is important to recognise that increased participation by the Europeans in their own defence has been underlined very often on the American side. It is time to debate these matters in a realistic spirit and in an atmosphere of goodwill. So far as I am concerned, I think that our work will be all the more useful if it does not remain at the level of rhetorical statements. We should on the contrary rather try to focus attention on the difficult problems of our transatlantic relations. There is no other alternative than a common crisis which would affect us all.

Chapter VII

Towards a New Relationship

NELSON D. ROCKEFELLER

THROUGHOUT THEIR HISTORIES, the great nations of the European movement have made enormous contributions to the creation of that philosophical base upon which rest our political institutions, our ethical and cultural values, our belief in human dignity; and we in Canada and the United States have grown from the seeds of European culture that were scattered abroad and have flowered in a new land. Our common purpose is to discuss the ways in which we can strengthen the unity of this family, and thereby add strength to each other: to explore ways in which we can continue to play our all-important collective role in achieving world stability. I have been involved for more than 30 years in the foreign policy and domestic affairs of the United States, and I realise the difficulties that have existed and do exist in our relationship. But I am also aware of our extraordinary accomplishments, examples of what can be achieved through unity and common purpose. Since World War II, based on this unity, the nations of the Atlantic Community have preserved their individual freedom and independence, safeguarded by their unparalleled military strength. Europe has achieved phenomenal economic and industrial growth, and now we have all entered a period of *détente*. However, in today's new atmosphere some tend to forget the fact that all this has been achieved in the face of a consistent effort by the Communist world to undermine our unity and individual sovereign integrity.

Now we are facing a new era, a new era of international relations; new conditions prevail, new policies exist. These new conditions are rooted not only in global and economic and political changes, but in the very success of the Atlantic Alliance itself. These changes have created new challenges for the West, both opportunities and dangers for the achievement of real international stability. We must guard against the serious danger that prosperity and *détente* can lull us into a false sense of security. We must face realistically the fact that we have achieved

53

these gains only because we had the will and the purpose to place our unity and our collective strength ahead of our individual selfish interests. In the face of these far more subtle dangers that exist today, we must more than ever have the will and the political courage to preserve the unity which is essential to ensure the survival of the Atlantic world.

Our survival is possible only if we adjust to the new conditions we face: economic, military and political. Western Europe has overcome incredibly complicated and difficult internal problems – political, social and economic – to achieve a phenomenal economic recovery and growth. As a result, the European Economic Community now has a gross national product of approximately 720 billion dollars, and is the second most powerful economic unit in the world. Western Europe, the United States and Japan are now the major determinants in the world's economy. This is the central fact of the completely new economic world. All of us now face new problems of competition and co-operation in trade and monetary matters. All of us now find ourselves increasingly dependent upon less developed nations for raw materials, particularly in the energy field. We have to deal with the implications of these new economic conditions.

We also have some hard realities to face in the security field. The most fundamental of these realities is that the United States has lost its overwhelming strategic superiority. Strategic parity now exists between the United States and the Soviet Union. This raises questions about the very nature of our security. The existence of strategic parity radically changes the deterrent effect of our nuclear weapons. This in turn requires re-examination by NATO and the European nations of the basis of their defences against Communist aggression.

Another new factor affecting our security is the increased domestic pressure upon the United States administration to reduce, unilaterally, the level of its force commitments to NATO. The latest discussion of this issue by the Democratic Party in the United States Senate endorsed almost unanimously a substantial unilateral cut-back of U.S. forces in Europe. This domestic U.S. pressure to reduce commitments springs from the combination of *détente* and the resulting trend towards isolationism, just as it does in Europe. However, in the United States there is an additional factor: the serious European balance-of-payments problem which has been only partially resolved within the framework of NATO. Thus the combination of the new strategic situation and our domestic pressures has created a new set of circumstances to which NATO must respond.

The final aspect of the new conditions relates to the changed political atmosphere. The major political changes have been the emergence of a period of *détente* in Europe and an expansion of relations with the Soviet Union and mainland China by both individual European nations and the United States. We should not forget that *détente* in Europe is based upon the solid diplomatic accomplishments of the West, rooted in the military unity and economic strength of the Atlantic world. It would be a mistake to assume that *détente* marked a profound alteration in Soviet policy, or that this period of lessened tension would survive a fragmentation of the Western Alliance. What *détente* does offer is an opportunity to create the stable environment in which democracies flourish. In so doing it raises the most profound challenge before the West – our ability to define a common political purpose and pursue it with will and determination.

Our goal remains immutable: it is to preserve our freedom, independence, and territorial integrity. The question is how can we, with the changed international developments, realise this aim?

First, we must recognise that in the light of the new realities our relationship must be readjusted. Our democracies must revitalise the dynamic nature of our partnership in order to shape common policies which reflect our overriding political interest. Unified action, particularly in East/West relations, is essential. No one could pretend to a diplomatic flexibility that exceeds our common base. However, we must recognise where our interests diverge and where a difference of perspective exists. We have got to have a political structure that makes this kind of co-operation possible, within Europe and between us.

In the economic field it is clear that the present monetary framework is collapsing, and the doctrine of free trade is being eroded by an increase in protectionism on both sides of the Atlantic. Obviously, the current structures are not capable of coping with these changing conditions, nor have they developed a consensus among us to meet our needs. Rather than commit ourselves to becoming enmeshed in the multitude of economic differences, we should re-examine the whole question of free trade. If we do not do this, if we do not reach an agreement, we are on the way to creating a jungle of economic blocks and special interests. What we need is an overall conceptual approach that can provide the order to avoid the emergence of such conditions. Of equal importance is the need to formulate common economic policies in relation to other areas of the world which seriously affect our future well-being. One example is the extent of Japan's phenomenal industrial growth and its ingeniously aggressive and expansionist trade policies. These present a totally new problem to us on both sides of the Atlantic, and we need to develop a common understanding and policy towards this phenomenon. Another example is the rapidly growing dependence of all industrial nations upon foreign sources to supply their energy needs. Already the United States imports 28% of its crude petroleum requirements; Western Europe imports 63% of its energy needs, and Japan over 90%. Given these circumstances and these trends, we must develop common policies which will ensure an orderly flow of oil at prices fair to both sides. Another important aspect of the energy problem is the currency problem which it creates for all of us. It is imperative that the consuming and producing countries work out a solution of these problems.

Perhaps even more serious than the economic problems is the need to readjust policies within NATO to the new realities in relation to our security. With strategic nuclear parity, greater reliance must be placed upon military forces within Europe, and our ability to co-ordinate and support them. We must also at last reach agreement on our strategic doctrine for the use of tactical nuclear weapons, and see in what way the British and French nuclear programmes can be made useful for the defence of Europe. In other words, strategic parity means that we must collectively develop a local defence of Europe which would include as many military options as possible. But we can only do this if NATO works out a common concept of security and if both sides of the Atlantic agree upon our defence requirements. In this connection, the present negotiations with the Soviet Union and the Warsaw Pact nations offer NATO an opportunity to clarify its defence needs. It must do this within the context of the mutual and balanced force reduction negotiations. Otherwise we face the dangerous possibility that the American Congress will force a unilateral cut-back by the United States. Only by a precise definition of NATO's security needs can the individual political leaders persuade their respective publics of the rationality of their NATO commitments. Europe, I repeat, must be aware of the political atmosphere in the United States. This atmosphere results primarily from the ill-defined requirements of NATO, both military and economic. But we cannot ignore the U.S. balance-of-payments problem because it exerts heavy domestic political pressure on the American administration. A more equitable arrangement must be worked out which would solve the economic difficulty without injuring security. Our success in adjusting NATO's policies to these current realities will affect our ability to conduct the diplomacy of *détente*.

The ultimate basis of *détente* is the West's military strength, but it must derive its sense of direction from our mutuality of political interest. The West must have the political will and effective institutions both to develop and present a united front in areas of common concern and negotiate with determination. A proliferation of East-West negotiations and the conduct of independent foreign policies with the U.S.S.R. in areas of mutual involvement can only increase the vulnerability of the West, and in the final analysis destroy the Atlantic community.

The need to re-align our relationships within a changed world is clear. It is not an easy task. It is made particularly cumbersome by the lack of political structure within Europe. Atlantic relationships are currently conducted on several levels: bilateral, inter-NATO, and with the EEC. This has compartmentalised and fractioned the various aspects of our relations within the Atlantic world. It has prevented the development of an overall political concept. It is for this reason that we all welcome the decision by leaders of the EEC nations to transform the whole complex of their relations into a European Union by the end of the decade. Under the present circumstances, Western Europe lacks a central, democratically-elected government that can produce an outward-looking European policy. In contrast, the present situation requires a complex system of compromises of individual national interests. This process makes it impossible for Europe to play a strong, purposeful political role as a global power. Political unity within Europe would not only increase its political strength but would eliminate the cumbersome framework within which Atlantic relations are now conducted. European union would facilitate the development of firm political policies. In the final analysis such political unity would contribute to peace and international stability; for a unified Europe would be able to assume international responsibilities commensurate with its real power.

We live in a fluid period, more so probably than any other period in history. This very fluidity offers unprecedented opportunities; but paradoxically, it contains equally great pitfalls. It all depends on whether we shape events or are overwhelmed by events. Naturally, in these circumstances, an atmosphere of uncertainty exists. Therefore there is a temptation, particularly in democratic societies, to draw back and as a result to become increasingly nationalistic and even parochial. It is a way of avoiding reality, and historically it has had disastrous results. We of the Atlantic world cannot allow this to happen: we must recognise the change in the world and have the courage to organise ourselves so we can look outward and shape our own futures. We are on the threshold of the most challenging period in history. No other era has held greater possibilities for improving the quality of life for all mankind. The youth of the world looks to us to seize this opportunity. We cannot fail.

PART TWO

Economic Issues in an Interdependent World

Chapter VIII

International Economic Policy as a System

HENRY H. FOWLER

WORLD PEACE AND PROSPERITY and the common interests of all nations will be served by preserving and improving the multilateral, open, and expanding international economic order which has evolved in the last 25 years, largely as a result of the collaboration of the nations of the Atlantic area.

This is as true for the developing as well as the developed nations, for those with socialist or mixed economies as well as those more oriented to private enterprise. It is even more true for the peoples in all nations and parts of the planet who suffer from poverty, hunger, unemployment, underemployment and a lack of economic opportunity as well as those who live in relative affluence and security.

Even before the current crisis began on 15 August 1971, which laid bare the cracks and flaws in the existing structure, it was recognised by many that the methods of loose and more often than not *ad hoc* consultation through which international economic policy had been developed and executed were no longer adequate. There were prescient and eloquent calls for a more effective and integrated co-operative management of the international economic order.

But today that system is threatened with a tragic breakdown or, at least, a dangerous paralysis that makes it highly vulnerable if the foreign exchange and gold markets of recent months are any sign. Retreat, to the accompaniment of continued inflation or threatened recession, into autarky, beggar-thy-neighbour tactics, narrow nationalism, neo-isolationism or retrogressive regionalism seems as likely as advance into an improved and modernised system of international co-operation.

What is needed is an open community of nations which is dedicated to a systematic and orderly utilisation of international economic policy for the common good. This will involve a far

61

more broadened application than we have yet witnessed of the principle of a limited pooling of sovereignty in specific areas of economic decision-making that substantially affect the world economy.

The increasing interdependence of the nations and economies and peoples of Western Europe, North America, and Japan is an important basis for this economic order. Their shared values, similar patterns of political and economic organisation and conduct, and common economic objectives are sufficiently compatible to form the basis for a high degree of consultation and collaboration. Their institutionalisation of this co-operation in many private as well as governmental organisations in trade, monetary affairs, financing and capital movements, international investment and development, tourism and general economic policy, is the nucleus of a vast and progressive international economic system. Its promise for the remaining decades of this century is as great as the progress of the past.

This interdependence is the fruit of success. Vast improvements in communication and transportation make the world constantly smaller in every sense but the physical. The past success of the international trade and payments arrangements since World War II has vastly increased trade, capital movements, and the movements of people across national borders. International monetary and security markets now influence developments in national financial markets, tending to tie them together. Interdependence has also grown outside the areas of trade, financial flows and movements of people across boundaries. Businesses increasingly look beyond national boundaries. So-called multinational companies lead to a declining national orientation of economic behaviour, at least within the developed countries.

This economic interdependence circumscribes national freedom to pursue widely divergent economic policies without sensitivity to their impact on other countries. This impact becomes increasingly important. The technological progress that has made the spaceship possible has brought home the elemental truth that our planet is but a spaceship and we are all its passengers.

This fact and the concept on which it is founded bring a degree of global interdependence that surely gives rise to the necessity for international economic and financial co-operation in the future, far beyond what we have had in the past. But this promise of the future is not a mere dream, for it is founded on the reality of past accomplishments.

Already the momentum of these accomplishments requires

many continuing activities – a persistent improvement of an international monetary system, a continuing assault on non-tariff barriers, a multilateral de-escalation of restraints on international capital movements, an expanding scale and efficiency of use of multilateral assistance by the developed countries to the less developed countries, a proper balance between national interests and the multinational corporation that will give the latter an opportunity to play its important role in international economic development.

But other areas and opportunities for international financial and economic co-operation do not necessarily flow from past experience and do not have the advantage of momentum from the activities of the well-established international institutions that dot the international monetary landscape. To seize these opportunities requires imaginative leadership, original action, and new international economic policy as well as national decisions by sovereign political authorities. Some of these newer challenges and opportunities where international economic and financial co-operation can play a decisive role are as current as today's newspapers. For example:

– the protection of the environment;
– the mining and utilisation of the resources under the oceans;
– an effective adjustment of excessive population growth to available resources, and the planet's ability to provide an adequate minimum quality of life;
– the utilisation of space for communications, weather monitoring and other services to this planet;
– and the development and utilisation of various forms and resources of energy to serve men's needs.

In all these and many other areas science, technology, and progress have given to men and governments opportunities undreamed of at the end of World War II. But, as yet, the processes of government and statecraft have not yielded an equivalent capability.

We must recognise that the primary cause of this long-recognised inadequacy of present methods of formulating and executing appropriate international economic policy and the existing crisis is a structural deficiency. We do not have a system capable of translating mutually advantageous international economic policy into meaningful and timely reality.

SOME PRESSING TASKS FOR INTERNATIONAL
ECONOMIC POLICY

There is a first and fundamental step in assuring a more effective
and systematic use of international economic policy. It is the
urgent and timely transition away from the existing pattern of
disorderly drift into separate monetary and trading blocs and a
world of floating exchange rates, and towards a modernised but
truly international monetary system.

This system must not abandon but build upon the Bretton
Woods Agreement and the principles it embraces. The objective
should be to strengthen the International Monetary Fund by
expanding the range and force of international decision-making
on monetary affairs, and by undertaking the structural adjustments that are necessary to make the institution equal to these
new responsibilities.

The Amendments to the IMF Articles of Agreement should
provide for a suitable degree of flexibility in exchange rates and
a more effective balance-of-payments adjustment process. This
process should apply equally to surplus and to deficit countries.
There must be no lasting abdication of national responsibilities
to defend stable exchange-rates appropriately determined under
rules of common application and to ensure a proper degree of
official convertibility. The system must provide adequate reserves,
internationally acceptable and usable, and supplementary sources
of international credit to facilitate these stabilisation processes
while adjustment to equilibrium is achieved without damaging
internal economic acts or restrictions on trade and useful capital
movements.

These and other necessary measures call for upgrading the
International Monetary Fund to the status and function of a
World Central Bank, rather than allowing it to become an
obsolete monument to a noble past. They call for an intensi-
fication of international co-operation rather than forsaking it to
rely upon so-called market forces and inward-looking national
decision-making on matters that affect the people of other nations.

The effective consolidation of the monetary systems of all the
nations concerned is indispensable to the tasks that confront an
international economic policy that will be truly responsive to
the world's needs in the last decades of this fateful century.

While we can all rejoice at recent progress towards European
monetary unification, its ultimate achievement must not be
accepted as an alternative or substitute for a viable international
monetary system.

The special role of the dollar as a reserve currency is no longer a barrier to a truly multilaterally operated and internationally governed system based on internationally created reserve assets. There seems to be fairly general agreement that, in a new, viable, and symmetrical system, balance-of-payments settlements in the future should be through conversion of officially-created international reserve assets rather than the random accumulation of officially-held national currencies.

The United States has expressed its willingness, after a suitable transition period and upon achieving a "demonstrated capacity" in terms of its reserve and balance-of-payments position, "to undertake an obligation to convert official foreign dollar holdings into other reserve assets as a part of a satisfactory system". It seems clear that a prerequisite for the establishment of this system will be some funding, multilateral or bilateral, of existing official reserves of foreign currencies, be they dollars, pounds, or francs.

The current efforts of the Committee of Twenty of the International Monetary Fund should be supported and invigorated. Recent events highlight the urgent importance of an act of political will by the governments most involved, at the highest levels, if these negotiations are to achieve the end immediately and urgently required. That end is the development of a financial institution through which the principal industrial nations can together manage their reserves and harmonise their economic policies in a manner consistent with a constructive international economic policy.

A rather large area of potential agreement on these and other related questions was reflected in the observations of ministers of finance and governors of central banks at the annual meeting of the International Monetary Fund in September 1972 when the Committee of Twenty was established to conduct formal negotiations.

However, we must not blind ourselves to the possibility that national decision-making in the ensuing negotiations may fail to achieve multilaterally agreed decisions that strengthen the ties that bind us.

Alternatively, unplanned or unexpected events such as those recently witnessed on the world monetary scene may overtake the negotiations, causing them to be downplayed, deferred, strung out or ultimately abandoned, leading to the easy way out – a permanent acceptance of so-called market-determined floating rates. This course dispenses with meaningful international cooperation in either the adjustment process or the creation and management of reserves – except on a regional basis.

The consequences of failure in either of these scenarios might be to dismantle or greatly diminish the effectiveness of any truly international monetary system, to encourage protectionism and trade wars between blocs, to refasten more tightly controls on capital in the manner of the old pre-war exchange control systems of Europe, and to weaken or drastically alter the alliances that have served the cause of peace and prosperity since World War II.

The world simply cannot afford the risks implicit in another major failure of international economic and financial co-operation such as marked the 1930s. Every effort must be summoned to maintain the momentum that began in the wake of battle when a war-torn generation had learned a bitter lesson.

In the International Monetary Fund, GATT, the International Bank for Reconstruction and Development, and the Organisation for Economic Co-operation and Development, there have been developed principles, policies, and precedents which lay a foundation for dealing with many related tasks of the international economic policy of the future.

The stabilisation and revitalisation of the international monetary system is a condition to success in every other field of international economic policy, such as trade policy, appropriate relationships with and assistance to developing nations, and suitable arrangements with nations where state trading is the current rule.

The current negotiations of the Committee of Twenty to restore and update a functioning monetary system should, therefore, be both a proving-ground and a beginning for institutionalising and systematising a co-operative management of the international economy which has developed in Western Europe, North America and Japan in the last 25 years.

For example, it will not be enough, to satisfy contemporary views of wise international economic policy, to modernise the Bretton Woods system in the particulars already discussed. The negotiatory momentum which that process generates should carry over into related negotiations designed to remove restrictions and discrimination in the field of international trade and investment. There should be a systematic prevention of the use of controls on trade and long-term capital movements to maintain a chronically misvalued currency or to provide long-lasting protectionism for an economy that is not being subjected to an effective adjustment process.

The importance of making a beginning on detailed trade

negotiations under GATT is generally accepted. Their results can be of great benefit to the international economy, but the need for action in the trade field is not dictated by economic considerations alone. There is a serious danger that if conditions are not provided for a continued expansion of world trade and a lowering of both tariff and non-tariff barriers for the benefit of nations generally, we may all face trade conflicts and jeopardy to the progress already made, with possible damage to Atlantic relations and those with Japan.

These trade negotiations will have to break new ground internationally both as to substance and procedure. Because of the constitutional division of power between the Congress and the Executive in the case of the United States, the authorising legislation should provide the Executive with authority to act when the objective can be readily defined. It should provide negotiating authority, subject to Congressional review in other cases, particularly those dealing with non-tariff barriers enmeshed in domestic legislation. Dealing with these problems will inevitably be a long-term continuing process, calling for negotiation, consultation and harmonisation of policies on a continuing systematised scale.

The same is true of the unique problems of agriculture. Nonetheless it is essential that international trade in agricultural products be dealt with as an integral form of a world trade system, particularly as regards non-tariff barriers, which are of great significance here. The Kennedy Round of negotiations was able to accomplish very little in this area, which is of particular importance to the United States in view of the efficiency of our agriculture and its role in our export trade. Agreements should be sought which would result in a substantial expansion of agricultural trade, particularly in view of the greatly increased demand that seems potential in Asia and the U.S.S.R.

Another example of the need for pioneering efforts in systematising constructive international economic policy is the need to develop internationally-accepted rules of good national behaviour to ensure the liberalisation and freedom of international investment flows. The result of an ambivalent and passive attitude towards controls on long-term capital flows, both portfolio and direct, has been a maze of controls, many added in recent years to the pre-war hangovers of exchange control patterns, whenever a nation found itself with a balance-of-payments deficit. Sometimes these were maintained long after the deficit disappeared. The adjustment process should be directed towards encouraging international investment and open capital markets; controls on capital flows should not be allowed to become a means of maintaining a chronically undervalued currency or avoiding an effective adjustment process.

In addition to the removal of long-standing barriers to international investment flows for balance of payments purposes, where the linkage is so close that the Committee óf Twenty must deal with it directly, U.S. policy sees a need for supplementary measures. U.S. Secretary of the Treasury Schultz has urged that group to help launch serious efforts in other bodies to harmonise the practice of nations with respect to the taxation of international trade and investment, the granting of export credit, and the subsidisation of international investment.

The implications of these policy assertions for both direct and portfolio investment over national boundaries, as well as the world's capital markets, are tremendous, if this U.S. policy suggestion receives any encouraging response. A GATT for international investment becomes a probability.

A sharp distinction must be drawn between long-term capital movements in the nature of bona fide international investment, and certain short-term capital movements which have played a very disruptive role as private parties in control of liquid capital move it from one currency to another in anticipation of changes in currency values.

These massive movements of short-term funds, some as a result of currency crises, some actually producing a crisis, and all intensifying the crisis, make it not only desirable but necessary to institute some measure of multilaterally negotiated and administered control over these flows, particularly when they are disruptive and not consistent with the adjustment process and appropriate rate relationships.

Of course, good economic policy, a modernised international monetary system, and a working adjustment process are the major tools to minimise these disruptive flows. But there are bound to be occasions when abnormal and destabilising short-term flows will occur if there are no measures to control them. While there is probably no practical way to prevent all of them, there are various techniques which can be employed to moderate such movements of funds even in periods of great unrest. Perhaps the most fruitful approach is one that operates to repel inward flows when they are primarily responsive to speculation as to currency rate changes.

In any regulation of inward capital flight, three important

points should be stressed. First, there should be genuine multi-lateral agreement that these measures to control inward flows are desirable in general, that they are not used merely to prevent overdue parity changes, and that they will be employed in timely fashion.

Secondly, the particular set of measures employed in one country may have to be different from those employed in other countries, simply because the internal institutional characteristics may differ. Therefore, multilateral agreement on measures may have to be in principle rather than in particular.

Thirdly, each monetary authority must have at hand the tools required to do the job, which may in some cases require the passage of new legislation.

It must be recognised that there may be occasions, one hopes very rare, when all the measures noted would prove to be ineffective but when something short of a formal change in par value may be indicated. In such a situation, a temporary float could be employed usefully either by a country experiencing outward flight of by one experiencing inward flight, or by both.

From the foregoing it will be clear that a far greater degree of co-ordinated effort by the central banks of the countries concerned, acting under the authority of their respective governments, will be necessary to draw an appropriate line between the allowance of constructive flexibility in exchange-rates and the disruption of the international monetary system. A key part of this co-ordinated effort by central banks must include a better co-ordination of monetary policy, which is an essential factor in the attainment and maintenance of a stable international payments system, characterised by fixed par values and freedom of capital movements.

This co-ordination need not take priority over domestic economic policy; but in turn, domestic monetary policy should not ignore the international consequences.

Space does not permit more than a brief mention of several additional pressing tasks for international economic policy.

The list must include among others:

– multilateral programmes to improve economic conditions in the less developed countries through both private and public capital and entrepreneurship;
– multilateral programmes to promote the expansion of trade and commercial intercourse with the state-trading nations on fair and equitable terms;

- intergovernmental approaches to the treatment of the multi-national corporation in view of the fact that the multiplication of these economic ventures and linkages across borders is proceeding so fast that some systematic harmonisation of threatened disorders of separate and defensive national reactions is necessary to promote and preserve the constructive integrative co-operation in this type of enterprise, and protect the good of all and the best interests of the people served;
- intergovernmental approaches to the problem of assuring adequate and reliable energy resources at reasonable prices, as well as other basic raw materials which may come into short supply;
- intergovernmental approaches to the international economic aspects of the problem of environmental protection.

SHARPENING THE TOOLS FOR INTERNATIONAL ECONOMIC POLICY AS A SYSTEM

Let us now consider how the tools for international economic policy as a system can be sharpened if our institutions are to tackle more effectively the tasks outlined and many others that may emerge.

In addition to my own reflections, I shall draw upon a few thoughtful U.S. contemporary commentaries from both the academic world and public affairs.

Naturally, much of the discussion focuses on the machinery of the international monetary system. Even before the Special Drawing Rights amendment, the International Monetary Fund was performing one of the functions of a world central bank. "It was exercising an influence over the economic policies of its member nations, in part a complement to its lending to them and in part independently of its lending."[1]

For the principal industrialised countries, a similar function of influencing the parts to improve the well-being of the whole is being performed in the consultation processes of the Organisation for Economic Co-operation and Development (OECD). A Forum is provided for close and regular consultations among senior officials of treasuries, central banks and economic ministries about the economic and financial policies of the industrialised countries. There is a periodic examination of the policy objectives and operations of the member countries for compatibility with

[1] Randolph Burgess, James Huntley, *Europe and America – The Next Ten Years* (Atlantic Council 1970).

each other and with the welfare of the rest of the world.

As William McChesney Martin has observed in his wise and stimulating lecture in 1970 entitled *Toward a World Central Bank?*: "Such operation, by influencing countries to modify their policies so as to make them more consistent with the pursuit of the welfare of the entire community, begins to resemble *one of the functions of a world central bank.*"[2]

Another example of these processes is the consultation and co-operative arrangements associated with the regular meetings of the central bank governors affiliated with the Bank of International Settlements.

In dealing with economic activities with substantial international implications such as the balance-of-payments adjustment process. Professor Richard Cooper has pointed out that there are five broad types, or stages, of co-operative arrangements among the members of an interdependent economic community.[3]

The first involves periodic international discussion about problems of common interest, reviews of developments in each country, explanations of the actions that have been taken. But each nation basically fends for itself. That is the basic pattern of OECD operations under its current authority.

The second level of co-operation also involves periodic discussion of problems of common interest, but it goes beyond the first in requiring consultation on certain kinds of measures to be taken and in calling for international justification of policies involving restrictions of international transactions.

Thirdly, national economic policy-makers may develop sufficient confidence in the policy judgments of their counterparts in other members of, for example, the Atlantic community to make them willing to go to considerable lengths to support their decision.

Fourthly, where regions have quite close economic ties and considerable mutual sympathy for each others' objectives, and where factor mobility is reasonably high, greater reliance may be placed on factor mobility among the members of the community to correct imbalances in payments.

Finally, for regions which have very close economic ties, where capital and labour as well as commodities move freely and where there is a high degree of agreement on economic objectives, close

---

[2] William McChesney Martin, *Toward A World Central Bank?* (Per Jacobsson Foundation Lecture, September 1970).

[3] Richard Cooper, *The Economics of Interdependence: Economic Policy in the Atlantic Community* (Council On Foreign Relations, 1968) pp. 264-8; See also Zbigniew Brzezinski, *Between Two Ages* (Viking Press 1970).

co-ordination of domestic economic policies will serve to reduce one principal source of imbalance – divergence in these policies – and will guide the region as a whole to its global economic objectives.

The types of co-operation envisaged in the fourth and final stages above, may come to apply to the countries of the European Economic Community as the process of economic unification evolves, but are not currently relevant to the collective group of industrialised countries of North America, Japan, and Western Europe.

Hence, the real heart of the problem of reconstructing a viable international economic policy to deal effectively with the tasks referred to above is the extent to which these developed countries, operating as free democratic societies, will engage in the joint decision-making envisaged in the third stage and accept the control of national restraints on international transactions implicit in the second stage.

The most recent and dramatic development to date in the process of structuring a system for joint decision-making in international economic policy and evolving a world central bank is the international agreement to amend the Articles of Agreement of the International Monetary Fund to provide for the creation of Special Drawing Rights.

The SDR mechanism provides a direct and clear-cut central banking function on a basis as wide as membership of the IMF. International money in the form of central bank reserves is created deliberately and systematically as a result of multilateral decision and distributed to the monetary authorities of the member countries according to an agreed formula for use by them under the terms set forth in the agreed amendment.

The issue tendered by the events of the last two years is whether or not the processes of joint decision-making in the International Monetary Fund can be extended to cover many additional attributes of a world central bank, including a facilitation of the adjustment process, exchange-rate flexibility, the protection of appropriate exchange rates from disruptive and destabilising forces, and the regulation of the total of the world reserves.

By the same token, much of the potential of wise and constructive international economic policy in areas which are outside the province of the International Monetary Fund or a world central bank, can only be realised if a system for joint decision-making on international economic issues of common concern, can be devised and developed.

As Mr Randolph Burgess and James Huntley put it in their valuable book published in 1970, *Europe and America: The Next Ten Years*, "In the 1970s it appears certain that the Atlantic powers will face an increasing need to overhaul, update and augment their methods and institutions for economic co-ordination." The OECD, the instrument most readily available to meet this need, has done valuable work, but it is not yet strong enough to serve the growing Atlantic business community or mediate in increasing competition in economic policy between national governments. Suggestions for a strengthening and giving of more authority to the IMF and the OECD raise squarely the question whether this process is acceptable to sovereign states located on at least three separate continents. As William McChesney Martin has observed,

> What we have been witnessing has been a willingness of nations by the exercise of their sovereign rights to recognise that the national interest can no longer be pursued in isolation, but is dependent on co-operative action in deference to the common good. It has become more and more clear that this involves no loss of sovereignty, but rather a pooling of sovereignty. It could even be said that what once were the principal objectives of sovereign powers, the maintenance of economic prosperity and of effective defence, can now only be achieved by the acceptance of co-operative international arrangements which by their very nature impose limitations on the sovereignty of all nations concerned.

The approach to a systematised practice of joint decision-making, in limited and selected areas of national behaviour, raises significant questions of structure and procedure. It seems clear that the International Monetary Fund will have to be substantially strengthened in its make-up and structure if it is to perform the functions of a world central bank. It follows that international decision-making within the context of a greatly strengthened IMF must be carried out by representatives in or to that organisation, who, in the words of U.S. Secretary of the Treasury Schultz, "clearly carry a high stature of influence in the councils of their own governments". It also follows that national governments will be intensively and continuously in-volved in the processes of making and executing the international decisions in an adequate performance by the IMF of a central bank function. Again, Secretary Schultz, in his address to the Annual Meeting of the Fund observed: "Without a commitment by national governments to make a new system work in this way, all our other labours may come to nought."

The same observations are equally pertinent to a strengthened and reorganised OECD and any other international organisation with particular functions, such as the GATT, which may be endowed with greater authority for the continued making and execution of decisions that constitute international economic policy.

In dealing with the area of broad consultations covered by the OECD, another important question looms, namely, whether the formation and execution of international economic policy should envisage any further proliferation beyond a greatly strengthened International Monetary Fund, OECD, GATT, and International Bank for Reconstruction and Development. A further dispersal of additional functions among other bodies might weaken the thrust of all. Indeed, it would seem that there is a stronger case for a more co-ordinated approach among the nations of Western Europe, North America, and Japan to give effective direction to the performance by these bodies of constructive international economic policy.

One interesting suggestion on this score was floated by Dr Brzezinski in his challenging book *Between Two Ages*. In discussing the structure for the concept of a community of the developed nations he observed:

> A case can be made for initially setting up only a high level consultative council for global co-operation, regularly bringing together the heads of government of the developed world to discuss their common political–security, educational–scientific, and economic–technological problems, as well as to deal from that perspective with their moral obligations toward the developing nations. Some permanent supporting machinery could provide continuity to these consultations.

Accordingly, such a council for global co-operation would be something more than OECD in that it would operate on a higher level and would also be concerned with political strategy; but it would be more diffused than NATO in that it would not seek to forge integrated military–political structures. Nevertheless a council of this sort – perhaps initially linking only the United States, Japan, and Western Europe, and thus bringing together the political leaders of states sharing certain common aspirations and problems of modernity – would be more effective in developing common programmes than is the United Nations, whose efficacy is unavoidably limited by the Cold War and by north-south divisions.

In summary, the thrust of opinion from some sophisticated Americans is that the tools of international economic policy as a system require the substantial strengthening of the International Monetary Fund, OECD, GATT and the International Bank for Reconstruction and Development.

This strengthening would involve:

– the enlargement of international decision-making authority in a limited number of selected areas, according to procedures that would pool sovereignty in accordance with the political procedures of the participating states;
– a far greater degree of participation in these international institutions by those in the top councils of their governments;
– a regular bringing together of heads of governments of the developed world to consult and exchange views on problems of global economic co-operation.

CONCLUSION

This is the time when the conjunction of various international events is likely to determine the future of international economic policy for some years and decades to come.

This is the time at which it will be determined whether a European can be a good European and a good Atlanticist at the same time.

This is also the time at which it will be determined whether an American can be a good American and a good Atlanticist at the same time.

It is also a time which will see Japan play a key role in the community of developed nations, commensurate with her trading genius and productive strength, or disappoint those who have held high hopes for full Japanese emergence into the improved multilateral governance of international economic affairs.

Acts of political will at the highest level in the countries concerned will be necessary to forge the tools adequate to convert our existing institutions for international consultation and co-operation into effective instruments for a system capable of the formulation and execution of international economic policy.

The future of an initiative of this nature depends on responsible and far-sighted leadership in the free democratic societies willing to lead.

It also depends upon an educated citizenship willing to support or, on occasion, to stimulate national leadership to establish and operate increasingly effective institutions for constructive international economic policy.

The future requires a global system that will intensify international co-operation and interdependence. If achieved in the period ahead, the results will mark another exciting step on the road to a modern world economic order of benefit to all peoples. This working together with benefits for all could in the words of President Nixon "help to shape the years ahead into a generation of peace".

COMMENT *by Jean Royer*

All of us who live on this side of the Atlantic should be grateful for the above very clear indication of the U.S. administration's determination to contribute, when this is practically possible, to a strengthening of international monetary system by a return to the convertibility of the dollar. Such an indication goes a long way to pacify those who have certain doubts about the ultimate aims of the present U.S. economic and financial policy.

The vision of a world in which the major governments would agree to pool their sovereign rights for a number of specific but important sectors is something which is absolutely new in international life. With the experience of more than 40 years in international relations, I may tell you that before the war we would never have dreamt of even mentioning that to governments; and even in 1947, after the war, when we tried to build up an international economic system we were very careful to limit any deviation from the principle of sovereignty to traditional matters such as commercial policy. Such a drastic pooling of sovereignty would be a very important breakthrough in the history of international co-operation. On the other hand, we have to realise that it is not something which is easy to achieve. Of course, from a technical point of view, all these problems have been thoroughly examined and practical solutions can be offered at a moment's notice by the competent experts. But the real problem is not the technique: the real problem is the political will of the governments. I think that governments are not at present prepared to give away a substantial part of their sovereign rights in any important economic function. They believe with some justification that their primary responsibility is towards their people.

They have to achieve the prosperity, the employment of their own people; and, quite clearly, international considerations have to take a second place. This is the drama of our present society.

This is not the only factor which is bothering us at the present time. Another very important factor is that these liberal policies, this feeling that we have to unite to be acting in a way in which we are part of a whole, are not today getting any real support from enlightened public opinion. Whether it be the opinion of business people or even of economists, or of other members of society, there is not the same enthusiasm that there was just after the war for any solution which would involve any limitation of the sovereign powers of their own government. This is a very serious affair.

We have to recognise that if we have the foundations of an international system which were laid just after the war, which if it didn't work as well as everybody expected has nevertheless done very useful work, we have to improve that present system. We have to improve, no so much the rules of the game but rather the readiness of governments to conform to their international commitments. We have seen that the governments are not really very keen on living up to their international commitments. I think this is a general phenomenon which can be seen anywhere, in any international organisation.

Today, the fabric of this international system has been stretched to such a point that its seams are falling apart. Some months ago the representatives of the banking and financial world meeting in a Commission of the International Chamber of Commerce were practically convinced, with the exception of some dissenting voices from our British friends, that it would be possible within a reasonably short period to repair, strengthen, and modernise the International Monetary Fund. Yet a few weeks afterwards we had a second monetary crisis. The staunchest lost heart and, despairing that anything would be settled, just jumped into the sea, some of them clinging together to a rather exiguous raft, others just drifting alone on a plank or on a barrel: only the Americans remained unperturbed on the ship although she had sprung a leak. This is what is happening in the monetary field today. People who should know better are listening to the counsel of despair and finding that there is no solution at all except to let the currency float and drift without any thought or form of control.

In the trade field the situation is not much more promising. For one thing it is impossible to do anything so far as trade and commercial policies are concerned unless there is a stable monetary basis. But in spite of the efforts which were made by the OECD group headed by Jean Rey some time ago, and by other bodies, we have to conclude that the major governments are not prepared to agree, either on the causes of the present troubles on the detailed objectives of the forthcoming GATT negotiations or even on some of the rules of the game. We may be heading towards a situation which could create serious problems for international co-operation in the future. This would not be too bad if the possible effects of such friction could be confined to the narrow limits of trade interests; but there is a serious risk that they may affect the general economic system and that our present Western economic way of life may be in jeopardy.

We learned in the 1930s, at a time when the international system of payments was out of gear, that unless you have a reliable yardstick for value then the governments are tempted to draw in their horns, to cut themselves off from other countries, to find that the price of international economic co-operation is too great. They simply become engrossed in the settlement of their day-to-day domestic problems. The ensuing Second World War nearly wrecked the economic system of the West. Unless we are very careful about what we are doing in the near future, we may this time be less successful than in the '30s. Our system is under very strong attack, in many European countries, from opponents of free enterprise and the market economy. They may win the day. If only for this reason, we should do everything that we can to convince not only governments, not only officials, but all sectors of enlightened public opinion in our countries, that there is something very important at stake; and that if we want to maintain our present system, if we want to strengthen relations between, let us say, the attentive countries and also with other parts of the world, it is essential that governments should forget about the present quarrels, which after all are only family problems, and sit at the negotiating table, not in the spirit of defending narrow parochial interests but as real partners, as members of a community whose interests are far more important for their peoples than the defence of national interests, legitimate as these interests may be.

Chapter IX

Future Problems of Trade Policy:
A Question of Political Leadership

ARTHUR J. R. SMITH

SINCE THE END OF THE FIRST WORLD WAR, the United States has been the leading commercial nation of the world. The implications of this for trade policy have not always been fully appreciated either within the United States or elsewhere. But over the past half-century, through its own national policies and through international groups and institutions of various kinds, the United States has in fact played the key role in the setting of international trade policy.

It has played this role in many different forms and through a wide variety of influences. Because of a general international failure to recognise the full implications of the key commercial position into which the United States had grown during the First World War, it played no leading role in trade policy developments immediately after that war. Hence, the stage was set for a troubled and turbulent interwar period in which rapidly expanding world trade could not become a salient engine of world growth and development, as it had been in the decade or two prior to the First World War. Through its protectionist policies at the end of the 1920s – exacerbated by the protectionist policies of other countries – the United States led the world into constricted and conflicting trading relationships that intensified monetary and other disruptive factors leading to depression and poor economic performance on a worldwide scale in the 1930s. Moreover, these commercial developments powerfully interacted with and reinforced other factors tending to produce strains on international political relationships that eventually culminated in the Second World War.

By the early 1930s, forward-looking leadership in the United States did succeed in gaining legislative authority in the Reciprocal Trade Agreements Act of 1934 for major reductions in tariff barriers. This provided the basis for beginning to reverse the previous steps towards protection. Although various initiatives were taken by the United States, Canada, and a number of European countries over the next few years to begin the process of tariff reduction, the process was slow and the lags were long before significant effects could be achieved. And this whole process was overtaken by the Second World War before even the pre-Depression basis for international trade had been generally restored. Moreover, the war, with its inevitable controls affecting not only international trade and payments, but also almost all aspects of international as well as national economic activities, plunged the world into a further round of trade dislocation.

THE POST-WAR ARRANGEMENTS

Even before the end of the war, however, the stage had been set for intensive and far-reaching efforts to move away from the growth-inhibiting policies of the interwar period towards a more open international economic environment. Three very basic factors contributed to the success of these efforts – success that, I venture to suggest, has subsequently turned out to be far beyond the fondest hopes of those who were engaged in seeking to construct a new set of policies and institutions designed to achieve an international basis for "peaceful prosperity".

The first was simply the fact that the economic disasters and policies of the interwar period had dramatically demonstrated the need for a totally changed system of international economic relationships: in short, the time was ripe for major reform.

The second was that, during the Second World War, when the basis was being laid for such reforms, relatively few countries were centrally involved in searching for agreement on principles and procedures. The United States, Britain, and Canada were essentially the three key countries involved. Canada at that time played a special role that was obviously out of all proportion to the size of its economy. This was partly due to the unique situation that arose when wartime devastation made it impossible for other leading industrial nations to play a full part in these initiatives. It was also partly attributable to the fact that Canada's participation was spearheaded by an extraordinarily capable group of senior public servants who were held in high international esteem, and whose intellectual coherence was respected because it was both slightly detached and yet totally involved in thinking strategically about the future rehabilitation and development of the economies of the Western world.

The third key factor that contributed to the success of the post-war international economic reforms – and perhaps the most important of all – was that, in contrast to the situation following the First World War, the United States as well as other countries basically agreed that the new system of post-war economic policies and institutions should be constructed around the United States as the country that must necessarily play a leadership role. Moving away from its earlier isolationist and insulationist moods, the United States took on the responsibilities and corresponding burdens of heavy involvement in international affairs on a global scale. This role involved much more than a capacity to persuade, exhort, or press other countries to act in certain ways; it involved a clear commitment to a number of basic principles in policy formulation and implementation, together with a willingness to deploy economic power to support such commitments.

In the quarter-century since the end of the Second World War, the United States has, in fact, obviously played this leadership role in the evolution of international economic conditions. Without such leadership, it is doubtful if the central principles enshrined in GATT, in the institutions that emerged from Bretton Woods, and in the operation of various other international institutions and policies could have prevailed in a practical sense. Without such leadership, neither the early rounds of reductions in tariffs, nor the subsequent dismantling of quantitative trade controls and major steps towards currency convertibility, nor the still later steps towards further tariff reductions under the Kennedy Round and towards closer multilateral and multinational consultations on trade and monetary matters, could have been so successfully achieved. Such leadership was also reflected in the Marshall Plan and strong support for European and Japanese post-war recovery and development, in the early initiatives for aid programmes to developing countries, and in a massive outflow to many parts of the world of capital, technology, skill, and other ingredients of economic progress. Of course, the obverse to all this was simply that other nations were generally receptive and responsive to U.S. initiatives. That, too, was a major constituent element in the leadership role that the United States played.

These new post-war international economic arrangements have, of course, not worked perfectly. Nor have they served fully satisfactorily the *national* aspirations of most countries. But, in spite of their imperfections, in spite of the emergence of new conditions and problems with which they have not been able to cope adequately, and in spite of perennial and increasing strains and crises in international economic affairs, they have served us well – and for a longer period than most authorities would have dared to hope a quarter of a century ago.

In sum, what they succeeded in doing was to open up the international arena to freer flows of "productive inputs" and of "production outputs" – providing what has perhaps been the most important of all conditions leading to strong and sustained world (and *national*) growth and development: the enlargement of opportunities for greater scale and specialisation in production based on comparative advantage and, more particularly, enhancing the basis for achieving the high-productivity gains which have constituted the key ultimate source both of unprecedented improvements in material living standards and of major new social policy initiatives.

THE PRESENT NEED FOR REFORMS

But it has become increasingly evident, especially since the mid-1960s, that significant reforms are needed in these arrangements to provide an appropriate basis for the vastly changed world conditions that have emerged and are in prospect over the next quarter-century. These reforms are proving to be very difficult to devise, agree upon, and implement. The main reasons are that the conditions in which these are being explored are almost diametrically opposite to those of the 1940s:

– First, we are seeking to work them out against a background of relatively high and well-sustained standards of economic performance, rather than against the background of the compulsions of the disastrously inadequate performance of the 1930s and the clear and essential need to dismantle severe wartime controls and constraints. The labour contractions that precede human birth appear to have a parallel in the crises that have been an almost inevitable precondition for basic reforms and adjustments in the fields of economic, social and political affairs.
– Secondly, we are attempting to design them in an arena in which a very large number of nations, with a wide variety of interests, not just a few nations as was the case in the 1940s, are involved in seeking to arrive at a consensus.
– Thirdly, in this context, too, we are seeking to achieve reforms when it is no longer feasible or appropriate to construct them

around the comforting and comfortable concept of expecting the United States – as the dominating and pre-eminent economy of the Western world – to play the same role of leadership and support that it was assumed it could and would play when the present arrangements were developed. More particularly, the European Economic Community and Japan have developed into large and economically very powerful entities, creating what some have termed a "multipolar" international economic structure.

— Fourthly, we are trying to consider reforms at a time when there has been an enormous growth in the size and economic power of national governments, a vast peacetime proliferation of government programmes and policies (many of which have increasingly come to intervene in private markets and private decision-making processes in disparate ways), and a considerable increase in national sentiment in various countries (sometimes embodying explicit anti-international attitudes, and sometimes focusing on the importance of dealing with perceived domestic problems as matters of essential priority).

— Fifthly, increasing international monetary instability, and the delays that we have encountered in achieving adequate and effective reforms in international monetary and financial arrangements, have been posing growing threats to the maintenance of an orderly and open world trading system.

— And finally, as a background to these reforms, we face a new sense of "mercantilism" abroad in various countries – a belief that exports *per se* are a particularly valuable route to new wealth and new employment, while imports are a serious threat to existing wealth and existing jobs. This is proving to be a fertile field in which to argue from the particular to the general. The real benefits of trade lie, of course, not in the creation of new jobs, but in the opportunities provided for overall increases in productivity and real incomes, and for greater satisfaction of tastes and preferences for new and more diversified patterns of purchases of goods and services – a proposition, incidentally, whose validity, even when fully appreciated, is often not very congenial for politicians or for particular industrial, labour, or other special-interest groups.

I emphasise these broader issues because it is highly important to bear in mind – as recent events have so vividly emphasised – that trade policy developments in the 1970s will necessarily be closely interrelated with developments in monetary and other aspects of international relationships, with other aspects of national economic policies and, most fundamentally of all, with political conditions and leadership. There is simply no way in which we can expect to achieve and maintain liberal, growth-promoting world trade conditions if our international monetary system is to come under increasing tension leading to a growing range of impediments to international financial transactions. Nor is there any way of retaining the real economic benefits of trade if increasingly nationalistic sets of domestic policies come to impede inflows of productive resources and the efficient operations of multinational corporations, or to distort trade in ways that, over an extended period, are designed to perpetuate or insert relatively inefficient industrial activities in a national economy.

THE CENTRAL TRADE POLICY QUESTIONS FOR THE 1970S

There are three central questions concerning trade policy for as poor domestic economic performance tends to place the heaviest the 1970s.

- or not?
- Do we wish to retain a relatively liberal trading environment
- Who will exercise political leadership to maintain such an environment, if the answer to the first question is affirmative?
- Will there be sufficient political will to provide adequate negotiating authority for maintaining such conditions?

For those who may have doubts about the first of these questions, now is an appropriate time to read some of the dismal commercial policy history of the 1920s and 1930s. A return now to a more compartmentalised trading world would clearly imply slower economic growth, especially productivity growth – and hence would imply fewer resources than could otherwise be available for expanding living standards and social programmes. The 1930s demonstrated dramatically how little scope there is for social progress under slow growth conditions. Along with this, it would undoubtedly also imply, as a practical matter, generally higher unemployment rates and, possibly, higher rates of inflation arising in part from the vastly greater institutionalisation of modern economies than existed 40 or 50 years ago. Finally, just as poor domestic economic performance tends to place the heaviest burdens on the weaker sectors and groups in a national economy, so a failure to maintain the benefits from a liberal trading environment would impose especially heavy burdens on the smaller and weaker national economies.

The economic arguments for a liberal international trading system are, if not impeccable, at least powerfully and practically demonstrable in historical terms. And governments which believe that their political strength can be buttressed by high and rising living standards and improved human welfare will therefore tend to place considerable emphasis on the importance of liberal trade as a means towards these ends.

But beyond these fundamental economic considerations, there are also broader political, security and other considerations – all of which also fundamentally argue for a liberal trading environment. Prospects for achieving and maintaining co-operative and well co-ordinated international arrangements for mutual political advantage and mutual security are not likely to be promising if they are set in the context of serious commercial strains. Discontents in any one area of relationships and policy inevitably tend to spill over into other areas – probably more so today than ever before as technological change in communications and transport is shrinking the earlier barriers of time and space to the "interrelatedness" of national economic and social systems.

However, there are now many forces and groups that, for tactical, shorter-term, or "special-circumstance" reasons, are looking for solutions to problems of a national or local nature and are prepared to allocate only secondary priority to preserving or enhancing our present liberal trading environment – unfortunately, in many cases, because it is assumed that the hard-won overall advantages of a freer trading environment can simply be taken for granted, and because it is not properly understood that the preservation of some jobs by reducing import competition is most likely to be paid for by the loss of existing or potential jobs of "greater value" in export-oriented activities. We are also in a situation in which the special interests and preoccupations of regional groupings, and the efforts to solve particular problems through bilateral and special arrangements of various kinds – illustrated, for example, by the preferential trading arrangements of the European Economic Community with various non-members, or by the Canada–United States automotive agreement – are increasingly infringing on what the founding fathers of our post-war liberal trading arrangements conceived to be in the long-term strategic interests of the whole community of major trading countries of the world. And we are also witnessing growing efforts by governments to pursue national policies of industrial, regional, social, and other development that are having various kinds and degrees of distorting effects on trade.

The totality of these and other trade-impinging activities and pressures does not appear so far to have had any very dramatic adverse effects on the overall growth and pattern of trade. But these pressures are giving rise to increasing concern among those who believe that it is *strategically important* for the future benefit of trading nations to maintain open trading conditions – and who recognise that any serious trade policy "crunch" which might produce setbacks in current arrangements would not be likely, on the basis of historical evidence, to be rapidly replaced by generally favourable trading relationships.

In some ways, the current situation has a number of parallels with that in the late 1950s and early 1960s when the post-war trend towards freer trading conditions appeared to have run its course, and when serious questions were beginning to arise as to whether national economies might have to look to factors other than trade policies to serve as the principal vehicles for improved economic performance and potential. Then, not unlike the Reciprocal Trade Agreements Act of 1934, came the rather spectacular initiative by the United States in the Trade Expansion Act of 1962, opening up new possibilities for retaining trade liberalisation and growth as a key element in economic advance through the 1960s. In short, we now face a rather similar situation to that of a dozen years ago. And the question is increasingly being asked: "Where will a new initiative emerge, if at all, for retaining rapidly growing trade as a key ingredient in good worldwide standards of economic performance through the 1970s?"

This brings me to the second and third central questions that I posed above – the need that exists in today's "multipolar" world for the political leadership and the political will and skill to revise, preserve and enhance trading opportunities as a means towards more fundamental objectives of modern societies. One of the most encouraging developments in the past year was the initiative taken by Japan to host (in September 1973) the ministerial conference of the 81 nations who are contracting partners of GATT. This reflected, obviously, the very large stake that the dynamically expanding Japanese economy has in international trade in its own interests – a stake that has been rightly assessed to be of almost overriding importance if it is realistically to aspire to be one of the industrially great and economically wealthy nations of the world. It was also, I believe, of great importance that the leaders of the new and enlarged European Economic Community stated that they are determined to ensure the harmonious development of world trade, and to contribute to a progressive liberalisation of international trade by measures based on reciprocity and involving reductions in both tariff and non-tariff barriers to trade. And it was likewise encouraging that President Nixon, in responding to a communique of the European Economic Community said:

I wish to reaffirm our commitment to work with the members of the European Community for reform of the international economic system in a way which will bring about a new freedom of world trade, new equity in international economic conduct, and effective solutions to the problems of the developing world.

The basis for political leadership in the field of international trade policy therefore appears to exist. But it will require a high order of statesmanship on all sides to carry these inflictions of leadership into effective and fruitful results – especially in the context of present commercial and monetary strains, and having regard to the wider and more basic sets of issues that must be dealt with in effective ways in the course of the next round of international trade negotiations. In the forthcoming GATT negotiations, there is, I believe, an urgent need for the closest possible prior contracts and consultations among leading officials of the world's principal trading entities to help set the stage for *comprehensive* and *adequate* negotiating authority to bring to the bargaining table.

THE ISSUES ON THE TABLE

This brings me to the question of "the issues on the table". It is a safe statement that never before has such a wide range of basic trade issues come forward simultaneously for examination and resolution. I have neither the knowledge nor the expertise to attempt to set out in detail the particular issues that need to be resolved. Nor do I have a neat and persuasive set of recommendations to propose for mutually beneficial results.

But I think that it has already become clear that half a dozen central issues must now be tackled in the commercial field. Moreover, it is now clear that these must be dealt with in a much more comprehensive and interrelated set of negotiating processes. Let me try to outline some of these central issues very briefly. Merely to do so stresses more sharply the underlying importance of the third central question I have already raised – namely, will there be sufficient political will to provide adequate negotiating authority to maintain a relatively liberal trading environment?

The first, and perhaps the least difficult and controversial, issue concerns that of further reduction in tariffs – especially tariffs on industrial products. The Kennedy Round succeeded in largely "breaking the back" of industrial tariff protection – at least for the world's key industrial agglomerations. The bulk of the industrial tariffs of the United States and the European Economic Community are now below 10 per cent, and in the case of many categories of trade the tariffs that now remain can be viewed as little more than "nuisance taxes". Yet, three key problems remain about tariffs as trade barriers: the fact that *effective* tariffs rates tend generally to be higher than actual tariff rates and still represent a serious impediment to the more efficient use of productive resources in most industrial countries; the fact that so long as tariffs exist for many commodities, closely linked non-tariff barriers (for example, matters of classification, valuation and other procedures) may constitute added impediments to trade; and the fact that for some industrial countries (and, unfortunately, my own country is one of these) relatively high tariff rates still prevail on many industrial products (often accentuating even further the economic distortions resulting from extremely high effective tariff protection). Thus, wide-ranging reduction in industrial tariffs – and, so far as may be possible, *elimination* of industrial tariffs – is, and should be, a major objective for the 1970s.

The second issue concerns measures for beginning to cope with the proliferating range of what are commonly called non-tariff barriers to trade – but which I prefer to call non-tariff "competition-distorting" factors. My preference in terminology is deliberately intended to reflect the fact that some of the most serious factors undermining the economic advantages to be derived from trade arise not from *barriers* of one kind or another, but also from measures designed to *promote* domestic activities and exports that may have equal, if not greater, distorting effects on a nation's economic development than any trade "barriers". Studies of non-tariff trade distortions have broken out all over the world in the past few years, and literally hundreds of these distortions have been identified (although it must be admitted that we still do not know very much about their actual economic impact). Among some of the principal categories of such distorting measures are: quantitative trade quotas (either on exports or imports), purchasing policies of governments or government-controlled organisations, aids to specific industries (including regional economic development programmes), customs valuation and classification procedures, arbitrary anti-dumping and counter-vailing duty practices and industrial and other standards. In view of the variety and extensiveness of such practices within different nations, these will undoubtedly prove to be extremely difficult to approach in international trade negotiations. But the time has now arrived when they must be tackled. The protectionist and economically distorting aspects of these practices will, I believe, need to be tackled at two levels. One is that we shall need to explore whether agreement can be reached on certain basic principles about appropriate "rules for international competition"; the other is that we shall probably need to create some effective surveillance mechanism for monitoring, examining, assessing complaints about, and reporting on, particular cases of non-tariff trade-distorting practices. Clearly implied in this view is that in their respective longer-term individual interests, the members of the community of nations will need to collaborate more closely on matters that concern their mutual longer-term collective interests. This will not be easy to accommodate in today's world, with its belief that growing affluence permits, and that growing complexities demand, more national-oriented solutions to various problems and more national-oriented policies to achieve increasingly ambitious and challenging domestic goals.

Also, it will be difficult to achieve since governments themselves have become increasingly involved directly in legislating, regulating, influencing, and promoting new objectives in response to political and social pressures. But this is a matter that I firmly believe must be tackled on a multinational basis. The alternative is simply that many of the present and prospective efforts to achieve national objectives will involve an enormous waste of scarce resources in a worldwide competitive escalation of measures that will largely offset each other. Without an open international economy, many national goals will simply not be attainable.

A third and partly related essential problem that needs to be confronted is that of "safeguard provisions" – in particular, safeguards against serious market, production, and employment disruptions. These safeguards will, of course, be all the more critical if very substantial progress is made towards tariff reductions and the amelioration of non-tariff trade distortions. The essential problem here is that, in any growing and developing economy, major structural changes must occur – changes in the types and processes of production, changes in the qualities of labour and capital and other productive resources, changes in the location of economic activities and in the salient thrusts of progress. *Change* is the essence of growth and development – no less so in the economic and social fields than in the fields of biology, engineering, and other scientific areas. But change is frequently a sudden and painful process, and economic and social change in the modern world appears increasingly to place burdens upon individuals through no fault of their own – burdens against which they cannot satisfactorily protect themselves and to avoid which they cannot readily adjust through transitions to new opportunities.

What is true of individuals is also, to some extent, true of nations which may feel that, for national security and other basic reasons, they should not be exposed to the full impact of international economic forces. But to leave "safeguard provisions" wide open to national decisions could well create a growing jungle of arbitrary actions that would neither be in the interests of individual countries nor serve the broader welfare of the community of trading nations. Here, too, I believe that the appropriate course must be to consider a two-tier approach: first, the possible development of general principles, criteria, and provisions that should govern national options and practices concerning the orderly transition to new structures and realities; and secondly, surveillance and reporting capacities on a multinational basis for averting abuses. Behind these, in turn, there must surely be developed much more effective national assistance policies and programmes – to promote effective and orderly adjustment to changes in commercial policy (as well as to technological and many other types of change that will inevitably be taking place in any progressive economy and society). This has been considered in some quarters to be such a fundamental issue that proposals have been made to make agreement on adjustment assistance policies the first order of business in the forthcoming round of trade negotiations – on the grounds that if this cannot be achieved, little effective progress may be feasible in other matters.

This point naturally leads to a fourth basic issue that must be taken up in the forthcoming efforts to review and improve trade-policies. This is the issue of trade in agricultural products. The field of agriculture is an outstanding illustration of both the results of high degrees of government intervention and protection for a special interest group, and the unfortunate longer-term economic consequences for national economies, and even for many of the farmers which such actions were designed to serve. In agricultural policies – especially those impinging on international trade in farm products – virtually every leading industrial nation has suffered from the unfortunate effects that have been produced over the longer run as a result of the failure to subordinate shorter-term national, political, and special interests to the larger-term interests of nations as a whole, and of their farming communities in particular. United States' farm policies in many ways, and perhaps the Common Agricultural policy of the European Community even more so – as well as Japanese policies that have slowed structural shifts to more efficient and more dynamically expanding non-agricultural development – are all remarkable for their failure to appreciate the long-term strategic opportunities for larger shifts of resources out of agriculture to the salients of modern economic progress. Through various ingenious devices, resources have been preserved in agriculture that have been enormously costly, both to those who have practised them and to other nations which had capacities for highly efficient use of such resources for the benefit of consumers on an international scale. In brief, the world market for agricultural products has been largely compartmentalised into national markets (and, within some of these, even into regional and local markets), with international trade essentially becoming a residual activity. Commercial barriers have been used – and usually with remarkably inefficient results – in an attempt to solve social problems, basically the low-income problems of farmers.

What disastrous overall economic waste has ensued! And what disastrous consequences have ensued, in countless situations, to farmers themselves, as trade protection has frequently proved to be just sufficient to maintain them at very low lifetime incomes. Here is a key problem which vividly illustrates both what the ultimate cost to individuals and nations would be if our present régime of relatively liberal trade for industrial products were ever to break down, and which cries out for major initiatives to begin to free international trade for agricultural products. This need is also strongly buttressed in current conditions by worldwide supply shortages for many important agricultural products and accompanying steep price increases for food. These are conditions in which it is critically important to allow agriculture to expand in those areas which can be most economically efficient in food and feed production and to reduce the severe constraints that now exist upon the flows of such products to international markets. Perhaps, after many earlier failures, the time is really ripe for a major dismantling of protective agricultural trade barriers, and for positive and substantial progress towards multinational harmonisation of agricultural policies. This should be one of the key items on the agenda of trade policy negotiations for the 1970s.

A fifth key issue on such an agenda should be that of invisible trade transactions. Just as service activities have been growing rapidly in importance as compared with goods-producing activities among the world's leading industrial nations during the past two decades, so international transactions in services have been rising in importance as compared with trade in goods. These developments are, of course, closely related in turn to the fact that modern societies are becoming increasingly knowledge- and skill-based, increasingly urbanised, increasingly government-dominated, and increasingly concerned with what have come to be called quality-of-life issues. In looking to the future, it would appear that many service activities – for example, recreational, professional, technical, financial, consulting and other activities – are becoming, and will continue to become, increasingly international in scope. Forward-looking trade policy negotiations could provide a timely and very useful opportunity to ensure that the economic benefits that will be available from increased trade in such "invisible services" accrue to national economies. This will be a new and difficult challenge to take up on a multinational basis. But it is, I think, a key challenge to which we should be addressing ourselves now.

TRADE OF THE DEVELOPING COUNTRIES AND EAST–WEST TRADE

The main thrust of my argument so far has been devoted to issues and questions that are of predominant interest and concern to the industrially advanced nations. But it is also vitally important to consider how trade policy can increasingly benefit and serve the interests of the developing countries, as well as the fundamental interests of the so-called "enterprise" and the so-called "socialist" countries. In a healthy world in the 1970s and 1980s – healthy in economic matters as well as in terms of broader and more basic political and social progress – rapidly growing trade between the industrially advanced and the developing countries, and between East and West, must be a crucial element. The most rapidly growing countries in the developing world have already discovered that expanding trade – *both exports and imports* – constitutes an extremely effective means for economic (and, indirectly, social) progress. The industrialised world – especially if it can establish better functioning adjustment measures, along with agreed criteria for safeguards against unduly disruptive market disturbances – should consider more generous and open trade opportunities for the developing countries. But in their own longer-term economic interests, the developing countries should also be prepared to see international competition help to shape the lines along which their most promising avenues for economic progress really lie.

Similarly, in the East–West context, in spite of different policy and institutional arrangements governing trade, there obviously exists a vast potential for mutually beneficial trade expansion. One of the most promising and rewarding developments of the past few years for the future welfare of humanity has been the opening up of new possibilities and initiative for trade between Western countries and the state-trading nations. To a significant extent, however, this has been proceeding under various bilateral arrangements. I believe that the time has now come to consider whether these could not be brought within a more multilateral and multinational framework in the longer-term interests of all parties concerned.

INSTITUTIONAL MACHINERY

The final issue to which I believe we must direct special attention is the creation of extended institutional machinery to cope with the more complex and different trade policy issues of the 1970s. Already, the present institutional machinery and inter-connections in this field are becoming somewhat confused – with the growing complexity of activities within GATT and in the OECD, with the evolution of the European Economic Community and some other trading groups, with closer involvement of trade policy issues in international monetary policy issues, with the emergence of UNCTAD, and in a vast array of bilateral connections owing to the proliferating scope of national policies that impinge on international trading interests. Beyond this, there is a matter of developing new elements of international surveillance and reporting to deal practically with some of the important but complex new issues to which I have referred above. How to bring all this within the framework of more coherent and consistent institutional machinery is clearly one of the most demanding challenges now confronting us. Progress in this direction will not, and cannot, be accomplished in an atmosphere of high priority to narrower *national* goals. What is needed, above all, is a new sense of *internationalism* that reflects the realities of an increasingly interdependent world economy and society. And, paradoxically, the greatest barrier to effective progress towards this appears to be the greatly increased affluence that rapidly expanding international trade has itself helped to achieve. For affluence itself provides both the means and the temptation to pursue policies and aspirations that are insular and isolationist in character.

CONCLUSION

And so I return to my central theme – the need for political leadership of a high order if we are to have opportunities for sustained and satisfactory advances for all mankind; for new initiatives in strategic thinking about where we can go over the next decade, *not* for manoeuvring for shorter-term tactical advantages that will prove to be illusory, even for those for whom such manoeuvring may be especially designed. This is a time for dealing with fundamental issues, not for "niggling at the margins" of commercial policy advantage. The next round of trade policy reform will require large capacities on the part of *all participants* both "to give" and "to take".

Prominent in this round will be the adjustments that will need to be made in European–North American trade relationships. At the core of the post-war arrangements developed a quarter of a century ago was the rehabilitation and strengthening of trade relationships across the Atlantic. Today, we must obviously be much more concerned about many issues and questions that were earlier not high on the agenda of commercial policy formulation – the key role of Japan, the vital interests and concerns of trade development for the developing countries, the promising potentials for swiftly expanding East–West trade. But still at the core of new arrangements – substantive and institutional – will be the trade connections between the newly expanded and economically powerful European Economic Community and the very economically powerful North American economy. Even after due recognition of the vastly greater trading interests of Japan and of other important trading relationships and potentials (including the huge expansion in oil trade with the OPEC countries), it will still be upon this trade axis that the future of world trade over the next decade will essentially be constructed. And, in turn, it will be essentially with European–North American trading relationships that the future international political and security issues of the Western world in the 1970s will be related. In none of the countries concerned will there be any real validity in assessing the future of the world through the 1970s and 1980s without prior assessment of the future of the "Atlantic World". Now, as in the 1940s, that is the first consideration in assessing our prospects for "peaceful prosperity" in our generation, even though we must now stretch ourselves to take account of other important relationships as well.

COMMENT *by Giuseppe Petrilli*

The repeated call for freedom in trade without doubt deserves all attention. Nevertheless it is important not to ignore problems arising in international trade through macro-regional unions in several geographical areas of our planet.

Some seem to consider this as a threat for the re-establishment of general liberalisation. But it seems to me that, in view of the need for trade safeguards, a return to total liberalisation would not at the present time be a realistic prospect, because it would be impossible to bear its social consequences without phasing it in time and without measures of reconversion and re-education of industry and its personnel. Without minimising the economic danger and wastage of resources which always go together with safeguard clauses, on account of the co-operative pressures of established interest, it is inconceivable that progress in liberalisation should not be accompanied by action on the part of public authorities to fulfill their social policy obligations.

As regards the European Economic Community, I think particularly that any subsequent measures for liberalisation of external trade there should go hand in hand with the establishment of political increased co-ordination within the area. If not we shall be perhaps exposing ourselves to serious political and social counter-currents. It may be true that its structured dependence on international trade requires the Community to retain the liberal attitude it has always maintained, at any rate as regards trade in industrial goods. Any customs union necessarily involves discrimination against other countries. To seek hastily to eliminate all discrimination of this type before achieving actual progress towards a true economic union would I think destroy the customs union and thereby compromise any possibility of political subsequent development.

It is not by chance that the treaties of Paris and Rome conceived the Common Market in the form of an institutional Community. In the present condition of our economies characterised by growing participation of the state in forming and disturbing the national income, it would have been senseless to seek to liberalise trade without at the same time providing for increasing political co-ordination. The main reason for the upsets that we have suffered so far is the lack of satisfactory parallelism between these two aspects of the Community.

I would stress, however, that my own attitude towards this does not imply a defence of certain aspects of Community policy. As regards for instance the common agricultural policy, I have often expressed criticism along the lines that the present level of protection could itself discourage any real effort towards constructive breaking down of these barriers. We know that agricultural world production remains well below the requirements of humanity and that it is impossible to meet these requirements without having recourse to the industrial countries' agricultural capacity. The latter can only exist if the farmers have a guaranteed average wage comparable to those of workers in other spheres of the economy. These major reasons and the safeguard of supplies in themselves seem to justify measures of support which weigh on the taxpayer rather than the consumer and which in any case give rise to problems. In the same way, we cannot deny that agreements between the countries of the Community and their former colonies in Africa risk, from the tariff point of view, maintaining distortions which belong to the colonial past. But development policy seems to require a reasonable system of priorities on the world scale and therefore a concentration of efforts on a macro-regional level for the main areas. A multinational framework is also a sure political guarantee both for the industrialised and for the developing countries. We also know that too early liberalisation of the foreign trade of these countries, far from making possible, according to classical economic opinion, division of labour based on the natural resources of the regions, would in fact perpetuate the structure of international trade on the basis of the levels of development prevailing in each economy.

I think, indeed, that it is insufficient to persist in conceiving problems arising from the regionalisation of trade in a purely negative way setting aside the political aims which are pursued. The phenomenon of the macro-regional economic phenomena cannot be explained if they are reduced to a mere lobby. On the contrary, they are the only means of reconciling the mandatory requirements of trade and guaranteeing them growth. I doubt whether it will be possible to solve all problems of discrimination by recourse to a kind of code of good manners with control measures or enforcement measures. I think it would be more realistic to think of subsequent measures of liberalisation as an aim to be sought by co-operation among the economic areas, which cannot be considered as something transitory, and which at the point we have reached should be the main future guarantee of international trade.

COMMENT *by Lawrence McQuade*

We desperately need effective political leadership and political will if we are to overcome the current decline and disintegration of the orderly system of trade and monetary rules which have guided transatlantic and world community since World War II.

To get such leadership, we need to change attitudes on both sides of the Atlantic. On one side, the European Economic Community has been deeply immersed in the birth pains of economic and political integration. Practical expedients and pragmatic adjustments have weighed heavier than international trading rules on a number of important issues, including the common agricultural and preferential arrangements with non-EEC countries. Moreover, the executive authority of the EEC itself has limitations militating against effective international leadership.

Across the Atlantic, the Americans have been embroiled with internal concerns and with the extended exasperation of Vietnam. Moreover, the various U.S. groups formerly allied in the fight for liberal trade have fragmented. Most prominently, American labour in the form of the powerful AFL-CIO has come out foursquare for protectionist legislation of the worst sort.[1] And the business community is ambivalent, infused with the feeling that other countries – especially Japan, but also Europe – are "unfair" to the U.S. exporter. (The accuracy is, for this purpose, less important than the feeling.) Of course, the shoe, textile, steel and some other industries have a clear-cut commitment to the programmes for import relief.

After two-and-a-half years of "benign neglect", President Nixon's administration woke up sharply when the 1970 and 1971

[1] Louis Kraar, "Labour's Big Push for Protectionism", *Fortune*, March 1967, pp. 92 et seq.

balance-of-payments deficit soared to unbelievable levels and
the balance of trade, which had been positive since before World
War II, turned negative. Feeling more sinned against than
sinning, the U.S. sent forth its tough Texan, Treasury Secretary
John Connally, to use its leverage to rectify things. Such a bully
attitude is a poor substitute for leadership.

Farther East, the Japanese have never quite accepted the underlying notions of world economics as conceived at Bretton Woods
and substantially followed by most developed nations over the
last 25 years.

The less developed countries and the Communist countries are,
likewise, too different in tradition and impact to be sensible
candidates to lead the world towards improved trading relationships.

So it comes back to the Atlantic community to escape current
parochialism (as we can) and to provide the leadership and its
counterpart – effective *response* to broad-gauged international
leadership.

Yet transatlantic discussions in recent years offer little hope.
The recently retired U.S. Ambassador to the EEC, Robert
Schaetzel has called it the "dialogue of the deaf", as both
"America and Europe are cursed by a preoccupation with their
own affairs and an inclination to deal with domestic problems in
ways that ignore their impact on the other side of the Atlantic".[2]

In contrast, Schaetzel quotes Jean Monnet: "Let's get everybody on one side of the table and get the problem on the other."

That is our leadership task. It begins with both sides of the
Atlantic accepting the importance of re-establishing sound rules of
the game. Then it will require serious listening to each other –
and to Japan, the less developed countries, and even the Communist countries.

Given these attitudes, I can see possibilities of effective
initiatives and effective co-operation from the United States, from
Canada and from the EEC countries.

The proper goal has already been defined: a liberal international trading environment. The Charybdis to be avoided is
the "constricted and conflicting trading relationships that intensified monetary and other disruptive factors leading to depression
and poor economic performance on a worldwide scale in the
1930s".

In essence, such a goal means a salvaging and revitalisation of

[2] Robert Schaetzel, "A Dialogue of the Deaf Across the Atlantic", *Fortune*,
November 1972, pp. 148 et seq.

the basic elements of GATT: trade substantially free of restrictions; the absence of discrimination as among traders in different countries; and a multilateral trading concept. It also requires monetary reform.

To be realistic, some compromises may be necessary. But the important thing will be to establish or re-establish *principles*. These principles (a) must be agreed upon at least by North America, Europe and Japan, (b) must be accepted by a large portion of the rest of the world, (c) must *be* fair to all trading countries, (d) must be *seen* by all to be fair, and (e) must include effective procedures as well as substance.

Such a systematic, orderly set of international principles provides national governments with a major and highly useful domestic political rationale for resisting internal pressure groups seeking incompatible benefits.

Moreover, an agreed, orderly set of principles tends to keep negotiations over trade and other economic relationships within their own context. The converse is also true. Less orderly – or chaotic – trade and economic relations invite bargaining in which political and security issues get mixed with – and counter-balanced with – the economic issues.

It would be regrettable for issues such as maintenance of U.S. troops in Europe as part of NATO to become bargaining levers over trade, monetary, or commercial issues. As things are going, I believe that this is quite possible.

Let me comment selectively on a few of the difficult issues with which Europe and North America must deal.

The common agricultural policy

Europe's common agricultural policy is flagrantly inconsistent with the principles of a trading system without subsidies and without excessive artificial barriers.

The variable levy on imports is a particularly offensive barrier.[3]

[3] Richard Cooper argues that it is not generally relevant to compare the U.S. agricultural support programmes with those of the EEC "because for many agricultural products the United States would, in the absence of price support and production controls, be a major exporter at prices well below its domestic support prices. This is in contrast to Europe, which for most agricultural goods would be a major importer in the absence of price supports and imports protection. Thus the American agricultural support system places the burden very largely on the American consumer, and therefore represents an internal redistribution of income, while the European system, in addition to burdening the consumer imposes major costs on residents of other countries as well, and thus represents an international redistribution of income." "Trade Policy is Foreign Policy", *Foreign Policy*, 9 (Winter 1972–73), p. 24.

(What a shame that the continent did not – or perhaps *could* not – adopt the British system of income support for its farmers rather than causing the British to adopt the CAP!)

In a practical sense, the United States has managed to increase its agricultural exports to the EEC despite the CAP. But the CAP commits the deeper sin of undercutting international trade *principles*, and thereby acting as a serious sore point and a major contributor to the current malaise of the international trading system.

Action within the EEC on this issue will be extremely difficult. High support prices have powerful domestic political support – especially in France. Moreover, the CAP has been important to political solidarity, particularly between France and Germany.

However, as Mr Smith argues, it is bad economics, because high support price subsidies without quantitative controls artificially stimulate production without proper market demand. It is also an expensive budget cost to the participants.

While abolition of the CAP at this stage may not be achievable, some modifications are surely a necessary price for progress towards the broader goal. The U.S. has proposed that all elements of protection be converted into fixed-duty equivalents and bound against increase; then negotiations for tariff reductions could be negotiated and implemented over a long period of time. The proposal merits careful consideration.

Special trading preferences

A second major dereliction from international trade principles is the EEC's special arrangements with former colonies, some non-EEC European nations like Austria and many Mediterranean countries. The political pragmatism – even the charitable solicitude – prompting such arrangements is perhaps understandable although it is hard to see why the EEC accepts reverse preferences from the less developed participants.

But the system is nefarious; pointing towards a world in which North America, Japan, the Far East and Latin America become a separate trading group or groups – the "outs". It is a precedent for regionalism rather than multilateralism. It should be phased out and thereafter prohibited.

Quantitative limits

The problem of quotas for industries which conceive themselves threatened by imports is classic. The United States sins mightily: it has quotas on beef, steel, petroleum (though this may change) and dairy products. It has sponsored the "voluntary" limitations on exports of textiles – using considerable political muscle to see that unwilling trading partners adopt such controls.

Europe and Canada, in turn, have quota arrangements with the Japanese which divert much of their exports disproportionately to the U.S. and similar open markets.

These sorts of things – including "escape clause" tariffs – are sometimes politically necessary expedients. To keep them under control, we must depend on international rules enforcing specific, time-limited phase-out plans – perhaps ameliorated by adjustment assistance payments or other help for those damaged by the transition. Such help, however, should be the responsibility of the country where the plant or people are located and should not be imposed upon the international community.

Institutional reform

Reviving international principles is particularly dependent upon effective procedures and effective enforcement. The GATT is fundamentally sound and has broad acceptance. More successful enforcement is perhaps the major improvement needed.

However, the industrial countries of the world need to work together to adopt more liberal trade measures among themselves which would then be extended, under GATT, to all others. To work out such arrangements – on issues such as those discussed here – we should seriously consider utilising the OECD machinery as the continuing forum.

Finally, let me reiterate the importance of attitude.

I worry about the United States' attitude. The "tough" line evidenced by Secretary of the Treasury John Connally's *Blitzkrieg* of 1971 has lots of appeal within the United States. This stems from the myopia found on both sides of the Atlantic and in Japan.

If less dramatic initiatives fail to overcome the current "dialogue of the deaf", both sides will no doubt negotiate with too much tough tactics and too little statesmanship.

Somehow, we must all get on the same side of the table – and soon. We must start listening to each other; start affirming agreed-upon principles by which we can all abide; and start living within those principles.

Chapter X

The Future of International Monetary Management

CLAUDIO SEGRÉ

INTRODUCTION

WRITING JUST NOW the aftermath of yet another international monetary crisis, one is tempted to rephrase the title of this paper as follows: "*Is* there a future for international monetary management?" At this juncture the answer would seem to be: "No".

Yet quite a different answer would have been heard at the end of 1958, when the return to convertibility for the major currencies ushered in what seemed to be a brave new world in monetary affairs. We have in fact been witnessing, ever since that time, the gradual build-up of the situation that was to lead to the succession of crises of the last three years. We now find ourselves saddled with an inherently unstable exchange-rate system, with the reintroduction of exchange controls practically worldwide, and finally with the threat of restrictions to trade and investment. Almost everything that could possibly go wrong did go wrong, and there is no point in trying to describe here a situation which is well known to everyone and which has been the subject of diagnoses that few would dispute.

The keys to the solution of the present difficulties are obviously not technical but political, both at the domestic level and in the international arena. Let me comment briefly on two points. Domestically, one can say that the proper and timely use of all the policy instruments needed to restrain inflationary developments or to stimulate the economy has much too often been sacrificed to considerations of political expediency. Thus, monetary policy, involving less of a political commitment, was made to carry the burden that should normally be that of budgetary policy. As a result, repercussions on the external accounts were bound both to reduce the domestic effectiveness of the measures and to lead to disturbances abroad.

At the international level, the major political difficulty was the reluctance, until recently, of the major interested parties to seek a solution together in the common interest by negotiation on such matters as exchange rates, rather than trying to make their interests prevail through the pressure of the market, sometimes stimulated by a skilful use of the mass media.

The awareness that the Western nations were on a collision course was perhaps most acute in the weeks following President Nixon's measures of 15 August 1971. A false step at that time could have meant a plunge into trade war, with immeasurable consequences for all concerned. The Smithsonian agreement, greeted with relief by everyone, criticised by many for its fragility, was in fact a noteworthy piece of international negotiation; this was the first time that the whole structure of exchange rates was recognised to be the common concern of a group of countries rather than the result of unco-ordinated unilateral action by each of them subject to quite theoretical control by the International Monetary Fund. It must be recognised that this approach was a step towards a more meaningful concept of international monetary management than we had ever known in the past.

The classical gold standard – if it ever existed – was supposed to embody the principle of an automatic discipline imposed upon domestic policies by external currency flows. The Bretton Woods agreement tried a different tack by admitting that countries could be allowed to change the par-value of their currencies without in fact being asked to justify the domestic policies which made such changes necessary. As has rightly been remarked, while the *size* of change was deemed to be a matter for international concern, the *intiative* of such a change was left entirely to the individual countries. They had the option of changing their par-values, if they so chose, or of undertaking instead domestic policies which would correct the disequilibrium in the balance of payments. In this case, provisions for external financing and exchange restrictions on a temporary basis were made. The case in which the country would neither adjust the external value of its currency nor undertake corrective domestic measures was not contemplated: yet this case was to become in fact the rule and bring about the downfall of the system.

We have just touched upon the first point which was to bring about the transition from the Bretton Woods system to the new emerging form of international monetary management: a way had to be found to prevent the strains and stresses which originated first from the "gold-dollar" and then from the "paper-dollar" standard endangering the survival of an orderly pattern of exchange rates.

The second major point which has influenced thinking in monetary matters in recent years has been belated recognition of the growing importance of capital movements, whether linked to direct or portfolio investment, to trade financing or to the management of liquid balances. I believe, contrary to a widely-held opinion, that this is not a pathological development, but the natural result of the closer interconnection of the major trading countries. However, there is little doubt that in a context where par-values tended to fall out of line for lack of quick readjustments, this could be (and in fact was) a destabilising influence.

The third factor compelling a reconsideration of the system and a new approach was the slow emergence of a new trading block, gradually evolving towards economic union, the European Economic Community. While the behaviour of its member countries has been far from harmonious in monetary affairs, a growing determination has been apparent that payment problems *vis-à-vis* third countries should not lead to a disruption of their mutual relations. One can point out incidentally that the problems of international monetary management which have been appearing within the EEC in the attempt to introduce a modest degree of solidarity in the movements of the member countries' currencies ("the snake in the tunnel") have provided an interesting testing ground for a broader approach. The point has been proved beyond reasonable doubt that a system of stable exchange rates among the member countries could only be obtained by subjecting the principal instruments of economic policy to a degree of co-ordination much greater than had hitherto been the case and probably greater than most countries were ready to accept.

If such then are the pressures impelling changes in the present international monetary arrangements, what system is likely to emerge from the current negotiations? Being too aware of the political implications of the problem, I can hardly rely on the conclusions that would emerge from a purely technical analysis; on the other hand, I believe the negotiations will want to build on firmer ground than simple expediency. Therefore I prefer to tread a middle path, that is to offer a view – which some may describe as wishful thinking – of what could be the final result, without setting a time horizon for the present evolution. Some of the features of such hypothetical arrangements are much to my liking; others I dislike intensely; but it may be useful for me to give a quick summary before commenting on specific points. The main characteristics of the structure which I think will eventually emerge are the following:

1. The par-value system will be maintained, although provisions will be made for temporary floating and for wider margins around the established parities: these will be expressed in terms of an international unit established within the IMF.

2. Rules of the game will be formulated to ensure timely adjustment in the balance-of-payments position of both surplus and deficit countries. It will be the central task of international monetary management to see to it that if domestic policy measures do not result in a correction, then exchange rates are adjusted so as to bring about the same result. There will be nothing automatic about exchange-rate adjustments, but if certain agreed indicators do not show evidence of correction, and if the country fails to comply with the rules of the game, then sanctions will be applied. In the case of a surplus country a unilateral surcharge might be imposed on its exports by other countries and in the case of a deficit country, both multilateral and bilateral credit facilities might be withheld.

3. Controls will remain in effect on capital movements, whether in the form of two-tier markets or of administrative restrictions. These will be lifted only to the extent that (and in those areas where) the stability of exchange rate seems assured and therefore speculative movements are not feared.

4. Additions to reserves will only take place in the form of international assets, such as special drawing rights: national currencies will cease to inflate existing liquidity. There will be a return to "convertibility", implying that reserve centres will be able to settle claims only by parting with assets and not by increasing their liabilities.

5. By appropriate measures of consolidation or by the creation of an IMF "substitution account'– or by a mixture of the two – the existing overhang of dollars in the hands of monetary authorities will enjoy an exchange guarantee in terms of an internationally accepted asset. We would thus get rid of the destabilising effect which the existence of the overhang has on private holders who will be reassured once the monetary

authorities stop the war of nerves at present being fought over intervention in exchange markets.

6. The long-standing demand of developing countries that some sort of "link" should be introduced between the issue of new international assets in the form of SDRs and the provision of development assistance will in the end be satisfied.

A certain consensus already exists on most of the points detailed above, but it stands to reason that the transition to new arrangements which would imply a much greater weight for international monetary management will not be easy: in fact, it will be punctuated by crises and setbacks. There will be times when a splitting of the present Atlantic community into opposing trading blocks will seem to have been consummated. Relations with Japan will continue to be a source of worry for both the United States and the EEC. Trade with the Soviet Union and China will develop to the point where they will ask for a say – or at any rate exercise an influence – in world monetary affairs. The oil-producing countries of the Middle East may also prove to be uncomfortable partners in the present context.

The critical issues in achieving a meaningful form of international monetary management should now be examined. To achieve a proper perspective, I have grouped them under three different headings: objectives, centres of power, and techniques and attitudes.

OBJECTIVES

The really difficult task in international monetary management is that negotiators must hammer out a compromise while a time-bomb that could set off a political as well as a monetary explosion is still ticking. If this defusing operation is successful, then managing whatever system will have been agreed upon ought, by comparison, to appear easy. The official objective of the present negotiations is to restore convertibility to the dollar, to substitute reserve currencies with some form of international reserve currency based probably on SDRs and to devise a system whereby international payments would be kept in balance at all times by properly timed parity changes.

The consensus that made it possible to draft the mandate for the Committee of Twenty left in the dark the divisive issues which still remain; and none is more divisive that the concept of "burden sharing" in balance-of-payments readjustment. This is a political concept, since it involves decisions concerning who shall have to take corrective action, not who shall eventually bear the economic consequences of such action. The Bretton Woods system, in its late "degenerate" version, was asymmetrical in two respects: there was no incentive to promote prompt adjustment in surplus countries and insufficient pressure was put on deficit countries that were reserve centres and therefore had privileged access to balance-of-payments finance. It has rightly been remarked that no country can escape undergoing an economic restructuring whenever balance-of-payments adjustment requires a change in real demand or supply. Why then is so much emphasis put on the need to build up a symmetrical system as opposed to the present asymmetrical one?

The reason is that, at any given moment of time, a number of alternatives are open to a country in balance-of-payments disequilibrium, the main branches of the alternative being to *finance* this disequilibrium or to *correct* it. Some of the corrective decisions may be very painful indeed and require an increase in unemployment or, conversely, in the rate of inflation. It is not surprising therefore that countries should consider it a privilege to retain as much freedom of decision as possible in this field. I would submit, however, that international monetary management can reduce the embarrassment of governments in taking unpopular decisions: it is therefore in their best interest that outside pressure should be exercised and incentives be offered in the framework of the reformed new international monetary arrangements. The EEC experience, where Community-level decisions are continuously invoked in order to justify the adoption of domestic measures, is quite revealing in this respect.

We have thus implicitly defined the task that international monetary management will have to face in the future: thanks to international control of liquidity creation and to the existence of agreed rules for exchange-rate adjustment, incentives and penalties will have to be provided for countries whose payments position does not seem to respond to domestic policy measures. It will require great skill to steer between two dangers: that of providing too much liquidity, so that there will in fact be little incentive to adjust, and that of adopting too strict criteria and withholding assistance, so that the exchange rate has to take all the strain even in temporary disturbances.

The role of international monetary managements will remain a marginal one, in the sense that decisions directly affecting the level of employment and price trends will continue to be taken at the national level. It will, however, be also an active one which will involve continuous international negotiations within some kind of body which we may for the moment assume to be the IMF in a new streamlined version.

CENTRES OF POWER

We now come to a second crucial question: who will in fact be entrusted with international monetary management? The idea of a central power endowed with a measure of control over international monetary affairs is bound to evoke the hostility both of those who want to safeguard national prerogatives and of those who are suspicious of "big governments" in whatever form, technocratic or political. By the same token this idea is bound to attract criticism from those that believe in the virtues of an automatic system which would impose an "objective discipline" on all the participants in the system.

Let us first dispose of this particular point by indicating that the much praised gold standard discipline has in fact never worked, except for the countries which were the satellites of the great financial centres of the 19th century and that, when it worked, it entailed consequences that would today be unacceptable. As for the other radical proposal of freely floating exchange rates for all countries, it has to be rejected out of hand and for perfectly good reasons. Exchange rate movements have a destabilising impact on domestic prices and wages and this impact is practically irreversible under modern conditions for price and wage increases prompted by devaluation.

A depreciation as well as an appreciation of the currency in the market may also be totally inappropriate – and indeed destabilising – to correct temporary balance-of-payments disequilibria which are unrelated to competitive distortions in prices and costs but arise for instance from capital movements prompted by political fears, interest rate differentials, etc. Countries should be able to choose in such cases other and more appropriate methods to correct their deficits or surpluses.

International monetary management will take place in the future, I believe, in the framework of rules and procedures that will strike a balance between the law of reason that would correspond to an intellectually satisfactory system and the law of the jungle which we have in fact seen in action in the past two or three years. Individual decisions will, however, still involve the exercise of discretion and that can only happen in a climate of co-operation between the major powers participating in this continuous process of negotiation.

Quite apart from helping to smooth the process of balance-of-payments adjustments among the member countries, the new arrangements will embody the principle that increases in internationally created reserves should be devoted to the financing of policies mutually agreed among the eventual reserve holders. We have here one further task for international monetary management. In the present system, where reserve accruals came from the United States deficit, one can say that the international community has been in fact financing American policies. As for SDRs, their allocation *pro rata* of the Fund quotas simply denotes the absence of a policy. I should venture to guess that in the new arrangements a link between SDR creation and development financing will be instituted, in one of several possible forms including the allocation of SDRs to development agencies either directly by the Fund or indirectly by the receiving countries with high *per capita* incomes. One could also include among the internationally agreed policies that would qualify for support, the recycling of reversible capital movements through open market operations conducted with SDRs.

This very tall order of business could certainly not be dealt with by the future reformed IMF if the relations among its member countries remained as unbalanced as they have been in the past. Negotiations will be easier and management more constructive if, as has been recognised by Secretary Schultz, "The European Community will accomplish sufficient progress towards regional monetary union to be able to speak with one voice and to be treated as a unit for the purpose of applying the basic rules of the international monetary and trading system." It may be appropriate in this context to mention this subject briefly, but it would be superfluous to go into details. Regional monetary union in the EEC is one particularly significant venture in the field of international monetary management. The road has been well mapped since 1971, the first steps have been taken and the first setbacks have also been suffered. The reduction of the margins of fluctuations among the member countries' currencies has faced them squarely with the problem of providing assistance to countries which may be experiencing difficulties. From there to the establishment of a European Monetary Co-operation Fund there was only one logical step. The next one will be the progressive pooling of the member countries' international monetary reserves.

To quote again Secretary Schultz in his IMF speech: "it is logical that countries in the process of forming a monetary union, with the higher degree of political and economic integration that it implies, should desire to maintain narrow bands among themselves and they should be allowed to do so." I would go further and argue that the gradual acceptance of the objective of monetary union among the member countries is the most powerful stimulus to the harmonisation of monetary, fiscal and other economic policies which is a condition itself for survival of the EEC

European monetary union would make the co-operation needed for international management easier also in another respect, after order has been restored to the world payment system. The strains and stresses affecting each of the member countries' currencies arise today less from their mutual relationship than from the relationship with the dollar. At the same time, trade among such countries currently encompasses 60-70 per cent of their total exports, as compared to a share of about 8 per cent only for their exports to the United States. Therefore, as has been remarked, exchange-rate readjustments with non-member countries would raise far less resistance when needed to restore competitive conditions with these countries if stability could be preserved among the currencies of the EEC. The same reasoning applies to the case of a "joint float" which may well appear in the future as an unavoidable temporary measure to cope with the problems of the transition period, while the United States progressively returns to balance-of-payments equilibrium.

TECHNIQUES AND ATTITUDES

It is customary for "realists" to dismiss monetary arrangements based upon international, rather than national, management as exercises akin to science fiction and entirely divorced from practical politics or economics. Yet, the much vaunted "pragmatic approach" – i.e. that problems should be tackled one by one and only when they become acute – has brought us to the brink of disaster. It seems imperative to try a new approach and I believe that the political will now exists to do so.

Will international monetary management involve the surrender of policy instruments capable of acting directly upon the national economies? Certainly not. However, strict limitations will have to be respected by everyone in order to avoid measures that would work at cross-purposes in the various countries concerned.

To a certain extent this is a problem of sorting out, among the possible alternative techniques of internal demand management in a broad sense, those that least risk setting in motion reaction in the external sector. Thus, the role of monetary policy and the notion that central banks have the obligation single-handedly to defend both internal and external equilibrium are clearly in need of a reappraisal.

A much greater effort will be needed to correct certain mental attitudes that have become deeply engrained after several years of what has been jokingly but accurately enough described as "international monetary terrorism". Official declarations, press reports and business opinion put forward on international monetary events an endless series of biassed comments that quickly become conventional wisdom. These comments reflect one common notion: that all inflationary pressures are of external origin and ultimately stem from the United States payments deficit – and lead to one common result: the sapping of confidence not only in the international monetary system but also in the domestic currencies.

This psychological climate appears far from favourable to a wide-ranging negotiation aiming to recast the principles of the world payment system. Yet there is no viable alternative to a joint effort, since no country or group of countries is today in a position to fend for itself. It would, be a sad paradox if, at the moment when the Soviet Union and China seem at last ready to join the mainstream of international trade, those countries that have enjoyed the greatest benefits throughout the post-war years were to opt out for lack of imagination and political courage.

COMMENT *by Richard N. Cooper*

Let me try to identify some of the issues which it appears to me involve disagreement. This is often posed in the form of technical issues but frequently involves much broader political issues, or in some cases is even a cover for political considerations.

My starting point will be the position taken early in 1973 by the financial ministers of the European Economic Community on the question of monetary reform. They once again emphasised the need to restore the convertibility of the dollar. At the same time they tentatively rejected a United States plan submitted to the Committee of Twenty in November 1972 that called for balance-of-payments adjustment, presumptively in the form of changes in exchange rates keyed to certain objective indicators over a country's balance-of-payments position and in particular to its reserve movements. The furthest that the Finance Ministers were willing to go was to suggest that movements in reserves should trigger off consultations, rather than adjustment: although they did not reject the idea of indicators as a basis for exchange-rate adjustment, they certainly rejected the exclusive use of the level of reserves. I am not sure whether the position that they took was merely tactical or whether it reflected a deep misunder-standing of the issues. In either case it revealed an imperfection in communication between both sides of the Atlantic. The facts of the situation suggest that the United States would be very unwise to agree to convertibility of the dollar without very tight assurances on the question of balance-of-payments adjustment mechanisms. This is also true of convertibility of the dollar that is achieved indirectly or by the back door, through a commitment to intervene in the exchange market.

The reason why it would be mad for the United States to make such a commitment is quite simple. There are roughly 80 billion dollars held in official reserves and at least an equivalent amount held in private hands in the Euro-dollar market and directly in the U.S. banks. How great are these sums? It is hard to know because there is some double accounting, but probably over 150 billion dollars are held outside the United States in various forms these days against U.S. reserves of a paltry 13 billion dollars, or some 17 or 18 billion dollars with drawing rights at the IMF. Many of the funds held outside the United States (and indeed held inside the United States) are highly mobile; and that means that at the first incentive for funds to move rapidly from one currency to another, dollars into marks and from marks into yen or whatever, a system involving convertibility without some kind of co-operating mechanism would simply break.

I am not one of those who feel that uncontrolled capital move-ments are an unmitigated good. It is no secret that much of international capital movement of today involves escape from national fiscal authorities, and that much of it involves escape from national monetary actions which are designed to stabilise domestic economies. The types of international capital move-ments that tend to thwart that design seem to me to serve no social purpose; and therefore it would not be a bad thing in principle to rein them in or indeed to stop them entirely.

But nevertheless I am not optimistic at all about the possibility of controlling them without so impeding normal international economic intercourse that we would do great damage to all our economies. There are simply too many channels, given the depth and the breadth of today's international transactions, through which capital movements can take place in practice if not in form. Even trade in raw materials, for example, increasingly takes place under long-term contracts and with credit terms which are stretching out over time; and by varying the terms of credit slightly, by what used to be called in the British context the "leads and lags", one can move enormous amounts of capital.

The best we can do, it seems to me, is to create some friction to slow down the movements a bit, but we cannot stop them. It may be we shall be required to create the frictions; indeed I think that as long as monetary policy is going to be used as an instrument of domestic stabilisation it is probably necessary to create some frictions against these capital movements: but in no sense will creating these frictions replace international monetary reform. Capital movement on a scale which we are not used to in our thinking and which we have only experienced in recent years, will continue to take place even with such impediments as we put in their way.

It seems to me therefore that we need to do two other things. One is to limit the incentives for capital to move; and the other is to have an arrangement to pick up the pieces after it has moved, if such movements are potentially damaging in one way or another. Let me take each one of these in turn.

The economic incentives are two quite different types. Leaving aside politically motivated movements in capital, the washing back and forth of capital takes place partly in response to expectations about exchange-rate movements, and the gains that can be made on such movements, and partly in response to differences in interest-rate differential. The first of these depends on the exchange-rate régime that we have and the second on the degree of divergence in monetary policy that different national economies have. What we have seen in the last five years or so, starting I believe just before the devaluation of sterling in 1967, is really large movements of capital in response to large changes in exchange rates. The régime of floating rates eliminates that type of capital movement, but on the other hand it may encourage a different type of capital movement, whereby those accumulative speculative movements may drive the exchange rates one way or another and then profit-takers sell out, while the less astute among speculators are still moving into a currency: a phenomenon that we see in land transactions on the stock markets and so forth or in other cases in which there are relatively free-markets. I myself believe that the risk from the second type of capital movement is very much less than the risk of damage we run from capital movements which are really betting against the willingness and capacity of national authorities to maintain a fixed rate which may well be a wrong rate. That, however, is a question of judgment on which I recognise that views differ.

As far as monetary problems are concerned, I think, as has been suggested above, that countries would be well advised to co-ordinate their monetary policies more, not allow them to get so much out of line. This, I think, is good advice – but it is also advice which is not likely to be followed at any time in the near future and for very good reasons, namely that the most important responsibility of national governments these days is to maintain a reasonable degree of economic stability in the domestic economy. The capacity to do this with a division of responsibility between executives and legislatures in the fiscal area is very much more sharply limited than it is in the monetary area; and for this reason I think monetary policy for some time to come will continue to be used especially in countries with federal systems, such as Canada, the United States and Germany, but to some extent in all countries principally as an instrument of domestic policy and in spite of the international consequences as far as the movements of funds are concerned.

This leads me then to the second part of the argument, which is that after whatever co-ordination that takes place we still need an arrangement to pick up the pieces. This, I would suggest, is a prime area for international co-operation. There is a very old idea but one which can be translated from the national to the international level quite comfortably: that is, to create in the IMF or in the BIS a true lender of last resort capacity. The IMF, although its quotas have grown over time, simply has not kept pace, in terms of the magnitude of its capacity to lend, with the magnitude of the problem. Indeed, the quota system of the IMF is much too cumbersome for these purposes. The IMF needs the capacity to lend quickly in very large amounts and then to make any necessary adjustments, tidying up after the fact. The swap arrangements grew up as a substitute for the IMF in this area. The swap arrangements themselves are too small, amounting now only to 12 billion dollars in U.S. swaps with around a dozen other countries. They could be greatly enlarged; but this is not simply a problem between the United States and other countries bilaterally but one that will involve pairs of other countries as well. I think that this is a natural area for internationalising the whole process and giving the IMF this capacity.

Let me return to the question of adjustment and argue that we do need much greater flexibility in exchange rates than we have had until recently, among the major components of the world's economy. I think that it is entirely a secondary question whether that flexibility is achieved through what are nominally floating rates in which the national authorities intervene in the markets to limit the flows or whether it is a régime which involves a declaration of fixed parities, but with rules and understandings which change those parities quite frequently. The key issue is the need to agree jointly on parity of exchange rates continuously or more or less continuously. Exchange rates that will have to be changed quite frequently and should be changed, if they have to be changed at all, should be changed by small amounts frequently rather than by large amounts infrequently because of the problem of capital movements.

The *de facto* system that we now have would be a workable system with one crucial additional component: that is rules for intervention. We have a system in which all of the major economic areas of the world are floating with respect to one another. I do not think that a freely floating system of this kind is sustainable, simply because the exchange rate is far too important an economic variable in most countries for governments to allow it to move freely in response to every pressure that may come through the exchange market; but if they are going to intervene, there must be some rules of intervention because the exchange rate is intrinsically and inherently a two-sided affair. Two parties are involved in it, and without some rules of intervention, there may be conflicting interventions by different governments operating on the same market, one country trying to drive its rate up and another country trying to drive the same rate down. Therefore we need a system with established rules of intervention. It is not hard, I think, to design such a system from a technical point of view. The more difficult part of designing it is agreement on the policies that underlie the choice of exchange rates; and that brings us back to the question of indicators of some type which would suggest when a country's balance of payments is out of line, such as the United States put forward in November 1972 and the EEC ministers partly rejected. It seems to me that this is really the core of the difficulties among the major participants in monetary reform now and something that has to be ironed out.

Let me conclude with a note on the question of sovereignty. There is, or seems to be, a lot of anxiety in all our countries about loss of national sovereignty. I think it is worth asking the question, What is it we mean by national sovereignty? Is it the capacity to control our own destiny, or is it the illusion of the capacity to control our own destiny? It seems to me that we have long since, all of us, passed the point at which we had the capacity to control our own destiny, or more accurately to control it without incurring such costs as would isolate us completely from the rest of the world economy and all the benefits that flow from it. It seems to me, therefore, that when we talk about pooling of sovereignty or even cession of sovereignty, in exchange-rate policy for example, we are not talking about something real, but about perceptions. We do not have "sovereignty" in that sense even now, and we never shall.

Chapter XI

An Atlantic–Japanese Energy Policy

WALTER J. LEVY

INTRODUCTION

THE PROSPERITY AND SECURITY of the whole non-Communist world depend on sufficient availability of energy on satisfactory economic terms.

During the next ten to twenty years, oil will provide the mainstay of the world's energy supplies.

In practical terms, because of the size of known reserves and the lead time for finding and developing new oil and other energy resources, the world's growing needs will be supplied predominantly by huge increases of oil imports from the Middle East – mainly the Persian Gulf area.

Directly connected with the anticipated large advances of oil imports, the consuming countries now face another set of problems which have developed very much as predicted last year.

The cost of oil imports has risen tremendously with extraordinarily difficult implications for the balance of payments of many consuming countries.

There are also very serious problems caused by unprecedented foreign exchange accumulations and the international use of such funds in the case of some of the major oil-producing countries, such as Saudi Arabia and Abu Dhabi.

We have also been witnessing a complete-change in the political, economic, strategic and power relationships between the oil-producing, importing and home countries of international oil companies and the national oil companies of producing and importing countries.

An energy policy for the oil-importing countries cannot be limited to the Atlantic Group of nations but must include Japan, the non-Communist world's second strongest single economic power and one of its largest oil importers.

It should also encompass other developed nations such as South Africa, Australia and New Zealand and should take account of the position of oil-importing developing countries in Latin America, Africa and Asia.

But the policy and organisation as suggested here will refer mainly to the Atlantic Group plus Japan as the nations with major world influence and responsibilities.

In the following review we shall deal as comprehensively as possible with the set of issues and changing relationships posed by energy–oil problems during the next ten years or so. The analysis will, I believe, demonstrate the urgent necessity for the early establishment of an energy policy for a new Atlantic–Japanese partnership.

SOME BASIC DATA ON ENERGY SUPPLY AND FINANCE

Many very competent studies have been devoted to the present and prospective position of energy supply and demand of the United States, Europe and Japan, as well as the non-Communist world as a whole.

I do not plan to repeat this analysis or to burden this presentation unduly with figures. I will only refer, as a point of departure, to the practically unanimous conclusion that from now on – certainly until the early 1980s – U.S. energy requirements can be met only by very substantial increases in oil imports. If present U.S. policies and trends are left to take their course, oil shipments from abroad will advance from about 4.7 million barrels per day in 1972 to over 11 million barrels per day in 1980.

As far as our allies are concerned, they would, except for the promising developments in the North Sea and the unknown potential in Japanese offshore waters or in other "safe" areas, have in general very limited, if any, possibilities of developing dependable alternative energy supplies based on synthetic oil or gas because of their relatively small coal, shale, and tar sands resources. But even with the most optimistic estimates for North Sea developments, the oil imports of Europe and Japan combined are estimated to advance during the same period from some 18 million barrels daily to 30 million barrels daily.

The preponderant part of all these imports – for the United States, Western Europe and Japan – would have to come from Middle East producing countries. Their output would rise from 18 million barrels daily in 1972, to an estimated 35 to 40 million barrels daily by 1980. The United States will, for the first time, compete with Europe and Japan for major oil supplies from the Middle East, whose share in total U.S. oil imports would, by

1980, amount to about 50-55 per cent and in those of Western Europe and Japan to about 75-80 per cent. There is little doubt that Middle East oil reserves are sufficient to cover these requirements, but without very large new discoveries this situation would change, probably during the 1980s.

The U.S.S.R. will most likely remain self-sufficient in covering its oil and other energy requirements and may, on balance, continue to be an exporter of oil and natural gas.

Let me cite two more sets of data that are most relevant for the formulation and urgent implementation of energy policy. The total value of U.S. net imports of energy materials, mostly oil, may, according to U.S. Department of Commerce data, easily reach $18 to $24 billion annually by 1980, those of Europe $23 to $31 billion, and those of Japan $12 to $16 billion – as compared with $2.3 billion, $8.5 billion and $3.1 billion in 1970, respectively. The revenues likely to accrue to Middle East producing countries can tentatively be estimated at about $40 billion annually by 1980 – as against $9 billion in 1972 – with Saudi Arabia alone accounting for as much as perhaps half of the 1980 total. In some of the countries, such as Saudi Arabia and Abu Dhabi, a large part of these funds could not possibly be absorbed in their internal economies.

The United States thus must share with Europe and Japan the deep concern about the physical availability, the terms of trade, the balance-of-payments impact, and the investment and monetary consequences of heavily increased oil imports. But the United States, as the only superpower of the non-Communist world with global commitments for its defence, carries the additional responsibility of protecting its capability thus to perform, especially since the Soviet Union and, for that matter, the People's Republic of China do not primarily depend on external sources of energy. The United States simply cannot afford an ever-increasing over-dependence for its oil supplies on a handful of foreign, largely unstable, countries. Otherwise, its security – and that of its Allies – as well as its prosperity and its freedom of action in foreign policy formulation, will be in jeopardy. But the United States does have a realistic and economically manageable alternative – and that is to point its energy policy towards accelerated development of its large domestic resource potential for conventional and synthetic hydrocarbons and nuclear energy.

Even though such alternatives may now look expensive, the cost of foreign oil imports is likely to escalate continuously, and will sooner or later – and probably sooner rather than later – approach the cost of alternative sources of supply that could be developed in the United States.

If all realistic actions to increase its domestic energy supplies were to be taken with utmost urgency, U.S. dependence on total energy imports by the early 1980s might be limited to perhaps around 20 per cent – instead of somewhat over 30 per cent if present trends were permitted to take their course. U.S. oil imports at that time would be substantially lower, perhaps about one-third, than they would otherwise have been, and probably would not exceed the "danger" level. But, as from now, continuing dependence of Europe and Japan on Middle East oil – and to an important degree the United States – appears to be inevitable. And the build-up of Middle East oil revenues will reflect that.

So much as a prologue for defining the statistical magnitude of the problems that the United States, as well as our allies, will have to face and that must be coped with by the new policies dealing with our developing energy situation.

CHANGES IN THE POWER STRUCTURE OF INTERNATIONAL OIL

In addition to the problems of security of oil supplies in terms of physical availability and the worldwide financial impact of ever-growing oil purchases by the importing countries and ever-growing oil revenues by a few producing countries, there are equally relevant issues affecting the economic, political and strategic future of the oil-importing countries. These are the result of a fundamental change in the relationships between the international oil industry and the producing countries, the importing countries and the home countries of the international oil companies.

Let us just set the scene by summarily describing the immediate post-war period. Based on a dramatic expansion of oil production and exports, mainly in the Middle East, the international oil companies effectively supplied the bulk of the ever-increasing energy requirements of the non-Communist world. From 1946 to say the late 1950s, the companies – on the basis of their rich Middle East oil concessions and at least indirectly benefiting from the immense strategic, political and economic power of the United States – were able to dispose of their oil reasonably freely and on favourable commercial terms.

Moreover, the United States itself was on balance independent of foreign oil imports and possessed a sizeable reserve productive capacity from which our allies could benefit substantially during the Iranian and with some short delays also during the first Suez Crisis.

By 1960, when the Organisation of the Petroleum Exporting Countries (OPEC) was established, the relative power position of the United States was beginning to decline as Europe, Japan and the U.S.S.R. acquired new strength. It was also the time when the developing countries began to play a more important role in world affairs. The timing of the establishment of OPEC and its ever-growing influence in international oil operations was beyond doubt also in part at least the result of a certain inability and inflexibility of the international oil industry and their home governments to anticipate, assess and adjust to the changes that had begun to erode their previous paramount position of political and economic influence in oil-producing countries.

During the next twelve years, from 1960 to 1972, OPEC and its members succeeded in achieving, to begin with, minor increases in the government take of oil-producing countries, and since the early 1970s in enforcing a quantum jump in the royalty and tax payments levied on their production, capped in 1972 by the so-called participation agreement. Without going into details – and assuming present arrangements are implemented – participation means an immediate 25 per cent interest for the Arab producing countries in the Persian Gulf in existing concessions, leading to 51 per cent control within nine years. National oil companies of the major Middle East producing countries will thus become the largest sellers of crude oil. By 1984, by the way, under existing provisions, most of the important Venezuelan oil concessions will also have reverted from the oil companies to the Venezuelan Government. Algeria, Libya, and Iraq have already taken over a very substantial part of the previously foreign owned production, and the current Indonesian oil contracts also leave the Indonesian National Oil Company free to dispose of a substantial part of the oil discovered by foreign oil companies.

During the same period, the U.S. domestic oil outlook underwent drastic changes and its reserve productive potential began to disappear. By 1972, with imports of close to 5 million barrels per day, the United States had become one of the largest importers of oil, with the prospect of a continuously increasing dependence on foreign oil.

With this background, let us now shortly review the new situations and constellations of the various countries – producing, importing, and home countries of the international oil companies

– in the international oil trade, and assess the problems facing the Atlantic world and Japan which must be considered in the formulation of a realistic energy policy.

THE DOMINANT POSITION OF THE MAJOR OIL-PRODUCING COUNTRIES

Culminating with the conclusion of the participation negotiations in 1972 – which may still turn out to be not the final round of negotiations – there is little doubt that the major oil-producing countries, especially of the Middle East, have acquired an immense potential for power – as long as at least two of the more important producers are able to maintain a reasonably united front. In the case of Saudi Arabia alone, we face a situation which, within a few years, gives that country, with its overwhelming lead in reserves and production, a pivotal role in supply.

As discussed, their power is based not only on their effective control over immense oil resources on which the security and prosperity of the non-Communist world have become dependent, but will in due course derive also from their control over unprecedented financial resources which they will be able to extract from the oil purchasers. Moreover, large monetary reserves will give them the freedom to restrict their oil production for political or any other reasons, even though they would thereby forgo current income.

The control which the producing countries will be able to exercise over their oil production and exports is not only based on their participation in the oil-producing companies, but stems perhaps primarily from the exercise of their sovereign power over companies operating in their countries. There is ample precedence for such use of power with the reluctant acceptance of the oil companies and their home governments: the Kuwaiti and Libyan restrictions on production; the prohibition of exports to certain countries, including in certain circumstances even the parent countries of the oil companies; the Venezuelan oil leglisation establishing practically complete control over oil operations, which were totally under foreign private ownership. This list could be extended nearly without exception to foreign oil activities in about any of the major producing countries.

To all intents and purposes, fiscal arrangements and payments to the producing countries are subject to nearly unilateral determination by the producing countries, as reflected in the demands leading to the Teheran and Tripoli "dictates".

Peremptory demands for national ownership of tanker transportation, reinvestments in oil exploration, refining, petrochemical, LNG facilities, and other related industries are bound to be made. The establishment of levels of production and the size and direction of exports for conservation, economic, political or strategic reasons are also by now "recognised" methods of controls as exercised by many producing countries.

In this connection it is perhaps noteworthy that the development of tremendous oil resources of the Middle East does not really reflect any extensive industrial involvement of the economies of their countries or any important contribution by their people to the huge flow of oil outward and of revenue backward. The oil-producing industry operations in these countries – whoever owns them – are limited fundamentally to a small enclave, transforming an export of liquid gold from underground into a reverse flow of solid gold above ground.

As mentioned earlier, national oil companies will in due course become the largest group of crude oil sellers in the world. Even though, under recent arrangements, a substantial part of the national companies' entitlements will, for some period, be sold back to their foreign partners for distribution through their marketing channels, it is only a matter of time before the national oil companies will probably dominate the market for non-integrated third party sales of crude oil. They will become major suppliers to national oil companies in many of the importing countries of the world and will probably also deal directly with the foreign refining and marketing affiliates of the international oil companies. In fact, effective competition in crude oil sales between the producing affiliates of the international oil companies and their partners, the national companies of the producing countries, may, from a practical point of view, become very difficult if not impossible, as the producing countries' governments might not only establish the levels of production but will also, through their policies, determine the tax-paid cost and the prices at which the greatly increasing quantities of crude to which their companies will become entitled will either be sold back to their foreign partners or offered by them to their own customers.

Coupled with the expansion of crude oil sales, the national oil companies of at least some of the major producing countries will obviously work out deals for joint refining and marketing in importing countries. Likewise, the producing countries, by taking over ownership or control of an ever-expanding tanker fleet to carry their oil exports, will thereby not only increase their revenues, but further enhance their power over the international oil trade.

With Saudi Arabia, which will probably become the largest Middle East producer by far, being unable to absorb its vastly expanding oil revenues in its local economy, it is quite possible that by the early 1980s the surplus funds annually available to it may be of the order of $15 billion plus. The large and continuously growing inflow of foreign funds that would accrue to the treasuries of a few Middle East governments, and to a small number of their privileged citizens, will far exceed any accumulation of foreign exchange holdings in modern times. Realistically, such amounts could probably not be placed into long-term or short-term investments year-in year-out without risking severe international repercussions and potentially extensive restrictions on the free flow of capital. It is most unlikely that the United States, or any other developed country, would permit continued massive foreign investments on a scale that could conceivably result in foreign take-overs of important companies and industries. Moreover, the reverse flow of dividends and interest would soon add an additional unmanageable balance-of-payments burden to the oil import bill of many countries. Nor could the short-term money markets handle such extensive and most likely very volatile funds without undermining the world's monetary arrangements.

The dilemma confronting us is acutely disturbing, as any proliferation of international restrictions on capital or short-term movements of funds would, in and by themselves, be most harmful to our financial markets and monetary system. In the affected Middle East oil and capital-surplus countries, any restrictions on their investments abroad would probably be accompanied by restrictions on the output of oil. Obviously, if the income of oil-producing countries were to be "sterilised", it would be more advantageous and completely rational for them to limit their oil exports. This would then further aggravate the world oil supply situation. However, controls over the level of oil production are unfortunately likely to be introduced anyhow, even without any hostile political or economic motivation of the producing countries, for reasons of conservation and wise resource management – at least in some of the major oil-producing countries – and certainly as soon as their reserve-to-production ratio begins to decline significantly. A recent pronouncement by the Saudi Arabian Minister of Petroleum has clearly suggested such a course of action. Interestingly, his statement was coupled with the suggestion that in order to assure continued supplies, oil imports from his country be given a privileged position in the U.S. market.

Some of the major Middle East producing countries will thus become two-pronged power centres; both as a supplier of oil and as an extraordinary accumulator of capital – with the latter further strengthening their ability to withhold oil from importing countries over a considerable period of time by drawing on their financial reserves for their budgetary and trade requirements.

The size of the funds which the producing countries have at their command is, of course, based on their control of an absolutely essential resource, through which, by combined actions of OPEC countries – or perhaps even with the planned huge increases of Saudi Arabian production, the latter solely by itself – could exercise a tremendous power. Moreover, by tying the price of their oil to say a commodity basket index, any changes in currency values as such will not affect their actual purchase or investment capacities. There is little doubt that this accumulation of oil and of money power – obtained so to speak like manna from heaven, and, at least for the time being, not accompanied by any substantial contribution in political, managerial, or technical competence – would bring with it tremendous and lopsided shifts in the balance of power of a potentially explosive character.

Not the least of the dangers posed by this extreme concentration of oil power and "unearned" money power is the pervasive corruptive influence which such concentration is nearly inevitably going to have on political, economic, and commercial actions and behaviour in both the relatively primitive and unsophisticated societies of the producing countries and the advanced societies of the dependent industrialised nations. Lust for immense power which is there for the asking and greed for money in unheard of amounts could easily corrode part of their – as well as our – political and social structure.

There are further complicating factors that must be taken into account in any assessment of the future dependability of the area as the centre for oil and money power. Within the area itself there are many deep-seated conflicts such as those of Iran versus Iraq, Iraq versus Kuwait, Saudi Arabia versus Oman and Abu Dhabi, Libya versus the traditional Arab countries, and so on. Also there is an underlying rivalry between Iran and the Arab States of the Gulf for hegemony in the area, which may sooner or later erupt into an open power struggle implicating also the Communist and non-Communist allies or sponsors of the various Middle East countries. In addition to these conflicts within the area, there are, of course, the perennial dangers and potentially explosive implications raised by the Israeli–Arab issue.

All these actual or potential confrontations also fundamentally affect the producing operations and government arrangements of the oil companies. When the activities of the companies extend to several of these countries, they will most likely be drawn sooner or later into any local area conflicts. Moreover, the producing countries will hold them responsible for their home government policies and expect them to support the producing countries' political, strategic or economic interests. The companies will nearly inevitably be asked to match any arrangements which either their affiliates or any of the other international oil companies (or sometimes even any newcomer company) make with governments of most other Middle East oil countries. And with the underlying rivalry between the Arab countries and Persia, either of them would feel compelled to be able to claim that it has struck the most advantageous bargain with the oil companies. National pride and jealously are bound to provoke a one-upmanship that would lead – in the case of different kinds of arrangements on the two sides of the Gulf – to endless escalations and no end of trouble. This is exactly what is happening as a result of the simultaneous negotiations on participation with the Arab nations on the one hand and on a differently structured deal with Persia on the other hand – and also in connection with developments in Iraq concerning the nationalisation of the Iraq Petroleum Company. Accordingly, the outcome in Iran and Iraq, any potential repercussions on the participation agreements with the Arab countries, and especially whether or not, and if so how long, the companies will be able to keep any equity interest in their various oil-producing arrangements are, as of the time of completing this manuscript, still undetermined.

Finally, it must not be forgotten that none of the national governments is really stable and that the societies involved are still largely backward; there are always serious doubts whether any existing arrangements would survive the end of any current régime.

THE LIMITATIONS ON OIL COMPANIES IN THE PRODUCING COUNTRIES

In the light of developments in the major oil-producing countries as previously described, there is no doubt that the position of the international oil companies has undergone a most fundamental change, with the participation arrangements highlighting, but not fully describing, the underlying metamorphosis in their functions and power relationships.

If for a moment we refer to the publicly-stated intent of what the producing countries have set out to achieve, it is clear that participation, if all the arrangements were ratified and would hold as negotiated in 1972, is mainly a device through which they, so to speak, smoothly and by arrangements with the international oil companies plan to obtain complete control over their countries' total oil operations.

It represents a grand design by the producing countries to forge an alliance with the oil companies in which the producing countries, while pursuing their national objectives, would still be able to take advantage of the large distribution outlets, the investment capabilities and the technical know-how of the oil companies. This is reflected perhaps most succinctly in the pronouncements of Mr Yamani, the Saudi Arabian Minister of Petroleum. His whole approach is based on the assumption, as stated already in 1968 and repeated since, that the oil companies would one day turn out to be the natural allies of the producing countries. As he explains it, he wants participation because the weight of the national oil companies in producing countries should be combined with that of the oil companies so as to:

1. Protect the concessions from nationalisation by providing an enduring link between the oil companies and the producing countries;

2. Gain control over the oil operations while maintaining the flow of foreign capital and expertise and obtaining marketing outlets for the output;

3. Prevent competition between producing countries as sellers of crude in open market, which would lead to a drastic drop in prices and producing government revenues;

4. Maintain thereby price stability, and through the implementation of participation even secure an immediate increase in world crude oil prices from which the producing countries would benefit;

5. Achieve through this combination a position of influence in the oil markets;

6. Make it difficult for any producing country to insist on an "abnormal" increase in production.

As the Kuwaiti Finance and Oil Minister plainly puts it, the true connotations of participation are nationalisation or take-over. "What we called phased participation is in fact phased nationalisation. This is precisely the situation and its implications."

It must be clear that even though the producing countries will start initially with a minority ownership, they will have a powerful voice in investment, production levels, size of exports and their destinations. As a corporate partner representing at the same time the sovereign, they possess all the power they need to control and direct the companies on all phases of the operations in the producing country and probably even on many phases of their operations abroad, holding their local interest in oil production as hostage.

In the immediate future, the bulk of the new participation oil will be bought back by the foreign companies for disposition through their own outlets and their profits on the resales together with compensation payments and the investment contributions of the new national partners will, to begin with, at least tend to protect their cash flows. But by 1976, the proportionate share of the quantities offered back by the national oil companies to the foreign companies will probably have declined substantially. As the Teheran agreement on government oil revenues terminates at that time, large new demands against the companies will undoubtedly be made then, and possibly even before.

In any case, the national oil entities of the various producing nations will in due course become practically the largest suppliers of oil – only somewhat delayed by the phasing out of "buybacks" by the foreign concessionary companies. They will thereby exercise tremendous market power through their terms of sales. In the meantime, they will apparently attempt to use their private company partners, whose interests they would try to tie up inextricably in joint production ventures, to assure market stability.

Perhaps sensing this, an American top executive of an international oil company in an early statement on participation demands said that the key role of the international oil companies to satisfy the needs of both the producing and consuming countries is

best performed when the commercial enterprise is freed from the pressures of conflicting ideologies and of the clashing political systems. These differences inevitably arise when governments of producing countries have a direct participation in running the oil industry or when government to government negotiations are substituted for the company bargaining with the host government.

The commercial framework of operations "would be subverted if we were to adopt an alternative of serving either group of nations exclusively". A top executive of one of the largest European international oil companies stated that a position of 51 per cent participation by the producing countries would be "almost intolerable" as the oil companies would have almost all the operating responsibility without any freedom of investment and without control of production levels.

Subsequently, another top executive referred more positively to the new participation agreement with some of the oil-producing governments in the Middle East as an example of building "more stable future relationships", though he conceded, "I won't pretend this was an easy adjustment." However, he added,

We believe that we now have a new basis for doing business which meets the needs of both consuming and producing countries. At the same time, we have maintained the essential intermediary role of the private international oil companies as the most effective agents for the production, transportation and distribution of oil products.

I am afraid that the earlier pessimistic evaluations and reactions of the oil companies' executives to the participation demand will unfortunately prove to be the correct one, notwithstanding the firm assurances by the present Saudi Arabian Government that Middle East oil should and will be viewed solely commercially and not politically. This is certainly not the position of most other Middle East producing countries and cannot realistically be depended on. A cold-blooded assessment of the real power relationships of the international oil company with the various countries where it operates must lead to the conclusion that its oil production, on which the continued operations of its upstream and downstream facilities are completely dependent, is now or will soon be under the effective control of the producing countries. At the same time, the producing countries will probably deliberately arrange their and the companies' affairs in such a manner that the industry's single most important after-tax profit centre will, as in the past, be located in the producing countries.

There is thus very little doubt about the change in the role of the oil companies from a buffer and bridge between producing and importing countries to what may in fact turn out to be that of junior partners of the producing countries. The oil companies would thus be unable to continue to act as an independent intermediary commercial force in international oil relations; instead the producing countries would tend to treat them as service companies under their control that would undertake admittedly essential worldwide logistic, technical, financial, production and distribution operations.

What we are facing, therefore is a subtle – or even not too subtle – shift of the major centre of power over international oil from the home countries to the producing countries. Whether the companies like it or not, they would be compelled to protect their huge interests in the producing countries by adjusting and co-ordinating their policies and actions in accordance with the directives and policies of the producing countries, hoping that nevertheless the pattern of their operations in their home countries and the importing countries would not be seriously upset.

The role which the oil companies will be able to play in any of their future dealings with producing countries concerning oil production and its availability to importing countries as well as with regard to future tax payments, is thus inevitably severely circumscribed. In the light of present power relationships and the extreme supply and profit dependence of the oil companies on producing countries, they cannot be expected to take a strong and determined stand in such negotiations with the sovereign of the country on which their whole prosperity depends and whose national companies are their partners and will in due course acquire the controlling interest in their operations. More over, they will have to argue that as long as they are able to secure the availability of supplies to importing countries – even at steeply escalating costs – they also serve the interest of their customers by not risking a confrontation that could lead to interruption of supplies; and as long as the companies are able to recoup such costs from the consumer, they would also protect their own commercial viability. As one top executive of one of the largest European international oil companies pointed out some time ago, "Pressure from the producing governments on costs is something we can live with, provided we are not at the same time denied freedom to move prices in the market so as to maintain a commercial margin of profit." It is obvious that in such circumstances the importing countries and home governments can simply not afford to remain passive. The companies, as private organisations and under the terms of reference applicable to commercial corporations, cannot possibly be expected to carry by themselves the burden of protecting not only their own interests but also those of their customers.

There are thus serious doubts whether the kind of negotiating problems we are facing now can be handled effectively solely through a common posture of the companies or by any other kind of inter-company arrangements. The approach followed in earlier negotiations, when most of the oil companies with foreign production negotiated as a group with OPEC producing countries as a group on matters that would vitally affect the tax-paid cost and oil supplies of about every oil-importing country of the non-Communist world, must thus be subjected to a most searching review in the light of the present realities of the power structure of international oil. In particular it would appear that a broad understanding on energy policy among the various importing and home governments involved is absolutely necessary to avoid or at least to contain unrestrained use or misuse of bargaining power by the oil-producing countries to impose excessive demands on the international oil trade.

THE NEW ROLE OF THE OIL COMPANIES IN IMPORTING COUNTRIES

Before reviewing the absolute necessity for a co-ordinated if not common approach of the Atlantic–Japanese group of nations to their energy problem, we may appropriately analyse the changed role of the oil companies in importing countries.

To begin with, it must be realised that the international oil companies will, during the next decade and probably much longer, continue to be a most important factor in the refining and distribution of oil in practically all the countries of the non-Communist world, based on their predominant investment position in all phases of the local oil industries. They will also represent the most diversified single source of crude oil supplies, even though ever-increasing quantities will be sold in the international oil trade by the national companies of producing countries. The international oil companies will also continue to make perhaps the most important contribution to diversified exploration, to technology and to expanded upstream and downstream investments. The logistics of their worldwide operations will be invaluable to the importing as well as producing countries.

Nevertheless, the international oil companies and equally their home countries, especially the United States, are now facing a serious lack of confidence by many of the importing countries not only with regard to their supply capabilities but also with respect to their intentions and concerns in so far as they may relate to the protection of the interests of their worldwide customer countries.

A course by the United States that would, through the exploitation of its domestic energy resources, lower American dependence on Middle East oil and thereby reduce the competitive bidding-up and depletion of Middle East oil reserves would, however, be a constructive contribution to the oil position of the Free World. Such a policy should thus be recognised by Europe and Japan as an integral part of a broader approach to oil issues that are the common concern of all.

But beyond that, the United States has additional possibilities to put – so to speak – a first mortgage on some of the richest oil resources in the Middle East. Saudi Arabia controls by far the largest known reserves developed by American oil companies; and the Saudi Arabian Government has already evinced its interest to conclude special deals with the United States for increasing oil deliveries. No doubt, Iran would be keen to do likewise. However, any acceptance by the United States of a preferred treatment as a customer for Saudi Arabian and Iranian oil would be extremely disruptive to its relations with other importing, and for that matter producing, countries.

The reactions of other importing countries to the Saudi offer is reflected in a statement of the French state-owned oil company Elf-Erap. In referring to the worries that such a policy would cause to all other importing countries, it comments:

> What an inducement to the raising of crude oil prices if the money paid by Europe and Japan should be invested through the producing state in the country of origin of these companies strengthening their power. Who would still be able to maintain that the companies which produce in Arabia are impartial intermediaries between these countries and the European consumer?

Along the same line of reasoning Italy's national oil company ENI suggests that the Common Market conclude direct oil supply agreements, in return for co-operation in the producing countries' development plans, to prevent a supply monopoly of the major international oil companies, especially so because American and European interests are not identical. Positions expressing similar reactions have been taken by several other major importing countries.

This prevailing fear is perhaps best summarised in a 1972 draft recommendation of the Western European Union which was unanimously approved by that body but apparently not endorsed by the Council of Ministers.

> ... much of the oil imported by Europe is shipped under the American flag. The Middle East oil question is therefore mainly a commercial matter for the United States.
>
> For Western Europe, on the other hand, it is a vital matter and the interests of consumers do not tally with the interests of the international companies. Increased participation in the capital of petrol companies by the Arab States or even national-isation would not necessarily be a catastrophe for Europe.
>
> A European oil policy should take account of these factors and in no case be linked with the international oil companies. This means Europe could reach agreement directly with oil-producing countries, help them to develop a national oil industry and purchase the oil thus produced ... Europe has no interest in becoming involved in a vain conflict for defence of the oil companies; its interest is to collaborate closely with the Arab States.
>
> The disadvantage of such a policy might be to make the European market over-dependent on the Arab States. But that is already the case since the Arab countries can cut off supplies of oil to Europe whether it passes through the international companies or is supplied direct ...

Individual European countries and Japan in those circum-stances might thus be tempted to outbid each other in an effort to curry thereby special favours with Middle East oil-producing countries and to secure a privileged position for themselves.

But whatever their motivation, the national companies of importing countries will, in any case, greatly expand their foreign supply operations. While such diversification might or might not provide a modicum of some added supply security, it should be noted that any such new ventures would be subject to fundament-ally the same kind of political and economic risks as those of the international oil companies. There may be some benefits in reducing certain contingencies that may arise from Anglo-American control over access to foreign oil by enhancing their national access to foreign oil; but the latter in turn will be subject to its own separate hazards. Suffice it to refer only to the French experience in Algeria or for that matter to the threatened expropriation of Belgian-held producing interests in Egypt because of Egypt's disapproval of the Congo policy of the Belgian government.

Also investments by the producing countries downstream in importing countries are unlikely to take place or to be permitted on a really massive scale; but even if this should occur, these investments are unlikely to provide a much higher degree of oil supply security if the producing countries for reasons of their own should decide to withhold oil supplies. Their downstream investments would not constitute an effective hostage in the hands of the importing countries because the latter's continued dependence on oil supplies would be of much greater urgency than the threat of expropriation, or the loss of current revenue from such investment would be to the producing countries.

Moreover, foreign crude secured by a national oil company of an importing country would most likely be given a preferred position in the home market. If such arrangements were to become an essential part of the total supply of an importing country, its dependence on what would most likely be a rather limited number of sources of oil imports would make it even more vulnerable to interruption – and to unilaterally imposed cost increases that it would then be compelled to absorb within its own economy. If the importing countries would follow a course of "go it alone" in a *sauve qui peut* spirit, each one of them would also become the target for potential political and economic blackmail, such as some of them have already experienced. They would run the grave risk that their policies and actions would be subverted by considerations of securing or protecting their access to foreign oil; ultimately such an approach will prove to be futile, and the price for the oil and the political or other terms under which it would be obtained might easily become untenable.

Obviously a continuous process of yielding valid rights, not through genuine bargaining but under threats by the producing countries, and a general posture of subservience by the oil companies and the importing countries – as has occurred in recent international oil "negotiations" – must undermine not only the prestige of the importing nations and of the companies but equally the respect for any arrangements concluded with them. Only a co-ordinated approach to energy policy by the relevant

importing countries could really prevent such harmful consequences.

THE INTERESTS OF THE HOME COUNTRIES OF THE INTERNATIONAL OIL COMPANIES

The change in power relationships affecting the operations of
the international oil industry also has a far-reaching effect on the
position of the companies in their home countries. The interest of
the home countries in their international oil companies have in the
past centred around their supply capabilities for their own
country and its allies, their support of the power position of the
home country that was implied in control over international
oil resources, the contribution of the companies to the balance of
payments, and the essential role the companies played in meeting
ever-increasing worldwide oil requirements.

Let us briefly review the changes that are now occurring in
the case of the two most important home countries, the U.S. and
the U.K.

The ability of the companies to provide secure supplies because
of their investment in foreign oil is now no longer absolute and
assured. Experience during the first Suez Crisis in the case of the
United Kingdom and France, and during the Six-Day War in the
case of the U.S. and U.K., has shown that even the U.S., British
or French controlled foreign oil could be and was – even though
for a short period only – embargoed for shipments to the home
countries. While in earlier years the United States was only a
marginal importer of Middle East oil, in contrast to the U.K., in
future the United States will become one of the largest single
importers of such oil. On the other hand, with the development of
the North Sea resources, the United Kingdom – if it could under
Common Market rules effectively reserve its domestic oil production for its own use – might be able to achieve a very substantial lessening of its dependence on Middle East oil imports.

The same questions hold for the extent to which Anglo-
American ownership provides supply assurance to our allies. As
a matter of fact, some of our allies fear that American ownership
of foreign oil might endanger their supply if there should be
political conflict between the United States and the producing
countries.

In the past, control over the international oil companies could
be and was used as a political instrument by their home
countries in their relationship to importing countries, such as

the United States apparently did during the first Suez Crisis or say for oil trade with Cuba, and so on. This possibility, to use the control over foreign oil for political–strategic purposes of the home countries, is disappearing fast. It is the producing countries which now claim the power to supply or withhold oil for their own political and other interests.

The contribution of the international oil industry to the balance of payments of their home countries is indeed substantial; but relatively more important for the United Kingdom than for the United States. In the future, with large increases in U.S. oil imports and the continued need for reinvestment abroad, the balance of payments concern of the United States with regard to international oil may be directed more towards the huge and escalating foreign exchange costs of oil imports rather than to the benefits of profit transfers from international oil operations. In the United Kingdom, on the other hand, the development of the North Sea resources may relieve its oil trade bill sufficiently so as to maintain a predominant interest in the profit transfers from British international oil companies.

In sum, therefore, the fundamental interest of the United States is moving somewhat closer to that of an oil-importing country. On the other hand, the U.K. might for the reasons cited above perhaps, in a narrow definition of its self-interest, pay more attention to the profit pattern of its companies from international oil operations.

There are, however, most important additional qualifying factors, affecting the security position of the home countries and especially the United States with regard to their oil supplies – independent of their position as home countries of worldwide oil companies.

What is relevant now is not so much any influence which the international oil companies may or may not be able to wield in producing countries, but the interest which producing countries have in maintaining an effective relationship with the United States. After all, the United States is the most important political, economic, and military power of the non-Communist world which, incidentally, also presents the highest priced and one of the largest markets for imported oil. This, above all, explains Saudi Arabia's and also Iran's interest in trying to conclude special oil supply arrangements with the United States – not the investment of U.S. oil companies in their country, which, as far as Iran is concerned, would anyhow be a minority interest. Moreover, the United States offers the most important potential outlet for their capital investments, and constitutes one of the largest sources for capital equipment, consumer goods, and military hardware; it can provide its customers with the most advanced technology.

Finally, the United States is the only power that can effectively assure protection against Communist – Soviet as well as Chinese – external and internal incursions. It is the one country which the traditional régimes of the two most important oil-producing nations of the Persian Gulf – Iran and Saudi Arabia – believe they can depend on for maintenance of their governments against subversion, and also for the security of the Persian Gulf area.

In the light of the U.S. possibilities for developing its domestic potential in conventional and non-conventional hydrocarbon and energy resources, and its opportunity for establishing a special oil relationship with the two most important Middle East oil producers – Saudi Arabia and Iran – there is little doubt that if it would ever so desire, the United States could go it alone.

The United Kingdom, as mentioned above, will after the development of the North Sea oilfields be less dependent on Middle East oil than any of its Common Market partners. It was, nevertheless, apparently the U.K., in the Paris Summit Meeting of October 1972, which was pressing for an early formulation of an energy policy for the Community guaranteeing certain and lasting supplies under satisfactory economic conditions.

This policy suggestion must be evaluated within the context of today's stark realities: that unilateral and diverse policies of the various European nations and of Japan cannot provide real supply security or contain the financial problems connected with the international oil trade; that the international oil companies can no more guarantee supplies to any of their customers in a crisis; that these companies no longer possess the bargaining strength, if left to themselves, to be effective negotiators with producing countries with regard to the availability and cost of oil; and that such a state of affairs would provide the most cogent reason for the various importing countries to work towards the establishment of an energy policy for a larger grouping of nations.

But the ultimate interest of the most important producing countries in the Middle East that have not fallen under Soviet domination is bound to remain the protection of their independence and that can only be achieved by close and friendly relationships with the United States. The United States will thus continue to be the dominant factor in world oil, not because of the foreign oil interests of its companies, but primarily because of its standing in the world balance of power. An energy policy applying solely to the Community would, we submit, be only the first step towards a really effective policy that must encompass the Atlantic group of nations and Japan.

THE NEED FOR AN ATLANTIC—JAPANESE ENERGY POLICY

Beyond doubt, U.S. relations with Europe and Japan are in disarray. There are many outstanding unresolved problems on defence, burden sharing, trade policy, the whole range of monetary issues including currency realignments, capital flows, and so on.

Perhaps instead of establishing a grand design which would encompass a resolution of all major contentions and areas of conflicts, it might prove to be more fruitful to proceed pragmatically on an issue-by-issue basis and try to tackle first those problems where the chances of an Atlantic—Japanese policy, or at least of an agreed-upon co-ordinated approach, would seem to be most promising. Incidentally, it is interesting to recall that the European Common Market was preceded by the establishment of a much more limited joint effort, the European Coal and Steel Community.

I should like to submit that the problem of the future energy position of the Atlantic—Japanese complex of nations is one of the most important issues confronting not only each of them individually, but also as a group. Obviously, an energy policy cannot be limited to the Atlantic nations but must include Japan as one of the major interested parties.

What is likely to induce the various countries to agree to co-operation and mutual adjustments is the existence of a severe outside threat to their security and prosperity, resulting from their dependence on oil supplies from a few foreign sources coupled with the potential danger of a flood of foreign funds that could harm their own economies and the world's monetary system.

The weak and unstable foreign political societies where the world's oil and money power centres are located could, for reasons of their own or stirred up by the potentially adverse policies of the Soviets and even perhaps the Chinese People's Republic, create great difficulties for the various countries of the non-Communist world. The United States as well as the United Kingdom would – shortsightedly to be sure – by themselves probably be able to resolve their energy problems, partly at the

expense of other importing countries. But as mentioned before
it is to the United States, more than any other nation of the Free
World, that pivotal producing countries look for their political
and strategic security, and this advantage could rebound to the
benefit of all oil-importing countries. Neither the Common
Market nor Japan alone or in combination could provide a
comparable total package of advantages for the political, strategic,
and economic well-being of the major Middle East oil-producing
countries

If, therefore, the United States abstains from any attempt to
try to obtain unilateral benefits, however short-lived they might
prove to be, and is willing to participate in an energy policy in
a new Atlantic–Japanese partnership, it might thereby provide
protection for its partners against potentially very serious oil
supply emergencies. Obviously the latter too must then forgo the
temptation of looking only at their immediate self-interest without regard to others, a policy that they could in any case not
pursue successfully over any period of time. Only then would
it be possible for the importing countries to pursue a rational
policy for their energy imports and avoid bidding against each
other or being played against each other with ever-escalating
political and economic demands being made upon them. Only
then would it be possible for Atlantic–Japanese and especially
U.S. power to become an effective countervailing factor in international oil without having been sapped by discordant and
conflicting attitudes of the individual importing nations towards
the producing countries.

The need for a joint or at least co-ordinated policy is indeed
most urgent because any delays in which conflicting approaches
to producing countries are made by the individual members of the
Atlantic–Japanese group of nations will accelerate not only the
disintegration of our partnership, but will even further encourage
arbitrary and dictatorial demands of the producing countries.
Moreover, as some of the producing countries accumulate large
surplus funds, it might become much more difficult, if not impossible, for the importing countries to influence their policies.

It would appear therefore that Europe and Japan need something from the United States which is in the interest of the U.S.
to give, i.e. its adherence to a co-ordinated Atlantic–Japanese
energy policy, in, as the game theorists would call it, a positive
sum game through which all sides would gain. This would provide
the most persuasive basis for an agreement on a joint policy

under which common problems could be resolved to the mutual advantage of all partners.

Needless to say that this should not imply that any of the partners should necessarily be inhibited from pursuing separate diplomatic and economic initiatives within the broad spectrum of developing Middle East relationships and within the framework of an Atlantic–Japanese energy policy.

The OECD Oil Committee has for many years served as the most significant international organisation encompassing the Atlantic–Japanese group of nations, providing a basis for the exchange of information and co-ordination and also for expert analyses on oil developments relevant to its members. Most important, it has established policies for emergency stockpiling and within certain limits for the emergency apportionment of oil supplies in the OECD European area; and during oil emergencies it has in fact served as a clearing body to achieve an equitable division of available supplies among its members.

The Common Market is at present engaged in a slow and difficult effort to establish an energy policy for its members that would secure certain and lasting supplies under satisfactory economic conditions. But in the framework of the Common Market, even including Britain with its large interests in world oil, national policies of the individual members could severely slow up the establishment of a Community policy, as long as there is no overriding conviction on the part of its members that the Community countries in combination would decisively add to their individual political and strategic bargaining strength.

In the light of the changed power relationships of today, an effective energy policy of a new Atlantic–Japanese partnership must inevitably go further than either the OECD or the Common Market have advanced so far. Obviously, however, such a policy would build on the valuable achievements of the OECD and the Common Market.

Fortunately there is, to a varying degree to be sure, a substantial consensus on the need for a co-ordinated or even joint approach to the energy problem in the United States as well as the Common Market and Japan. It is reflected in many official pronouncements during the last year or two.

The United States, in a 1972 statement before an OECD Council Meeting, officially expressed its readiness for such co-operation.

It is imperative for the world's major consumers of oil and

other forms of energy to take joint and co-ordinated action – starting now – to increase the availability of all types of energy resources; to lessen, to the degree possible, an overdependence on oil from the Middle East, to co-ordinate the response of consuming countries to restrictions on the supply of Middle East petroleum, and to develop jointly and co-operatively a responsible programme of action to meet the possibility of critical energy shortages by the end of this decade.

The OECD itself is again engaged in a study of the world energy situation, hopefully leading to concrete recommendations for actions by the member governments. The Common Market Commission considers it necessary to substitute or extend liaison in the energy field between the Community and other energy-importing countries in order to provide a better exchange of information and produce common solutions.

Japan, through its Overall Energy Council, an advisory body to the Minister of International Trade and Industry, recommended in 1971 that, while it was necessary for Japan in order to assure stable oil supplies at low cost to behave independently of any foreign influence in all aspects of her oil industry activities, she must co-operate with other consuming countries.

To this end it is necessary for Japan to promote with them and their national oil companies exchange of information and mutual understanding and to explore possibilities for constructive co-operation on the part of oil-consuming countries towards the formation of an organisation in which debates are held among the countries with international oil companies and the oil-producing countries on the basic policy concerning the world oil situation.

As the Natural Resources Survey Mission, sponsored by the Japanese Foreign Office, put it in its report published in 1972, Japan must engage in active participation in international co-operation with advanced countries on oil matters and "must refrain from being passive as has been the case thus far. It must take full advantage of opportunities such as an OECD Oil Committee meeting where industrially advanced nations meet, through which Japan could clarify her oil policy on international co-operation before the OECD member countries."

Building on this awareness of the energy problem by all the importing countries and their consensus on the need for joint discussion, co-ordination, or actions, as the case may be, we will

now submit our suggestions for an energy policy for an Atlantic–
Japanese partnership.

AN OUTLINE FOR AN ATLANTIC–JAPANESE ENERGY POLICY

The major goal of an energy policy for a new Atlantic–Japanese
partnership must of course be to try to cope with the common
problems of the security of oil supplies and the financial issues
related to it. While nobody can guarantee that such a policy will
lead to a completely satisfactory resolution of all the problems,
it should at least be possible to contain them. Future bargaining
in international oil would no longer be lopsided, i.e. between the
producing countries as a group and the oil companies (be they the
internationals or the national companies of importing countries),
with the latter "negotiating" under the threat of being treated as
virtually the captives of the producing countries – but would also
engage the extraordinary political, strategic and economic power
of the Atlantic–Japanese group of nations.

If such "countervailing power" to OPEC should really become
a factor in international oil, which indeed it must, there is some
reasonable hope that international oil and financial arrangements
could be set up on a rational and manageable basis; and that
OPEC would no longer be able, as Mr Yamani put it in October
1972, through its co-ordination and unity to "prove time and
time again that it can enforce its demands".

Some fear has been expressed that such a grouping of oil-
importing countries might unnecessarily provoke a confrontation
with the producing countries. But circumstances have significantly
tipped the balance of power during the last few years. It was the
producing countries which, through the establishment of OPEC,
created a producing countries' organisation which as a group
formulates policy guidelines for major producing countries and
through the threat of withholding supplies to companies that
would not submit to its demands and through other means,
provides enormous power and overwhelming bargaining leverage
for each of the producing nations. Moreover, the Organization of
Arab Petroleum Exporting Countries (OAPEC) has stated its
intention to establish official relations with countries of the EEC,
either collectively or individually. To this purpose, it announced
in 1971 that it is setting up a committee to co-ordinate the
relations of its member countries – in the Arabian Gulf, represented by Saudi Arabia, and in North Africa, represented by

Libya and Algeria – with the EEC countries.

The subject matters to be covered by the energy policy could perhaps be put under the following broad categories:

1. Study and review of energy demand and supply including tanker, pipeline, and refining availabilities. A programme for optimum diversification of supplies.

2. A co-ordinated and/or joint research programme for the development of new energy resources, especially of atomic energy and from non-conventional sources.

3. Investment review and national or multinational incentive and guarantee programmes for the development of conventional and new energy resources.

4. Review of arrangements by importing countries for oil supplies from producing countries, be it through purchases, service contract arrangements, concessions or otherwise. The establishment of broad terms of reference and/or of parameters for arrangements, acceptable to importing countries.

5. A programme of arrangements for stockpiling, rationing, and equitable sharing of import availabilities between all members in case of an overall or specific country emergency.

6. A co-ordinated and/or joint research programme on conservation of energy and on its implementation if called for, including research on battery-powered cars, nuclear-fuelled shipping, savings in motor car transportation, etc.

7. Review and co-ordination of programmes of economic development and technical assistance for producing countries.

8. Review of prices, costs and balance of payments effects of oil imports of member countries and also of developing countries. A programme of arrangement for support and adjustment if called for.

9. Review of government revenues of major oil-producing countries and of their impact on world trade, world capital flows and short-term money markets; and a programme of financial co-operation – if called for.

10. A review of the dependency of Middle East producing countries on the exports of industrial and agricultural goods and of military equipment, on shipping, services, technical know-how,

etc., from the non-Communist world's oil-importing countries; and a continuous assessment of mutual interdependence and of the means that might be available to cope with an oil supply, trade, or finance emergency.

The administration of the energy policy might conceivably be entrusted to a special new high-level international energy council, composed of member states with a top-level permanent staff with generally recognised and incontestable professional and practical experience. The timing and method of its establishment, its organisational structure, the range of its executive and/or advisory powers, the procedures on voting and the rules governing ratification and implementation of its decisions or conclusions and its relationship with the various member countries and their oil companies would of course be determined in a process of give and take through international negotiations. It will, obviously, be very difficult indeed to achieve any such agreement; but it may well be the only remaining chance to attempt to safeguard the interests of the importing countries, the home countries and those of their oil companies. Whatever the odds it must certainly be tried, and there is no time to be lost.

The above proposal presents of course only one of several possible approaches to an Atlantic–Japanese energy policy and its implementation. In particular, a great deal of thought must obviously be given to the problem of whether or not it would be feasible and advisable to restructure the present OECD Oil Committee or its High Level Committee so that the conclusion and implementation of an Atlantic–Japanese energy policy could be handled within the framework of the Committee. While this might require substantial changes in the powers and functions of the OECD Oil Committee, it might perhaps be more expeditious and easier to reach an agreement on a revision of the terms and conditions governing an existing international organisation concerned with the oil policy of importing countries rather than to start from scratch and try to establish a completely new international body.

The competence and functions of the International Energy Council, however it were to be set up, as well as those of the member countries and those of the oil companies, must of course be clearly delineated. The policy framework established by the Council would set the limits within which the countries as well as the oil companies would handle their affairs, taking into account their changing responsibilities and capabilities.

At the same time it would try to provide an effective basis for protecting the supply security of the oil-importing countries through encouraging the development of added supplies, diversification, investment incentives, research, assuring sufficient tanker and refining availability, etc. Through stockpiling, co-ordination of rationing policy, and especially through an emergency import-sharing agreement among all members, an oil embargo by producing countries against selected countries would become much more difficult, if not practically impossible; in such circumstances the producing countries would have to be prepared to cut their oil supplies to all member countries – with unpredictable, dangerous consequences to them.

The conclusion of an effective arrangement for emergency import-sharing between the Atlantic nations and Japan would presuppose that each member country, including of course the United States and Japan, would be prepared to share with its partners its own import availabilities in an equitable manner on the basis of agreed-upon principles. The establishment of substantial stockpiles of oil by the various importing countries, again including the United States and Japan, would provide them in case of emergency with time for possible supply–demand adjustments, for efforts to resolve equitably any underlying conflicts with the producing countries, or, if everything else fails, for initiating whatever measures are required to protect their security. Arrangements on sharing of import availabilities and stockpiling applicable to all nations of the new Atlantic–Japanese partnership may well prove to be the touchstone and provide the foundation for a broadly conceived energy policy such as outlined above; they may well be considered as the essential initial step on which it should be possible to achieve more easily an early international agreement.

Likewise, a joint or co-ordinated policy on dealing with supply, trade, and financial problems related to oil would have the best chance to lead to rational and manageable solutions of the very difficult issues that are bound to arise. The producing countries could no longer, so to speak, pick out consuming countries one by one; OPEC itself has, in its own resolutions, introduced similar measures of solidarity among the producing countries.

Moreover, the companies in their negotiations on prices and payments to producing governments which will come up for revision at the latest by 1976 – and which OPEC's Secretary General has already described as the next major issue – would no longer be as exposed to unilateral dictates, as in the past. Their negotiating stance would be based on broad terms of references such as recommended or formulated by an International Energy Council similar to the practice OPEC is applying in suggesting the basic position for producing countries. There need no longer be the hectic and somewhat improvised discussions and confrontation between oil companies and producing countries, as experienced between 1970 and 1972 in the Tripoli–Teheran and participation arrangements, brought about by ultimatums of the producing countries rather than through genuine negotiation.

Under current conditions, as pointed out earlier, there would be very little if any bargaining leverage left with the oil companies if, in their negotiations with the producing countries, they were to depend solely on their own strength. Only a firm backing by all major oil-importing countries could provide the necessary countervailing power which would permit the oil companies to establish a credible negotiating stance. The companies, acting within their terms of reference and within the framework of a co-ordinated energy policy, could thus count on such backing that should enable them to handle international oil negotiations and their implementation.

In this connection, an additional factor in the assessment of the respective bargaining leverage by either side would undoubtedly be the awareness that there is a limit to which the oil companies, together with the importing countries, could be held hostage by a threat to access to reserves in producing countries; that it might in certain circumstances be preferable to abandon the hostage and to turn away from the reserves and reappear as competitive buyers of crude from the producing countries. Since captive concession-holding companies would no longer be at their behest, one might expect that OPEC unity would erode and that producing countries would eventually compete with each other for export sales to the companies whose purchasing power would derive from past investment in and current control over transport, refining and marketing facilities – the power to dispose.

The importing countries, through extending economic and technical co-operation to the developing producing countries, should contribute to the advance in their standard of living, the diversification of their economic activities and the expansion of their general import and export trade. Hopefully, the producing countries will in due course become such an integral part of the world economy that they will be much less tempted to take radical measures which might sever these links. If the dependence of the producing countries on continued oil revenues, flow of trade and friendly political and economic relations with the non-Communist world is such that they could not risk more than a very short interruption, then and only then will the producing countries act with circumspection and probably be sufficiently discouraged from attempting to impose an oil embargo.

In particular, the producing countries would be constrained to exercise great caution not to confront importing countries or their companies – if firmly backed by all major importing countries – with unreasonable demands if the turmoil resulting from a confrontation is likely to undermine the régimes of the oil-producing countries, or if they would have reason to fear that their actions might provoke dangerous international repercussions affecting their integrity and security.

Moreover, the producing countries are fully aware that if their relations with the major importing countries should deteriorate gravely, they may have to rely on Soviet support, which not only could not provide anything comparable to the benefits they are enjoying from dealing with the non-Communist world, but would also confront them with political and other risks.

Obviously, too, the more essential oil supplies from the Middle East are becoming to the rest of the world, the more attractive a target would it offer for Soviet subversion and control. For the Communist world, the concentration of oil and money power in a few small countries in the Persian Gulf, at their back door so to speak, presents an enviable opportunity to attempt to undermine the political and economic strength of the non-Communist world by "peaceful means" through encouragement of all the nationalistic and centrifugal tendencies that already exist in the area. However, any serious threat to Middle East oil supplies could, in such circumstances, easily lead to a confrontation between the major powers. Only friendly relations with the non-Communist world, that would include the United States, can hold the Soviets at bay. A united or co-ordinated Atlantic–Japanese posture with regard to oil provides the most persuasive safeguard for the security, prosperity and integrity of the importing as well as producing countries.

COMMENT *by Sir Derek Ezra*

What I think is agreed for a moment among all who think about energy policy is what is likely to be the trend of future demand for energy by the three groups in question, namely, the United States, Japan, and the enlarged European Community. On certain fairly well agreed assumptions about general economic growth in those three groups, it is generally accepted that whereas at present the total requirement in those groups is of the order of between 4 and 5 thousand million tons of coal equivalent, by 1985 it could be over 8 thousand million tons of coal equivalent.

That seems to be fairly well agreed.

But immediately one has stated that, of course, one then raises a number of obvious questions.

The first is: Where is this energy going to come from? Is there going to be enough of it altogether? Well, in all probability, yes. As Dr Levy has shown, if one takes account of the substantial reserves in the Middle East and North Africa, and of what is available elsewhere, there would probably be enough.

But that immediately raises other issues. The main issue is that during this period one is going to get an increasing imbalance between supply and demand if trends go on as they are. At the present time, the three groups in question depend on imported energy very largely from the Middle East, to about 30 per cent of their overall requirements. In some cases rather less, in some cases rather more: for example the United States is importing about 10 or 11 per cent of its total requirements for the moment, whereas Japan is importing something like 85 per cent. By 1985, on present trends, that could well get to nearer a half of total requirements which would have to be imported – a half, of course, of double the total needs of the present time. The main reason for this is not only the increasing growth in demand generally, but the funda- mental change that has taken place in the United States, which has hitherto been pretty well self-supporting in energy supplies but which is going to become increasingly dependent on external sources. So this situation immediately raises the first problem, that of security of supplies. Whereas they might be in total sufficient, the degree of insecurity is bound to increase as supply and demand get out of balance.

This in turn raises the question of price. Whereas during the 1960s it was generally felt that plentiful energy could be available at low price, we are now entering an era where there is some doubt about the security, if not about the quantity, of total energy supply; and almost certainly that is going to lead to an escalation in price. So one has to get used to an entirely new relationship between the user of energy and the supplier of energy, in terms of price.

And the price question, allied to the security question, seems to me to raise a very important issue. Eventually we are going to have to pay very much more for energy than we do today. But in order to correct that, there are certain things which could be done now, which will mean that one could have to pay more now, in order to control the trend of prices later. I think there is a lot to be said for spending more today in order to safeguard oneself against this later trend.

The question of price, as I have suggested, seems to me to be a question of usage. During the period of cheap energy, efficiency and the usage of energy were not regarded as one of the most important things. From now on, they are going to become very much more important. Generally speaking, about 50 per cent of the heat content of the energy we use is wasted. This is a very broad generalisation, covering wide disparity between power stations and other consumers, but that is broadly speaking the situation. A relatively small percentage improvement in efficiency of usage, of course, will make an enormous difference in the quantities required. So this is another important factor in the situation.

I do not need to underline the question of the monetary problem that could well be created by this situation of imbalance, because Dr Levy has very clearly shown what could happen if one simply takes the situation as between the United States, Europe and the Middle East, if the trends we envisage really take place. The present monetary crisis in the world has in large part been created by an American imbalance of payments of something like 6 billion dollars. But what is at issue here is more than the possibility of imbalance, purely on energy account, amounting to up to 25 billion dollars by the early 1980s. One can see the very grave implications of that situation. And of course, monetary imbalance raises in turn the whole question of international politics, which I shall not discuss here, but whose implications are obvious.

What should we do about all this? I would emphasise the question of security of supply, which I think is going to become increasingly a problem, the solution of which cannot be cheaply obtained. It means paying more now than we otherwise would in order to achieve a greater security later. I believe that the ways in which one should seek to achieve that greater security must first be to maximise the controllable resources of energy among these three groups that we're talking about: to maximise the controllable resources by seeking to exploit whatever they have readily to hand, or can obtain from other sources of greater reliability.

This in turn is going to involve a good deal of additional investment in what, on purely current commercial and economic grounds, might not seem desirable, and a great deal more research.

These are very central issues. These policies, in my opinion, need to be devised concurrently within the enlarged Community, the United States and Japan, and at the same time should be co-ordinated between the three groups. This co-ordination should take place not only at governmental levels, but also at what one might call technical or professional levels.

We are entering a period when one is not only concerned with overall policies and the co-ordination of one's approach to the Middle East supplier and so on, but also very much involved in what could well amount to an increasingly technical revolution – a revolution in the sources of energy, and in the conversion of primary energies into secondary energies. An enormous amount of work, for example, is now being done in the United States to convert coal into high calorific gas, and to burn high-sulphur fuels in a non-sulphur way. A great deal of work needs to be done. Therefore, I would suggest, one needs to bring these various strands together on an international basis between the three groups at both levels. If one were to tackle the problem in the way that I have indicated, on this broader base, bringing in the controllable fuels, launching into a much greater degree of research and development, particularly from the point of view of supply, conversion, and usage, and thus reducing this trend towards imbalance between supply and demand, then, I think, one could bring the situation into a more controllable form. That action really has to take place today. It should have taken place yesterday.

COMMENT *by Ronald S. Ritchie*

I should like to comment briefly on what has been happening so far as the oil-producing countries are concerned; I should like to touch upon the capital issues; and then I should like to discuss the proposals for an international energy council.

As to what has been happening: the oil-producing countries have recently been playing from an overwhelmingly strong hand, and one which reflected the fact that we are in the early stages of a very important shift in the energy picture, a shift which means that the kind of energy on which industrialised countries are most dependent today is going to have to be supplemented over the next few years by new kinds of energy which are going to be much more costly. Even in the field of conventional oil and gas, we are at a stage where the new supplies yet to be created of oil and gas are themselves likely to be much more costly – in an economic sense, much more costly than the Middle East reserves. Because the Middle East countries have had a supply on which all the industrialised countries of the world are going to have to depend, for the next two decades at least, to a major extent, they have been in a position to get the price that the market would bear. In effect they have been able to do two things. One and, except perhaps for certain people, the less important, has been to extract from the oil companies the major part – some would say all – of what the economists call economic rent. Beyond that, however, and more important to the consuming countries, they have been able to push the price of oil up by raising their tax take in various ways, one of which is participation, to levels which more closely match what energy was going to cost from other sources. They have gone a long way towards that achievement, to the point where Middle East oil is not cheap in North America today by comparison with indigenous sources of supply, whereas it once was. The question is, could that have been prevented? The hand that was very strong would have been just as strong had governments been doing the negotiating. The fact that companies were doing the negotiating at least has saved us from some of the more difficult international situations that might have resulted if it had been governments.

What do we have to look forward to for the future? First of all, can we hope that OPEC will break down? If we look at it realistically, it is easy to see that over the next decade or two, two very large producers, Saudi Arabia and Iran, could themselves almost individually dictate the terms within the limits of what other competitive constraints there are, so that we should not be looking towards a breakdown in their cartel so much as a hope for getting a better deal. More relevant, I think, is what would a rational owner of reserves try to obtain from them in the picture which faces us? The most probable conclusion is that he will try to obtain the maximum that he can get in competition with other sources of supply, not just of oil and gas, but of other kinds of energy, taking account of the fact that there are substantial delays involved for obtaining some of them. This analysis does not suggest that the increases to come, over and above what are already built into the arrangements, will be as startling as those that have happened in the last few years. One of the effects of what has happened and what is scheduled to happen is that these other sources of supply will be brought into play more rapidly. In North America, for instance, there will be an immediate incentive to push ahead with alternatives. These in turn set a ceiling on what Middle East oil can be worth in the future.

The capital questions, secondly, have been raised in a rather foreboding manner, and fears may be fully justified; but I suspect that they may be overstressed. The country which is likely to have the largest supplies of capital from oil sales over the next two or three decades available for use outside the country is Saudi Arabia. Iran will have tremendous revenues, but it also has very large domestic capital needs if it is to achieve the domestic programmes it wants. I do not know how the Saudi Arabians will handle their huge supplies of capital; I believe that the record to date is that they have been very cautious and conservative. So far as any indications from their words are concerned, they expect to be major investors abroad. They may not contribute significantly to international monetary problems. So far most of the comments that one hears are that this kind of capital, to the extent to which it is invested abroad, will be invested in downstream oil and gas projects. This may well be true: certainly, as has been pointed out, the capital requirements for energy for the industrialised world are going to be tremendous, and it would not be illogical for some of them to be financed from this source. On the other hand I have often thought that, if I were involved in managing the affairs of a country which had all its eggs in oil, I might think about investing some of my capital in other industries around the world.

Finally, a brief word about close co-ordination, and perhaps something more, among Western Europe, North America, and Japan. It is evident, I think, and beyond debate, that these countries share to some significant degree a common destiny, a common intense interest in Middle East oil during the next two or three decades and perhaps beyond, and a common stake in the development of other sources of energy, on I would think a more economic basis than otherwise. This suggests that at the very least they should be in close and continuing consultation to ensure so far as possible that they recognise what the real facts of life are and see them clearly, if possible through common eyes. This at least would, if it did not ease their minds, give them the satisfaction of a common understanding, and it might avoid their individually trying to do things that would be more disruptive and counter-productive than otherwise. I think that it is evident just from the history of the last decade and a half that they do have some interest in shared planning for emergency purposes. However this form of co-ordination evolves, it should not begin with, and let us hope does not end with, an effort at joint confrontation, with producers opposed to consumers. The two share an interest which is almost as great as that which the consuming countries share together; and if co-ordination among the consuming countries can be handled in such a fashion that the producing countries have this continuously in their minds, we shall all be better off.

Chapter XII

Policies for Technology Transfer and International Investment

HARVEY BROOKS

TRENDS IN THE INTERNATIONAL TRANSFER OF SCIENCE AND TECHNOLOGY

Internationalisation of Pure Science

SCIENCE HAS ALWAYS BEEN A worldwide co-operative activity, characterised by both intense competition and close collaboration. The improvement of communications and transportation and the trend of many fields of science towards large-scale activity have both contributed to the increase in international collaboration, especially in "pure" science, i.e. science whose strategy is governed primarily by the internal logic of the field itself rather than by externally determined practical goals. In general, the "purer" or more "fundamental" a field of science, the more likely it is to be a candidate for strong international collaboration. Thus we find worldwide integrated scientific communities most strongly developed in those fields of research which are generally regarded as being on the "intellectual frontiers" of science – high energy particle physics, radio astronomy, molecular biology, pure mathematics, and theoretical physics. It is in these fields that the most intense international exchanges of people and ideas occur, and in which there is the greatest collaboration in the planning and use of the most sophisticated modern instrumentation.

Much of this international circulation of people, ideas, and research technology occurs at the non-official level, i.e. with the blessing and funding of national governments, but with the explicit initiative coming from working scientists. This is as it should be. Government ought to step in only when it can facilitate co-operation which is beyond the resources or organisational capabilities of the professional associations of science. But as pure science becomes more expensive and far-flung, government agreements become increasingly necessary, especially when crossing of the various "iron curtains" may be involved.

The movement towards worldwide co-operation in science is, perhaps, best illustrated by the field of high energy particle physics. This stems from a long tradition of international community in nuclear physics which goes well back into the pre-war period, when Copenhagen, under Nils Bohr, was the world centre for theoretical nuclear physics, and Cambridge, England, under Ernest Rutherford, the centre for experimental nuclear physics. The majority of the most active nuclear physicists in the world spent some part of their careers in one or both of these great centres. Much of this international community retained its identity and collaboration even through World War II, when many European and British physicists joined in the U.S. atomic bomb project at Chicago or Los Alamos.

Today the worldwide effort in particle physics is centred in five major facilities – the U.S. National Accelerator Laboratory (NAL) at Batavia, Illinois, just coming into operation with 400 Gev. protons; the 72 Gev. proton accelerator at Serpukhov in the U.S.S.R.; the Stanford linear accelerator producing 20 Gev. electrons; and the older 33 Gev. proton synchrotron at Brookhaven, Long Island in the U.S. and the 28 Gev. proton synchrotron of the European nuclear organisation at CERN, near Geneva, which now has the unique capability for colliding beams of protons which produce the highest effective proton collision energy in the world. These instruments are soon to be joined by the new European 300 Gev. accelerator which is also being built at CERN.

Although built with national or consortium funding, these machines are open to the entire world scientific community on the basis of the scientific merit and interest of the experiments which are proposed. For example, there have been about five U.S. research groups participating in experiments at the CERN intersecting storage ring. Following extensive discussions at the governmental level, there is an agreement for reciprocal participation of U.S. physicists in work at the Serpukhov accelerator and Soviet physicists at the National Accelerator Laboratory, with each supplying its share of support and special instrumentation, including an American computer at Serpukhov. Soviet physicists will move with their families to Batavia. Direct teletype communication for exchange of data has been set up between Palo Alto (SLAC) and Serpukhov. Through agreement the French also undertook to build and deliver a giant hydrogen bubble chamber for use at Serpukhov, as a contribution to a collaborative research effort involving Russian and French physicists.

In radio astronomy a new subject of long base line interferometry has developed which involves close dovetailing of measurements between groups all over the world. Each group records radio signals from space timed against a highly precise local "atomic clock". These clocks can be synchronised by worldwide VLF radio signals. The separate recorded signals from space can then be synthesised in one location to study the fine structure of radio sources in space, at a resolution far finer than can be achieved with optical telescopes.

The U.S. is now constructing a new highly precise radio astronomy array, the VLA, which will be capable of generating high resolution images of radio sources in space, with a discrimination somewhat superior to that of the largest optical telescopes. Already international groups are making plans to make use of these facilities, which will be available to the world scientific community.

Molecular biology is a field of "little science", i.e. not requiring large complex instrumentation, that has benefited greatly from the rapid circulation of information and people on a multinational basis. News of new discoveries travels rapidly, and new experiments are planned in close informal co-ordination virtually without reference to distance or national location of laboratory, as laboratories both compete for priority and exchange their latest findings in the kind of co-operative competition which seems a unique characteristic of science.

International collaboration has also developed rapidly in the so-called "environmental sciences", the sciences of oceanography, meteorology, and geophysics. Here collaboration is motivated by the fact that worldwide co-ordinated observations are scientifically much more meaningful than isolated studies of a local part of the environment. The global approach has been facilitated by a number of technological developments – the ability to take soundings of thermal and chemical properties of the atmosphere from satellites, the ability to observe the ocean surface from satellites, so-called constant pressure balloons that can circumnavigate the globe following the global atmospheric circulation and transmit data automatically to a central point via satellite, instrumentation that can automatically measure and record ocean currents *in situ*, and above all computers that can manipulate an enormous amount of observational data, and carry out computations with complex physical models of the global atmosphere. These computations require worldwide data, with a minimum of geographical gaps. Out of these technologies has precipitated a plan for GARP (the Global Atmospheric Research Programme), which will involve worldwide collaboration of atmospheric scientists. Similar programmes have been organised in oceanography through the IDOE (International Decade of Ocean Exploration), in ecology through the IBP (the Internationl Biological Programme), and in the Arctic and Antarctic regions. More than a decade old, and supported by an international treaty which dedicates the Antarctic continent and its environs to science, the Antarctic programme is widely hailed as an example of the successful exclusion of national rivalries from a whole domain of exploration and research.

In geology a deep-sea sediment coring programme, supported largely by U.S. funds, has produced samples of ocean-bottom sediments which have been studied by scientists all over the world, and have helped to establish on a firm scientific basis the once discarded hypothesis of continental drift, now the starting point of the first comprehensive unified theory of the geological history of the earth. Recently an agreement has been reached in principle with the Soviet State Committee for Science and Technology to contribute funding to the coring programme, and the Russian Institute of Oceanology has become a member of the U.S. consortium (JOIDES) which plans and manages the effort, conducted by the ship *Glomar Challenger* under contract to the Scripps Institution of Oceanography of the University of California.

As apparatus becomes more complex and expensive, and as the potential advantages of co-ordinated global observations in some fields become more apparent, the internationalisation of many sciences is likely to accelerate. Even a country that has a near-monopoly on the research technology, as do the U.S. and the U.S.S.R. in space science, has more to gain than to lose from opening up its capabilities to the use of foreign scientists. This is not only a prudent use of resources; the wider sources of ideas lead to a competition which is likely to be more productive of interesting scientific results than a national monopoly. In this sense knowledge, and even scientific prestige, are entities whose aggregate is increased by being shared. This is most true, however, when each of the participants has something unique to bring to the collaboration, so that the whole is greater than the sum of its parts. Because of the gradual retreat from the support of fundamental science in the U.S., many U.S. scientists now fear that collaboration between them and their European or Soviet colleagues will suffer as they come more as suppliants than as partners to the international scientific enterprise. Furthermore, lack of stability in programming has made it increasingly difficult for U.S. scientists to live up to the requirements of international collaborative programmes, which usually require more advance long-term planning than the average scientific programme. It may well be that European and American governments need to agree to more concerted long-term plans regarding the funding of basic research, if you will, an international "policy for science" to replace the present individual national policies, which are often out of phase with each other. This should be high on the agenda for the next decade.

Internationalisation of Industrial Technology

The internationalisation of pure science has been paralleled by an analogous development in industrial technology, the international trade in proprietary technological information. This grew dramatically during the decade of the 1960s, much more rapidly than trade as a whole, and somewhat faster even than multinational production, which itself grew at more than twice the rate of the GNPs of the nations involved. A variety of factors is responsible for this development. Most are economic or political in nature. Clearly the Common Market provided an unusual opportunity for American multinational corporations. The undervaluation of the dollar undoubtedly facilitated American direct investment in Europe and elsewhere, as did certain features of the American corporate tax law. However, it is also clear that the nature of technology transfer and of technology itself had much to do with the vigorous growth of all forms of technology transfer in the 1960s. First was the great improvement in transatlantic communications and transportation, brought about by coaxial cable and jet aircraft. These factors facilitated central control and planning for European affiliates, and the rapid transfer of market information. Secondly, technology itself was of a sort that could more readily be "packaged" for transfer than in the past. The new technology rested on a more theoretical scientifically structured base, and was less "arty", a situation conducive to effective and easy transfer because information could be more readily codified. This was especially true in high-technology areas such as computers. Thirdly, travel and mass communications had probably created a much more homogeneous market, in the sense that tastes were less locally or regionally idiosyncratic. Since much technology transfer takes place in the field of capital goods, there are cumulative effects which tend to make successive transfers of technology easier. As one national industry becomes accustomed to foreign technology, it is easier to introduce it to another. The general culture becomes more receptive to ideas and practices from abroad.

All the technological developments in the rest of the century are likely to favour technology transfer. This will be especially true of technologies having to do with the transmission, manipulation and utilisation of information and data. One characteristic of modern communications is that to an increasing degree its costs do not increase very rapidly with distance between the points of origin and reception. The cost of satellite communications, for example, is virtually independent of distance. Moreover, it is almost certain that the unit cost of both data storage and data transmission will continue to decline rapidly with further improvements in technology and with the economies of scale realised as the volume of data transmitted and processed increases. Unlike the situation which probably exists with energy, we have not reached the end of a long historical period in which relative cost has been steadily declining. We probably still have several decades and several orders of magnitude to run before unit costs in the handling of data begin to level off. We are thus likely to see a continued rapid spread in the use of information technologies, including long-distance telecommunications. The impact of this trend is only just beginning to be felt in the international sphere. The total volume of international telecommunications is still small relative to domestic communications, and such operations as telecopying are still expensive compared with the mails. But the time is probably not far off when, for example, international access to data banks of various sorts will be taken as routine. Marketing and sales information will be easy to store and retrieve in this way. Training packages for sales of application engineering will be easy to make and to market. Central inventory catalogues can be queried and processed telegraphically. Even large labour forces might be trained through computerised or packaged programmes of various sorts. To an increasing degree design information will be encoded for computer, rather than incorporated in blueprints. As computer-controlled production machinery spreads it will become possible to remotely control and programme production runs. There will be strong trends towards the development of international standards for product safety, environmental protection, and effective performance.

Another trend that is likely to develop is international trade in services. There seems little reason why the present international division of labour in manufacturing could not be extended to the service sphere, and the packaging and marketing of what might be called "management software", even in areas traditionally regarded as the province of the public sector, such as solid waste management or postal services. I will return to this subject later.

John Diebold has expressed the opinion that in the future the most important export of the United States is likely to be "know-how", and that traditional manufacturing activities will increasingly move from the rich northern countries to the poorer southern countries. This is likely to occur for several reasons. In the first place, the technological organisation of many of the older traditional manufacturing industries is better suited to the less educated labour forces available in the less developed countries. In these industries mass production tends to be organised in a rather authoritarian fashion, which is increasingly unacceptable to the highly educated and high-aspiration labour forces of the most developed industrial countries. While some sporadic efforts are under way in both Europe and the United States to redesign work to fit better the character of modern work forces, it may prove more efficient in many cases simply to transfer certain kinds of production elsewhere, thus developing a kind of international division of labour with respect to the quality of working life. It is generally much easier to fit new, high-technology production processes to the aspirations of American and European labour than it is old, low-technology processes. In addition, of course, the normal evolution of the "product cycle" will tend to make foreign production in less developed countries economically more efficient. Finally the growing concern with environmental protection in the industrialised countries is already causing a shift of the more polluting types of production towards less developed countries, and this trend is likely to accelerate in the future. The very uncertainty regarding future tightening of environmental requirements will lead corporations to favour long-term investments in manufacturing facilities in locations where they can be free of new requirements imposed during the useful life of the plant. The more polluting industries tend to be the older industries which are also candidates for export to less developed countries on other grounds. What complicates matters is that these industries include some of those usually considered basic to the economy such as steel and non-ferrous metals, as well as oil refining and some basic chemicals. There is a question as to the degree to which industrialised countries will permit a large fraction of such basic industries to escape their sovereignty, even though it may be more efficient from a purely economic standpoint to permit them to settle elsewhere.

Global Technologies

By global technologies I mean technologies which can be sensibly deployed only on a global basis. The most conspicuous examples are the technologies related to space, such as communications or broadcast satellites, meteorological satellites, and earth resources survey satellites. However, there are other less spectacular technologies which have similar characteristics, for example, technologies which enhance the efficiency of fishing in international waters, and, in the future, technologies aimed at the exploitation of natural resources on the sea bed or on the outer parts of the continental shelves. The international transport of oil and liquefied natural gas may also be considered as global technologies, primarily because they have a large potential impact on the global environment. These technologies have the common characteristic that, to be intelligently managed, they require some kind of international agreement, since they utilise the world's "commons" in one way or another, and it is necessary to develop some means of limiting total national or private claims on these commons. An area which is as yet less clearly global is that of weather modification. It has potentially global effects, but is not yet developed on a sufficient scale to be of real significance. As international information systems and data banks begin to be developed, as seems likely, they may also be considered as global technologies, as a need develops to manage access to them as well as the collection and validation of the information that goes into them.

It may also be expected that the present research programmes related to the understanding of the global atmospheric and oceanic circulation and the earth's heat balance and atmospheric composition will eventually evolve into operational forecasting and monitoring services with well developed systems for the dissemination of data and related interpretation thereof. There will be problems of how the costs of such services will be shared among nations, and by what methods and to what extent their costs will be paid for by users. There are, of course, precedents for such services; the international ice patrol is a good example. But the costs have seldom been high enough to constitute a major political issue. This may not remain true in the future.

In many ways the world energy supply is assuming the dimensions of a global problem in the sense indicated above, and hence new technologies for energy generation have increasingly global aspects. For fossil fuels the major industrial nations are becoming less and less self-sufficient. Sixty per cent of the fuel oil burned in the world moves by sea, with attendant risk of pollution of the oceanic "commons". Energy resources are for the most part the property of sovereign states, but are almost as vital to the maintenance of modern societies as the air they breathe. The sources of energy do not coincide with the areas where it is most used.

As nuclear energy begins to replace fossil fuel, new problems related to the international control of technology are raised. There are the problems of the possible diversion of plutonium. There are the problems of management of high-level radioactive wastes. Since these have to be stored in geological formations for thousands of years, questions of how this storage is to be managed and monitored are of more than national interest. We cannot assume that national political boundaries will last that long. The reprocessing of fuel can lead to the emission of some materials, such as Kr^{85}, which could eventually contaminate the atmosphere to a dangerous degree. There will thus have to be international standards for the removal and storage of this particular gas. Through the IAEA this subject appears to be under better control than many others, but the future potential growth of nuclear energy is enormous, and there is uncertainty as to how it will be managed.

In the United States today there are many cries for a "national energy policy". What this really means is not always clear. But it does seem that long before the century is out we shall need an international energy policy to ensure that every nation has access to the energy it needs, and that if resources are limited they are shared on some basis that does not threaten the survival of national economies. Especially during the next two decades the competition for fossil fuels could become a serious irritant in international politics, both among the developed countries themselves, and between the industrialised nations and the countries that have most of the supplies. Unless we get together on policy ground rules before serious shortages develop, then negotiations will be much more difficult. A fruitful area for the sharing of technology may lie in the efficient utilisation and conservation of energy, from which everyone stands to gain.

As one looks to the long future there are many options available for the world's energy supply – fast breeders, thermonuclear fusion, several forms of solar energy, dry rock geothermal energy, conversion of agricultural wastes. From a technological point of view there is no reason why we should run out of energy for thousands of years. Yet we do have at least a perceived short-term energy crisis; whether it is a political or a technical crisis is not so clear. With so many technical options for the future there would appear to be a strong case for a better international division of labour in the necessary research and development. At the present time, however, all the advanced nations appear to be concentrating on a single line, the liquid metal fast breeder reactor, with the next most effort going into thermonuclear fusion. Europe, the U.S. and the U.S.S.R. all apear to be embarked on the construction of LMFBR prototypes. Given the global nature of the energy problem, one may well ask whether this is a wise strategy. Yet it is the natural strategy as long as we think in terms of a world of sovereign nations. The LMFBR appears to be the most promising as well as the most imminent option at the present time, and under present conditions it is natural that each nation should choose this most promising route. Yet if it fails, as it well could, the whole world will be worse off than if some of us had chosen to try a different route, such as the gas-cooled fast breeder, the molten salt intermediate breeder, or some mixed thermal–fast reactor configuration. Yet, given the stakes in terms of international trade, nobody wants to be caught with the "runner-up" technology. In these massive global technologies it seems that competition, far from producing technological diversity, tends to generate a single approach. One wonders whether we should not design a system in which at least some of us would pursue alternate technologies, while being insured in some way against the international trade impact of choosing the losing option.

The above remarks apply to the present generation of breeder technology, but they apply even more to the more "far out" options which are much further from engineering feasibility. Perhaps one of the central questions for European–American discussion in the field of technology is how do we achieve a sensible division of labour in technological development, enabling the exploration of more options without unreasonably penalising the nation that happens to choose the option which proves to be less viable in the long run. It may be that the best way to handle this problem is not to do such global developments on a national basis, but rather deliberately to create several multinational groups which work on competing options. In this way each nation would own a share in the winning option, and there would be less incentive for technological imitation along national lines. I am sure this is the way things will go in the end, but there may be a good deal of pain in the process of getting there. Indeed, for a proposal of this sort to work would require some sort of multinational assessment and planning structure, capable of evaluating and comparing progress on the various technical options and recommending changes in the relative allocation of resources to them.

RESISTANCES AND OBSTACLES TO CONTINUATION OF CURRENT TRENDS

Introduction

This paper is put forward on the premise that the maximum international division of labour in technology and production is desirable, on both economic and political grounds, and that a primary objective of European and American policy should be to facilitate technology transfer and the international movement of capital, particularly venture capital for the development and deployment of new technology. This does not mean that both capital and technology transfer are not without their undesirable side-effects. The greater the permitted circulation of capital and technology, the greater the hazard that imbalances of trade will develop which may have negative political repercussions. Perhaps the present disarray of the international monetary system is a good illustration of this problem. But I believe these are dis-benefits secondary to the great benefits of technology transfer, and therefore policy must aim at cushioning and controlling the negative effects rather than limiting the primary processes of transfer.

Indeed, any effort to limit the circulation of technology would be an example of the "tragedy of the commons" in reverse. It seems clear that world society has a stake in the free circulation of technology, and that resistances to this process occur largely when the costs of this progress fall unevenly on different groups and organisations within countries. In other words the benefits of the international division of labour are spread rather evenly among all members of the population, while the secondary dis-benefits often fall with special impact on relatively few people who are nevertheless quite potent politically. One can hardly blame these groups for resisting what they see as the fundamental trends which have caused their discomfiture. The problem, then, is to find ways of facilitating the compensation and adaptation of the disadvantaged groups so that they will not cause so much political friction in the process which is a net benefit to all.

One can identify a number of sources of resistance both to technology and capital transfer. Briefly listed, they are:

1. Organised labour, which sees foreign investment and the sale of technological know-how as the export of domestic employment opportunities.

2. The political drive for self-sufficiency in raw materials and energy, prompted by national security considerations.

3. The increasing volatility of capital movement, and its potential disruptive effects on the international economy.

4. The growth of political nationalism and ethnocentrism, accompanied by a fear of foreign influences and control.

5. The "not invented here" syndrome.

6. The threat of the free movement of capital and technology to national social objectives.

Let me look at each of these in turn.

Organised Labour

It is unfortunate that in the United States organised labour is strongest in precisely those industries, generally characterised as "low technology", which are most threatened by import com-petition, and by the migration of production abroad. Most of the political power of labour is based in these industries, and it is this fact which largely accounts for the recent switch of labour from a free-trade to a strongly protectionist political stance.

Labour sees the licensing of technology to foreign firms, and even more, foreign direct investment by multinational corpor-ations, as illegitimate methods for exporting domestic employ-ment opportunities. However, the evidence for this view is unconvincing. In fact the U.S. multinational corporations as a group have shown superior performance as compared with the average for the economy as a whole in both the creation of new domestic employment and in increasing exports. In most cases it appears that foreign investment and technology transfer have enabled U.S. firms to capture or retain markets from which they would otherwise have been excluded.

Most of the loss of employment in domestic industry owing to foreign competition has been in industries with relatively static markets, such as textiles, and certainly not in those industries which have large foreign affiliates.

On the other hand, there is a strong case for developing methods of compensating or facilitating the adjustment of firms and employees which are adversely affected by foreign competition as the result of increased freedom of trade. A precedent for this was set in the U.S.–Canada Trade Products Agreement of 1965, which contained assistance provisions for adversely affected firms, and temporary financial compensation for affected employees. Such adjustment costs are quite properly borne by society as a whole, but they must be designed so as not to be permanent. Otherwise they simply build inefficiences into the economy. There is probably good reason to undertake more comprehensive adjustments, if necessary by international agreement, to ensure that adjustment costs resulting from a more socially efficient division of labour are shared by society as a whole.

On the other hand, there is a danger that adjustment mechanisms will be gradually corrupted politically until they become permanent subsidies for an uneconomic allocation of resources at the expense of the consumer, as has proved to be the case with agriculture in virtually all the industrial countries. It is a challenge to political wisdom to steer a course between the irrationalities of the situation in agricultural trade, and such indifference to the problem of adjustment as to court a protectionist reaction. It would seem that a scheme which provided adjustment compensation from a multinational fund might provide a more neutral mechanism than a purely national approach. The benefits of freer trade and technology transfer are essentially multinational in character, and it seems fair that their secondary costs might be borne multinationally. Perhaps a small percentage tax on all international transfers of capital, goods, and services could be used to support an internationally controlled fund for such compensation of sufferers. If the fund were administered by a multinational board, it would be less subject to parochial national special-interest groups.

Self-Sufficiency

If free trade is permitted to run its course, would some countries altogether lose their position in certain basic industries such as steel or energy? Since the middle 1950s the U.S. has maintained an oil import quota for the purpose of maintaining the price of oil at a level compatible with the maintenance of a viable domestic production capacity and reserves. The argument was that we could not afford to let domestic capacity fall into disuse and the exploration for domestic reserves to stop, because the country would then become vulnerable to arbitrary political actions by foreign suppliers. Similar considerations might apply to other basic industries such as metals, and indeed there are now substantial political pressures in the U.S. for import quotas on steel. In a world of sovereign, and sometimes hostile, nations, this argument is hard to counter. It is particularly persuasive in a nation such as the U.S. which has been long accustomed to self-sufficiency in most of its essential raw materials, and which has only recently become a major importer of raw materials and energy. The argument is easily extended to basic refining and steel ingot production capacity. It seems to be less persuasive in Europe, long used to importing most of its raw materials, and perhaps trusting to the U.S. military presence to ensure its supply lines. A somewhat similar argument was used by De Gaulle in his insistence that France had to have an independent computer capability, because computers were so basic to the whole economy, that it could not afford to be wholly dependent on foreign suppliers. Some such argument probably partly motivates European investments in nuclear energy, particularly separation plants for enriched uranium.

The question arises whether self-sufficiency is any longer an attainable goal for any highly industrialised country. Its possibility seems long since past for an economy the size of Japan's, and for most of the economies of Western Europe. The volume of international trade, even on a percentage basis, is much higher than ever in world history. In the 1930s it was still possible for the world to revert from interdependence to autarky, but it is doubtful whether such a reversion is possible in the much more interdependent world of the 1970s. Even if full self-sufficiency is not possible, however, some domestic capacity provides a political insurance policy. Within its own borders Europe decided to forgo the possibility of individual national autarky when it created the European Coal and Steel Community. Perhaps one must look forward to the day when certain basic industry consortia will be set up comprising the whole Atlantic community. Such a larger community could even afford to ensure its supplies through the development of standby common technologies which might be uneconomic on a worldwide basis. Surely the time will eventually come when the nations of the world will be forced to negotiate agreements assuring the access of all peoples to certain basic raw materials and industrial products necessary for a viable industrial society. It seems difficult to believe that the self-sufficiency argument can outlast the 20th century. As the world economy grows, its absurdity will become too patent. It is not too early now for the developed nations of the world to start talking about these problems seriously among themselves.

Volatility of Capital Movements

Since 1970 rapid shifts of capital between countries have become an increasing problem for the international monetary system. Much of this shift is probably in funds held by multinational corporations. Certainly such shifts have been facilitated by modern communications and data management. The problem is to put some limits on the rate of such shifts without inhibiting normal trade flows and foreign investments of a long-term nature. This is a technical question for international economists which I am not competent to comment on, but there is one aspect which directly relates to technological matters. The increasing dependence of the Western countries on oil from the Middle East inevitably results in the transfer of large quantities of capital to countries whose economies are structured so that most of the money enters international capital markets. By the mid 1980s U.S. oil imports alone will exceed $30 billion, and the fate of these funds is a matter of not inconsiderable concern for the management of the international monetary system. Such funds are likely to be even more volatile in their shifts than the normal operating balances of multinational corporations. They may also be used to buy ownership in European and American corporations. In some instances, of course, the money may be used for economic development in the supplying countries themselves. But the question of these balances remains a serious concern for international monetary managers. Efforts to protect the system against this kind of volatility may also inhibit normal and desirable capital movements and investment. Thus the situation may provide an indirect source of resistance to the further diffusion of the international division of labour.[1]

Nationalism and Ethnicity

Isaiah Berlin has pointed out that virtually all the intellectual prophets of the 19th and 20th centuries have tended to ignore the phenomenon of nationalism, treating it as an anachronism that was always just about to depart from the scene. Yet today nationalism and, even more, local ethnocentricity seem to be on the rise everywhere. Berlin connects this with the rising mood of "self-protective resistance" against the rationalist integration of world society which he sees as having triumphed everywhere on both sides of the "iron curtain". In his words, nationalism or ethnocentrism "expresses the inflamed desire of the insufficiently regarded to count for something among the cultures of the world". We see this strain strongly in the rhetoric of the leaders of the Arab world and of the Arab guerilla movement. It is an element in all the revolutionary movements around the world, every one of which appears to have strong ethnic or nationalist overtones.

The revolt that Berlin describes is contrary to the rational material self-interest of the people involved. It raises the question of whether we can count on the stability of the rationally integrated and interdepedent world which we have been discussing. Perhaps this will prove the single most important and significant resistance to the international division of labour. Even among the more sophisticated populations of the highly industrialised countries, are the undoubted benefits of world integration sufficient to continue overcoming the particularism which rears its head as soon as society feels that it has nearly solved its material problems? Perhaps the world has enjoyed nearly 30 years of relative peace, punctuated only by distant colonial wars, because it was populated by a generation fed up with the chaos created by particularism in the '30s and '40s. As the memories of the Great Depression and World War II fade into history, national and group interests may become increasingly important relative to the rationally integrated world society whose stability is now taken for granted.

[1] For detailed development of this point, see Chapter X.

"Not Invented Here"

One of the benefits of a worldwide technical community, both in technology and in science, is that national scientists and engineers are exposed to the cold winds of a worldwide standard of performance. This is a remarkably effective tool for sweeping away inefficiencies. But it is also resisted. This is a particularly serious problem for Americans who, accustomed to superiority in technology, are less disposed to learn from others than technical people from elsewhere in the world. It may well be that the great secret weapon of the Japanese in technological competition is their sense of technological inferiority, and consequent lack of psychological resistance to learning from others, and adapting the innovations of the whole world to their own needs. Cultural habits die slowly, and it may take a whole generation before the sense of technological hubris characteristic of the '50s and early '60s gives way to sufficient humility for Americans to learn from the rest of the world the way they have from us in the past. It is indeed remarkable that only a few years after publication of *Le Défi Américain* the technological gap should appear to have been reversed.

It is also disturbing to see the revival of the pathetic illusion that secrecy and the control of information can prevent the acquisition of American know-how by foreigners, except in the very short term. This is the reverse aspect of the "not invented here" syndrome, the belief that our ideas are bound to be better, and that if somebody comes out ahead of where we expected they would, it must be because they stole our ideas, or somehow did not play fair. The most important fact about a new technology is the knowledge that it can work. With that knowledge any nation with reasonably sophisticated technical capability of its own can duplicate a technological development more cheaply than its originator, even without technology transfer. Indeed, efforts to prevent the export of technology are likely only to accelerate the development of an indigenous capability, as has been demonstrated over and over again. It seems clear that the failures of new technology in Britain and Europe that have occurred have been commercial, not technical, and it is unlikely that they would have been overcome by better technology transfer.

The most usual net effect of controls on the export of technology is simply to induce others to develop an indigenous technology at somewhat higher cost than if we transferred the technology, but at lower cost than that at which we developed it ourselves, with the result that the U.S. loses revenue and sales resulting from technology transfer, while the rest of the world pays somewhat more for the technology or the goods resulting therefrom, and hence has less money left over to pay for other imports from the U.S.

Regulation of Multinationals

Particularly from the U.S. standpoint, the multinational corporation has been the main instrument for the transfer of technology both to the industrialised nations and to the third world. Exceptions occur for nations which are hostile to or do not accept foreign investment. Japan, for example, has ordinarily only permitted joint ventures with less than majority ownership, and then only under carefully regulated conditions set by government.

The MNCs have begun to create serious political problems around the world. The hostility to them has focused on American-based corporations only because they grew up first, but in fact MNCs based in Europe or Japan are now growing considerably more rapidly than the U.S.-based group, and similar political problems are likely to arise. The problems arise simply because of the difficulties in reconciling the objectives of the centrally determined economic and technical strategy of an MNC with the diverse social and economic policies of a variety of independent host nations. A particularly sore point, especially in the LDCs, is the tendency of MNCs to do their R. and D. and advanced design work in the mother country, so that the host country has access only to the mature technology, and feels excluded from the possibility of participation in the earlier and more prestigious phases of the innovation process. Such centralisation of technical work often makes sense from the strict standpoint of economic efficiency, but it exacerbates feelings of political or cultural inferiority.

As long as MNCs are in the position of bargaining individually with independent, sovereign governments, the latter will be at a disadvantage. They will be in competition with each other to induce the MNC to locate its facilities in one nation rather than another. This sort of bargaining for concessions to outside firms is, of course, not unknown domestically within the developed countries. It has been particularly prevalent in the United States, where it is facilitated by a high degree of state and community autonomy. Some such competition, of course, is part of the process of optimising the international division of labour, and should not be discouraged. What may be needed is agreement among, say, the OECD countries in regard to minimum standards of behaviour for the MNCs both within the member countries and *vis-à-vis* the LDCs. Such agreements would cover matters like transfer of funds to avoid taxes, but would particularly concentrate on matters of technology transfer. For example, they might establish general guidelines as to minimum amounts of R. and D. and advanced design work that would be performed in host countries, training of indigenous personnel for technical and management positions, conduct of training for skilled labour, possibly in excess of immediate company requirements, and other forms of technical assistance and upgrading to accompany the conduct of business operations in the host country. If such standards were set by agreement, competitive undercutting in responsible corporate behaviour could be reduced, and the MNC could become an increasingly important channel for technical assistance, which in most instances would be more efficient and politically more acceptable than more direct forms of aid. This is obviously a very complex matter, and would require a great deal of work and perhaps many years to settle. The important point is to secure immediate recognition of the principle of mutually agreed standards of the MNC behaviour, and start the process of negotiation leading to its implementation. The creation of a climate which legitimises such negotiation of multilateral limitations on corporate behaviour may be more important than the details of the final agreements.

Government Subsidy of Industrial R. and D.

Among the developed countries themselves there is also a need for agreed ground rules regarding governmental subsidy of industrial R. and D. directed at products and services for the commercial market. Among the advanced industrial countries there is an increasing trend towards such government subsidy of technological innovation in the private sector, and competition in this area could get out of hand unless there are understandings as to the degree to which development costs must be incorporated in the sale price of the final product. This is a very difficult and touchy area. As the basis for technological innovation becomes increasingly scientific, the results of industrial R. and D. tend to have more "external benefits" which cannot be captured by the firms making the original R. and D. investment. This provides a justification for some form of social subsidy for certain kinds of industrial R. and D., especially in the areas such as safety, environmental protection, or methods of meeting performance standards, where improvements benefit all the firms in an industry equally, and where it may be economically inefficient for each firm to carry out research competitively without sharing its knowledge. In other words, without a social subsidy, firms will tend to under-invest in certain kinds of research. But in practice it may be very hard to draw the line between legitimate subsidies of this sort, and subsidies which are merely hidden subventions enabling firms to compete unfairly on price. There may also be a case for encouraging, by agreement, the internationalisation of certain kinds of industrial research which benefits a whole class of industries, and for which exclusion of some firms from the benefits is either practically difficult, or economically wasteful because it leads to unnecessary duplication. If research co-operation between firms in an industry is desirable at the national level, it may be even more desirable at the international level, but in either case there is a need to develop objective standards by which one can decide when competition in research stimulates innovation and when it merely results in unnecessary duplication.

If the trend towards the disappearance of tariff barriers continues, the effects of non-tariff barriers on distortions in the pattern of international trade will become increasingly important, and will tend to become the focus of negotiation and, alas, recrimination. The relationship between government and the private sector in R. and D. innovation could become an important field of controversy, and requires study and multinational discussion before it becomes problematic.

COLLABORATION IN THE PUBLIC SECTOR

Backwardness of the Public Sector

In the United States the fastest growth of employment has been in the government sector, with the non-profit service sector being a close second. About 15 per cent of the labour force is directly employed by government, and about 31 per cent of the GNP is in the form of government services and purchases at all levels of government. In Europe the public sector is even larger, generally around 40 per cent of GNP. Although measures of worker productivity in the service sector are generally unreliable, there is a general consensus that the growth of productivity in the public and non-profit service sectors has lagged seriously behind that in manufacturing and in such private service sectors as transport, public utilities, finance, and trade. The very sectors showing the least productivity growth are those that have experienced largest growth in demand, so that they absorb a rapidly rising share of national income. It is generally believed that this situation is an important contributor to the inflation experienced in all the OECD countries, since average wage and salary levels tend to be paced by the growth of productivity in the more productive sectors of the economy.

The lagging economic sectors in question are also those in which there is very little technology transfer or sharing of knowledge and experience at the international level, and often not at the local level either. Since the services provided are either monopolies, as in the case of national governments, or non-competitive because of geographical jurisdictions, as with local and state government, there is little incentive to increase productivity or even to measure it. For the same reason there is little transfer of experience about more efficient ways of doing things.

Although 25 per cent of the manufacturing production of the free world is by foreign affiliates of companies based in other countries, each nation has its own school systems, hospitals, local governments, and judicial systems. Thus we have the paradox that information and results from basic scientific research flow freely across national boundaries, and highly proprietary technological information which can be purchased on the assurance of full exclusion of non-payers can be freely traded internationally, while the intermediate kinds of information which are neither pure science nor proprietary are relatively much more immobile. Thus every industrialised economy has a rapidly growing sector which is sheltered from the bracing winds of international competition, or even regional competition. Yet this is the very sector that is increasingly connected to the "quality of life" which is the rising concern of affluent populations whose immediate material needs have been met.

Thus a major challenge to international co-operation for the next two decades will be how to make the public and non-profit service sector internationally competitive and more efficient in the same way that the manufacturing sector has become more competitive. This includes the problem of technological and administrative innovation in these sectors, and that of stimulating the circulation of innovations on a worldwide basis. At the present time such exchange as does take place occurs largely through the mediation of intermediate inputs such as computers, communications systems, office equipment, and other capital goods sold to the service sector. Some areas of the service sector, such as insurance, banking, and credit, have shown spectacular productivity increases owing to computers and other intermediate inputs, but others, including virtually all publicly provided services, have shown very little net gain. I suspect one of the major developments of the next two decades will be the appearance of new institutional mechanisms for providing various kinds of services, including governmental services, in such a way that they can be standardised geographically and exported across regional and national boundaries. There is already a brisk international trade in such services as management consulting, geophysical exploration for minerals, plant engineering design services, and credit and banking services. Is it too fanciful to imagine that the day will come when a few specialised multinational corporations will provide solid waste management systems for many of the world's major cities? Is it out of the question that a large American city might contract with a Japanese corporation to manage its mass transit system, and that Japan might contract with an American corporation to lay out a new national highway and traffic control system? The Americans have forgotten how to run railways, while the British and Japanese do not appear to be very good at managing highway traffic. Why cannot we develop institutions to apply each other's special skills on a worldwide scale, and thus enjoy the efficiencies of an international division of labour in the service and government sector, as we have done in the manufacturing sector? One can argue, of course, that peculiarities of local conditions, local employment priorities, different national or local legal or administrative systems, etc., block this kind of integration in the service sector. This is indeed true, but a few decades ago much the same thing could have been said in regard to many activities in the manufacturing and consumer goods field. There seems no reason in principle why the same evolution will not and should not take place in the service sector, including many services traditionally publicly provided. Any service that does not have a heavy component of allocative decisions in it should be a candidate for the substitution of private or quasi-private transnational institutions for civil servants. When allocation of benefits or costs among competing individuals and groups is involved, there is clearly the necessity for a political process, and therefore it is not appropriate to substitute quasi-private for public institutions in such cases, but once the allocative algorithms have been specified by the political process, there is no reason why the execution cannot be carried out by non-governmental institutions which can be subjected to objective performance measures. And there is absolutely no reason why such non-governmental institutions have to be confined by national boundaries.

COMMENT by John Pinder

I can only welcome the opportunities for international co-operation which have been identified and which will surely be fruitful for all our countries. I have one very slight reservation about the above proposals for co-operation in the public sector; this is the suggestion that the running of city mass transit systems in the U.S.A. might be turned over to the Japanese. Rush hour on the Tokyo underground is a forbidding prospect.

When it comes to the subject of relations between multinational companies and governments, I feel less happy. If one yearns after a world where intervention is just a slight ripple on a smooth surface of free trade, I think one should feel prepared for the rougher seas where intervention by government is the norm. Governments, after all, have important economic and social objectives, and symbiosis between governments and business is the basis of the economic world that we live in; but I feel that this needs to be a starting point rather than something built in on the way. Of course, most multinational companies are extremely well aware of this situation. They accept the need to be good citizens; and they are, for the most part, good citizens, obeying the laws, bargaining where necessary with the governments, because laws cannot lay down every last detail, and complying with the informal rules of behaviour in the countries where they work. Some multinational companies doubtless do not behave quite like that. I think I detect some reservations about tens of billions of dollars of American stocks being owned by Arab governments, and this I think because these holders of shares are expected to be very volatile. I do not think that would be the only trouble. I suppose that the governments of countries such as Libya or Iraq, if they owned large sectors of our industries, might not have the same idea of social responsibility towards our people as the companies which own our industries at present.

However, I do not think that the behaviour of multinational corporations has caused any great problem in Europe in the post-war period. If anything, multinational corporations have a reputation for better behaviour as employers and producers, and for setting up in accordance with the regional policies of the governments concerned, than other companies do; and in the European Community we have an instrument which is becoming well adapted to cope with such problems as there may be. Also, American multinational corporations have on the whole a very good reputation in Europe for the way they have behaved. One can make a short list of cases where there have been serious complaints about their behaviour, but it remains short. So, from the point of view of the European side of the Atlantic, we do not, I think, feel that there are great problems regarding the behaviour of individual multinational companies.

I do think, however, that there is a considerable unease at a macro level. This is because the flow of capital into ownership has been so largely one-way in the post-war period; there has been a massive taking over of European assets by American companies, and there has not been a massive taking over of American assets by European companies. No doubt this does not create any problem, and fears are inappropriate; but beyond a certain point, fears of increasing dependence do seem to take on more reality. The right answer, surely, is to reverse the flow, to have more European multinational companies taking over assets or establishing operations in the United States. This is of course already taking place to an extent, and I am sure it will take place more in the future, but it does seem to me important that the United States should encourage this tendency by removing the legal obstacles which are placed in the way of foreign companies that might wish to invest there.

If we look at the other large partner in the OECD, Japan, we find a case of extreme protectionism as far as foreign investment is concerned. If the Japanese were any respectors of liberal economic theory, they would have been bankrupt long ago; instead, they are very prosperous and getting richer very fast. However, although their treatment of foreign investment does not seem to have made them suffer in an economic sense, it does seem to be very important that if they are to be full members of the OECD fraternity of market and mixed economies, they should come into the open world economy in this respect; and I do not think it would be wise for Americans and Europeans to be too forthcoming in their negotiations, even on the trade side, if the Japanese do not concede something on the side of welcoming incoming investment. Here it seems to me that the proposal for an OECD statute assumes great importance. If the Japanese are just told "You must adopt some rules, but we are not having general rules", there will probably be a degree of acrimony, and the Japanese will feel they are being singled out. If, however, the OECD countries can develop something analogous to the GATT with respect to treatment of foreign investment and multinational companies, then the Japanese are offered a statute which is the same as that of other countries.

On the European side, I think it would be best if the European Community *per se* were to negotiate about such a statute, just as the Community negotiates in the GATT; and I hope that Americans would understand that and would not resent Europeans acting collectively in this matter. The way forward, in my view, therefore would be increasing adoption by the European Community of common policies regarding the treatment of multinational companies in its own area, the development in the OECD, by agreement among its members, and principally of course the United States, European Community and Japan, of a statute of the kind that is suggested above.

COMMENT *by A. E. Safarian*

Obviously, there is a conflict between national regulations and national fiscal policy of different kinds, on the one hand, and international specialisation and exchange of trade, capital, and technology on the other. There is no point in saying that one of these must prevail over the other. They serve different and equally desirable purposes. Where I think we run into difficulty is in trying to agree on the minimal constraints on the use of national regulatory and fiscal powers, if the gains from international specialisation and exchange in trade, capital and technology are to be preserved and extended. We should try to be a little clearer, I think, about the national objectives that are being served by national regulation. Merely to say that there are political and social objectives that must be supreme, without any specification, is I think not nearly good enough. I would agree that there are large gains from technological transfer and multinational production. Both parties can gain from this: it is not, except in some cases, a zero-sum game.

There are qualifications which are important, however, to this basic premise. One of the qualifications is that there are obvious national costs. Some of these are fairly direct: payments of various kinds to the parent country. Others are not as obvious, but are easily described. I am not impressed by the nationalistic arguments one sometimes hears on this subject, but I do think that there are difficulties for certain quite desirable national policies in a world of multinationals, whether they are foreign or domestically owned. There are certain costs involved in dealing with such companies in the attempt to secure other national policies.

I would also suggest that the gains are strictly potential gains. Whether they are realised and how much they are realised depend on how adequate are the tax policies in the host countries, how adequate are their industrial policies in general, and whether there is in fact enough competition or sensible regulation in the system, so that the benefits of technology actually do come through in price decreases, product improvement, real wage increases, and so on, rather than simply being captured in the profits of the firm. Finally, there is the very important question of how the gains are divided between the home and the host country. This is becoming more and more important as each set of contracts tends to secure more of the gains to the domestic country involved; and here, I suspect, we may be on a collision course.

For some time to come, moreover, the costs of information storage and dissemination, will come down; and this means that the multinationals and transfer technology are going to be with us and spreading for some time to come, unless of course governments deliberately restrain them. And in particular it means, as has been pointed out, that there may be a major breakthrough for the less developed countries, in the sense that many of them will become a very efficient source of production through trans-national, multinational organisation, based on the rapidly falling costs of certain kinds of information, on the processing of production and management knowledge and so on. There is a very great opportunity here, I think, for a breakthrough in the development problem for many countries, provided that their hostility to certain kinds of multinational can be overcome, perhaps by varying the ways in which multinationals move to those countries, and also depending on the kind of policies that the industrial countries follow.

Let me now raise one or two questions. I think that we should not underestimate the importance of conflicts between groups within countries, and the effect this has on policy towards international and multinational companies. One of the difficulties is that competing local capitalists, who might benefit in the first instance from the introduction of foreign technology and capital, eventually find certain disbenefits; for instance they may not be able to enter certain modern industries, which have become developed very substantially by outside interests and where the costs of entry are fairly substantial after development. There may also be hostility on the part of highly skilled persons whose services may not be in as much demand because the host country is importing a great many services with the technology, or with the product. It is these group conflicts, I think, which are the essence of the political attitudes towards multinationals.

The benefits of the international division of labour are in fact not evenly spread within a country. This is true both of the import side and of the export side; and it certainly is in the rational, material self-interest of those groups which are adversely affected to challenge the spread of technology through technical transfers and multinationals. It may not be in the national interest, but it certainly is in the material self-interest of the groups involved; and we need ways of ensuring that the costs do not fall wholly on particular groups.

On the policy level, I think that the many criticisms one hears in all countries of the performance of multinationals are so systematically at variance with the studies which are done of behaviour performance that one despairs of ever getting this point across. I am not suggesting there are not some fairly significant problems, but they often come from misapplied domestic policy of one kind or another which is then translated into a performance problem for the multinational. At the same time, I can see that the mere attempt to try to improve performance, whether on the R. and D. side or in other ways, is something that governments will and should attempt; but if this is done between pairs of countries a real problem arises. The host country is trying to increase R. and D. and exports; but the home country may feel that it is losing something in the process, and will therefore set up a countervailing process. This, I think, is eventually going to give rise to some very serious problems, of the kind that we subsume under the heading of non-tariff barriers. We could in fact virtually emasculate the contribution of multinationals if we do not reach some agreed policies on what governments can do to persuade multinationals to locate more of certain kinds of production in their territory, rather than in someone else's territory.

About the energy problem, I am not sure that I would agree entirely that every nation must have access to the energy it needs and share it on a basis that does not threaten survival of national economies. At one level that is obvious. At another, the language could be misinterpreted, I am sure unfairly, to suggest that the United States and some other consuming countries are going to pay less for energy than the straight economics of the situation would dictate for the next decade or two; or that some countries, which might be interested in trying to retain the energy and build industry on the basis of that energy, may be prevented from doing so. We have been through periods before when the cost of certain inputs has risen, and countries have adjusted to these; we have also been through periods when relative shifts in the costs and sources of inputs have led to shifts in the location of industry.

There is one more point that I think is rather critical as regards the nature of technology transfer. This is a conflict. The production of knowledge – which is what technology and technology transfer are about – generally requires some incentive. People have to invest and experiment long before the knowledge is useful. And so one needs incentives to get it created. On the other hand, once it is created, the advantage to the community, surely, is to disseminate that knowledge as widely as possible; to have it imitated as quickly and widely as possible. And this is a basic problem, because the national or multinational firm's interest, is to preserve its control of the knowledge as long as possible so as to get back its returns and more; whereas the country's interest very often is to enforce in various ways, through competition policy, through regulations, and so on, the rapid dissemination of this knowledge. It becomes a public good at the point where it is created, and public goods, from one point of view, should be supplied as widely and freely as possible. And this is going to create some conflict if we get specialisation and exchange of knowledge on a wider basis. Those who are essentially importers of certain kinds of knowledge must have some guarantee that their dependence on the importation of knowledge which has been created in these large corporations will not yield results in terms of the price, and in some cases outright exploitation, which would force them to begin to try to produce the knowledge themselves. What this leads to, I would suggest, is that we should start harmonising some major areas of national, regulatory policy, which interfere very heavily with the flow of knowledge. We should also look at the taxation by governments of the profits of multinationals, and the whole problem of transfer pricing. These, I think, are areas where more agreement is possible.

Finally, of course, we really should be thinking of different ways to transfer technology. There are many such ways: joint ventures, licensing agreements, turnkey arrangement, management contracts, even state purchase and dissemination of knowledge. We ought to know more about these: we ought to make it easier to have a variety of transfers. Some are certainly more suitable to certain industries than others; and my guess is that the multinational is better suited to some of the very dynamic kinds of industry. But by looking at and encouraging variety in this area we should be able to make the transfer of knowledge acceptable, both economically and politically, to a much wider range of rich and poor countries.

COMMENT *by Lane Kirkland*

In many cases the flow of capital and technology is in no sense a reflection of free trade but rather the contrary. It is designed to get around barriers to the flow of goods. Because of the existence of barriers to the sale of goods in a particular country, a firm may find it expedient to build a plant and produce in that country. I find it hard to see how that makes a contribution to the liberalisation of trade in any real sense. Nor is the free exchange of technology always an expression of a liberal ideal in trade. The sale by the MacDonald Douglas Corporation of the Thor Delta rocket to Japan, for example, is far from an expression of free trade or an ideal of the untrammelled flow of technological expertise. It reflects, I think, the fact that Japan wanted self-sufficiency and missile capability for the launching of satellites, rather than purchasing those services from the United States. And in many instances the attraction of capital, frequently by inducements that can in no sense be regarded as liberal trade policies, is often designed to give the host country a degree of self-sufficiency or an export capability in areas other than those which it is best fitted to pursue. Reference has been made to one of the reasons for American direct investment in Europe and elsewhere, i.e. certain features of the American corporate tax law. Perhaps that ought to be overcome and a little balance restored to the very different tax treatment faced by a domestic producer and a runaway producer.

I am also somewhat appalled by the suggestion that the technology of certain industries lends itself to transfer to, say, the less developed countries of the south as a means of avoiding the environmental restrictions of the northern countries; and I am bemused by the further suggestion that these industries are ill-fitted to the educational and aspirational level of workers in those countries. In reality, a worker can be found in the United States to perform any job that exists in that country if the price is right; and that of course is the rub. The real reason for the flight of these industries to less developed countries is the pursuit of cheap labour. Nor is it true that organised labour is strongest in precisely those industries generally characterised as low-technology, which are most threatened by import competition and by the migration of production abroad. I do not know how one defines which of those industries is most powerful politically. The one that certainly has suffered most directly and visibly, for example, is the American shoe industry, which I would not characterise as politically very powerful. That industry has been virtually wiped out – not by the products of European capital, technology, resources design or skill, but because plants in Connecticut and Massachusetts have been dismantled, lock, stock and barrel and taken by their owners to other countries, to Brazil and to Spain, where their products are manufactured and shipped back to the United States. They did not lose in the face of competition from foreign goods, but in the face of competition with American capital and technology located in the area of cheap labour.

We have no particular hostility to the fact that corporate enterprise pursues its best interests as well as it can: we expect that. If we were convinced that the growth of the multinational corporation and the flow of capital and technology abroad did result in the expansion of employment opportunities in the United States, then we should embrace it. We are not so insensible to our best interests as to resist such a boom. But, my experience is to the contrary. We have seen a Philco plant in Philadelphia making television sets: the executives of that company entered into a commitment with the National Alliance of Businessmen to employ underprivileged, undereducated ghetto residents in their plants located in the area of the United States which has a very high level of urban poverty; and yet we have seen them close that plant down and simultaneously reopen a television plant in Taiwan. That is what the worker sees, and it is going on, on a substantial scale; and our position is a reaction against those facts.

I believe that the perception of people who are affected must and should have some influence on policy in a democracy: it is not necessarily true that they stem from some primitive delusion or inability to see where one's best interests really lie. Our position stems in large part from the fact that in many industries the old principle of comparative advantage appears to have been supplanted by other forces. Comparative advantage is now movable and saleable; it can be dismantled and packaged for shipment to avoid taxes, to avoid minimum wage standards, to avoid the full range of social laws and responsibilities. We used to think that comparative advantage meant that Taiwan should produce rice, that Brazil should produce coffee, and not Philco television sets nor Florscheim shoes. I suggest that those who wholeheartedly, as we do, embrace the idea of free competition and trade between one nation and another, can still reasonably take a different view of competition between American domestic corporations – with their wage levels, their standards, their tax charges, and their obligations – and American firms located elsewhere not meeting those obligations, but evading them. It seems to me that there are circumstances in which the flow of capital abroad, the development of multinational interests, and production behind barriers to the import of goods, militate against efforts by my country to expand exports, including rather drastic measures such as devaluation. If a U.S.-based company is producing an automobile in another country, it will obviously think twice before shipping its domestically produced automobile to that country in competition with the locally produced one.

Our view of the trade policy question also stems from a rather long and very dismal experience with the adjustment features of the Reciprocal Trade Agreements Act, designed to cushion the adverse impact on employment. This experience produces no confidence whatever in the value of such measures and promises. Our position here stems from a growing sense of outrage at the manner in which governments – my own government, this and previous administrations, these and previous political leaders, and the governments of other countries – have facilitated, defended, subsidised, aided and abetted the flight of American capital, technology, and jobs, for the ultimate benefit only of private profit, at the expense of working people. There is a feeling throughout our ranks that, over the years, our strong and consistent support which enabled the Reciprocal Trade Agreements Act and extensions of it to survive, and we have been pretty badly gulled.

I do not believe that American labour has to apologise for the way in which it has proved its commitment to a humane internationalism: its record of support for trade union movements, and for social progress in other countries – in Europe after the war, today in Latin America, North Africa, and the Far East – demonstrates that. But we are seeking a way in which we can draw attention to some real problems, and maintain a posture that will avoid our being forced into isolationism, which is the danger today.

Chapter XIII

Developing and Industrialised Countries: a Generalisation

PIERRE URI[1]

THE FOLLOWING PROPOSALS stem from the theme that it is high time for the developing world, in particular for Latin America as a whole, to steer a new course and, as some of the countries have already begun to do, build up industries able to compete on export markets. That is the surest way of reducing dependence on foreign aid and financing. From this premise, a generalisation springs to mind: the political precondition, without which development will still be blocked, is that the developing world should be relieved of its posture, and its feeling, of dependence on the developed world.

First of all, bilateral dependence should disappear: that of Latin America on the United States, which is due to the unwillingness of Europe and Japan to involve themselves beyond sheer profit-seeking in trade and investment. But just as obvious is the danger of too close a dependence of Africa on Europe and – although memories from the past commend caution on both sides – of the rest of Asia on Japan. It would already be a great leap forward if the main powers acted jointly in giving aid to the various developing areas, creating a network of multilateral relationships in which Latin America, Africa and Asia discovered their own identity and, by the same token, made an original contribution to world affairs.

But even this joint action, or an increase, as envisaged by the United States, in the channelling of aid through such international institutions as the World Bank, would not eliminate the asymmetry between the obligations accepted by an industrialised debtor country and the conditions imposed on the developing ones.

[1] The present chapter is an excerpt from the author's contribution to *Latin America: Time to Regain*, by Adalbert Krieger Vasera and Xavier Pazos, published by Ernest Benn; it will be elaborated into a full-length study for the Atlantic Institute, under the title *Development Without Dependence*.

This point is crucial. As long as the countries of the third world feel that they depend on discriminatory conditions of aid or investment from the industrialised world, they will put the blame on others for their setbacks. The rivalry of nationalists from the right and left will substitute for a common national purpose.

It was opposition to the well-to-do that first drew the developing countries together. The Group of 77, and now of 95, which formed at the UNCTAD conferences, has led to a confrontation of indiscriminate demands and collective refusals. But this common front was composed of countries of very disparate conditions and levels of development, and it began to disintegrate in 1972 at Santiago, when several of its members realised that the advantages that were being extracted from the developed countries, especially generalised preferences, benefited some more than others and were in fact widening the gap between the most and least advanced among them.

Three major themes emerge from these observations: development without dependence, recognition of diversity in the third world, and the search for a common interest among developed and developing countries.

These basic ideas are political, and they must be carefully followed through into application. In other words, we must try to find the means to deal with issues rather than with countries, and to create the general conditions, often in indirect ways, in which each country could discover its opportunities, and with them its responsibilities.

There is no need to review all the problems and policies of development and to repeat what other, first-rate minds have already expressed. The objective here is to make a few precise proposals on certain points, which would change the overall context in which development takes place and in which relations are established between countries at different stages of development.

The first proposal concerns the administration and financing of aid. Today, whether aid is bilateral or comes from international institutions, it goes to governments. This produces a dilemma, in that too frequently funds go to governments that one is ashamed to support, yet withdrawing them would only deprive the people they tyrannise. The dilemma can be avoided only be rethinking the basic function of public aid. For the poorest countries it serves to raise the subsistence level. Beyond that, it should create hospitable conditions for investment, i.e. infrastructure and education. It is thus the transposition to a world scale of the essential ingredients of a domestic regional policy. Such a conception is all the more adapted to present circumstances as a freer flow of trade and capital brings the world increasingly together. It also shows the way to practical arrangements. Regional development banks should be set up everywhere, with special responsibility for particularly depressed zones in large countries, such as north-east Brazil, or for a region comprising a number of countries in the case of small contiguous states. Let us not delude ourselves that this new form of aid could begin without a modification of the statutes of the World Bank and other financial institutions dealing with the third world, or without joint guarantees by the states concerned. But if this proposal were adopted, at least aid and loans on favourable terms would be channelled directly into regional development, without passing through the hands of national governments.

The needed changes in the international monetary system could also be a first step towards improving the system of aid. It is surprising that international liquidity, in the form of SDRs, is created according to the allocation of quotas in the IMF, i.e. largely as a function of wealth and trade. Equity and efficiency would call for different priorities. Developed countries have normally to earn their growth in reserves. The only cases in which they benefit by a windfall are when there is a revaluation of the price of gold or the devaluation of their own currency. Allocations in the form of gifts should be reserved for developing countries. But there is another obvious source of development finance. An increase in the price of industrial gold is profitable for countries with large reserves, but they would lose nothing *vis-à-vis* their current positions if the IMF were charged with progressively liquidating stocks of gold and transmitting profits to development institutions or otherwise earmarking profits on the sale of gold to finance aid. This would be a free source of finance on a world scale for years to come.

These basic sources of finance are a necessary complement to private investment, and especially direct investment, particularly by firms which, owing to the size and spread of their operations, accede to a multinational status. Such investments could theoretically best achieve a rational distribution of resources, both with respect to the location of production and the sources and allocation of funds. This distribution, however, is completely distorted by various national policies, some of which raise difficulties – expropriation, for example – while others, on the contrary, offer

various facilities and tax incentives. This distortion, as well as
rivalry in the developing world, would be avoided if joint
guarantee councils were set up by groups of countries, which
would provide insurance against default in the case of a loan,
or against expropriation without suitable indemnity in the case
of direct investments. This mechanism, which would enable aid
to be distributed otherwise than through the states, would also
increase the negotiating capacity of developing countries *vis-à-vis*
the big companies.

A complete analysis of the advantages and disadvantages of
direct investments in developing countries, especially those of
multinational businesses, would involve a study of the contribution of capital and the cost of servicing it; of the increase in
exports and savings in imports; of resources provided to or
removed from states, according to the supplementary taxes they
collect or the subsidies they grant; of the incentives or obstacles to
the formation of domestic savings and an entrepreneurial class –
the whole being mainly prospective, and being balanced by a
comparison with other, purely domestic, solutions. But statistics
are rarely available for such an analysis of costs and benefits,
which in any case would involve many problematical elements.

A scheme exists that has every possibility of maximising the
benefits and of minimising the costs, and even more, of reducing
political friction. The large corporations of the industrialised
countries have taken the intiative in implementing it, first in
Latin America under the name ADELA, then by PICA in Asia
and an organisation now being formed in Africa. These groups
are constituted via the subscriptions of large firms from the various
countries, with no one of them having a predominant position.
Thus, they are genuinely multinational. They form associations
with local partners, who participate in the management. After a
period of development, all the interests are turned over to the
local partner. In this way, local savings and management potential
are encouraged rather than stifled. The financial capabilities of
the participating corporations allow for loans and credit in
addition to direct capital. As money becomes available, it can be
reinvested in new projects, so that the impact of development
is more widely diffused and the burden on the balance of payments caused by debt servicing or profit remittances is as limited
as possible. If all the developing continents adopted this scheme,
there would be a basis of agreement that would eliminate a great
number of risks and conflicts.

It is imperative that development be not hindered by sudden

losses of income from exports. Many developing nations are exporters of primary products. Contrary to what has long been believed, there is no long-term trend disfavouring these products and favouring industrial products of which these same nations are buyers. In fact, the last decade has in general proved favourable for primary commodities, except for agricultural products, which are in any case exported mostly by industrialised nations. And increasing demand, along with the exhaustion of resources, can only tend to raise prices. On the other hand, the fluctuations are violent. For food products, they are due primarily to variation of supply, for example an abundant coffee or cocoa harvest. For primary industrial products, price tendencies are a function of the industrial growth-rate of the developed countries. Indeed, industrial activity being constant, substitution and technical economies of utilisation will reduce demand. This reduction should be compensated for by increased industrial production. A further increase is then necessary to absorb the growth of production of primary goods.

Thus, the trend of primary products reveals not only the situation of the producers but also the risk of inflation, or on the contrary of deflation, in the industrialised countries themselves. In other words, it is the prime indicator of the world monetary situation. From this, one should infer an essential element for the reform of the international monetary system: the creation of SDRs might be accelerated or decelerated as a function of the trend of primary products. This would also provide for compensatory financing, in as much as the export losses of each country are attributable to the weakness of the international market for its products. Such a mechanism would serve as a stabiliser on a global scale, giving primary producers the means to sustain their demand for industrial goods and industry in turn to maintain the demand for primary products, which would uphold their prices.

Not all developing nations have a large base of exportable natural resources at their disposal and, anyway, with increasing productivity, employment cannot be guaranteed on this foundation alone. Thus it is imperative that industry develop and that it find new outlets. What has been demanded by the third world, partially accepted by the European Community and Japan, and not ratified by the United States, is the system of generalised preferences. Within certain quantitative limits and with the exception of some sensitive products, the European Community has abolished duties on manufactured goods from developing countries. But no sooner is the system implemented than it proves disappointing. The most advanced of the developing countries fill all of the available quotas, further reducing the access of the least developed nations to the international market. Moreover, preferences are granted at the expense of other exporters; they offer no guarantee to developing nations that they can compete with the internal producers on the national markets they seek to penetrate.

A totally different scheme would solve the initial difficulties of new industrial exports and gradually transfer the advantages from the countries in a position to benefit from them initially to others at various stages of development. These countries should, in one way or another, be allowed to apply to their new exports a rate of exchange different from that prevailing for their traditional exports. One practical way would involve the choice of an intermediate rate of exchange, the imposition of a tax on traditional exports, and a use of the proceeds of such a tax to subsidise the new exports. It is immediately clear that the rate of subsidisation per unit of merchandise would tend to zero while exports of new products grew in comparison with exports of traditional products. In other words, the dual exchange-rate would be only temporary and a single rate would gradually re-emerge as the device proved effective. However, other less developed nations would in their turn benefit from these new opportunities for export and development.

Such mechanisms will still not allow for the development of industries where they are most economical if developed countries continue to respond through increased restrictions on exports which compete with their internal production. They have no right to accuse developing nations of pushing import substitution too far if they condemn them to do so through their own tariff structures, which impede the processing of natural resources where they originate. This is evident in industrialised nations which receive primary products without duties but impose a duty on semi-refined products. These duties may, at first glance, seem minimal; compared with the margin of transformation, that is, the added value, they are on the contrary prohibitive. Two examples come to mind: refined copper versus ore, and soluble versus green coffee. Quantitative restrictions of all kinds and customs duties varying with the stage of processing converge under the notion of effective protection as distinct from nominal protection. This effective protection is the greater, the larger the gap between duties applicable to outputs and inputs. It is all the greater if restrictions of one sort or another, or preferences in public procurement, make internal prices higher than international prices. In other words, effective protection is measured by the excess value added in the internal price over the would-be price under free competition. We shall not here go into the various corrections that should be introduced in order to take monopoly effects into account, nor the modifications of exchange-rates that would become necessary if effective protection were reduced. The principle should be adopted, in the forthcoming international negotiations, of putting a ceiling on effective protection and then reducing it.

In the developed countries, effective protection is especially great in industries employing unskilled labour. An end to this distortion and the establishment of a rational international division of labour will come about only if the industrialised nations decide to give the needed breadth to methods of conversion. Labour must be protected from the risks of the changes without which there is no progress. Better still, any change of employment ought to become a chance for promotion. An analysis of the disparities in wages among economic sectors and firms reveals the advantage to labour of such a progressive conversion, of abandoning underpaid jobs and transferring to more productive economic activities at normal salaries. Such a policy, if pursued with the necessary vigour and continuity, would raise the standard of living in the industrialised nations themselves inasmuch as they would allow its improvement in the developing countries.

The developing nations can grasp this opportunity for export-oriented industrialisation only if they are also assured of a market extending beyond their national boundaries, and with more than their own feeble purchasing power. For them, regional integration is even more necessary than for the nations of an advanced continent such as Europe. Appropriate means still remain to be found for countries constantly threatened by balance-of-payments difficulties. The inequalities in size and in stages of development of countries within the same continent must also be taken into account. For political at least as much as for economic reasons, sub-regional groupings may be a prerequisite for small nations, in order to establish a substantial initial market, create new industries and approach equality with larger or more populous neighbouring states.

Beyond this, still another idea is worth consideration. It would not demand the same firm commitments to reduce trade barriers that the Europeans could agree to, knowing that the diversity and dynamism of their exports would furnish them with the means to pay for freer imports. Developing nations, as parties to an agreement, would undertake to increase the share of their imports from each other each time they achieve an increase in their overall exports. The impact and the double consequence of such a policy are obvious. It rests on a genuine possibility of increasing purchases, and it is flexible enough to allow, when necessary, the import of needed investment goods from the most advanced producers. A primary effect would be to provoke a chain reaction. If A buys more from B, B can in turn buy more from A or from C, and so on. At first, each country would opt for what it most sorely lacks; but soon a process of integration of pro- duction itself would get under way. There would also be another crucial effect. For one or more industrialised country to allow imports or generalised preferences would have but a pinpoint effect on the developing nation which reaps the benefit. This scheme, however, would spread the advantage among a greater number of countries. Thus, as with the conditions that will make a new international division of labour acceptable, the common interest of the developed and developing worlds might be sub- stituted for their confrontation.

COMMENT *by William S. Gaud*

How can we carry on development programmes in order to achieve development without dependence, give greater recog- nition to the diversity in the third world, and search more effectively for a common interest among the developing and the developed countries? There can be no quarrel with those principles. The question is how do we get from here to there? Obviously, there will be many differences of opinion on that.

A subject that has been debated among us all for many years is how best to administer and finance aid. We started out, primarily, with a bilateral aid programme; and most people would agree that that is the worst way to do it – the way most likely to create a feeling of dependence – of Latin America on Europe, of certain parts of Africa on Britain or on France, of Asia on Japan. And so we moved fairly quickly into the establish- ment of the World Bank and its affiliated institutions. These institutions, despite their considerable advantages, are still not the final answer. For one thing, the developing countries tend to look on the World Bank as being run by the industrialised countries, and this in itself is a decided disadvantage.

The key, it seems to me, in avoiding as much of a feeling of dependence as possible, is increased participation, on the part of the recipients of development assistance, in the decisions which are of such great importance to them. It has been suggested that regional development banks be set up throughout the world, to avoid dealing with individual governments, and to deal instead with areas. If I understand this proposition, I am afraid that I disagree with it pretty completely. Let us consider a member of the Atlantic family of nations, Ireland, which is somewhat less developed than its neighbours, which is working hard on increasing its industrialisation. Let us suppose that the rest of the Atlantic community set up a development bank, of which Ireland was a member, to decide how to develop Ireland, that it worked out a programme, and instead of dealing through the Irish government it went in and started making loans inside Ireland. I hate to think of what would happen; and in this respect I do not believe the Irish are any different from the Indians, the Nigerians, the Brazilians, or the Indonesians, or anyone else in the developing world. I think that we must deal with governments, whether we like it or not. There may be some we do not want to deal with; but let us not try to short-circuit governments, if what we are trying to do is to avoid the "Papa knows best" philosophy of development assistance. It does not seem to me that immediate neighbours, or regional neighbours, have any more right to make decisions for a developing country, than do distant neighbours.

I do subscribe wholeheartedly to the proposition that regional institutions are very important, and that we should give them more emphasis than we have to date. We now have the Inter-American Development Bank, the Asian Development Bank, the African Development Bank, the Caribbean Development Bank, the East African Development Bank. They are significant institutions – largely, as I see it, because the regional members have a substantial say in their activities, and for my view, the more so the better. If I were to write a prescription for the future of aid, of development assistance, I should route much more development assistance through those institutions, and much less through a centralised institution such as the World Bank. We should do everything that we can to build up the capacity of these regional institutions, and perhaps devise, or help to establish, some more. Again, the Inter-American Development

Bank should not be a bank to which the Latin Americans and the U.S. belongs: it should be a bank in which all of us belong, and to which all of us contribute. Japan should not run the Asian Development Bank; no one country, or two countries, or three countries should run the African Development Bank. Let us multi-lateralise those regional institutions, in terms of both the industrialised nations and the recipient nations, and let us give the recipient nations more of a say on how development assistance is distributed.

Another means of avoiding development assistance is private investment in the developing countries. Putting aside the question of whether that is aid (and I feel it clearly is not), I for one think that private enterprise, private investment, private initiative, have a very large role to play in development. They provide resources, technology, management, opportunities for training, and perhaps, very important, access to markets to which these countries would not otherwise have access. In this connection, investment insurance is useful as an incentive. But the trouble with investment insurance, as I see it, is that it takes into account only the interests of the investor, not the interests of the host country. Obviously, it will be better if it is a multilateral insurance scheme, than if it is bilateral. If it is a bilateral scheme, one is liable to get into the situation the United States is in with Peru or Chile today: an economic problem, or a problem between one corporation and another country, is converted into a major political issue, and all sorts of relations between the two governments come to a halt until that particular issue is settled, if it ever is. So that a multilateral investment scheme is greatly to be preferred to national schemes. But, unhappily, the climate for such schemes does not seem to be very good. The World Bank has been trying for some six or eight years to establish such a scheme, without success, because many of the industrialised nations are not interested, and the great majority of the developing countries will have nothing to do with it.

It seems to me that if we are seriously interested in the role of private investment in the developing countries, we, the industrialised countries, and the developing countries alike, have to tackle the basic question of mutual lack of confidence between foreign investors and the developing countries: a lack of confidence which grows out of a lot of history in the past. Both have to realise that reasonable investment terms for the investor and economic benefits for the country are not mutually exclusive, that they can readily go hand in hand. The host countries have to recognise that all foreign investors are not ogres; that they can provide badly needed capital, technology and managerial experi ence; and that they are entitled to fair treatment. By the same token, foreign investors have to take into account far more than most of us have in the past, the needs, the sensitivities of the countries in which we are operating. I think that this should be, in the years to come, one of the major preoccupations of all of us in the industrialised countries: to try to improve the climate for private investment in these countries; and it is going to take concessions on our part, just as it is going to take concessions on their part. The bridge between us and the developing countries is paved with all sorts of good intentions about general trade preferences – which I incidentally think my country should get behind, all sorts of notions about using SDRs – although I am a little concerned about whether SDRs are ever going to be used for a link now that they are talking about using them as a reserve asset, or perhaps as sopping up some of these large pools of money that are lying around the world. But there are all sorts of pro- posals and schemes to take the place of, or to be additives to, the transfers of resources to which we have been accustomed in the past. I am rather sceptical about these things happening within a reasonable time frame. I think the most important job for us today, in terms of development assistance, is to keep at what we are doing. Take for example the International Develop- ment Association, IDA. It may seem unambitious to discuss something as specific as this, but there is another replenishment of IDA coming up next year, and if we really wish to do something serious about our development assistance programme, I think the thing to do is to get together and increase the amount of resources that are passing through IDA to the developing countries.

Finally, I should like to emphasise the diversity of the third world. We make a mistake, in a sense, in discussing it as "the third world". We tend to lump all these countries together. In fact, there are approximately a hundred widely different countries in all stages of development. It is also very dangerous, it seems to me, to think of our relations with the developing countries only in terms of development assistance. This is a great mistake. Our poor country cousins around the Persian Gulf and elsewhere, who are going to inherit 50 to 60 billion dollars a year in the not too distant future, are also developing countries. They can be tremendously important in contributing to the development of the rest of the developing world. We have not thought too much in the past about being dependent on developing countries for things like copper and other minerals; we are going to think much more about that in the future. How long is Brazil going to remain one of these one hundred anonymous countries? How soon can Brazil start taking its place with us – and helping other countries? Above all, we should not only recognise that we have many interests in common with these countries other than interest in providing assistance to them but we should also give them a voice in the matters in which they are involved. They forced their way into the Committee of Twenty. It is a very good thing that they did. And there are many other issues, it seems to me, on which we do not give the developing countries enough to say in matters in which they have as deep and as much of an interest as we do.

PART THREE

Processes of Change in the Field of Security

Chapter XIV

Perceptions of the Military Balance

DAVID PACKARD

WORLD AFFAIRS are in a transition period, a time of change more rapid and more far-reaching than has occurred for some time. This is a time that calls for a new look towards the opportunities of the future and a reappraisal of the policies of the past. It is in this context that this is a very appropriate time to review the course of the Atlantic Community and to revalue and strengthen plans for its future.

The record of the Community under the wing of NATO over its nearly two-and-a-half decades is one of great success. There have been many problems, but the alliance has served its purpose well. It has provided the security and kept the peace in Western Europe. This was an absolutely essential ingredient to make possible the great economic and social progress of the nations of the Atlantic community during these past 24 years.

There was wise and firm leadership through the several crises of the 1950s and the early 1960s, but confrontations were containable on every occasion because the overall military balance weighed heavily on the side of the non-Communist world. It was a decisive balance because of the vastly superior United States strategic nuclear power. This was backed with worldwide naval superiority of the NATO forces, and what has turned out to be an adequate air and ground force posture in Europe.

But the strategic nuclear balance has changed radically since 1962. In that year the Soviet Union had fewer than a hundred nuclear missiles which could reach the United States. The U.S. missile force was over 400, and the U.S. bomber force had more than a three-to-one superiority in numbers and much greater superiority in terms of its capability. The Soviet Union could not risk a nuclear exchange with the United States. Today, the Soviet missile force has grown to over two thousand – 1,530 ICBMs and 560 SLBMs. This exceeds both in numbers and in destructive power the U.S. missile force of 1,710 strategic nuclear missiles – 1,054 ICBMs and 656 SLBMs. Today neither the Soviet

Union nor the United States could risk a nuclear exchange.

This shift in strategic nuclear power as well as other factors influencing the military balance pose a considerably different, although not necessarily more difficult, problem for the Atlantic Alliance in maintaining a satisfactory military balance in the future than it has had in the past. It is essential to recognise that great changes have taken place and to try to comprehend their significance in charting a course for the future.

Let me summarise some of the changes that must be taken into account when considering what must be done to help assure a peaceful environment for the Atlantic community in the years ahead:

1. As I have mentioned, in the decade of the 1950s the superiority of U.S. strategic nuclear forces tipped the overall military balance heavily in favour of NATO. This strategic nuclear superiority was lost in the decade of the 1960s and it cannot be regained short of a major technical breakthrough, which no one can foresee.

2. This change in the nuclear force balance has been accompanied by a substantial increase in the destructive power of both sides. The Soviets have increased both the number and size of their weapons and the United States has increased the number and quality of its weapons. This vast increase in destructive power, combined with the rough equality which has been achieved, severely restricts the utility of nuclear forces for the kinds of confrontations which are probable in the future.

3. The United States, supported by its allies, has had virtually absolute control of the oceans and seas around the world. This favourable balance is being threatened by the current build-up of Soviet naval power. There is no need for naval balance to swing away from the Atlantic community, but this matter deserves a very high priority. A favourable naval balance may be as critical to the future security of the Atlantic community as any other factor, including the strategic nuclear balance.

4. The role of tactical nuclear weapons as an element of the military balance has never been resolved in a satisfactory way and must be re-examined in the light of the changing situation.

5. There will continue to be many factors, including techno-logical improvements in non-nuclear weapons, which influence the military balance. In this regard, evaluating the balance of conventional (non-nuclear) forces by simply adding up the men,

the guns, the tanks, the planes, and the ships on each side and expressing them as ratios, in my view serves no useful purpose. There are many other factors which counterbalance an apparent advantage in numbers. Technology is and will continue to be an important factor – probably one of the most important factors – in the future.

6. The Sino-Soviet confrontation required the deployment of considerable Soviet forces to the East and thus has already had an effect on the military balance in Europe. Whether this situation will make a more difficult problem for the Warsaw Pact is hard to say. But this confrontation, whichever way it goes, will continue to influence the balance of forces in the European theatre.

7. There have been political changes of great significance. Increased trade and a strengthening of communication between the non-Communist world and the two major Communist countries are examples. This changing political climate will influence what needs to be done, as well as what can be done, about the future military balance.

8. The very significant economic progress of all nations in the Atlantic community makes it quite feasible to do what is needed to maintain an adequate military balance in the future with an equitable distribution of the load.

THE CHANGED STRATEGIC NUCLEAR BALANCE

The most important element of change in the NATO–Warsaw Pact military balance is the decisive and irreversible change in the balance of nuclear forces.

In the early years of NATO the military balance was strongly in favour of the West because of the vast superiority of United States strategic nuclear power. Conventional NATO forces in Europe had no need to be capable of handling alone a massive Soviet thrust into Western Europe. As long as these forces contained a reasonable number of U.S. military personnel, they would serve as a "trip wire" to bring forth American nuclear might should any expansionist venture be attempted.

The United States strategic nuclear superiority made the trip wire strategy credible. The conventional NATO forces were a key element, but they also had many shortcomings, both potential and real. Although the Alliance worked hard to maintain an effective conventional military force through this period, there was always the satisfaction that the nuclear umbrella was there should it be needed

There is no doubt the leaders of the Soviet Union felt this U.S. nuclear superiority to be a serious constraint to their freedom of action, and that it was in their national interest to change the situation. They attempted to accelerate their corrective action by a bold venture into Cuba in 1961, and even though this venture failed, they continued a very substantial effort to achieve an equality, to achieve what even might be called a conspicuous superiority in nuclear capability. This they have now done, and what exists is a nuclear balance. Both the Soviet Union and the United States are now very effectively deterred from using their nuclear capability against each other for any reason short of a dire threat to their very national survival.

With the strategic nuclear forces now in place on each side, it is almost certain that neither nation could survive as a viable society after an all-out nuclear exchange. This is a very sobering fact which I hope is reasonably understood by our friends in Europe. This nuclear balance means that both sides are now effectively constrained to the use of non-nuclear force in nearly every conceivable situation in which force may be needed.

The SALT negotiations can in no way change this fundamental situation. In the long run a further agreement could result in lower nuclear force levels for both the United States and the Soviet Union and less drain on their economies. It can be assumed that this nuclear stalemate will not be changed. Neither side can agree to a reduction which would bring into question the effectiveness of its nuclear deterrent. Neither side can do anything with present technology which would break this stalemate.

In the early years of the decade of the 1960s it was recognised that the nuclear balance was changing and that the massive retaliation strategy had become much less credible. Thus there was the ill-fated attempt to strengthen the NATO nuclear capability with a multilateral force. This was followed by an alternate strategy based around a flexible response, including the use of tactical nuclear weapons.

These strategies of the 1960s assumed that the so-called nuclear umbrella provided by the United States was either a credible deterrent or a possible course of action of last resource. Most of the thinking about conventional forces involved escalation to nuclear forces in one way or another, and that conflicts which resorted to force would ultimately be resolved at the nuclear level.

We have now reached the point with the rough equality and the greatly increased destructive power of the United States and the Soviet nuclear forces that the strategy from now on must be designed to minimise the possibility of escalation of a conventional force conflict to nuclear forces. This requires that conventional forces be adequate to handle the range of all probable confront-ations without the use of nuclear weapons.

Such a strategy is consistent with the Nixon doctrine to resolve future conflicts with negotiation rather than confrontation; it is consistent with the aims of arms control, SALT and MBFR; and is the most realistic strategy for the alliance to follow in the decade of the 1970s and beyond.

Thus the Atlantic community is faced with the need to support a more effective conventional military capability in the future than it has had in the past. This need to reorient emphasis to conventional forces is already accepted by military planners. You may recall that Secretary Laird made this point very clear at the NATO meeting in Brussels in autumn 1972.

In this regard I believe naval power can play an increasing role. Specifically, if NATO can maintain worldwide naval superiority, this can add a great deal of realism to the credibility of the NATO conventional force deterrence even though there may be factors of uncertainty in the balance of conventional forces along the central front.

Naval forces in this new environment are essential to keep the lifelines open to the European countries and in denying the Warsaw Pact access to the outside world during a conventional force conflict. What I am suggesting is that this nuclear stalemate has, to a very large degree, restored the importance of traditional military concepts.

The increase in the level of nuclear forces is also relevant to the utility of third-party nuclear forces in the European theatre. The present level of nuclear forces of France and Great Britain, even if they could be combined and placed under effective command and control, would have very little deterrent or war-fighting capability against the Soviet Union except as an addition to U.S. nuclear forces.

The British force of 64 Polaris A-3 missiles would not be very convincing against the Soviet force of 2,000 larger and more powerful missiles in addition to some 700 Soviet medium-range missiles, and the French force would appear no better. Even the Soviet ABM system might have some credibility against these small forces, if they were used alone. It is difficult to postulate any situation in which these third country nuclear forces will have much independent impact on the NATO military balance.

These European nuclear forces do add somewhat to the overall NATO nuclear capability even though they have very limited capability standing alone. Until there is a better understanding of and a confidence in what is meant by the United States commitment to provide the nuclear umbrella for the Atlantic community in the era of the new nuclear balance, it would not be desirable, however, to propose a reduction in these indigenous nuclear forces. In the long run, the resources which are now used to support these indigenous nuclear forces would be more effective if applied to the NATO conventional force capability.

There are those who have suggested that the countries of the enlarged Common Market might feel impelled to develop an independent European nuclear deterrent. This would require vastly expanded nuclear forces for the European NATO countries and poses so many problems as to be almost unthinkable. I am absolutely convinced the United States will remain firm in its nuclear commitment to the Alliance. The present nuclear umbrella is not only adequate for the Alliance, but even with the new problems which must be considered, is far better than any conceivable alternative.

I have said that I believe the United States will remain firm in its nuclear commitment to the Atlantic community. I have also said that with the present nuclear balance the United States would not use its nuclear forces against the Soviet Union short of a dire threat to the survival of the United States. These statements taken together imply my faith that there will be a strong and continuing interdependence between the United States and the European nations of the Atlantic community. This impact of interdependence on the credibility of the United States nuclear umbrella is one of the reasons why what happens to the Atlantic community in the future is so important to all of the member states, including the United States. I do not want to imply that this is the only or even the most important reason for working to continue and strengthen the Alliance, but I am particularly troubled by the suggestion that this is a motive for the United States to encourage the Alliance when, in fact, if it is a motive at all, it is much more relevant to the European countries. I do firmly believe that to the extent the nations of this community work diligently to resolve the common problems, to build on the common interests, to increase their interdependence and strengthen their sense of unity, this will do more than anything else to assure that the United States nuclear umbrella will be available to them should it ever be needed.

But let me again emphasise that this nuclear umbrella will be useful only in conflicts at the highest level, and the only safe course is to keep conflict at the level which can be handled with conventional forces, and to make sure those conventional forces are adequate for the job.

THE NAVAL PROBLEM

Until the last few years the naval strength of the Atlantic community was not thought to be a serious problem. There was concern about the large Soviet submarine fleet, and there were thought to be naval problems in some contingencies – for example, what is the role of a navy in a nuclear war? NATO essentially ruled the seas. The Soviet Union has been taking steps to attempt to redress this balance. They have increased their naval shipbuilding. They have developed a surface-to-surface naval missile force of considerable capability with at least 11 new surface-to-surface missile ships added in the past five years. They have also increased their capability in anti-submarine warfare and seem intent on developing a navy capable of challenging hostile forces anywhere on the oceans of the world.

This Soviet naval build-up must be viewed with great concern by the Atlantic Alliance. I do not see how the Alliance can survive unless it has effective control of at least the Atlantic Ocean and the Mediterranean. If the Alliance can maintain a superior worldwide naval capability, this can be a strong factor in maintaining an acceptable conventional force balance in the future. NATO naval superiority could be a major factor in limiting or dealing with low-level confrontations. This need not be a difficult job, because the only barrier to an adequate naval superiority through the foreseeable future would be the lack of a determination in the Alliance to take the necessary action.

The United States and European naval technology and shipbuilding capacity are quite adequate to keep ahead of the Soviet Union. NATO naval forces have a good history of working together and can continue to do so in the future. It would be helpful to have France on board, but even without France, NATO can easily afford to maintain a superior naval balance – in fact, the Alliance cannot afford not to do so.

Control of the Mediterranean by NATO requires more attention to one very important problem. Soviet aircraft based along the African Coast can severely limit the operation of NATO forces in the Mediterranean. For the same reason, NATO aircraft based in Spain, Italy, Greece, and Turkey are absolutely essential to NATO to control the Mediterranean. Land-based aircraft from these countries working with NATO naval forces could assure almost absolute control. Spain and Turkey are especially critical because they oversee effective choke points for any Soviet naval forces going into or out of Mediterranean waters.

The United States has increased its naval shipbuilding pro- gramme during the last four years, and a number of very im- portant development and procurement programmes have been accelerated to increase the effectiveness of the U.S. Navy. Co-operation between the United States and its friends in Europe on naval affairs has been excellent in recent years, but the naval problem must continue to receive a high priority in the Councils of NATO, and should include at least informal co-operation with France and Spain as well.

In emphasising the need to keep a naval force balance favourable to the Alliance, I have not attempted to delineate all the reasons why this is so important. I have pointed out that the naval power can be a major element in the conventional force balance. Naval power provides a force mobility that is an effective element of deterrence in addition to its role as protector of the lifelines.

Looking to the decade of the 1980s, a superior NATO naval force may be the most important element in the military balance. I believe some of the reasons that support this view will come out in the session at this meeting which considers the Economic Issues in an Interdependent World. The most visible factor is the dependence of Europe on middle-Eastern oil today, and the projection that the United States will be in the same situation by 1980, or shortly thereafter, when about half of U.S. oil and petroleum requirements will have to be imported. No known source other than the Middle-East can meet these requirements. This lifeline must be kept secure for the Atlantic Community and this consideration alone dictates a strong naval superiority continuing into the future.

THE TACTICAL NUCLEAR SITUATION

In the early years of NATO, when it appeared difficult to counter the considerable Soviet ground force capability with non-nuclear weapons, tactical nuclear weapons were introduced into the theatre. They were thought to be a way of greatly increasing the fire power and, therefore, the effectiveness of NATO forces in Europe. These tactical nuclear weapons included warheads for artillery, for rockets, for bombs, and demolition weapons. A nuclear warhead on a tactical weapon does not increase the probability that a given military target can be destroyed. If the enemy co-operates by massing his forces – his tanks, for example – tactical nuclear weapons would be very effective. If tactical nuclear weapons were used to attack bridges or airfields near cities, the bridges and airfields would be destroyed. But so, in all probability, would the cities, unless very small warheads and very accurate delivery systems were used, in which case there would be much less need to go to nuclear fire power.

The devastating argument against the use of tactical nuclear weapons is that those which both the United States and the Soviet Union now have in place would create vast destruction of civilian population and non-military installations, and the destruction would be very severe in NATO countries, although there would also be much damage in the Warsaw Pact area, particularly those countries close to the front. If both sides agreed to limit themselves to very small nuclear warheads with accurate delivery systems, and agreed there would be no escalation to strategic weapons, tactical nuclear weapons could have some utility. These are, clearly, improbable conditions to postulate.

Tactical nuclear weapons have been discussed many times over the past decade and by many sincere and knowledgeable people. I have never heard what I thought was a satisfactory description as to how they could be used. Probably the very uncertainty about their use makes them somewhat effective as an element of deterrence. They should be maintained and taken seriously if they are to remain an element of deterrence. They should not, in my view, be considered simply as an extension of non-nuclear military capability.

One argument for tactical nuclear weapons is that they provide a coupling from conventional forces to strategic forces and are therefore an important element of conventional force deterrence. If this were ever the case it is less so now, and a conventional force will be a more realistic deterrent if it can be adequate to control a confrontation without the need for tactical nuclear weapons.

THE ROLE OF CONVENTIONAL FORCES

As I have said, the nuclear parity which we now have is, in fact, a very effective stalemate between the United States and the Soviet Union. This nuclear stalemate must be preserved at all cost. Fortunately it can be preserved without much, if any, higher cost and probably at a lower cost through tough and realistic negotiations in SALT. This essential stand-off cannot be preserved under any course of unilateral disarmament. Tactical nuclear weapons must, in my view, be considered an important part of the nuclear stalemate. These weapons cannot be neglected, although as I have pointed out, they cannot be thought of as simply a useful extension of conventional theatre forces.

The result of this situation is that the essential national security priority for the Alliance is to maintain an acceptable balance of conventional military force in Europe, and a superior naval force in the Mediterranean and the Atlantic – and preferably world-wide. This security priority must be addressed in the atmosphere of the growing *détente* and in the environment of discussions to limit or reduce the level of military forces. One goal is to reduce the burden of military arms on the member states on both sides. This is not the only goal, nor even the most important goal of arms control. If the stability of mutual deterrence is lost in the course of arms control or in the course of *détente*, both will have failed. I am convinced there can be smaller forces on both sides in a stable balance, and to the extent the smaller forces are strong forces, stability will be enhanced. I have said on a number of occasions the United States can safely have smaller forces, but it cannot safely have both smaller forces and inferior weapons. The same applies to NATO, and this brings me to the role of technology.

THE CONTRIBUTION OF TECHNOLOGY

One very important ingredient in maintaining an acceptable future military balance is technology. The Western world holds a considerable superiority in technology of all kinds, including that which contributes to military capability.

It is not necessary to match forces man for man, tank for tank, plane for plane, to maintain an effective military balance. Some of the so-called "smart" weapons which have been used recently in Vietnam are from ten to a hundred times more effective than the weapons now in the inventory of either the Pact or NATO. It is probable that modern anti-tank weapons can, to a large degree, neutralise the effectiveness of a massive tank force. Air-to-air and surface-to-air missiles now in the inventory of both sides are primitive in terms of what can be done with the latest technology. There are many more examples.

This means that the military balance of the future will be determined even less by the number of men, planes or ships on each side. It will be determined by how effectively each side applies the latest technology to the weapons those men, planes or ships carry.

For many years after World War II the United States held a very dominant position in technology, not only in nuclear technology but also in all aspects of aeronautics and electronics. The Soviet Union made a great effort to catch up, and indeed made great progress as we all know. Europe was busy with rebuilding and West Germany was prohibited from working in some important areas of technology – microwave electronics, for example. During the decade of the 1960s the European nations began to make progress in all areas of technology, and can now compete effectively with both the United States and the Soviet Union in many areas of weapons technology. Some success has been achieved in improving the co-operation in this important area between the European nations and the United States and among the European nations as well. Continuing co-operation and emphasis on technology can have a major impact on the future military balance.

To maximise the potential of technology will require understanding by both military and political leaders. Weapons involving advanced technology often appear to be very expensive. It may be difficult to convince both the political and the military leaders that a "smart" bomb which might cost $50,000 is more desirable because it is much more effective in destroying a military target than 100 "dumb" bombs costing $500 each. There is uncertainty about the new; there is safety in numbers. But in the end, it is relative effectiveness that must determine the choice. With the "smart" weapons comes a very great bonus – as the probability that these kinds of weapons will destroy a military target goes up, the probability that they will kill civilians and destroy non-military targets goes down.

Manpower costs of United States military forces are increasing rapidly and there is lessening interest in military service among young people. These trends are also present in the European countries of the Alliance. The Warsaw Pact countries are less constrained in their use of military manpower and are also less capable in technology, particularly in its practical application: these factors clearly dictate that the planning of NATO forces to

maintain the military balance must be in the direction of fewer
men and better weapons. NATO does not have to match the Pact
man for man, tank for tank, or plane for plane provided it stays
ahead in the application of advanced technology to its weapons.

There is also another bonus. Research and development on
military equipment has great potential for fallout of technology
useful in non-military fields. There are many examples of this
effect in recent years. I would go so far as to say that the great
progress made by the United States in technology since World
War II is to a very large degree the result of the extensive military
research and development programmes during this period. This
is clearly the case in my field of electronics, as well as the more
obvious ones of aeronautics and space.

The Warsaw Pact and NATO are closely matched in total
population and in total economic strength even if the United
States is not included. The Warsaw Pact encompasses a population
of 350 million people, while Western Europe has a combined
population of 330 million. The Gross National Product of the
Pact is estimated to be about 700 billion U.S. dollars, while
Western Europe is at least 740 billion. If Canada and the United
States are included, the combined gross national product of the
Alliance is nearly $2,000 billion – over two-and-a-half times the
economic strength of the Warsaw Pact. There is absolutely no
question about the ability of the Alliance to do whatever is needed
as far as resources are concerned.

The Atlantic community can more than match the Warsaw
Pact in economic strength. The Atlantic community has a
tremendous advantage in technology and in the ability to put
technology into practical use. This is where the effort must be
directed. This is both the least costly and the most certain way
to maintain an adequate military balance in the future.

We must also look at the consequences if NATO should fail
to take advantage of its great technological superiority. If the
Soviet Union and its satellite friends should seize the initiative
in technological warfare, the military balance could swing against
the non-Communist world in a decisive way, particularly in the
environment of *détente* and arms control.

We are standing on the threshold of a major breakthrough
in military capability through technology. This will be the factor
second in importance in determining whether the non-Communist
world can maintain a viable military balance into the years
ahead. I say second because the most important factor is the desire
and determination of the non-Communist world states to do so.

There are, of course, many problems involved in doing what will be needed to meet the future security requirements of the Atlantic community and its member nations. There will even be problems in reaching a consensus as to what should be done. There are conflicting interests of the member states – but only to the extent the member states perceive and maintain a common purpose will it be possible to agree on a common security plan. The United States alone has the capability of providing a substantial share of the security of the Alliance without requiring the full effort of the other member states. It is not reasonable to expect the United States to do this in the future. The United States will maintain the nuclear stalemate which, of course, it must do in its own self-interest. At the same time, no individual European nation can alone match the military might of the Soviet Union. This, then, is the national security imperative that must continue to help cement the Atlantic community into a viable organisation in the decades ahead.

I have purposely avoided giving a great deal of statistical data about the NATO–Warsaw Pact forces. For those interested in more detail, the International Institute for Strategic Studies' publication *The Military Balance 1972–1973* is reasonably accurate from what I know of the situation. Military experts might find some errors in the figures, but they are quite adequate to convey a good impression of the actual situation on both sides in some detail.

Section 3 of that publication discusses "Balances". It covers some of the qualitative factors of different forces and points out that there are geographical advantages, training, logistic support doctrine, philosophy and other factors which can have a large effect on the balance in the effectiveness of military zones. These matters are very important; they have been subject to endless debate, and they must receive continuing attention. Some of these considerations tend to weigh on the side of the Warsaw Pact, some on the side of NATO. In my view, the most important intangible factor of all is one hard to define and impossible to qualify. That factor is the resolve of one side versus the resolve of the other. It is the territorial imperative that strengthens the defence of the homeland. To the extent the Atlantic community can continue to progress towards common goals and develop strong common interests, it can and will maintain the resolve to defend itself. That is the essential ingredient of military strength. To the extent the Atlantic community deteriorates into a loose coalition of nations with cross-purposes and without a unifying spirit, to the extent the community is carried away on the euphoria of *détente*, it will be very difficult to achieve and maintain an adequate balance of conventional military forces and unrealistic to expect the United States nuclear commitment to remain firm. In these terms, an adequate military balance is essential for the survival of the Atlantic community and a strong and cohesive Atlantic community is essential to build and support a military balance adequate to assure the generation of peace which is now finally within reach of this troubled world.

COMMENT *by S. W. B. Menaul*

There is a great deal in the preceding chapter with which I would agree. Certain aspects of it require in my view a different emphasis; and there are parts of it with which I profoundly disagree. The theme of the chapter is quite straightforward: it is that in this era of strategic nuclear parity, both sides are now effectively constrained to the use of non-nuclear forces in nearly every conceivable situation. But Secretary of Defence Melvyn Laird only five months ago said this: "the expected mutual limitations on strategic weapons would of necessity place higher importance on tactical nuclear weapons, and conventional land, air and sea forces assigned to defend America's allies in Europe". That is the view with which I side. One of the great dangers in writing about what is required for tomorrow is to apportion yesterday's technology to tomorrow's requirements, and I believe that we must resist the temptation to talk about strategic and tactical nuclear weapons as if they belonged to an era long since past. I would suggest that it simply is not possible to conceive of scenarios in which a war in Europe could be fought solely with conventional weapons and that the European allies would win. On the contrary, the Soviet Union has persistently practised the use of tactical nuclear weapons in all its conventional operations and the latest of course was Shield '72 in August 1972 which I and others like me watched with great interest. That operation, which took place in Czechoslovakia, used tactical nuclear weapons from the outset of the attack. Quite recently I was talking to Professor Kulish, from the Academy of Sciences in Moscow, and I said to him: "Now you will be able to get rid of some of these masses of troops that you have and these masses of tanks and use new technology." He smiled and looked at me and said: "We'll have both." Of course, new technology can go some way towards redressing the imbalance of conventional forces between the Soviet Union, the Warsaw Pact and the NATO Alliance. We talked about the "smart" bomb – the laser-guided seeker bomb – an example is a laser seeker pinned on to the nose of an ordinary conventional iron bomb, the difference being that in this case the bomb can be made to hit its target, which bombs have notoriously failed to do in the past. We have therefore got at our command what may be called zero-error bombs and missiles. In other words, if one selects a target for attack, and uses either a laser-guided or an electro-optically guided weapon, of which the Mark 84 is a laser example used in Vietnam, the Maverick television-guided missile is another, then one can select a target with the minimum force requirement, knowing that one will hit it. As an example, the famous Than Ho bridge south of Hanoi was attacked 600 times between 1965 and 1968 and not one of its five spans was damaged. In May 1972 two Phantoms carrying laser bombs destroyed it in one afternoon without loss. That is a measure of the technology that can now provide accuracy such as we have never had before. Anti-tank missiles are another. In my view, it is the helicopter with the airborne anti-tank missile that will almost certainly become the primary anti-tank missile system in modern armies. Regrettably, only the United States today has them as only the United States has the laser bomb and the electro-optically guided bomb. We in the West have spent hundreds of thousands of pounds on research and development, each in his own little cell, and until we get together to use that money and brainpower we shall always be trailing behind.

On the question of tactical nuclear weapons, what they do, and what they do not do, I would agree with Secretary Packard's statement that he had never found a convincing reason for their use. I accepted the philosophy of flexible response because it turned out to be the only strategy that NATO could put into operation. But it could not or would not afford the conventional forces required to stem a Soviet onslaught. It will not afford, in the future, to provide those massive conventional forces. We cannot hope in the West ever to match the Soviet Union and the Warsaw Pact in mass, but we can hope to match them in technology and in tactical nuclear weapons. But the tactical nuclear weapons to which I refer are not those which I think many people have in mind when they discuss this subject. The mention of a tactical nuclear weapon usually conjures up Hiroshima and Nagasaki, with millions of civilians dead all over the area and possibly the target not even destroyed. Today, there are weapons called, for lack of a better description, "mini-nukes". They represent a new approach to nuclear weapons. They can be less than 0.1 of a kiloton. They can be the equivalent of 50 tons of T.N.T. They can be radiation-suppressed so that one can use them against any target. There is no fall-out: one destroys the target by putting them on the end of a smart bomb or missile, and they do not kill the civilian population, nor do they devastate the area surrounding the target.

This is the new approach to technology in the nuclear field. It is not a dream. It is available now. All it requires is the will and the money to put it into operation. So there is a choice. One either pays the money for technology in both the conventional and the nuclear fields and then one has some chance of restraining any Soviet advance that might be made into Western Europe, or Europe goes on as things are, depending on the United States, with NATO as 13 separate nations trying to design its own weapon systems, always falling behind and never really achieving the sort of defence of which it is capable.

Nobody wants to see nuclear weapons used at all; and here is the second paradox. By moving these nuclear weapons into the spectrum between the bullet and the thermo-nuclear bomb, getting rid of the old and the dirty ones, one can improve deterrence *and* improve defence. This is done with less manpower but more technology; and in the process one opens up the prospect of reducing, in the Mutual and Balanced Force Reductions discussions, the numbers of forces actually needed to give what is required in MBFR, that is mutual security at less cost. Europe will have to move towards this sort of consideration as it develops in the economic and political field. The triumvirate of economic, political and security considerations is inseparable. One cannot discuss security requirements without discussing economics, and until the European nations come together and produce some sort of common procurement approach, perhaps from a common defence budget, we are not going to be able to afford the weapon systems we ought to have. As each year progresses we fall further and further behind. These weapons and the technology are available in the United States. We must make up our minds whether we want them or not. I believe that we are moving towards that goal. The Eurogroup Ministers at their last meeting said that some form of European procurement organisation was clearly going to be required in the future. The sooner that we get it the better.

Chapter XV

Threats to Security in Europe

NEVILLE BROWN

A DOZEN OR MORE YEARS BACK the belief was widespread, especially in Democrat circles in the United States, that the impending disappearance of the U.S.A.'s margin of strategic nuclear superiority would encourage the Russians to be more daring in regard to local probing actions. Thus General Maxwell Taylor wrote in 1959 that in the years ahead the Russians, blessed with what he apprehended would be an actual superiority in intercontinental ballistic missiles, "... may be expected to press harder than ever before, counting upon submissiveness arising from our consciousness of weakness."[1] Meanwhile Sir Basil Liddell-Hart, too, was warning that "Nuclear nullity", as he called it, "... inherently favours and fosters a renewal of non-nuclear aggressive activity."[2]

The impression made on him by these two scholarly and by no means illiberal students of strategy was one of the mainsprings of President Kennedy's drive to build up American and allied conventional war capability. Indeed, General Taylor was to serve in his "New Frontier" administration first as presidential adviser and then as Chairman of the Joint Chiefs of Staffs.

Yet after just a few years' actual experience of a superpower nuclear stalemate rooted in hard technological reality and lately underlined by the first SALT agreements, a different prognosis is widely accepted within the Atlantic Alliance. Spurred on by some of the self-same members of the liberal intelligentsia who so fervently endorsed the original Kennedy vision, mainstream opinion in Washington and other Alliance capitals has waxed sanguine about future relations with Moscow and her allies. Confrontation is deemed to be dissolving into dialogue and thence into *détente*.

Accordingly, Europe's future security is currently being

[1] Maxwell D. Taylor, *The Uncertain Trumpet* (Stevens & Co., 1959) p. 136.
[2] B. H. Liddell-Hart, *Deterrent or Defence* (Stevens & Co., 1960) p. 43.

discussed mainly in terms of Mutual and Balanced Force Reductions (MBFRs) and collateral political accommodations
between East and West rather than with regard to the opportunity
provided by the EEC's enlargement to reshape NATO and thus
consolidate the existing pattern of collective defence.

Moreover, pressure continues to mount within the United
States, not least in Congress, in favour of big cuts in the American
garrisons in the European theatre in the course of the 1970s, these
cuts often being sought regardless of what progress may be made
towards genuine *détente* through such channels as the multilateral Conference on Security and Co-operation in Europe (CSCE)
now anticipated, and Federal Germany's *Ostpolitik*. Similarly no
less than 10 of NATO's 13 European full members have either
abolished conscription or reduced the period of service within
the last decade. Then again, the annual military expenditure
of NATO Europe stayed virtually constant in real terms from
1963 to 1971, whereas the Warsaw Pact aggregate rose by over a
third.

True, the latest indications are that the downward drift in the
national defence expenditures of the Common Market area,
measured as a proportion of the respective GNPs, is being halted.
On the other hand, in several of the countries concerned there
is a growing reluctance to accept compulsory enlistment in time
of peace.

Obviously in both Western Europe and North America the
current mood is more the result of broad changes in society and
in intellectual attitudes towards permissiveness, Vietnam, etc.,
than ever it is of any concerted reappraisal of Soviet aims in
Europe. In association with it, however, a subtle revaluation of
the impact of Soviet-style Communism can be discerned.

One strand in this is a romantic notion, reminiscent of that
entertained by certain members of the British Left in the 1930s,[3]
that the spartan regimen to be found beyond the Iron Curtain is
somehow more dynamic and purposive than that of a West which
is felt to have become, in all senses, too indulgent. Were violent
crime, drug-addiction and the other emerging or residual ills of
our affluent society to grow much more prevalent, this notion
might enjoy a powerful upsurge of support, at any rate on the
Left. Over the last few years, however, the main hypothesis, both
in radical circles and elsewhere, has been the contrary one that
the "obsolete Communism" of the Soviet Union has grown too

[3] See Sidney and Beatrice Webb, *Soviet Communism: A New Civilisation.*

benign or, if you like, too weary and introspective to pose a threat to anyone.[4]

Usually this view is sustained by some rather generalised thinking about the relaxing effects of economic growth. What does need far closer scrutiny than it has yet received, however, is whether the rigidly monolithic Soviet political system can hope to adjust to ever-more-affluent life-styles and the rising expectations of freedom of thought and action which appear to be their inevitable concomitant.

In this connection the course of the political debate in the U.S.S.R. itself is highly indicative. Certainly there is much talk of ever-greater technological efficiency leading to a golden age of socialist affluence, to what Mr Khruschev used to call "Goulash Communism". Yet behind the recurrent political contests over how rapidly to switch from heavy industry to the manufacture of more consumer goods one may readily discern an anxiety on the part of many in positions of influence and authority lest iron discipline be thereby fatally corroded. So maybe the U.S.S.R. has, in a sense, become the latest victim of the puritan paradox: the vigorous economic growth that a puritan way of life facilitates tends continually to undermine its basic ethic. Inordinately heavy defence expenditure is one way in which she might hope to square this circle.

Where the resistance to change has been least ambivalent is, of course, in the sphere of individual rights, a sphere in regard to which there has – in my opinion – been far too much talk of "de-Stalinisation". No doubt the secret police has never been quite the same since Lavrenti Beria, then its chief, was executed a few months after Stalin's own death in 1953. Likewise literary dissent has occasionally been subjected to a rein less tight than was ever the case before. Even so, such basic liberal prerogatives as free expression, electoral choice, the right to withhold one's labour, and freedom to travel abroad, have still not been conceded.

Yet, especially since the fall of Khruschev, there have been manifold signs of the tensions which may be generated by such inflexibility in the face of internal change. Official or quasi-official warnings against the spread into the U.S.S.R. of the New Left youth revolt are among them. So is the upward trend in the labour camp population which has lately been apparent.

Still more noteworthy from the longer-term standpoint, how-

[4] See the author's article "Arms for Peace" in *The Times* Supplement, 26 February 1973.

ever, is the revolt against the Soviet establishment by a small but determined minority of Soviet intellectuals backed by a proliferating underground press. Perhaps the most penetrating analysis of the predicament faced by this "neo-Czarist" régime is that by Andrei Amalrik, the young historian who is now in prison. He writes of "... a caste-ridden and immobile society" and of "... the rigidity of the governmental system which has openly clashed with the need for economic growth".[5]

As yet these literary rebels operate somewhat in isolation from the mass of the Soviet people. But in due course they may collectively become a focus for a broader dissidence. Evidence of this from within the managerial and technocratic classes may be seen in the subtle but continual pressures for the use in economic planning of such Western techniques as marginal analysis and also for a devolution of decision-taking in order to tackle more effectively such problems as regional imbalance, impending urban congestion, and sluggish agricultural expansion. Nor should we forget that these and all other radical issues are always liable to be interwoven with the nationality question, particularly in such sensitive areas as the Western Ukraine and the Baltic States and among the U.S.S.R.'s two or three million Jews.

Accordingly we can all too confidently anticipate that various vested interests operating within the Soviet body politic will be ever more anxious to slow down this incipient consumer boom and, even more particularly, to sublimate it in some way. In addition, they will at best adopt an equivocal attitude towards the increased contact between the U.S.S.R. and the West seemingly inherent in political *détente* and in a number of economic and technological trends. A more expansive external policy is one route round the dilemmas thereby posed, notwithstanding the evident concern of the present Soviet leadership to avoid the nuclear confrontation in which such a course might culminate.

Indeed, grounds exist for believing that already this reaction has begun. Among the more specific indications are the following: the sharp acceleration in the long-term rise in real defence expenditure which took place during the late 1960s; the global extension of Soviet naval power since 1963 or thereabouts; the resurgence of tough attitudes towards dissident states within the Communist world itself – e.g. China and Czechoslovakia; and a sustained drive in certain aspects of advanced technology, both military and civil.

[5] Andrei Amalrik, "Will the Soviet Union Survive Till 1984?", Survey No. 73, Autumn 1969, p. 67.

So might not the time be ripe to examine more stringently the sweeping revision of the received wisdom of the Cold War years which has been taking place of late? Undoubtedly a disposition did develop in the late '40s and early '50s to see the U.S.S.R.'s external ambitions as less moderate than they really were, as witness the then common but entirely erroneous belief that Stalin encouraged the Communist uprisings in Greece and China in 1946. Yet to concede this is not automatically to endorse an over-reaction which, in its turn, may have been no less simplistic.

Both sanguineness and apprehension could well be justified in the current situation. For quite possibly the truth of the matter is that in this age of superpower nuclear parity the U.S.S.R. will both "... talk softly and carry a big stick". When in exile in London during World War II, Charles de Gaulle was wont to advise his Anglo-Saxon colleagues: "I am too weak to compromise." But those who rule the Soviet Union in 1973 have no military reasons to harbour such thoughts. From this the inference may be drawn that they will not only feel secure enough to sustain a more frank and extensive dialogue with the West over arms control and many other topics of common concern, but also be less inhibited about brandishing their conventional military force in earnest from time to time.

Confirmation that the outlook for relations between the U.S.S.R. and the West remains unsettled can be gleaned from even a brief examination of the chief geopolitical argument adduced in support of the modish complacency: it is that increasingly the U.S.S.R. will be diverted from Europe by the enduring and ever more menacing hostility of China. First let us consider whether this hostility will necessarily prove so very enduring. Were the Communists eventually to be completely triumphant in Indo-China – a possibility that still cannot be ruled out – Moscow and Peking might thus be drawn closer together again. This is partly because of the fillip that would thereby be given to the morale of Marxists everywhere and partly because this outcome would vastly enhance the prestige of Hanoi, a capital that has long struggled with fluctuating success to minimise this split by keeping on good terms with each protagonist. In any case, the approaching demise of Chairman Mao could well usher in a new Sino–Soviet relationship.

Nor would it be wise to discount the possibility of such developments leading to a total *rapprochement* between the two leading Communist powers, on the grounds that they are now too deeply entangled in a mutual competition for influence in areas as far afield as Southern Africa and the Indian sub-continent to reach any general accommodation. After all, France and Britain have competed with one another in Africa throughout this century, but this has not precluded their fighting as allies in two world wars.

And what if the Sino–Soviet conflict does continue unabated? Surely a key reality is that, until the early 1980s at the very least, the configuration of Peking's nuclear deterrent will make it susceptible to elimination in a surprise attack by either super-power. For basically this force consists of a modest number of cumbersome liquid-fuelled rockets in static and known locations, just as its Soviet counterpart did at the time of the Cuban crisis.

Nor is China's demographic superiority of much avail, given not only the possibility of nuclear dissuasion but also the nature of her common border with the U.S.S.R. Peasants from the rice-lands will never infiltrate Siberia across the Gobi desert.

That inwardly the Kremlin understands all this is suggested by the moderation with which its Far East sector has been reinforced. Only a fifth of the Red Army's divisions are in the Sino–Soviet frontier zone even now, whereas well over half are west of the Urals. Likewise only a tenth of the 700 medium-range strategic missiles in service in the U.S.S.R. cover the Far East: the rest are still directed against European targets.

What makes Europe so paramount and perplexing a concern to Russia is, of course, the U.S.S.R.'s quasi-imperial nexus with the rest of the Warsaw Pact, a network of new or comparatively new states reorganised along Marxist lines after 1945 and now characterised by quite rapid industrialisation and by intense national and communal feeling. Needless to say, the problems involved in maintaining stability in the face of dynamic change are considerably greater in this region than they are as yet in the U.S.S.R. itself. One complication is that Communism itself is widely and not unfairly regarded as an alien imposition. Another is more general contact with the West, as witness the extensive spread of the "pop culture" among East European youth.

On the other hand, the sheer diversity of culture and of historical experience across the area in question not infrequently enables the Kremlin to apply the classic political strategy of "divide and rule". An additional factor working in its favour is the ambivalence displayed towards the Soviet presence by indigenous Communist leaders. At times they see the Red Army and all that it connotes as an overhanging threat to their own position. At other times many of them apprehend that Soviet intervention may sooner or later be needed to buttress them against some kind of internal challenge. So how will the U.S.S.R. react to this complex and fluid situation? Dare she try and entrench herself further in flat defiance of the winds of change?

Among the more ominous of recent signs was the impromptu formulation in 1968 of the Brezhnev doctrine of the collective solidarity of the Socialist Commonwealth, a move that was readily endorsed by most of the other Warsaw Pact governments as a means of according a sort of legitimacy to the invasion of Czechoslovakia. For in essence this was a firm reiteration, in the context of the Soviet bloc, of the "domino theory" that if any one territory has fallen under a hostile influence, its immediate neighbours are liable to follow suit. As such it was the logical extension to the regional plane of the critique developed by Leonid Brezhnev of Alexander Dubček's internal policy. Thus the latter believed his "socialism with a human face" would be more popular and so less insecure than a Stalinist posture. But the former, adopting the usual Kremlin standpoint, contended that such actual or proposed reforms as the restoration of freedom of assembly, of the press, and of travel abroad would generate more aspirations than they satisfied and so usher in progressively greater instability.

Certainly all the indications are that the Russians launched the 1968 invasion only as a last resort. In like manner, however, they had been reluctant to invade Hungary in 1956 and had condoned without enthusiasm the erection of the Berlin Wall in 1961. Yet on each occasion the narrow logic of the Leninist way of government presented little alternative. So too much store should not be set by current assurances that the Brezhnev doctrine no longer applies.

Any major renewal of armed conflict in Eastern Europe might directly threaten some of the territories which lie just outside the Iron Curtain, even though the risk of an actual overspill of fighting – e.g. through the pursuit of refugees by Communist troops – may well be quite low. Romania and Yugoslavia are two Communist countries that happen to be not only adjacent but also much in harmony on the basic question of national autonomy. So it is not too difficult to imagine circumstances in which, say, a Soviet march on Bucharest would be accompanied or followed by pre-emptive action against the Yugoslavs, this action being either economic or military. Presumably the temptation to undertake some such action would be greater if, thanks to the departure of Marshall Tito or some other crisis, communal antagonisms were deepening inside Yugoslavia itself.

Nor would it be sensible to assume that the ratification of the Berlin Accords gives West Berlin an absolute guarantee against ever again being subject to coercive action. On the contrary, greater contact between this exposed enclave and East Germany could well compound the danger of the former being pilloried as a "spy-nest" under certain circumstances. So could a further development of the *Ostpolitik* and of the inevitably ambiguous response of Moscow to it.

After all, the Soviet–Czech treaty of October 1968 stated that some of the newly arrived Soviet troops were "temporarily" to remain on Czech soil "... in order to ensure the security of the countries of the socialist community against the increasing revanchist stirrings of the West German militarist forces" (Article 1). So much for the big effort Willy Brandt, as the Foreign Minister in Dr Kissinger's "grand coalition", had even then been making to improve relations with the East.

Thinking in more general terms, it is reasonable to suppose that any marked rise of tension throughout the Warsaw Pact area, including perhaps the Soviet Union, could induce Moscow to try and "Finlandise" various other parts of the continent – i.e. to use all means short of physical occupation to render them compliant on matters of diplomacy and maybe of ideology too. In this connection it is as well to bear in mind that uneven economic and political development leaves not just Yugoslavia but the whole of the Mediterranean flank very much a "soft underbelly", susceptible to various types of harassment. Thus since 1960 virtually every country in Mediterranean Europe has been subject to at least some armed terrorism by small but ruthless groups of either Left- or Right-Wing extremists.

Another threat to European and, indeed, North American security inherent in the fractious state of the Mediterranean theatre is that by the 1980s the Arab world will be more willing and able to apply crippling oil sanctions against the West in order to make the West in its turn oblige Israel to relinquish East Jerusalem and other areas occupied in 1967. For by 1985 the non-Communist world is authoritatively expected to be consuming two-and-a-half times as much oil as it was in 1969, in spite of the advent of nuclear power in electricity generation, etc. In consequence, its dependence on the vast Middle East and North African fields will inevitably increase, notwithstanding the big discoveries continually being made within the Arctic Circle, the

North Sea, and elsewhere. To be precise, it is anticipated that the percentage of Western Europe's needs coming from the Middle East and North Africa will continue to oscillate between 80 and 85 through 1980. Concurrently the corresponding figure for the United States may rise from a mere 3.5 in 1970 to around 20 to 25.[6]

In some respects, of course, the Middle East-cum-North Africa arc can be regarded as a very special case. At what may be a deeper level of analysis, however, its unique political problems appear in essence to be the manifestation within this particular region of the economic and social stress that is endemic to the developing world as a whole. Salient among the causes of this stress are the population explosion in general and the urban implosion in particular. Also the revolution of rising expectations. None of these trends show much sign of slowing down significantly between now and the turn of the century; and when they are together related to certain technological trends with strategic connotations – most notably the rapid diffusion of nuclear reactor capacity which seems now to be impending – all the prerequisites would appear to exist for a great deal of international violence in the decades immediately ahead.

Even the briefest glance back to the 1930s is enough to show how readily violent and successful defiance of international law and world opinion in such regions as the Far East or Africa can lead on to similar behaviour in Europe. One way in which this could happen under present circumstances is by the U.S.S.R. moving against either West Berlin or a portion of NATO Europe in response to Western policies in some other part of the world which it dislikes but cannot easily impede: a pattern of conflict perhaps best described as limited world war. During the Suez crisis of 1956 Bulganin spoke, albeit belatedly and so not very plausibly, of rocket retaliation against London and Paris. At the time of "Cuba", Khruschev obliquely threatened reprisals against Turkey. Meanwhile, plans were being laid in several capitals lest action be taken against West Berlin. Nor are these the only recent examples of limited world war which could be adduced.

One aspect of the assortment of possible confrontations which no survey could exclude is maritime conflict. For one of the most striking, and indeed ominous, anomalies of the nuclear era to date has been that, notwithstanding a very low incidence of conflict at sea, the world's aggregate naval power can be seen to

[6] See P. E. L. Fellowes in Brian Crozier (ed.) *The Arab–Israeli Dispute* (The Institute for the Study of Conflict, 1971).

have grown conspicuously, even when the simple yardstick of manpower is used. Thus over two-and-a-half million sailors and marines are serving with the colours in all the different navies of the world at the present time. Furthermore, even non-nuclear naval action can cover a wide range of possibilities. And Western Europe is more vulnerable than any other major region to interference with its maritime trade.

COMMENT *by Pierre Hassner*

It has often been said that the negotiations relating to Europe at present, the Conference on Security and Co-operation in Europe, MBFR and the SALT 2 negotiations, refer less to security than security appears in their title, and I think that this has a meaning. It seems to me that if we consider the attitude of the European public today with regard to these matters, security problems and negotiations referring to security meet with considerable indifference. There are neither hopes for a change in the European order as, without much conviction, the Eastern side tried to push through propaganda, nor is there any fear that experts might say something against the deteriorating balance of power or the failure of our political will regarding a Conference on Security. Eventually, it seems to me, public opinion takes it for granted that the balance is more or less guaranteed, that we are living in a *status quo* situation and that we need not fear a war by accident or aggression,

But within this there are dynamic factors of political change, which in the final analysis might call in question the *status quo* and the military balance itself. In other words, it seems to me that the problem is that of the consequence for the military balance of new political conflicts within the Alliance, both political and economic, and of new social developments which raise the problem of the place of defence in society. It seems to me that Europeans are not so very much concerned by nuclear parity, nuclear response, and so on; and that the problem arises from the fact that security and balance are taken for granted, whereas this may not necessarily be the case for all eternity. Moreover, political conflicts, and disputes on monetary and trade matters, could poison the political and psychological basis of the Alliance and of American commitment in Europe. In Europe as in the United States, moreover, there is a certain structural instability in society and a certain loss of priority in security and defence problems. Finally, it seems to me that the *détente* period of contacts which are increasing between the two societies in the East and in the West contribute, contrary to what may be believed, to this instability. I myself react against the idea that the era of negotiation is automatically an era of peace and stability. Personally I would rather support the opposite thesis, which I have expressed elsewhere, by saying that we are moving from a cold war to a hot peace.

In the cold-war period the two Alliances, the two camps, the two societies, were solidified so to speak by their mutual hostility and by their absence of communication. In the era of *détente* or negotiation political possibilities are opening up, but also dangers. To adopt a military comparison, one could say that in the cold-war period primacy was given to the defensive, military factor and there was a certain invulnerability on the part of the societies, the one with respect to the other. Today, each society is more vulnerable to the influence of the other, and this is indeed our problem. From the Western standpoint, we see that when there is no longer a direct threat of aggression, there are factors of disruption, ideological and political reactions which could move in the direction of what has often been called Finlandisation; while on the Eastern side there are problems not of erosion, but of ideological and social vulnerability for régimes faced by contacts with the West. One can see the extraordinarily mistrustful attitude of the East Germans or the Russians towards any Western tourist who might bring the ideological plague from the West. On the other hand, this feeling of weakness or vulnerability does not necessarily mean that there is a political–military attitude which is either more on the defensive or more peaceful. If on both sides the essential problems for the time being are within the Alliance themselves, in the West this is more in the direction of an erosion and negligence of military factors, whereas, in view of the legitimacy problems of the Soviet régime, the trend there will be to seek in outside successes, or in the increase of political or military weight, a response to internal ideological problems.

So it is in the dialectic between expansion on the one side and erosion on the other, but also in the possibility of an explosion of the Hungarian or Czech type, owing to the rigid nature of the Soviet apparatus, that arise the real problems which face us in Europe. As far as Russia and China are concerned, either mutual conflict or mutual convergence may be possible: but I would emphasise less these two extreme possibilities than the probability of continuation of violent hostility without any war.

What are the effects of all this on us? It seems to me that we can consider four hypotheses.

The normal hypothesis is that since the Russians are concerned with China they will disregard Europe: that they are aware of the fact that they are a European power, and that this leads them to leave aside their Empire in Eastern Europe.

As regards Eastern Europe there is another interpretation which is more probable: that the more the Russians feel themselves in conflict with China the more they will wish to avoid a risk in Eastern Europe: that they want an Eastern Europe which is stable, which is under their full domination. One can see how nervous they are at any idea of a possible Chinese influence in Eastern Europe. So on this hypothesis they want a *détente* with the West, but on the basis of a very rigid *status quo* in Eastern Europe.

In the third place, it can be believed, as Michel Tatu does, that indeed the Russians are rather seeking reconciliation with China and that the essential dynamic is rather towards Europe than towards the Middle East.

In the fourth place, it can be believed, and this is my own opinion, that the degree of hostility is even greater towards China than towards the Western world, that indeed the dialectics of the Chinese–Soviet conflict lead the Russians rather to act with a certain dynamism and to seek, both through diplomacy, through economic factors and a whole series of means, to encircle China – rather as the containment of the Soviet Union has led to a considerable presence of the United States throughout the world.

In any case I think that it is perfectly right to question the automatic and simplified optimism as to the effects of the Chinese–Soviet conflict. If so what hypotheses can be formed as to the role of security and the role of strength in Europe? I think that, owing to the combination of nuclear deterrence and the military force, the deliberate use of force, particularly between nuclear powers, has very considerably decreased in probability. Nevertheless, there are three possible ways in which the indirect use of force might lead to political influence in Europe. In the first place there is the escalation of internal conflict, that is to say inside the societies and inside the Alliances, because of the instability already mentioned, and here I would refer again to marginal situations like those of Yugoslavia, Berlin and others. There might be an overflow from a conflict inside the East towards concerns which might affect us, both on the European level and on the world level. The degree of instability and conflict has not diminished throughout the world. However, the will to exploit them on the part of the great powers has diminished considerably and there is a certain fragmentation of the diplomatic field: there can be a Vietnam war and a Middle Eastern war or Biafra or whatever without this leading to generalised conflict. Therefore the idea of limited war on the world level, in which, if the Soviets don't like something the Americans are doing in Asia they block Berlin, is a somewhat abstract hypothesis. Even in Europe, what is striking is that there can be intervention in Czechoslovakia or elsewhere without this necessarily creating a reaction in East/West relations except for a very few months. So until there is a true conflict within the Soviet Union at the summit, so to speak, it seems to me that the possibilities for a conflict within the Soviet world without an escalation with us are fairly great and even, in the case of conflicts like those in the Middle East, there is something in Moscow's allusion to agreement by the great powers to avoid being dragged into local conflicts.

But the possibility remains, nevertheless; and the case of Yugoslavia is very worrisome, though there also it seems to me that once again, fortunately or otherwise, the Soviets are much more subtle in their approach. They are very capable of distinguishing between real threats and the proposal to nominate Tito Nobel prizewinner. What is essential in Europe is the threat of the two other forms of projecting military force. The more indirect form I referred to as the notion of Finlandisation; and it seems to me that in the case of both Finland and Yugoslavia one can see how without a direct military pressure one has a possibility of exerting political influence owing to the superiority of military forces, by expressing displeasure over this or that development or this or that candidate for the Presidency. In Yugoslavia I do not know if there was any Soviet threat, but it is clear that the internal vulnerability of Yugoslav society pulls it in a certain direction. This is perfectly implicit: there is no scenario of threat or resistance; but in the back of their minds the various actors know full well that the problem of power is not absent from their relations.

In an even broader and more general sense, it may be that Albert Wohlstetter can rightly say that he does not know what superiority or parity means, that all the analyses break down if one carries out a very precise strategic analysis: but since it is less a matter of war than of the psychological protection of the power relationship, there is political importance in the feeling, often badly expressed, often obscure, of balance or superiority, so that in interpretation of both the German *Ostpolitik* and European policy there is a certain ambiguity. In other words, one does not know whether the novelty of the present age is due to the fact that the Soviets are no longer dangerous or whether it is due to the fact that American protection is no longer as sure as it was, and one should adopt the more reassuring interpretation of Soviet intentions, because indeed we are not sure and we should not like to have to consider other possible interpretations. There is a deep ambiguity in the European consciousness between optimism and a certain vague worry and concern. The problem here is that of balance, of will, of the balance of hopes, of balance in the dynamism and unity of the countries and the various alliances, and the problems of security and defence must first of all be considered in the present phase as a very important component, but only a component, of this total equation, which is first of all psychological and political. It is one component in the true competition which is that of the past few years. "Competitive decadence" is a useful label for what I am discussing, and I believe it will play an important role in the essential problem; that of knowing which of the two alliances will better resist the forces of deterioration and disruption which derive from the crisis of authority and legitimacy and which express themselves in various ways in modern society throughout the world.

COMMENT *by Frank Barnett*

I should like to comment very briefly on certain intangible non-military threats to common security. In doing so, it is necessary to ward off an intellectual disease called "hardening of false categories". As everyone knows, Soviet definitions of key political terms differ radically from our own. For example, in the Leninist lexicon peaceful co-existence is by no means the correct antithesis of cold war, but rather the formula for pursuing somewhat similar objectives through somewhat muted means. Some will argue that Leninist rhetoric in the context of modern Russia is no more than hollow incantation and not meant to be taken seriously. On some occasions undoubtedly this is so, and certainly the Party line is often bent to the Politburo's convenience. But no one who is obliged to read Soviet publications can be entirely optimistic that Brezhnev and Podgorny and Suslov became Russia's chief ministers in order to liquidate Marx and Lenin. Where militant rhetoric is underlined by increased defence budgets and continued large expenditures for propaganda warfare, it would be unwise to postulate that dogma and doctrine, reiterated through all internal channels of Soviet communication, afford no clues to the behaviour of their élite.

Thus, despite *détente*, Russian leaders openly promise to pursue more ideological conflict, and one might hypothesise that in an era of nuclear parity Soviet propaganda and psychological warfare operations are a low-cost, low-casualty and low-visibility weapons system, which are rather effective and which can create further imbalance. Since the Soviets do not seem to be dismantling this twilight apparatus, perhaps the West needs to become more sophisticated in coping with the dialectics and semantics of this form of electoral struggle. Not with the crude anti-Communist sloganeering of the past, but with more subtle discourse and more credible symbols which we are capable of evolving. Surely we need not fear to engage in a wide spectrum of East–West contacts on this front, even though our adversaries are trained Marxists: for the West has learned to live with dissent and pluralism and controversy and the East is very wary indeed of that sort of engagement. We need to remind ourselves that the propaganda gap in favour of the U.S.S.R., at least in terms of manpower and sheer expenditure, is even wider than the gap in ICBM launchers or armoured divisions. While the democracies take a good deal of comfort from the climate of *détente*, the Kremlin takes great pains to explain the current of negotiations to its own people as simply an instance of capitalism bowing to the changing balance of power. We really get no credit inside the Soviet Union for being nice guys, and we should be very unwise to assume that we were. Will and motivation in the West more-over, relate to the defence budgets and conscription policies of the democracies. How does the West create positive public opinion in support of policy scenarios that have neither heroes nor villains? Here again there is little symmetry between the rival social systems. It is true that a handful of Russian literary figures and scientists have dared to question their own government's policy, but the whole machinery of the Russian state still domin-ates Russian media and the school system. Inside Russia, massive hate propaganda against the West is still part of the routine educational curriculum A recent very interesting monograph on the military indoctrination of Soviet youth indicates that over the past few years as many as 14 million Soviet young men have been taking part in military war games at the weekend, supervised by Red Army Officers. There are also museums of military glory in many Soviet high schools, and the study of World War II military heroism is part of the curriculum. This is much more than what we have come to think of as routine indoctrination in the Marxist–Leninist ideology: it is indoctrination in patriotism and military heroism.

I should like to conclude with a word about the type of political insecurity which we create for ourselves by our remarkably perverse habit of believing all the bad news about each other. At one season it is alleged that America is so hopelessly divided by racism and the Vietnam war that she cannot and will not keep her commitments in Europe. Next season, everyone is sure that France will be governed by a popular front dominated by Communists; and at still another time it is taken for granted that Bonn is following Vienna into neutralism. Previously we have many times mourned the demise of Britain and suffered convulsions over the nonstop catastrophe of Italy. Yet somehow, with all their flaws, battle-scarred but still with great innovative skill and *élan vital*, the parliamentary democracies persist; and we can do more than persist: we can prevail, with our values rooted in wide options for humanity rather than all power to the state, if we take the pains to become better informed about the strength and recuperative virtues of our respective institutions. Perhaps we can help each other by putting Western friction and vulnerability in perspective. If we focus always on the indecisiveness of democracy, if we overstate our differences and persistently proclaim our own weakness of will, then the Finlandisation of Europe may become a self-fulfilling prophecy. But our disadvantages should be weighed in the context of the difficulties, divisiveness and potential vulnerability of the Communist bloc, which is not a bloc at all. We should remind ourselves that dictatorships always look more efficient than they really are. There is nothing inevitable about a Soviet way for the future: there is nothing written in the stars that says we must meekly detrain in the Finland station. And while this should not make us complacent, at least there is no reason for us to lose our nerve.

Chapter XVI

Nuclear Threats and Allied Responses in an Era of Negotiation

ALBERT WOHLSTETTER

MILITARY THREATS AND PROMISES OF PEACE

Promises

WHETHER OR NOT we have left behind the era of confrontation, we are plainly in an era of negotiation. We are in the midst of a great scurry of private and very public comings and goings and conferences among adversaries: Chancellor Brandt's *Ostpolitik* and West Germany's opening to East Germany; the American opening to the People's Republic of China; the conclusion of the SALT 1 agreements in Moscow and the preparations for SALT 2; the completion of a variety of lesser agreements between the United States and Russia (such as the one avoiding collisions between naval forces at sea); the overtures on Mutual and Balanced Force Reductions and the Conference on Security and Co-operation in Europe; moves for a variety of forms of co-operation in scientific, technical and cultural exchanges; and, in the economic field, the expansion of trade and investment relations with Russia, East Europe and China, initiated long ago by Western Europe and Japan, and joined last year by the United States when it concluded a half-billion dollar sale of American wheat on credit to the Soviet Union. These are only some of the moves to relax relations of antagonism and increase communications with the Communist world.

Negotiations with adversaries for the limitation or reduction of military forces and the increase in exchanges, including economic exchanges, all tend towards a sense that there is a diminishing danger of military conflict. Indeed, so knowledgeable a commentator on the relations between the Communist and non-Communist world as the Foreign Editor of *Le Monde*, while cautioning that war is still a continuation of politics through other means, interprets the SALT 1 agreement as "now definitely ruling out a ... confrontation between the United States and the

Soviet Union", and as consolidating the slow-down in the "strategic arms race".[1] According to Michel Tatu, the two superpowers have neutralised each other.

Even if the superpowers had effectively "neutralised" each other's nuclear forces by agreement, this might or might not mean that neither could use or threaten to use nuclear weapons against a third country. However, more than a few, like Michel Tatu, interpret SALT 1 to mean quite simply that nuclear war is ruled out altogether, and many take its probability as negligibly small. Some put a good deal of hope on the prospects that MBFR agreements will permit drastic reductions in general purpose forces. Finally, much of the aura of good feeling centres on future trade and investment relations between the non-Communist and Communist powers, on the "primacy of economics".

In Europe as well as in the U.S., economic relations have frequently been taken as tending essentially towards peace, if not by simply increasing communications and thereby understanding, then by creating an interdependence too large to be sacrificed for military adventure. Secretary of Commerce Peterson, for example, cited the authority of Alexander Hamilton for the first possibility: "the spirit of commerce has a tendency to soften the manners of men and to extinguish those inflammable humors which have so often kindled into wars".[2] And Mr Peterson clearly endorsed the second possibility, of an economic vested interest in peace:

> Our purpose is to build in both countries a vested economic interest in the maintenance of an harmonious and enduring relationship. A nation's security is affected not only by its adversary's military capabilities but by the price which attends the use of those capabilities. If we can create a situation in which the use of military force would jeopardise a mutually profitable relationship, I think it can be argued that our security will have been enhanced.[3]

This optimistic view of the irenic effect of expanding economic relations appears to be more than the official rhetoric that fits occasions for signing large-scale trade agreements. At any rate, many scholars who hold no government office and who have

[1] Michel Tatu, "The emergence of a New International System: Prospects for a New International Order". Paper delivered in June 1972 at the Peace in Asia Kyota Conference.
[2] Peter G. Peterson, "U.S.–Soviet Commercial Relationships in a New Era", August 1972, p. 6.
[3] Peterson, op. cit., p. 3.

earned a reputation for political realism say much the same. Professor William E. Griffith of MIT, for example, recently cited the example that the West Germans used trade to get the East Germans to ease their harassment of West Berlin. He suggests that its new expanding economic arrangements will offer the non-Communist industrial societies great political leverage. "The more the Soviet economy becomes involved with the West, the less likely Russia will be to return to hostile tactics that would endanger these contacts. Such contacts, ranging from spare parts to exports of wheat and gas, can be cut off just as easily as they can be made."[4]

Doubts

This all sounds very promising. We've had more than enough of the overhanging fear that in spite of our best efforts, war, even nuclear war, might come. We should welcome a moderation of these old antagonisms.

Then why do we feel uneasy? It seems we continue to be bothered by a sneaking suspicion that dangers of military conflict will persist; and even more, that threats to use military force, either implicit or explicit, will continue to figure in the relations among states; that, on occasion, such threats if unchecked may mean a coerced political accommodation, a surrender of independence. Even the most glowing announcements of the new era of negotiation and peace tend to be qualified by the warning that peace will be neither "instant" nor "permanent".

Many of our purposes continue to diverge from those of the communist countries we have thought of as adversaries, quite as much as their aims differ among themselves. Not *all* of our purposes, to be sure. Avoiding a nuclear war in which both sides are devastated continues plainly to be a common interest. Professor Marshall Shulman suggested recently that the current U.S.–S.U. relation that has succeeded the cold war might be designated a "limited adversary relation". But the qualification applies also to the luridly titled "cold war". That was not a case of unlimited or strict opposition. And even in a *hot* war, since some outcomes could worsen the position of *both* sides, the two sides have a common interest in avoiding at least those outcomes. Even hot war opponents are "limited adversaries".

If our opposition is not total, neither are our points of agree-

---

[4] William E. Griffith, "Summitry and the Prospects for Peace", *Readers' Digest*, Jan. 1973, p. 54.

ment. Treaties for limiting or reducing strategic or general purpose forces can be helpful or damaging depending on their content. In any case, they will not replace the alliance.

Nor does the increase in trade and investment necessarily tend towards peace. Increased flows of capital and commodities are a good thing. We should favour them. The economic benefits that stem from comparative advantage and the division of international labour are a classic case of the possible mutuality of gains. But the political benefits are something else. They may be mutual, one-sided or negative, or all of these at different times.

It seems doubtful surely that the political leverage provided by economic arrangements will be all on the side of countries where private businesses play the principal role; or that the *net* political leverage will accrue to Western governments. It seems especially dubious should Western firms undertake massive capital investments that the East can repay only by a return flow of trade continuing for many years. Businessmen in general have an interest in doing business. They like political arrangements that are good for business, even if they run counter to their government's policies. This has long been a tradition in the West. In the 18th century, British companies insured French owners of French merchant vessels against the loss from capture by the British. A free enterprise economy trading with a state-controlled one tends to build a political constituency for expanding that trade and for political arrangements that facilitate it. In state-controlled economies, on the other hand, economic transactions are inherently political, and by definition pro-government. The size and direction of trade and investment then varies much more sensitively with varying governmental purposes.

Sophisticated Japanese understand this very well. The history of their relation with the Peking People's Republic of China illustrates it. In Japan in the 1950s Peking had a constituency of "friendly firms" opposing the government's stance with respect to Taipei and Peking. Sino–Japanese trade grew rapidly in the 1950s and then, in 1959, when it suited Peking's political purposes, that trade was cut nearly to zero. Trade recovered, but was again cut drastically during the Great Cultural Revolution of 1967.

State-controlled economies, moreover, have exhibited a long-term interest precisely in limiting their dependence on foreign powers, and, in particular, capitalist powers. The Communist countries have been essentially autarkic. They have a strong motive for buying goods in sudden short supply, like wheat, to take care of emergencies. And, to effect longer-term improvements in their economies, they at present have reason for buying technology to improve their lagging productivity. In the next while, both of these interests will probably mean a substantial increase in trade and in investment in joint enterprises of various sorts between the Communist and the non-Communist world. For the U.S., which has hardly traded at all with Communist China and whose trade with Russia dropped drastically after World War II, this will undoubtedly mean a large percentage increase, even though it will be modest in absolute terms. None of this, however, persuasively suggests that Russia and China will put their economies and the political power of their ruling élites at the mercy of the world market, or at the mercy of capitalist governments. Moreover, the economic movement of goods and capital and possibly labour, while good in itself, has never assured peace, even among the countries dominated by market enterprise. After all, World War I (to take one example) was fought among countries that did a considerable amount of trade with each other. It was war between trading partners.

Indeed, the most famous argument for the pacific effects of trade and investment appeared shortly before World War I. It was Norman Angell's *The Great Illusion*.[5] Angell argued that the need for military power was an illusion. Measures for defence assumed someone was likely to attack. That assumed in turn that someone had a *motive*, for attacking. But this was all an optical illusion since no one could actually benefit from a war, even at the expense of someone else.[6] An invader who destroyed natural wealth and population would thereby destroy his market.[7] A German invasion that disturbed British capital and destroyed credit would also lead to the collapse of German credit, and so on. Modern technology of transport and communication, the increased division of labour in the world, the international financing of trade and industry, all had bound countries together into an interdependence that made it impossible for anyone to gain from a conflict.

The argument had a reassuring plausibility. Truth, however, it quickly developed, was *not* on the side of Angell. The first edition appeared on the eve of the Balkan War. The "illusion" in the title, Winston Churchill did not fail to point out, belonged mainly to the author. Angell's fuller explanations in an expanded

[5] G. P. Putnam & Sons, New York and London, The Knickerbocker Press, 1913.
[6] ibid., p. 330.
[7] ibid., p. 30

edition duly appeared on the eve of World War I. It seems that
some governments can find reasons for serious disputes that can
expand and lead them into war even when it is not a matter of
cold cash, and even if it is bad for trade.

Indeed, while we talk today of trade with the Communist
powers as opening up a new era of negotiation and peace, we
are increasingly aware that trade and investment practices among
allies in the non-Communist industrial world can be quite bitter;
they appear, in fact, steadily more acrimonious. Now they strain
alliances. It seems that economic exchanges are expected to pacify
adversaries and make allies belligerent. Barriers are erected,
retaliation threatened, surprises sprung, ultimata issued, currencies raided, communiques agreed on, and misunderstood. In
these trade and money wars, blood may not flow, but the noise of
battle is deafening. It is something of a paradox that in recent
years the United States may have invoked its "Trading with the
Enemy Act" prominently in dealing with its allies, including the
two who are its largest trading partners.

One can approve of the expansion of economic as well as other
contacts with Communist countries then and still be sceptical
of the current euphoria. Neither the newly rediscovered primacy
of economics nor treaties to reduce or limit arms imply either that
the end of military conflicts is at hand; or that the probability
of war will be negligibly small for the next generation; or that
conflicts between Communist and non-Communist powers can
be ruled out.

Optimism about peace in Europe derives in part from the
feeling that negotiations between NATO countries and Warsaw
Pact countries soften Russia's hostility towards the West, and
in part from the knowledge that Russia's conflict with China
keeps her occupied in the East. War, this suggests, has not been
abolished, but just redirected. If there is not to be a generation
of peace, it is hoped that belligerence might be aimed at someone
else. No one seems to rule out confrontation between the two
principal Communist powers.

However derived, this diminished sense of immediate danger
in Europe is a central fact of the alliance today.

Threats

Paradoxically that raises problems. For good reasons, it is harder
for allies to cope with distant, less palpable dangers. If, like
humankind in general, the members have a positive time rate

of discount, if they value present enjoyments more than future ones, they may spend less and quarrel more about sharing present burdens. The dangers seem less immediate now than the enjoyments that might be sacrificed, and the lessened sense of danger leaves more room for abrasive dealings among allies on money and exchange rates, on tariffs and non-tariff barriers to trade and on hindrances to capital flows. Then, again, distant dangers are more uncertain in shape and direction. For that very reason, the dramatic summit meetings between Washington and Moscow and Washington and Peking that are characteristic of the new era of negotiation can themselves have an unsettling effect. This effect is emphasised by their suddenness, and partial secrecy, and by the accompanying press and official rhetoric proclaiming the emergence of a new international system, a new balance of power in the world. What will the new balance look like? At Moscow did the superpowers really "rule out" nuclear war altogether (whatever that means)? Or did they only "rule out" unconditionally confrontation and nuclear war with each other?

For some Europeans the text of the May 1972 Moscow statement on basic principles of relations between the U.S.A. and the U.S.S.R. is less than reassuring, precisely where it announces mutual restraint, where the superpowers say that they will do their "utmost to avoid military confrontation". It illustrates the uneasiness that stirs just beneath the placid surface of *détente* that, for some, even this seemingly innocuous statement evokes the nightmare that de Gaulle envisaged in 1959 of a U.S.–Soviet condominium – if not an agreement between the two superpowers "to divide the world", then an agreement by each "not to launch its missiles at the main enemy so that it should itself be spared" but leaving open the possibility of "an awful day [when] Western Europe should be wiped out from Moscow and Central Europe from Washington".[8] Or the concern may be less extreme, but nevertheless serious. Europeans may fear that while the comings and goings between Washington and Moscow or Peking and the talk of changing balances of power do not imply a full-fledged shift in alliance, they do mean a very damaging change in American priorities: a willingness to "sacrifice some of the partnership relation with her allies in order to negotiate with ex-enemies". (That is the way a distinguished Japanese phrases it; such concerns are not limited to Europeans.)

Such shifts are a natural alliance concern, because they might

[8] Transcript of de Gaulle's news conference statement and replies to questions, *New York Times*, 11 November, 1959.

affect the value of the American guarantee to its allies. In fact, a shift that ruled out the possibility of any U.S. confrontation with the Soviet Union – even when Russia threatened an American ally – would revoke the guarantee. NATO depends for discouraging coercion or attacks on a willingness to answer them in military terms, by conventional means if these suffice or by nuclear means if not. American conventional and nuclear forces in Europe are there to make clear that a threat to Europe might lead precisely to a nuclear confrontation between the superpowers. If a sense that the immediate threat had diminished led to a lessened credibility of U.S. response, as well as to increased division in the alliance, the military threat might grow.

ALLIED RESPONSES

Strategies that strengthen and those that loosen alliance

For myself, I do not believe that SALT 1 or any East–West agreement current or impending will lessen either the essential interests that the U.S. shares with its allies in their safety and independence, or the continuing need to keep threats to their safety low by responsible strategies of defence that strengthen alliance ties.

But there is reason enough today to re-examine in good faith both strategies that might strengthen alliance ties and those that might loosen them. For one thing, the forthcoming negotiations call for a degree of unity and clarity about defence objectives that has not been conspicuous in the past. (I agree with Ian Smart that the coming talks in MBFR might themselves greatly intensify divisions in the alliance. This could be true not only of the process of negotiation, but also of some possible end results, either in MBFR, or indeed in SALT 2.) For another, some essential military technologies are changing rapidly in both the nuclear and non-nuclear field. They should be taken into account in any rethinking of alliance defence. They will present opportunities to deter a war more effectively at any level or (if nevertheless war comes, by miscalculation or design) to bring it to conclusion with less devastation. Greater clarity about these technologies as well as the goals of alliance defence will help in the negotiations.

The alliance needs a coherent doctrine covering the use of non-nuclear as well as nuclear weapons, of weapons based in as well as outside the theatre, and systems of both short and long range, employing small as well as large yield explosives. Such a doctrine should call for the discriminate use of weapons and would carefully distinguish between military and civilian targets; but it must avoid any invidious discrimination based simply on territorial distinctions among the allies. Such a strategy would tend to strengthen alliance ties. It can be understood by contrast with strategies that divide an alliance and tend to weaken the guarantee of one member to the others.

1. A member of an alliance would weaken his guarantee to other members to the extent that he lessened his short-run stake in the integrity of the alliance so that it less adequately reflected his long-run identity of interest. This would be so, for example, if the guarantor were to reduce the size of his forces based in or near the immediate path of likely attack.

Various allies and adversaries may weigh diversely the importance of keeping this immediate stake high. The Federal Republic (and France) prize a massive American force on the European central front. But Japan would prefer to reduce further an already diminished American presence. Norway has permitted neither nuclear weapons nor any NATO forces on its territory, but worries, as the Soviet presence in the North-East Atlantic grows, about any lessening of the U.S. activity off their coast, or any reduction in the American ability to engage quickly in the defence of Norway. The Soviets clearly want foreign (that is, American) bases removed. However the People's Republic of China likes them there now precisely as a diversion and counterweight to a potential Soviet threat – not only in Europe, but also in Japan and even in Taiwan. (So Chou En-Lai has informed visitors.)

2. A member of an alliance would also weaken his guarantee to other members to the extent that the limits that the guarantor sought to impose on his own use of force were designed to save himself at the expense of his allies.

This would seem a substantial possibility if

(a) The guarantor had forces on allied soil but were to draw an absolute distinction between such "theatre" forces to be used in allied defence, and "strategic" forces based outside the theatre that were to be used only in defence of his own homeland.

(b) If his doctrine and strategy were to make the homelands of the guarantor and the adversary sanctuaries.

3. A member of an alliance would also weaken his guarantee to the extent that he had only an "unlimited", essentially suicidal,

response to aggression against his allies; or no response at all.

This would be so if the guarantor had a reckless strategy calling for a response to attack on allies that, in the event it was executed, would plainly serve no function for any member of the alliance and might even worsen the position of all. The chief example here, in my view, would be a doctrine calling for only one strategic course of action – the annihilation of an adversary's population. When unrestrained, such a response is pointless as well as brutal, even if the guarantor's own territory were attacked. It is pointless even as a "last-ditch" response to an attack on one's own territory, since it can accomplish nothing. But it is *at most* a last-ditch response.

I have phrased the above in deliberately general terms. They have nothing intrinsically to do with the United States rather than any other guarantor, nor with the Soviet Union rather than any other potential nuclear adversary. These terms apply, for example, to the possible role of France and of the United Kingdom as guarantors in an alliance. If such forces are to supplement or if they were to replace the American nuclear guarantee to Europe, they would have to avoid the same potentials for disconnection from their allies.

Such questions of political–military strategy plainly go to the heart of alliance debate. Past alliance debate has generated an imposing museum of military metaphors touching on problems of sharing decisions for collective defence and making them convincing in an age when nuclear devastation is possible for defender and attacker alike: trip wires, plate-glass windows, triggers, safety catches, bridges, firebreaks, ladders, escalators, shields, swords and the lot. One should not assume, however, that such metaphors settle or even adequately define the persisting problems that generate them.

Moreover, some things have changed since the debate began, including the technologies. I should like to discuss first some relevant technical changes, and then address several of the issues of political military doctrine. (For example, the choices between preparing only a massive response or having a range of choice of various levels of violence; between the use of tactical nuclear weapons and non-nuclear explosives; between the use of "theatre" and "strategic" forces; and the choice or lack of choice between deterring a war and being willing, if necessary, to fight it.) And finally I should like to touch upon coming arms negotiations and the alliance.

Technologies of Discrimination and Technologies of Destruction

Since I am concerned to emphasise the importance of these new technologies, I should say that I do not in general take a "gee whiz" view of the wonders or terrors of technical change. A variety of other factors shape our choices. And I am as far as possible from the technological determinism that sees our choice among strategic policies as simply foreclosed by "the technical realities". In fact my point is almost the precise opposite of that foreclosure presumed, for example, by proponents of a policy of basing the deterrence of war exclusively on a threat to annihilate population[9]: technologies of discrimination and control increasingly offer alternatives for choice. But that of course only emphasises the importance of technology in our time. Those who doubt this should recall that it was a technological change increasing the yield of explosives by a factor of a thousand that introduced us to the dilemmas of policy in the atomic age.

But technical change has not stopped. Nor is it likely to. I want to underscore the importance of what David Packard has to say in Chapter XIV about our standing now at the threshold of major breakthroughs in military technology. He has mentioned several. Here I shall focus in particular on the large variety of precision-guided munitions, such as the so-called "smart" weapons that were a small fraction of the total weight of bombs used in Vietnam near the end of the war; and on the other greatly improved and rapidly improving technologies that would permit a much more effective and discriminating application of force. These will have essential though still uncertain effects on nuclear as well as non-nuclear combat.

First, as David Packard indicates, precision-guided modern non-nuclear munitions might serve many of the purposes originally foreseen for tactical nuclear weapons in defending against invasion. They might destroy critical segments of a force gathered for invasion and so discourage it. After the initial shock of an invasion, they might be used to destroy the means of support and reinforcement and so isolate the battlefield and limit the depth of penetration by the invading force.

Secondly, it is clear that these new munitions can do their work with much less by-product damage than the familiar, much less accurate, non-nuclear weapons. (Not to say, nuclear weapons.) This is of utmost importance and that should be most obvious

[9] One such proponent recently expressed surprise that "critics seem to imply" that mutual threats to kill populations are a "consequence of policy and . . . therefore subject to change".

to defenders fighting in their own territory. It directly affects the will as well as the ability for territorial defence. But it can be critical also in inducing restraint in adversaries.

Thirdly, at a time when military forces have increasingly to depend on volunteers rather than conscripts, and when personnel costs may account for most of the increase in defence budgets, such precision-guided munitions might economise on manpower, especially if we maintain our technological lead. These economies are still uncertain; the equipment has yet to be fielded, and in any case the prospect should not serve simply to rationalise unilateral manpower cuts.

Fourthly, if agreements with the Warsaw Pact should bring about numerically lower limits to manpower, these weapons (together with some much needed redeployments) might help maintain the effectiveness of a responsible alliance defence.

Fifthly, these are technologies that can and should be developed by or made available to Europeans. The West should try and should be able to maintain a substantial technical advantage in this respect over the Warsaw Pact powers.

But sixthly, I believe these technologies might help stability in Europe even if the Warsaw Pact powers had them too, and with equal sophistication. They can be a powerful discouragement to invasion. But NATO has no desire to reach Moscow.

Finally, improved technologies of discrimination will greatly affect nuclear as well as non-nuclear force and therefore they are worth viewing in long perspective.

The most striking and familiar development in military technology in the last 30 years has been an enormous increase in the destructiveness of bombing: an increase in explosive yield by six – and in destructiveness by four – orders of magnitude.

But during the same period and recently at an increased pace there have been major changes in the possibilities of discrimination: the vast increase in the potential for acquiring precise information on the location and identification of targets and the co-located structures that is permitted by reconnaissance satellites and aircraft with high resolution optical cameras and other sensing devices; the progress in control and communications and the enormous increase in the ability to process information permitted by the computer revolutions; and the development of extremely precise means for delivering munitions at long, medium and short ranges. These changes are very much in process. They complement each other, but are proceeding at different rates. They will continue to develop in accuracy, reliability, range, all-weather performance, and in controllability, but exactly how and how rapidly will depend on our will.

The nuclear explosive revolution settled for most purposes one of the two principal issues in the controversy about bombing that started with World War I: it made clear that bombers, when equipped with nuclear weapons, could unquestionably be effective in destroying targets. On the other hand, it hardly helped solve the other major issue involved in bombing. If anything, it seemed to worsen the undesired by-product damage, the destruction of things one might want to preserve. It did this in part because the increased destructive area made possible by nuclear explosives was used at first by planners not simply to overcome the resistance of targets aimed at, but even more to make up for errors of location and aiming, to compensate, that is, for our ignorance and our mistakes. But this indiscriminateness raised more than ever the question of the appropriateness of bombing in response to provocations of various sorts.

The second sort of technical change then may be as important: the development of precise means for selecting, locating, and destroying military targets or facilities that directly support an adversary's means of conducting a war, while not destroying civilian targets that have no direct relation to the conduct of the war. However, this second revolution has not been well understood, nor even adequately noted. Some of the changes in delivery precision have come about quietly as the cumulative result of progress in neighbouring technologies and the many complementary small changes that reduce the "error" of weapons delivery systems: improved gyros, better data processing and computer programmes for onboard computers, better geodetic estimates, etc. These have not been announced by the spectacular effects of nuclear blasts. But delivery precision has a squared effect on point targets; hence improvement by a factor of ten in precision can increase effectiveness by a hundredfold: the same result as a thousandfold increase in explosive yield,[10] the difference between the largest non-nuclear weapons of World War II and the A bomb! The precision of some major systems has improved by a factor of more than ten.

In part the stress on explosive revolution and the neglect of the possibilities of discrimination has been conscious; or if not thoroughly conscious, it has at least not been accidental. It

[10] While changes in accuracy have much more than proportional effects, changes in yield affect results less than proportionately – as the two-thirds power.

stems from a kind of distrust of the possibilities of any genuine discrimination and control; a fear that any large war, or any war in which nuclear weapons were used, would be so destructive that differences would not matter. It rests on the slender hope that if any large-scale war is dutifully described in apocalyptic terms, it will not occur at all; and if, on the contrary, anyone were to suggest such a war might occur and that it might mean some-thing less than the end of the world, then it *will* occur and it *will* mean the end of the world. Hence, all of the recriminations against Herman Kahn for making nuclear war "thinkable".

But this is exorcism and moralising rather than deliberation or morality. We cannot assure that a nuclear war will never occur simply by repeating that it would be an unlimited catas-trophe. And we cannot eliminate the possibility simply by assur-ing that if it occurs it will be an unlimited catastrophe. We may instead make it more likely, and may make almost certain that if it occurs, it will be more brutal and more terrible than was necessary.

There are some relevant parallels from World War II. Scientists in England before the war were for the most part re-luctant to work on military problems at all. When in the mid-1930s, as the menace of Hitler became clearer, several outstand-ing scientists did begin to work on military problems, they turned to the problem of air defence. The Committee for the Scientific Survey of Air Defence sponsored Watson-Watt's devel-opment of radar for air defence. This was all to the good. The reluctance to have anything to do with bombing except to counter it by air defence, however, was symbolised by the late start and desultory efforts of the Committee for Scientific Survey of Air Offence. As a result of this and also because Bomber Command itself felt no urgency for improving precision, radar lagged in its application to bombing navigation and guidance. But the reluctance of the scientists to develop precise modes of bombing did not mean that the British avoided bombing. It meant only that Bomber Command was reduced to area bombing of cities at night with very little discrimination.

A failure to exploit the possibilities of discrimination today would not mean that a nuclear war would be impossible. It would only mean that it would be more indiscriminate. But today the difficulties of facing up to the problem of discrimina-tion and control are reinforced by much more universal dogmas (current especially in the American academy) suggesting that there is a virtue in indiscriminateness and a danger in the ability to discriminate, and that even defensive actions as well as restraint in the offence are bad things. Present academic dogmas advocating "Mutual Assured Destruction Only" are much more extreme than those that influenced choices in World War II, or indeed in any prior time. Not even Genghis Khan tried to avoid military targets and to concentrate *only* on killing civilians. The cruelty and recklessness of such a policy can be kept below the conscious level by the hope that it will never have to be executed. By making the deterrent awful, it is hoped, we assure it will not be used. We threaten to kill only to be kind. Such terror is kindly even to adversaries since we will never actually fight.

But can we so separate deterring and fighting?

Some Persistent Issues

DETERRING V. FIGHTING?

It is tempting to describe a decision to prepare to fight at a lower level of violence – say the level at which an adversary might attack – as a preference for fighting at that level of violence rather than deterring. But the temptation should be resisted. Many Europeans place a considerable importance on tactical nuclear weapons and on NATO preparations to use them as a bridge to strategic weapons. This is hardly because they prefer to fight a tactical nuclear war rather than to deter it and have no war at all. They think that the initial use of tactical nuclear weapons is more credible than the immediate use of long-range high-yield nuclear weapons in large numbers. It is more credible because there is a chance that the war might stop there and for that reason the decision to use them seems more likely. But because the decision is more credible, this is expected to help deterrence.

Similarly, a good many Americans have placed a considerable importance on conventional weapons and NATO preparations to use them as a possible stopping point or as a bridge to the use of nuclear weapons of any kind. This is hardly because they prefer to fight a conventional war rather than to deter it and have no war happen at all. Rather, they think that in response to a conventional incursion, an initial use of conventional weapons is more likely to be believed than the immediate use of nuclear weapons. Again, the decision to reply is more credible because it leaves open the possibility that the war might stop while there is something to save. For that reason an adversary may be more deterred. He may recognise that a decision to resist his advance is more probable. Because the prospect of that decision is more credible, it is expected to help deterrence. On the other hand a threat to destroy oneself along with one's adversary in an orgy of mutual annihilation can dissuade only if the threatener is believably reckless about committing suicide. But then one must establish a record not merely of brave words, but also of adequately rash acts to continue to be convincing. And the war might start because the record of recklessness was not convincing enough; or through recklessness.

The transition to the first use of nuclear weapons is a particularly difficult one to arrange so as to have the right mixture of a high likelihood that they will be used in case they are really needed and of a low probability that they will be used when they are unnecessary – without authority or by miscalculation in the heat of crisis or battle. Pre-delegation to a military commander, even a high military commander, has been unlikely. The rules for releasing such weapons have remained firmly under political control. It is this fact above all that has made especially important arrangements for a conventional response in the early stages of a war. Tactical nuclear weapons cannot replace conventional ones.

I doubt whether differences between Americans and Europeans (or among Europeans) can be accurately characterised as a difference in preference for fighting a war as distinct from deterring it. Everybody would prefer to deter a war.

Nor do I think one can accurately say (as one of my British associates has recently put it) that West Europeans generally assume that "nuclear weapons are exclusively destined to deter" while Americans characteristically view them, at least in Europe, as "reasonable and effective" for fighting. An instrument that destiny or disposition plainly made unreasonable and ineffective for any actual use and so quite certain to remain unused, could hardly deter. It would then make war more likely, not less.

MASSIVE RETALIATION V. FLEXIBLE RESPONSE?

There has been a good deal of myth-making about the era of massive retaliation announced by Secretary Dulles in 1954. Some recent European references suggest that it was a kind of Golden Age when the United States was invulnerable to Russian attack, when U.S. policy, to the harmonious applause of all Europeans, promised convincingly, unambiguously and inflexibly

to use SAC instantly against the Russian heartland in response
to any local incursion into Western Europe. Then it seems,
came the Fall, at the end of the 1950s, when the U.S. is supposed
to have become vulnerable for the first time to Soviet attack
and the U.S. adopted a policy of flexible response, of using conventional weapons and raising the threshold at which it would
use nuclear weapons; and so undermined the credibility of the
nuclear deterrent.

There is very little reality that corresponds to the myth.
American cities were vulnerable to Russian attack in 1954 and
American strategic forces were less vulnerable in the 1960s than
in the preceding decade. The massive retaliation doctrine was
extremely ambiguous from the time of its first announcement.
But almost immediately after the initial statement, it was made
clear that the retaliation would not necessarily be "instant"; it
might not involve SAC, and it did not necessarily mean the
bombing of the Russian or Chinese homelands. And though it
seemed to lower the threshold at which nuclear weapons, particularly tactical nuclear weapons, might be used, it did not exclude
the use of conventional forces. Indeed it called for creating an
adequate local defence of the continent of Europe. To deter
aggression, it seems our response would be – prophetic word –
"flexible". It is important, Secretary Dulles made clear in 1954,
"to have the flexibility and the facilities which make various
responses available". He did indicate, though quite vaguely, that
the nuclear threshold was being lowered, and that in particular
we might use tactical nuclear weapons early.

A policy of lowering the nuclear threshold did not meet with
uniform applause among either Europeans or Americans. The
stated motive for massive retaliation was to find a strategy that
would lower the long-term cost of collective security. This was
the era of "a bigger bang for a buck", and it reflected the desire
to reduce costs, following the Korean settlement. But when the
Carte Blanche exercise in 1955 indicated that the early introduction of tactical nuclear weapons might kill nearly 2 million
West Germans and wound many others, the Germans, in particular, did not applaud. In fact, Chancellor Adenauer rejected
massive retaliation as a policy for NATO and changed his mind
only when at the end of 1956, it became clear that the conventional build-up in Germany would be drastically limited by
the difficulties of getting an 18-month term for army conscripts.
Chancellor Adenauer had not come to look more fondly on the
possibilities of nuclear devastation in Germany. He yielded to

the apparent difficulty of providing adequate manpower to do battle at less than nuclear levels.

When the new strategy of "flexible response" raised the allied nuclear threshold again in the 1960s, this responded to a searching criticism in Europe as well as America of the credibility of massive retaliation, a criticism that cast severe doubt on whether it would actually always deter. The stress on selected response all along the line was motivated by a belief that the massive retaliation threat might look like a bluff and so might be called.

FIREBREAKS V. BRIDGES, OR
TACTICAL NUCLEAR V. CONVENTIONAL WEAPONS?

A conventional war or the conventional phase of a larger war would in general be fought on the territory of the allies of the Soviet Union and of the United States. Emphasis on conventional war therefore seems to some Europeans to separate the U.S. further from Europe. However, here the implication must be subject to analysis. It is worth dealing explicitly with the problem of separating or linking lower and higher levels of violence than we normally treat in terms of one or another or several of the mixed bag of metaphors listed earlier: "firebreaks", for example, when we think of separating the levels, "bridges", say, when we think of linking them.

In general, recognition of the importance of a conventional phase to war, after which the war might be brought to an end or raised to nuclear violence, is no different in principle from recognition of a possible "tactical nuclear" phase, after which the war might conceivably move to levels of violence involving longer range or larger yield weapons in greater numbers. Tactical nuclear weapons, like conventional forces, have been thought of primarily as being used in West or East Europe, not in the U.S. or the S.U. Many Europeans favour tactical nuclear weapons because they think of escalation as extremely likely and they think therefore that an emphasis on tactical nuclear weapons will help deter the Russians.

However, every "bridge" spans a possible "firebreak". As a metaphor for decision, the only reason we might want to introduce a bridge, in fact, is because the gap it covers might still serve as a firebreak. But metaphors can sustain only part of the weight of analysis. Firebridges do not always ignite the other side. If escalation from the use of tactical nuclear weapons were plainly and simply inevitable, then the decision to use them would be the *same* as the decision to use strategic weapons and they would serve little or no function at all. In particular, the decision to use them would be no easier than the decision to use strategic nuclear weapons. What might make it easier is that there is some *chance* that matters might be settled, that the war might be brought to an end at that stage. At the edge of any bridge or firebreak one has the choice to do nothing, to move across, or to take a longer leap. There is a threefold choice. The purpose of having an intermediate action is to make it *less* likely that one would simply decide to do nothing. Any head of state would be concerned if the alternatives were simply "humiliation or holocaust". Having something in between makes it much *less* likely that the head of state would choose humiliation. Because there is a chance of stopping the war at an intermediate level, he is more likely to enter the process of increasing violence. That improves the deterrent.

But what has been said applies equally to the conventional inbetween steps and not just to the tactical nuclear inbetween steps. The emphasis on conventional forces at the beginning of the 1960s was motivated by a belief that the leap from any small incursion, even a local one that persisted, to a massive use of long- or short-ranged nuclear weapons, was too large a jump to be believed. The conventional step was intended to make it less likely that nothing would be done at all and it recognised specifically that, once a conventional war was under way, a decision to use nuclear weapons was made more likely because it raised the stakes. The same principles apply today. But the basis for such a strategy is greatly improved by new technologies of discrimination and control.

THEATRE FORCES AND STRATEGIC FORCES

Europeans are justifiably concerned about any decoupling of the fate of the United States from the fate of Europe. They are therefore concerned about any decoupling of U.S. "theatre forces" from U.S. "strategic forces" or any sharp distinction between "theatre" and "strategic" war. They may see this as implying an absolute discontinuity between the risks that the United States might undertake in the event of an incursion into Western Europe and the ones it might undertake in the event of a violation of U.S. boundaries. The Europeans would then tend to interpret American strategic policy as implying that the U.S. and S.U. homelands would be sanctuaries in the event of an attack on Europe and that the war would be fought out in Europe. Naturally, they are not happy about this prospect, (*a*) because they think that the Russians will be less deterred, and (*b*) because Europeans would bear the brunt of the conflict.

Some Europeans then equate "war fighting" with "fighting in Europe". And this drives them towards hopes for "deterring only" – deterring somehow by promising to retaliate without any possibility of really doing it.

However, a policy of restraint in response to Russian attack is called for, whether the attack is against an ally or against the United States. It does not imply a decoupling of U.S. territory from that of West Europe. I think it of vital importance that there be no absolute distinction between strategic and theatre forces. Strategic forces should in all cases be used with restraint and they should include as possible targets adversary theatre or other general purpose forces.[11]

It is equally true that a policy of unrestrained, indiscriminate attack on Russian civilians, executed without reserve, without any attempt to induce restraint in the Russians, can serve no purpose of state at all under any circumstances. If "Mutual Assured Destruction" (for which Donald Brennan proposes the acronym "MAD") means a policy of using strategic force only as a reflex to kill population, it calls for a course of action under every circumstance of attack that makes no sense in any. To take the destruction of civilians as the only strategic response would decouple Europe from the U.S. The unsuccessful Democratic Party nominee in the last presidential election in the United States and his technical advisers, basing themselves on Mutual Assured Destruction theory, defined "strategic forces" as those used in response to an attack on the United States, and defined "general purpose forces" as those *conventional* forces used to deter or fight in defence of allies. Since forces are either "strategic" or "general purpose" and these two categories exhaust the field, the implication for Europe could hardly have been more ominous.

Some less drastic adherents of MAD, who see some role for tactical nuclear weapons, nonetheless, reserve "strategic forces" for the last desperate, futile spasm against the Russian cities

---

[11] It has become customary to treat "strategic" nuclear forces and the "general war" in which they are used as indiscriminate by definition. It seems exotic therefore for strategists even to consider limitations. A U.S. army field manual defines "General War" as "characterised by a lack of restraints". (See Army Field Manual FM 100-5, *Operations of Army Forces in the Field*, 6 September 1968.)

after a Russian attack on the U.S. This too would separate Europe from the United States.

But any such doctrine would decouple not merely the United States from Europe, but all the rest of Europe from any European country operating an independent strategic force under that doctrine. Indeed, the prototype, "Minimum Deterrence", originated in justifying the spread of nuclear weapons as a substitute for alliance guarantees. Would that doctrine govern the use of the French strategic force or of the British strategic force? Would they be "last ditch" forces to be used only against Russian cities? It is questionable whether they make sense for that purpose, but there is hardly a doubt that if they are pure, spastic population killers without reserve or restraint, they are quite decoupled from the defence, say, of West Germany. If the French in World War II did not fight to the death for Paris, it may be doubted that they will commit mass suicide for West Berlin, especially if it did nothing for West Berlin.

The assumptions underlying minimum deterrence doctrine presuppose a territorial definition of national interests in abstractly absolute terms. On the one hand it cannot be taken seriously if it implies that any violation of national boundaries will make certain an unrestrained response by "the terrible swift sword". As an act of suicide that could hardly protect the undestroyed part of the national territory, it would be without a purpose; and since purposeless, it would by no means be certain; and, since uncertain, the possibilities of "salami slicing" would always be present. On the other hand, one cannot take it seriously if it implies that there is an absolute dichotomy between national interests inside and outside national boundaries, that the damage done to interests of allies, no matter how large, would be less important than damage done to U.S. territory no matter how slight. I would agree with President Nixon that an incursion into Little Diomede in the Bering Straits would do less immediate injury to the United States and might also portend less ultimate damage than an attack on West Europe.

The time may come when the boundaries of "Europe" will be national boundaries. Mr Heath has suggested that the British and French nuclear forces should be held in "trusteeship" for that day. But that day is quite far off. When it comes Europe's interests will extend beyond those boundaries, and incursions inside them will still call for some reply other than suicide. For Europeans, then as now, an absolute distinction between strategic and theatre war makes least sense of all. Their homelands are the potential theatre of combat. For them it is essential to respond in a way that would minimise the by-product damage in West Europe and also leave something standing in an adversary's territory so as to induce him to leave something standing in Europe.

ARMS NEGOTIATIONS AND ALLIANCE

Europeans with whom I have talked now tend to put security problems – and especially nuclear security problems – either out of their minds, or off in a small uneasy corner of their minds. The likelihood of an attack seems small and remote. This encourages promises to reply to attack that have a low probability of execution if the attack occurs. Part of the ambivalence felt about SALT and MBFR has to do with the fact that, on the one hand, negotiations with adversaries might further decrease the probability of attack by building a community of interest with the Russians and that, on the other hand, they might lessen the credibility of reply to attack by revealing and intensifying divisions in NATO, especially between the U.S. and Europe, and by shifting NATO to lower-cost, more fragile, higher risk strategies. For the trouble is that these *two* probabilities – the low probability of attack and a decreasing probability of reply – are not independent. If the reply to attack becomes plainly reckless and therefore unconvincing, the likelihood of attack will increase, and of more immediate importance, so will the effective use by adversaries of implicit threats of force to constrain and shape West European external and internal policies.

Nevertheless, budget pressures and balance-of-payment considerations might push us towards high-risk strategies and agreements, as do the stereotypes about an "ever-accelerating arms race". If arms control agreements with the Warsaw Pact powers should make it possible to reduce budgets without increased danger, that would be all to the good. But the interwar history suggests how easily such arms negotiations can rationalise the desires of one side to reduce budgets even at increased risk. As for the current talk of an "ever-increasing arms race", let me be blunt: there is nothing in it.

So far as their total defence budgets are concerned, NATO countries, including the United States, are on the whole spending smaller percentages of their GNP than before. What is even more significant, the absolute amounts have been decreasing. The

United States' overall defence budget, for example, has been declining not only in relation to GNP, but in real terms. In 1974 dollars, it is at its lowest point for over 20 years.

The stereotypes about an ever-accelerating arms race are most often applied to strategic budgets, and here they are farthest from the mark. In this connection there is space only to summarise some recent unpublished research results:

1. U.S. strategic budgets in constant prices have gone down, not up. In the Eisenhower years (a useful benchmark since, improbably enough, Eisenhower has become something of a hero on the New Left for his supposed quietism[12]) they were two-and-a-half times what they are today.

2. The number of strategic defence vehicles, which current dogmas about the exponential arms race claim to be particularly destabilising, peaked a decade and a half ago at seven times their present number.

3. The number of offence vehicles has remained roughly the same for many years.

4. Strategic offence and defence mega-tonnage has gone down drastically.

5. The total number of offence and defence warheads has declined sharply since 1964 and today is somewhat lower than at the end of the Eisenhower administration.

6. The aggregate destructive area of the total number of warheads of varying yields are at their lowest point since 1956.

Nonetheless, large innovations were introduced into the American strategic force during this period. Though they involved no overall – much less an exponential – increase in strategic budgets or stocks, the American strategic force was better controlled and better protected in the 1960s than it had been in the 1950s. This was a period in which key stabilising innovations were made – for example, silo-protected land-based missile forces and mobile submarine platforms for medium-range and intermediate-range rockets. These major new systems did not simply buck the strong trends in the state of the art, symbolised by the conjunction of fusion and ballistic missile technologies: they made adjustments to and exploited these trends – a historical example of some interest.

[12] For this odd development, see the appreciation of Eisenhower in Gary Wills, *Nixon Agonistes* (1969), and Murray Kempton, "The Underestimation of Dwight D. Eisenhower", *Esquire*, September 1967.

Much of the arms control literature of the past decade and a half – especially that written by technologists – has had a Luddite character. It would try to halt military technology altogether if it could or, if not, slow it down as much as possible. But progress in military technology is indissolubly connected with technical progress in non-military fields; and "for progress", as John Von Neumann said very well, "there is no cure". Curing it is neither possible nor desirable. We can exploit technology intelligently by continuing to emphasise stabilising innovations that fit our political aims. In this way we may restrain arms budgets in the 1970s and 1980s, as we did in the 1960s, even without large-scale agreements with our adversaries. And we need not move towards reckless last-ditch strategies that fit no political purpose whatsoever.

While it is not possible here to go into the technical details of SALT and MBFR, what I have suggested above about technical trends and about strategies that strengthen and those that loosen the alliance offers some guidance for these negotiations.

First, the validity of alliance guarantees derives much of its strength from the presence of the guarantor's forces in the immediate path of likely attack. This has implications for MBFR as well as SALT 2. Since we want to keep the destinies of allies entangled with each other, any force reductions in the West European theatre must not only be balanced against Warsaw Pact reductions, but the remaining forces had best also be left free for redeployment within the European theatre. If U.S. forces are reduced, it might be good, for example, to relocate them in the North German plain even more directly in the traditional invasion path. And Europeans looking towards a European Defence Community will want various European national forces to move freely within Europe. Finally, in SALT 2 it is important to continue to reject the Russian definition of what is "strategic", to continue to recognise among other things that the role of U.S. bases in Europe has less to do with increasing U.S. effectiveness against Russian homeland targets than with keeping the *immediate* American stake in Europe high. And it is important to look sceptically at claims that American "forward bases" in Europe give the Americans an unfair advantage, for which the Russians deserve to be compensated.

Let me offer one example: the SALT 1 interim agreement allows the Russians nearly half again as many submarine-launched ballistic missiles and missile-launching submarines as the United States. It is sometimes argued in Western Europe, as well as in the

United States, that this is only just and hence, by implication, might be embodied in a permanent agreement in SALT 2, since NATO bases permit the U.S. to keep half as many again of its submarines on station as the Soviet Union. In that connection a well-regarded British publication,[13] which which I am associated, says that the U.S. maintains 60 per cent and the Russians 40 per cent on station at all times. These percentages on station are not accurate for either party, but the current ratio of U.S. time to Russian time on station would not in any case justify a permanent U.S. inferiority. First, the time on station is affected by the fact that the Americans use two crews for each submarine, the Russians one. But this is a matter of choice, and easily changed, rather than a matter of permanent geographic advantage. Secondly, as missile range increases, the percentage on station has less and less to do with the location of submarine bases. For example, the Russian SSN8 was announced in November 1972 as having a 4,300 nautical mile range. That puts it on station when it is at home in Petropavlovsk and Murmansk, from where it could cover essentially all of the United States! Finally, the more permanent geographical advantage has nothing to do with base location, and it accrues to Russian rather than American submarines. Submarines reduce their vulnerability to open ocean search by the amount of ocean area in which they can hide. Points in Russia are protected by a very large land mass much of it non-Russian, that must be overflown by a submarine launched missile; so for any given missile range American submarines have less ocean in which to hide. At 4,300 miles from each other's capital, Russian submarines have three times as much operating area.

In general, territorial distinctions enshrined in agreements with adversaries have a very large potential for loosening alliance ties. They should be handled most soberly and gingerly.

Because we want to be freer to determine the location, composition and equipment of our forces, we should favour agreements that limit or reduce gross aggregates on both sides and avoid agreements that try to freeze forces in specified places and with existing equipment. We should stress aggregate throw weight in strategic forces and aggregate budgets for manpower or forces in MBFR, and consider how SALT and MBFR complement each other to make sure that some gross disparities do not appear in a crack between them.

One of the problems of coping with strong technological trends is that we get to understand them only bit by bit as we go along. The extraordinary, wild oscillations by the technologists them-

[13] *The Strategic Survey* of the International Institute of Strategic Studies.

selves on the political and military implications, for example, of fission, fusion and other post-war technologies, should have induced a certain modesty about our ability to understand these matters once and for all at any given time. Trying to fix and enshrine a transient state of the art in a treaty of indefinite duration is asking for trouble. The final reason then for a focus on aggregates is that it would leave us free to take incremental advantage of, and to direct, the new and rapidly developing technologies including the technologies of precision and control described above. In this way we might preserve and improve the possibility of a variety of responses that make some political sense, and we could avoid drifting into dependence on the unrestrained annihilation of adversary populations as the only strategic course of action other than compliance. Such a threat, in any case, can hardly contribute to the building of a community of interest with adversaries in the long term.

COMMENT *by General Jean Houssay*

I do not think that the development of commercial or financial exchanges amongst people is very much a factor for peace. It seems absolutely necessary to me and hopeful, but that this is something which could avoid war is questionable. History is full of conflicts based on rivalry. But what I believe very deeply is that the exchange of ideas, and the exchange of people among nations, are indeed factors for peace; and in this Alliance, whose concern is to guarantee the defence and the security of our common good, it is essential that we should grasp all possible opportunities for exchanging our points of view: that the great should place themselves in the position of the small, that the small should try to understand the opinions of the great powers. This exchange of opinion is the very basis for the solid nature of an alliance.

On the problem of response and deterrent, I think we should go back to the very definition of the purpose of the Alliance. I believe that whatever hope we may have as to the development of a peaceful spirit among people, and while trying to develop the links which enhance this hope through *détente*, we must envisage the possibility of a confrontation and prepare for each country its own defence and its own security. This is being done. Faced by the danger represented by the Soviet Union after World War II, various countries came together, the Europeans first in Brussels, then the same group enlarged in Washington by the participation of the United States and Canada. This led to the Atlantic Treaty.

This Treaty has two main points. The first is the geographical area of the guarantees which are envisaged by the Treaty itself: this area is defined. The question has often been asked whether one should not try to extend it, since the risks which might derive from a threat to the peace of the Western countries might not be limited to the area indicated in the Treaty. I have heard naval people discussing this problem and it seems very pertinent to me. Threats to the forces of NATO north of the Tropic of Cancer, for example, might be considered as an act of war, but not if the attack occurred south of the Tropic of Cancer. This of course, is not marked on the sea and on the border areas one might hope to see the area extended. But the negotiators I think were right to define the area of the Treaty very precisely and to refuse to envisage any possible extension.

But what is the scope of this guarantee of an intervention in the case of an armed attack? The Treaty gives no automatic indication with regard to the action to be undertaken. Three Articles are the very Charter of the Atlantic Treaty. The allies commit themselves to maintain and increase, each one with the help of the others, their capacities of resistance to an armed attack. This is under Article 3, in time of peace. Under Article 4, in case of a threat, they commit themselves to consult each other; and finally under Article 5, in case of an armed attack against one or several of them, they consider that the attack is addressed to all, and each will aid the country under attack, taking immediately, and in agreement with the others, the actions which they consider necessary, including the use of armed force. It is on these two terms, "agreement with the others" and "the action deemed necessary", that the whole strategy of the Alliance is based, whatever the deterrence and defence envisaged.

Concerning deterrence, if the deterrent is fairly new in the vocabulary of political strategy, the notion is as old as the world. There are many classical examples of this. Nobody could question its significance for the Atlantic Community. But the fact that the Treaty exists is a deterrent in itself. It can be argued that the last two wars might have been avoided if in both cases the aggressor had been sure that his action would have led to the joint and immediate intervention of all those states which, joining in the course of the conflict, managed to defeat him. The aggressor must believe in the Alliance, must have a sufficiently clear idea of the force and the speed of the reaction which his initiative might give rise to. These actions will be those which each ally deems necessary. Each ally has resources, some of which are permanent, others of which vary according to the situation, for instance the trends of its public opinion during the period which preceded the crisis. The United States alone have a strategic nuclear capacity with no common measure in respect of their allies, and two of the other Atlantic powers have also developed a nuclear capacity of their own which, without being comparable to that of the two superpowers, is nevertheless capable of introducing a nuclear element into a conflict.

Moreover whatever theory there may be as to the virtues of graduated response or massive retaliation, it should nevertheless be said that, since this is an action of force, it is in any event wise not to leave the opponent time to develop any successes which will lead to further success on the part of the troops which obtained it. Following limited aggression, to which there was no response, one would be faced by a situation which could no longer be stopped. Has one sufficiently thought of the effects of panic which might be brought about in men who expect to perceive the terrible effects of a nuclear bomb? The appreciation of risk, and the vigour and energy of the response, might vary according to the possibility of having sufficient time to take a decision. A measure of discretion can certainly be allowed to the military in evaluating the threat and manoeuvring with the forces they have at their disposal. Certainly the use of sophisticated arms and more precise selection of targets without having to reach the nuclear level can enable the defence forces to have more effect without calling for a political decision – which would of course be ideal. The problem of the nuclear decision, however, remains. Obviously this takes place at two levels which are not necessarily consecutive. The decision to use tactical nuclear arms which can enhance the action of the battle troops and is integrated with the manoeuvrable forces themselves is a political act, and represents an escalation in itself because once one of the opponents has crossed the nuclear threshhold one cannot see what would stop either side going further. Subtleties of this kind certainly avoid escalation, but it should be recognised that the use of nuclear weapons is unavoidable from the time the devices capable of launching them are part of the organised stockpile of the armies. So once the battle has started and once the aggressor uses the advantage which his initiative has given him, escalation from the level of tactical nuclear weapons does not appear to be avoidable. Failure by the aggressor to push his advantage could be the result of a second-degree deterrent. The first was unsuccessful, since he attacked; the second might make him fear a nuclear apocalypse, once he was convinced of the determination and decisiveness of reaction to his initial action. The fact that the decision to use nuclear strategic weapons may derive from three separate national wills which it is more difficult for the aggressor to evaluate increases the deterrent capacity of the Atlantic Community.

But we are not concerned only with deterrence. I will not go into the matter of the increased power deriving from the combined forces of France and England added to that of the United States. By them, the Atlantic bloc is being defended and not only one's own territory or a part of the territory.

But today only the very deep-rooted feeling of the danger for the national community can really mobilise public opinion. One should therefore try very wholeheartedly, in the consciousness of citizens, to raise the instinctive feeling of the interests of the national community up to dimensions of Atlantic Community. This is a necessary condition for the effectiveness of a common defence and security. Certainly the task will be easier once the political entity known as Europe, which we are hoping for, has developed to the full. But this is not for tomorrow and in the meantime this concept of collective responsibility must ripen, and in an environment further complicated by the search for *détente* which is necessary also. These contradictions underlie all the problems of the defence of Europe and America.

Chapter XVII

NATO, the European Community, and the Transatlantic Order

JOHAN HOLST

AN IRONICAL VANTAGE POINT?

IT SEEMS A LITTLE IRONICAL, perhaps, for a Norwegian to be asked at this juncture to present his views on the interrelationships between NATO and the European Community in the evolution of the transatlantic order. However, I trust that I may approach the issues not as an outsider but as a member of the family. From the perspective of the main flow of history, I am convinced that the Norwegian referendum of September 1972 will seem like but an aberration, a temporary detour, caused by the insecurities of a people still extremely protective about a sovereignty gained less than 70 years ago and so brutally rescinded during those dark years of the last senseless internecine war in Europe. The exacting pace of social and technological change which moulds the conditions of modern man produces a mixture of anxiety, estrangement and resistance to change which was felt particularly strongly, perhaps, in the peripheral communities in Norway where the "future shock" is a rather recent phenomenon.

Norwegians have always been good navigators, and I feel confident that in due course they will realise that they have a role in the construction of the good society in Europe; that sovereignty has to be established rather than abrogated at the level of transnational politics, and that the road towards a meaningful devolution of the power of decision and right of participation goes via sharing in Community deliberations and decisions.

In the same way as the problem confronting my country is to realise what our interests and responsibilities require, the future evolution of NATO and the EC will be determined by our perceptions of what are the requirements for adjustment and change. Unfortunately, the necessities of history never become necessities before it is too late. It is the mark of true statesmanship to recognise what is required and translate it into action before it becomes a necessity

The political order in Europe has entered an era of transformation. The post-war period is now behind us. The '70s and '80s will be a period of political construction. That construction, hopefully, will transcend the divisions and fissures of the cold war. It will have to transcend also the distribution of obligations and responsibilities of the post-war epoch. Superpower patronage can no longer enfold the political order in Europe. But superpower commitment and involvement remains a *conditio sine qua non* for the viability of that order.

There is, it seems to me, a need to avoid false analogies and prescriptions based on a narrow gauge of possible alternatives. The European Community constitutes a political entity *sui generis*. It need not develop according to the logic and traditions of either the American or the Soviet unions. There is nothing at all inevitable about the EC emerging as a superpower patterned on the standards set by Washington and Moscow. Any facile notions about a pentagonal world structure wherein the enlarged European Community shall occupy the position of an equal contributor to the maintenance of a power equilibrium, imply demands on performance which the Community is unlikely to meet, and, in my view, should not aspire to meet. The Community is not a state but a community of states acting in concert rather than by fiat. It exercises civil power rather than military power.

THE NUCLEAR PREDICAMENT

A European nuclear force would not be the virility symbol which many observers seem to assume. It is much more likely to be a project which would cause the Community to disintegrate rather than federate. Nuclear weapons carry demands for central decision-making; there is no way of sharing decisions about when and how to use them. For this reason nuclear weapons do not make very good cement for community construction.

The nuclear balance will remain the privileged concern of the superpowers. But it is a limited privilege which is not easily converted into valid political currency. In fact the management of the central balance is becoming something akin to a rich man's burden which does not lend itself to redistribution because of the adverse impact on the existing world order, limited though that order may be. The shared burden, which does, of course, include competitive aspects and hegemonial potentialities, implies also a sort of objective solidarity between the two superpowers. SALT is a living monument to this solidarity which seems to be driving Moscow and Washington in the direction of stability at parity levels. But that objective solidarity harbours possibilities for interference with the subjective solidarity upon which the Atlantic Alliance is based. The issues associated with forward-based systems (FBS), technology transfer, and constraints on anti-submarine warfare (ASW) illustrate the point.

The nuclear weapon does not, of course, lend itself to dis-invention. The security of Europe is inextricably linked with the nuclear peace. The recurring problem within the Atlantic Alliance has been to arrange for "special drawing rights" on the American nuclear deterrent. Great Britain and France have taken out their own insurance against long-term uncertainties while the other states of Western Europe have found a role in the Nuclear Planning Group (NPG) in NATO. In the years ahead it may well be that a closer co-operation in nuclear matters, based on the complementarities of British and French achievements, will develop between Paris and London. It is likely also that Washington will accept if not applaud such a development. It would seem important, however, that a Franco–British *entente nucléaire* should not have any formal link with the European Community. Such a link would involve a privileged and pre-eminent status within the Community which would imply delicate problems of comparative status and influence. It could open the nuclear issue in Germany or, alternatively, affect the relative priorities of *Ostpolitik* and *Westpolitik* in ways which would seriously dampen German enthusiasm for Community construction. This problem will be compounded as the negotiations on force limitations in Europe may produce another set of internal frontiers which will separate the non-controlled nuclear powers of the EC from the rest.

It should be recognised that neither Paris nor London are about to dispense with their nuclear deterrents. It is quite obvious that such forces contribute at least somewhat to the overall deterrence via the residual uncertainties. And uncertainties extend also to the future of the transatlantic relationship. To hold the British and French forces in trust for Europe does seem to me a reasonably prudent course of action. It does not mean that they can be instruments in the construction of Europe. But they do to some extent constitute instruments for the protection of that construction should the American guarantee be less viable under a future President under altered circumstances. Nuclear weapons should not become a major source of Community attention at a point in time when the EURATOM countries are completing the process of ratification of the Non-Proliferation Treaty.

Franco–British nuclear co-operation could extend to joint procurement, planning and targeting. The latter is not as impossible as it is sometimes depicted. It was practised, apparently quite satisfactorily, between the U.S. Strategic Air Command and the RAF Bomber Command in the '50s and early '60s. Such a "solution" would act as a link between the French and the American forces and could conceivably pave the way also for French participation in the NPG.

DEFENCE: A PREREQUISITE FOR POLITICAL UNION

It seems unlikely that the European Community can make genuine progress towards political union without including defence. Its members' expressed and structured willingness to preserve and defend their cohesion against external threats will in itself constitute a powerful force making for political union. The area of concentration ought to be that of conventional defence. It is one in which all the states can participate on an equal basis; it does not imply internal frontiers. On the contrary, it could serve to counteract those which may emerge from arms limitation agreements. The institutional problems are not easy, but nor do they appear to be paramount. A useful beginning would be the establishment of an EC Defence Committee as a counterpart to the Political (Davignon) Committee. It could possibly be brought into being through a reconstitution or re-location of the Eurogroup in NATO. It would thus provide a framework for renewed French participation in multilateral measures for the defence of Western Europe. The tasks of the Committee should, in my view, at least initially, be rooted in concrete problem areas such as joint training, logistics, research and development, procurement as well as standardisation of equipment and harmonisation of tactical doctrine. There is also a need to evolve some sort of analytical rather than negotiated consensus about strategic doctrine. A useful step in such a direction would be the establishment of a European Defence Research Institute.

A co-ordinated effort in the defence area could provide a basis for closer co-operation with the United States within NATO.

Influence on defence planning problems within NATO has always been closely correlated with the insight and independent assessment which the allies of the United States have been able to bring to bear on the issues at hand. One of the problems in NATO has been that there has prevailed too sharp a division between the political and military hierarchies within the organisation of the Alliance. The working procedures of the EC Defence Committee should be such as to result in a close and steady contact between the various working groups and the relevant sections of the bureaucracies of the participating governments. The direct co-operation with the United States could then take place within a non-nuclear planning group patterned to some extent on the NPG. In the longer term it is possible to envisage the crystallisation of a European Nuclear Defence Committee which would provide also a European nucleus in the NPG, but that is not a priority item on the agenda for Europe.

The approach suggested here is that of a gradual and pragmatic transformation of the Atlantic Alliance into an alliance structured around a U.S.–EC axis. What is envisaged is also a kind of dialectic growth pattern where the transformation of NATO would stimulate and be stimulated by community construction in Europe. Small steps in the direction of defence co-operation in the EC will serve not only purposes of internal growth and consolidation but also those of external deterrence. Some progress and the establishment of joint procedures and working habits imply a potential for expanded co-operation should the Community be subjected to external pressures.

From the point of view of international society at large the way the nuclear issue is handled in the transatlantic context is of seminal importance. Here will be decided to a considerable extent perceptions about the role of nuclear weapons in the process of international politics. It is of great importance also to the future of the European Community. Statesmen will have to steer a careful course between the dangers of fractionalising the Community by adherence to a *tous azimuts* strategic concept, immobilising it by accepting an active U.S. preponderance, or breaking its back by attempting to compete with superpower paraphernalia in the "big league". There is always the problem of maintaining a credible link with the nuclear balance between the superpowers. However, the requirement that the link be credible will necessitate some important changes in the structure of the current arrangements. The NATO nuclear posture in Europe contains important elements of pre-emptive instability which would become salient if ever a serious crisis were to occur. The quick reaction aircraft are vulnerable targets which might precipitate disarming attacks. The present nature and number of so-called tactical nuclear weapons in Europe defy inclusion in any coherent strategy. They promise to destroy rather than defend Europe and thus tend to deter the possessor as much as or more than the aggressor. They should be replaced by the new generation of small precision weapons which permit a high measure of deliberate control and target discrimination. They should be brought into the inventory in reasonable and not excessive numbers. These weapons are needed not as a means for reflex escalation but rather as a link in a continuous chain of options. They do not obviate the need for effective conventional defence in Europe. For very good reasons statesmen are going to be extremely reluctant to transgress the nuclear threshold. It takes two to do the nuclear tango and we shall never be in the position of fighting controlled antiseptic nuclear wars with high confidence assurance against very dirty eruptions. There is an urgent need to fashion a strategy for the possible use of nuclear weapons which would have a terminatory rather than an escalatory impact on a war. A viable strategy should contain incentives for the opponent to desist from offensive actions.

There is, in my view, also an important moral issue involved in the formation of the strategic nuclear doctrine of the Atlantic Alliance. It is doubtful, indeed, that the doctrine of "mutual assured destruction" will prove viable as the ultimate expression of our ability to attain security in the nuclear age. Men of conscience, humanity, and a sense of aesthetics will want to transcend the twisted logic of the present state of affairs. For a generation which seems, at least ostensibly, committed to uncovering and removing the hypocrisy and irrationality of their fathers, "mutual assured destruction" is unlikely to have much appeal. Some may seek solutions by way of disarmament, others by different systemic transitions away from the point of holding civilian populations as hostages and as collateral for the good behaviour of governments which are not invariably responsive to the needs and wants of these same civilian populations. There remains the ethical, intellectual and, in important ways, technological challenge of constructing a more rational order consistent with long-range political objectives and with human compassion. There is an urgent need for Europeans to take up the problems "beyond" deterrence before the options are frozen and pre-empted by superpower agreement at the level of SALT.

THE AMERICAN COMMITMENT AND SECURITY IN EUROPE

American military presence in Europe remains essential both from the point of view of the structural problem of the balance with the East and as a psychological collateral for the U.S. commitment to Europe. However, for a number of years now the possibility of unilateral U.S. force reductions has cast ominous shadows over the security order in Europe. Talks about possible mutual force reductions between NATO and the Warsaw Treaty Organisation (WTO) have served as a deflector of Congressional assaults on the President's position on the troops issue in Washington. Thus what is fundamentally a West–West issue has been transferred to the East–West level where the outcome will be determined by dynamics different from those which are designed to strengthen the transatlantic security arrangements. There is, it seems to me, a general danger inherent in the current flexibility of the international system and the novel American fascination with balance of power politics, that the processes of the diplomatic game come to overshadow the erection and maintenance of viable co-operative structures.

The Nixon administration appears to be intent on fighting off Congressional pressures for troop reductions in Europe as long as the Europeans continue to exhibit willingness to carry their share of the burden and the Russians continue to be willing to talk about mutual reductions. However, a combative position on the part of the President could have a polarising impact on the American political scene and remove the U.S. presence in Europe from the realm of bipartisan consensus. The unsettling impact of such a development is obvious. From the point of view of credibility in Europe it is the permanence of U.S. presence rather than the exact level of troops (although the level must be substantially more than symbolic) which is primary. Thus the troop presence ought to be pegged at a level which can obtain broad support in Washington. Long-term confidence in U.S. military protection is an important political and psychological precondition for Community construction in Europe.

If I am right in believing that the level of U.S. troops in Europe will change over the next five years it seems imperative to come to grips with the ways in which we may be able to manage and limit the scale and impact of the American disengagement. We need to fashion compensatory adjustments to American troop withdrawals in terms of more coherent European efforts. Such efforts would have to be in the realm of conventional forces and involve an expansion of territorial forces, fortifications, modern anti-tank weapons, etc. They would have to be directed also towards stemming the tide of reduced conscription. But we should consider American compensatory adjustments as well. Such adjustments could involve the prepositioning of heavy equipment and the sharing of advanced military technology. Of particular importance here are precision-guided munitions for attacks against point- and area-targets which promise significantly to improve the fighting power of modern armed forces and to raise the nuclear threshold.

A reduction of ground forces could be offset in part also by home-porting portions of the U.S. Atlantic fleet in the North Sea. The growth in Soviet naval power is perhaps the most serious threat to the coherence of transatlantic defence arrangements. It is a problem which is not confined to the Mediterranean. It is even more acute in the North-East Atlantic. Naval forces and operations are perhaps the most promising short-term focus for joint European efforts in the military area. Here is a major role for Britain to play, a role which would serve *inter alia* to preserve the internal balance between Mediterranean and North Sea Europe in the construction of Europe. It would be relevant also to the protection of off-shore gas and oil at source as well as in transit in the North Sea. Here, joint efforts on the part of the North Sea powers could extend from joint training and operations to research, development, and procurement of specialised vessels and equipment for the surveillance and protection of petroleum installations.

THE NEED FOR A BROAD ATLANTIC FRAMEWORK

Transatlantic relations are entering a conflictual stage just at the very time when the process of *détente* is reducing conflict across the East–West division in Europe and at the level of superpower relations. The conflicts are sharpest in the realms of money and trade, and therein lies a danger of escalation. The very compartmentalisation of transatlantic relations and of the national bureaucracies may cause conflicts in one sector to spread to others by spill-over or accident. The problems are endemic and can probably only be remedied by instutional reconstruction. There is an obvious need for a transatlantic institutional framework which will facilitate joint management and conflict resolution through the construction of cross-sectoral package solutions and compromises. As long as transatlantic relations are channelled through single-sector institutions there can be little bargaining and the institutional incentives for evolving overall policies are missing.

In the current phase of international relations the Atlantic states need to establish joint EC–U.S. institutions to handle the broad spectrum of interstate and inter-societal relations. NATO would be but one element of a larger structure in the institutionalisation of the transatlantic order. An Atlantic ministerial council should be vested with the competence and authority to deal with the issues across functional frontiers and, at the level of permanent representatives, serve as a forum for continuous consultation and bargaining. The build-up of transatlantic institutions should be tailored to the pace of institutional reconstruction and policy co-ordination in the European Community. Atlantic co-operation could become a catalyst for the growth of the EC in the same way that the growth of the EC into the defence area could give NATO a new lease of life.

Conflict may, of course, occur. The Atlantic and European perspectives may pull in opposite directions and the process of East–West *détente* may deflect from the broadening of West European–American relations. But *détente* may also work in favour of consolidation of the democratic system of the West. The external requirements inherent in such undertakings as the Conference on Security and Co-operation in Europe (CSCE) have already had the effect of intensifying and giving substance to the work in the EC Political Committee. The pattern of caucusing and consultations during the Multilateral Preparatory Talks (MPT) in Helsinki has been such as to cause the EC procedures to cut into the established NATO processes and provide an EC–U.S. axis as the dominant structural element. A broadening of the CSCE canvas will cause the challenges to multiply. A co-ordinated multilateral approach to the East will be chosen for purposes of preventing bilateralism from escalating into a race for *détente* and in order to prevent the CSCE from pre-empting joint EC policies in such areas as trade, energy, transportation, and pollution.

There is also the dilemma associated with the likelihood that a concerted approach on the part of the EC will structure the bargaining so that Soviet control over Eastern Europe will be strengthened rather than weakened. In this realm a long-range view is necessary, however. The evolution of the political order in Europe will be determined more by the flow of transactions across the old divisions than by the format of the negotiations which establish the ground rules. The Soviet Union is not about to accept any negotiated weakening of its imperial hold on Eastern Europe. A fairer deal for the East European states will be possible only in a situation where the Soviet Union does not feel compelled to give absolute priority to maximum control in Eastern Europe or tempted to expand her influence in Western Europe. Hence a viable European Community with a strong accent on civil power and anchored in a broader system of Atlantic co-operation, which promises stable military security, can provide a basis for partnership and counterweight *vis-à-vis* the Soviet Union and Eastern Europe. In the long run a strong European Community – and strength here refers to internal cohesion, political content, and moral authority – is a necessary condition for the emergence of a European order wherein the two collective defence organisations in Europe are tied together in a collective security system. Such linkages would, of course, contain requirements for modification of the collective defence organisations. But the need to adapt and adjust to changed conditions and the implementation of long-range structural objectives is a permanent one in international relations. We cannot plan for the future of Europe and forget about Eastern Europe. Europe extends beyond the Elbe and the Danube, and the inherent instability of the present order in Eastern Europe constitutes a latent threat to the stability of the total order in Europe. But the problems cannot be eliminated overnight. They can only be transformed within an evolutionary process. There is a constant need to preserve a sense of priority and long-range vision about the political order in Europe in the coming years. The era of negotiation will contain inferential pressures which may cause the states of Western Europe to deflect from the priority of Community construction. The necessity for choice, for weighing short-term gains against long-term benefits, is part of the challenge we face.

A reduced level of forces in Western Europe, whether it be brought about by negotiated mutual force reductions, by unilateral U.S. withdrawals, by a reduction of the West European forces in being, or any combination thereof, will necessitate a freer location of forces in the European area. This imperative could, if it be recognised, have a catalytic impact on European defence co-operation, as an optimised deployment would have to be based on strategic rather than national frontier considerations.

TOWARDS A TRANSFORMATION OF NATO:
WHO IS LEFT BEHIND?

There are, of course, a great many problems connected with
the transformation of Atlantic institutions and processes along
the lines which I have suggested. Europe of the Nine includes one
non-NATO state, namely Ireland. But Irish membership in the
EC is more than a commercial arrangement; it is a political commitment. It is too early to tell whether Ireland will act as a
brake on the extension of community co-operation into the
realm of defence. Denmark may be more of a minimum factor
due to the non-membership of Norway. Hence it is possible that
Norway's staying out of the EC will have the indirect effect of
slowing down the growth of Community activities into areas
like defence. Denmark, however, is likely to be undergoing an
important process of "community socialisation" in the years
ahead which may change outlooks and priorities.

A series of more serious problems involves the position of non-
EC members – apart from the United States – in NATO. For
NATO members like Greece, Turkey, Portugal and Iceland,
membership in the alliance has by and large served the function
of obtaining bilateral protection from the United States. The
problems are more serious for the two northern flank members of
the Alliance, namely Canada and Norway. Both of these countries
have taken a very active part in the political deliberations of
the alliance. For Norway, isolation from the main axis of intra-
alliance communication and bargaining would, of course, be
the result of her own making, although the broader political perspectives involved were not particularly well presented and frequently denied in the campaign preceding the referendum.
Norway occupies an important strategic position in relation to
the defence of Europe, particularly in the light of the substantial
increase in Soviet naval power and activities in the North-East
Atlantic. Prospective force limitation agreements seem likely to
be focused on Central Europe and would thus add to the separation of Norway from the main structure of European security
arrangements. The cumulative impact of the frontiers drawn as
a result of the East–West *détente* and the West–West reconstruction may breed a sense of estrangement and aloofness in Norway
which might entail dangers of a permanent separation detrimental to Norwegian as well as European interests. There is a
need for bridges and links across the "internal frontiers" of the
Western democratic system. For Norway it is particularly

important to preserve the notion of the indivisibility of the peace in Europe, and to that end any arrangement for force reductions in Central Europe ought to be integrated into a broader system of constraints on military movements and dispositions which would apply to all of Europe. There is also the need for the Norwegian political leadership, which so predominantly favoured membership in the European Community, to preserve and explicate their vision of Norway's role in Europe.

For Canada, the problems of a bilateralisation of the main axis in NATO are even more intractable. Canada does not have the option of joining the EC. The competence and enlightenment that Canada invariably brings to bear in her participation in the Alliance are as important as the location of that vast country from the point of view of strategy. The bicultural links with Britain and France as well as the intensive involvement with the United States provide a broad basis for special relationships in the Atlantic context. There would also seem to be good reason to structure special relationships among the Arctic countries of the Alliance, Canada, Denmark, Norway and the United States. In the years to come, activities around the Arctic basin are bound to multiply and intensify. There will be need for joint management and conflict resolution in regard to many of the issues which may emerge in connection with developments in the realms of resource exploitation, transportation and environmental protection. There are also important strategic interests which would give substance to the suggested co-operative pattern.

THE EUROPEAN COMMUNITY AND WORLD ORDER

It may seem contradictory, perhaps, to claim that the European Community is and ought to remain primarily a civil power, and then proceed to argue that defence should be included in the affairs of the Community. There is, however, no real contradiction here, since the impact of the EC on international society will continue to be concentrated on the realm of civil power and social organisation. The emphasis in the defence sector should be on general purpose forces for the defence of the Community area. Such a "low posture" will be viable only so long as the United States continues to underwrite the security of Western Europe. Such underwriting will in turn necessitate equitable burden-sharing and institutionalised co-responsibility for the broad pattern of transatlantic relations. The ability of the EC to steer such a course will carry important examples and suggestions about the postures which other major powers, such as for example Japan, may choose to adopt.

There is an urgent need to deal constructively with the nuclear issues. The EC can contribute significantly to non-proliferation and world order by de-emphasising the political importance attributed to nuclear weapons in the European political process. France and England will remain supplementary nuclear powers. They cannot replace the United States' nuclear umbrella for Europe. Pragmatic Franco–British nuclear collaboration outside the Community framework could remove the "independent" national deterrents from the area of intra-alliance conflict, particularly if it would lead also to co-ordination with the United States. However, should a Franco–British *entente nucléaire* be thought of as a means of creating Franco–British hegemony within the Community, the damage would be irreparable. I have been arguing for a consolidation that is consistent with a long-term posture of nuclear de-emphasis on the part of the Community. The Nuclear Planning Group in NATO will remain of critical importance in this connection.

From the viewpoint of long-term stability based on nuclear de-emphasis it seems important also to fashion a nuclear strategy which will shift the accent away from offensive punishment to defensive protection. Such a shift in emphasis would seem to make substantial reductions in the nuclear arsenals of the super-powers more likely. Here I have tried to identify a direction for future developments from the point of view of politics and ethics. Economics and technology will continue to operate as constraints on our ability to accomplish desirable objectives. But our efforts ought to be oriented at driving developments in the desired directions. The European Community can hardly afford to ignore such paramount issues of the human condition.

We are in the midst of a transitional period between the era of the cold war and what could be the era of partnership and reconciliation in Europe. NATO and EC will be important institutions in the construction and management of a viable peace order in Europe.

COMMENT *by Guido Colonna di Paliano*

I would buy this scenario right away because in fact it would be the continuation of the situation in which we have more or less happily lived in the whole of the post-war period. The trouble is that the first assumption on which the scenario is based concerns the attitude of the United States in regard to Europe and I am sure that my American friends will not deny me when I say that this attitude has changed and that this change of attitude of the United States in regard to Europe marks the end of the post-war period. I mean by this that if we in Europe desire to have the continuing involvement of the United States in Europe we cannot any longer take it for granted, but we have to acquire it, almost *ex novo*.

Mr Holst believes that the notion of the so-called pentagon is unrealistic because it would imply demands and performances which are unlikely to be met. But this notion does represent the current political strategy of the United States, whether we like it or not, and it is already applied, not without positive response, in regard to the Soviet Union, China and Japan. We Europeans may wish, or we may be forced, to stay out of the pentagon, but this would not prevent the other four from pursuing a policy based on the balance of political power. There is an edge in the notion of the balance of power insofar as we are concerned in Europe. The objective of this policy, in my opinion, is the preservation of peace and the advancement of the interests of the parties concerned through diplomacy of great complexity, supported by the strength of each of the centres concerned. Should Europe fail to develop into a centre of power, this would be from now on our affair, not the affair of the Americans. It should not recriminate against the Americans because of deals concluded with others behind our backs. In such a perspective the duration of effective protection of Western Europe by the United States would depend upon the relative importance, in the eyes of the Americans, of preserving the present political order in Europe as against other objectives and priorities. No doubt the affinities existing between the United States and Europe may prevail, but we cannot be sure.

In other words, American involvement in Europe cannot any longer be taken for granted: it must be acquired. It seems from everything we hear and read about the negotiations that are beginning in various directions and on various themes that the United States will be hard bargainers. There have so far been more valid reasons, in my opinion, for dissatisfaction in the United States in regard to Japan than to the European Community – I refer now of course to economic affairs. One senses, however, the growing impatience of the Americans, in the face of a Community which in their eyes has been able to this day only to organise discrimination against the outside world, without being capable even of a start towards an effective co-ordination of national economic policies, and without the will to assume full and effective responsibility for its actions. The common agricultural policy, the non-tariff barriers, the preferential agreements, could and should have been handled in the first place with the United States in a way which would have avoided their rising to the level of emotional issues. The monetary chaos in which we live could have been avoided, at least to a certain extent, if the members of the Community had established between themselves in good time a common discipline and a solidarity corresponding to the ultimate objective of the Community, which is still supposed to be political unification. Mr Holst remarks that men become conscious of the necessities imposed upon them by history too late. Well, it is perhaps not too late for us in Europe to look after our own future, provided that we face realities and do not take refuge in any more wishful thinking.

There are four areas in the world wielding tremendous power, political, economic and military. The U.S. and the Soviet Union possess this power in its three dimensions. It may take time before China emerges as a military and economic power, but it already has a great political influence and there is nothing short of pre-emptive aggression to prevent China from becoming a nuclear superpower. Its immense internal market and the industriousness of its people should make possible the gradual development also of an extraordinary economic potential. As for Japan, already an economic superpower, its position with regard to the U.S.–Soviet Union–China triangle offers political opportunities of the first magnitude, while no physical limitation would exist to the creation of a Japanese military power including a substantive nuclear component. Other areas may emerge wielding a new and menacing form of power. I am thinking of the countries which have in their soil essential raw materials, such as oil. We in Europe, with our scarcity of raw materials, shall have to think about our future relations with these countries and decide whether we shall try to secure supplies and stability of prices, negotiating with these countries on our own, and in competition with other areas, such as the United States and Japan, or in concert with these other great consumers.

These are hard facts, no less real than the direct threat to Western Europe from the East of the late '40s and '50s. It is perhaps not unreasonable to think that the European nations could draw from these facts a new sense of urgency, a revival of the initial drive towards cohesion. Thus I would for my part link the question of the viability of the existing political order in Europe above all to the capacity of Europeans to overcome the barriers which have so far prevented them from integrating their nations in some European entity. This is for me basic assumption No. 1. At the risk of being criticised for being superficial and shallow I would sum up all these obstacles to political union in two simple facts: lack of mutual trust and lack of solidarity. By and large every member of the European Community, including my own country, has up to now regarded the Community as an opportunity for exploiting its own national interests, while reserving its right to act on its own when it appeared that the bargain was not advantageous. This may sound a hard judgment, influenced by recent events. The fact remains that at least since 1965 the members of the EC have not considered themselves any more bound by decisions agreed by the majority simply because they have given up deciding on the basis of a majority vote. The notion of mutual trust embodied in the initial supranational structure of the Community has thus disappeared. Without mutual trust there cannot be lasting unlimited solidarity; and how could solidarity develop in a purely national context without the guarantee of multinational and supranational democratic institutions responsible for the impartial promotion of the common interest?

This brings me to two issues which in my opinion are central: the inclusion in the Community of a common defence structure and the *a priori* renunciation by the European Community of the creation of a common nuclear force. I too dislike the idea that one day Europe might develop a nuclear deterrent of its own. As has been pointed out, nuclear weapons demand central decision-making, or sharing decisions about when and how to use them. This statement goes along with the previous remark that the Community is not a state but a community of states acting in concert rather than by fiat. There lies the whole problem. The notion of the Community can and has been interpreted in different ways. For my part, I have always considered that the Community in its ultimate stage of achievement should be an entity endowed with the powers and responsibilities of a federal state. Be that as it may, if we are unable to visualise the establishment, gradual as it may be, between the members of the Community, of unlimited solidarity on the basis of which if necessary, and I underline if necessary, the creation and management of an independent nuclear deterrent could be considered, we should remain indefinitely in the unsatisfactory situation in which we are – or rather, we should begin to disintegrate. I agree that we should not pick the nuclear deterrent as the indispensable symbol of European virility. I also agree that it would be highly desirable, if possible, to de-emphasise the role of nuclear weapons in general. But such an attitude should be dictated by a free choice and not by resignation to the impossibility of an alternative. We should not forget that for the time being nuclear weapons are there and that they carry, for the time being, a precise political connotation. The building, in the context of the Community, of common adequate conventional forces stands to reason as long as there is the certainty of securing the right combination of nuclear and non-nuclear defence tactics. A decision by the Community to limit its defence to conventional weapons pre-supposes indeed the so called United States/European Community axis. I personally would have nothing against this, but there are several hundred million people in Western Europe who would have to agree to spend a great deal of money – conventional forces are expensive and are becoming more expensive all the time – for achieving a defence system which would be worth while only to the extent in which there would still be a nuclear commitment on the part of the United States. And so we are back to assumption No. 1. Would it not be better, in any case, for the Community to go on acquiring the political capacity for creating and managing a nuclear deterrent of its own and then negotiating an alliance with the United States?

One word about the two national deterrents existing in Europe. I am afraid that, whether or not they are included in a European Defence Community, the discrimination between nuclear and non-nuclear members of the Community that is implied in their existence would remain. This discrimination could become divisive if as a result of economic interdependence within the Community the non-nuclears could be induced by certain circumstances to believe that they were called upon to finance deterrents over which they would have no control and from which they would draw no political dividend. This is perhaps the most difficult of the issues involved. I believe that these European national deterrents should be committed to NATO and supervised, along with the other nuclear forces committed to the Alliance, by appropriate organs open to all the members of the Community who agreed to participate in a common defence effort.

Let me make clear, however, that I visualise the role of the Community as centred on the promotion of social progress in Europe and in the world as an instrument of international reconciliation and as a means for preserving peace. No other role would be acceptable to our public opinion. I ardently hope that relations between the Community and the United States become, as time goes by, more and not less friendly, and their views more and not less convergent. But to be able to exercise this role, to be credible for such a role, to become a friend of the United States as a result of a spontaneous and deliberate choice and not just out of necessity, Europe should put an end to its internal quarrels, rivalries, and suspicions.

I have, together with others, advocated as a medium-term objective for commercial relations between the industrialised countries, a zero tariff goal, supported by a monetary system admitting adjustment as required, under international control. I am indeed convinced that the Community must free itself from the narrow mercantilism of which it has become a prisoner. Cohesion in the Community cannot be secured for ever by the advantages of a preferential area. The acceptance of a zero tariff objective would force the Europeans towards the real goals for which the Community was created – mutual trust and solidarity. It would give Europe the authority required to negotiate with the other industrialised areas of the world, and eliminate at least some of the main causes of friction between Europe and the United States.

In conclusion, it seems to me that the time is ripe for a Euro–North American summit which should clear the atmosphere between both sides of the Atlantic Alliance before the various negotiations become substantive and possibly divisive. I am convinced, indeed, that unless the approach to the various issues on the table is a global one, such as only a summit would make possible, the solutions might remain out of reach. Globality entails also the offer by Europe and the United States to Japan, and the acceptance by Japan, of some sort of joint responsibility for responding to its position as a free, highly industrialised area of the world.

PART FOUR

New Perspectives in Foreign Policy

Chapter XVIII

Future World Systems

EUGENE V. ROSTOW

THE SUBJECT OF THIS CHAPTER recalls an anecdote about Churchill. As he stood with a friend in the lobby of the House of Commons, the story goes, one of his political opponents passed by.

"Isn't he a modest man?" Churchill's friend remarked.

"He has much to be modest about," Churchill is supposed to have replied.

No doubt Churchill's quip was unfair to his rival. But its force is self-evident for anyone who is required to peer through a dark glass towards a particularly murky aspect of the future.

Churchill's observation applies also, and with splendid impartiality, to the record over the last 29 years of all our nations in making and carrying out foreign policy – the activity which has had a great deal to do with determining the present shape of world politics, and will necessarily have a great deal to do with determining its future. We cannot, of course, remake the world to our heart's desire. But the future systems of world politics will depend in large part on what Europe and America are willing to do in the next few years – on their perceptions of reality, their generosity of spirit, and above all on their will.

As we review the basis of our relationships, and try to understand the circumstances which make this decade so different from those which immediately preceded it, the first thing to be said, I submit, is that we have the capacity to assure our own tranquillity and prosperity in the world which is emerging. Together, we have something more, and perhaps something more important. As children of common civilisations, committed to the faith in individual freedom, in racial equality, and in social justice, we have both the capacity and the obligation, as responsible citizens of the world community, to contribute significantly – substantially, perhaps even decisively – to its peace and development.

Will we in fact succeed? As we try to answer the question in the light of what we have in fact accomplished, the answer, I suggest, is that we have much to be modest about.

I do not mean to imply by this comment that everything we have done or tried to do since 1945 has been misconceived, or badly managed. On the contrary, I am convinced that on the whole Western policy has been on the right track during that period, and achieved a good deal. Indeed, one of our problems as we face the novel and unfamiliar issues of the future is a certain subliminal complacency – a confidence that because we have avoided ultimate disaster for the last 28 years, we are bound to do so indefinitely.

But we do have every right to draw some encouragement from the many sensible and successful programmes we have conceived and carried out together since the end of World War II. Indeed, we can draw encouragement as well from some of our proposals which were not accepted at the time they were made. They stand as monuments to our purpose, ideas to which men may yet rally – the offer of the Marshall Plan to the Soviet Union and the nations of Eastern Europe, for example, and of the Baruch Plan for the international control of nuclear energy, whose time may come sooner than we think.

The North Atlantic Alliance, surely has been and is an important success. With a minimum of the kind of friction which has historically bedevilled alliance relations, it carries out, more effectively than ever before, the immensely difficult task of harmonising the policies of 15 nations on a number of the most sensitive problems of security policy and diplomacy – deterring attack, and preparing the way for *détente*.

The progress of the European idea has been a brilliant achievement – a great victory of the spirit, reaching far beyond the humdrum world of tariffs, taxes, and exchange rates. Against the background of history, it represents an aspiration that stirs men's hearts as well as their minds. Its vindication should contribute to the balance and vitality of the Atlantic world, and of the world beyond. The recent enlargement of the Community, and its rededication to the ideal of a political Europe, are heartening events, which are bound to give a fresh impulse to the processes of world politics.

In economics, too, we can look back with satisfaction to what has been accomplished, even though the very success of these policies has precipitated a new situation, requiring new measures and indeed new institutions, if we are not to retreat into autarky or worse. Through 25 years of imaginative co-operation, the bankers, businessmen, trade unions, economists, and governments of Western Europe, North America and Japan have created something new – a closely unified economy of the industrialised nations. That economy functions as the nucleus of a vast and progressive Western economic system, embracing many smaller industrialised nations, and large parts of the third world as well. The Western economic system is both planned and decentralised, directed but also flexible: planned, through the use of fiscal and monetary policies to maintain high levels of demand; decentralised, in its reliance on the free and unplanned responses of competitive markets to economic opportunities. For all its problems and shortcomings – and I have no wish to gloss over them – the international Western economy has proved to be by far the most successful of all the economic systems now functioning in the world. It has raised living standards, and promoted both a wide dispersal of power and opportunity, and an equitable sharing of the fruits of progress among all classes of the population. Its character as a social order has been deeply and favourably influenced by our own humane movements for social justice, which have helped to mitigate inequality, and assure welfare, on a scale which would have been unimaginable a generation ago.

I recall these bright pages from the record of the last 29 years simply to encourage the doubters among us as we face the challenge of the next 29.

In attempting to describe the challenge of the next 29 years, let me start with the questions implicit in the topic assigned to me: "future world systems".

Let me start as well by stating briefly my own answer to the question. Many perceive the world as being divided by all kinds of pressures into a more and more diffuse pattern of diverse autonomies – a multipolar system of diffused power. While there are of course centrifugal and centripetal forces at work in world politics, as there are within each separate society, my own view is that the forces, the values, and interests drawing the world together into a single society, necessarily governed by a single system of law, are far stronger than those tending to divide it into its individual atoms and molecules. Whether the centrifugal or the centripetal forces will prevail depends to a large extent, I should suggest, on the world outlook of our peoples, and those of a few other key nations in the world – Japan particularly – and on the decisions our governments take within the next few months and years. In short, I see the world as becoming smaller and smaller, pressed together by factors of technology and fear towards a system of union by necessity.

What do we mean by the phrase "world systems"?

The notion of a world system or of world systems is a novelty in world politics. Even Rome, after all, did not embrace the world. The 19th century was the first moment in human history when one could actually visualise the world – or nearly all the world – as included within a single political and economic system, or series of related systems. The explorers, the colonists, the imperialists, the missionaries, dreamed of a world system, to be sure. But it only became a possibility the day before yesterday. It has not yet become an actuality, although that too may happen, of necessity, before long.

It is illuminating to measure the passage of time in history by noting the changing scale and scope of the relevant social units – the atoms and the molecules which compose societies. When 70 or 80 per cent of the population of all countries lived by farming, social life was necessarily circumscribed and stable. A certain amount of interregional and international trade and travel took place, of course. And, equally, there was a certain amount of interregional war. And there were always wanderers, adventurers, restless spirits. But these events did not involve many people. Most people lived within the supportive routines of established custom, a fate to which many modern writers look back with nostalgia, although at the time most of the participants found it dull.

The modern migrations on a considerable scale began in the 17th century, and have increased rapidly ever since. But most men never wandered far from their farms and villages. It is still common in rural districts to find older men and women who have never seen cities 50 or 100 miles away. It is inconceivable that this could be said of their children.

The effective unit of social life has grown larger and larger, under the impact of changing technology, improved methods of transportation and communication, and the other factors we include under the general rubric of "industrial revolution". Initially, the effective unit of social organisation was a self-sufficient farming district and a market town, save for the exceptional cities dependent upon international trade. Under these circumstances, small dukedoms, free cities, and principalities were viable, sometimes linked together in leagues, or alliances, or loosely defined nations, sometimes not. Then the operative unit became regional, later national, as nationalism became a consuming religion. One can see the history of this process visually as one travels in Europe, and indeed in the United States and Canada as well, and passes between districts which are still somewhat different in architecture, in place-names, in dialect, and in economic activity. In the United States the balance of influence between the states and the national government changed radically over a century, with a steady decline in the importance of the states, and a steady increase in that of the nation. Now even the largest countries can hardly function at all without sustained access to world markets, not for silk and spices, but for necessities.

There are, of course, other forces behind the steady enlargement of the representative social unit: religion surely, the idea of nationalism, and, above all, military technology and its impact on political organisation. The same intellectual revolution which produced the railway also produced the machine-gun, the aeroplane, and now the nuclear weapon. Fear has not disappeared as an influence on men's behaviour. The search for security against the possibility of external attack has required ever larger units of political organisation.

The 19th century, which in retrospect seems a golden age in so many ways, came close to achieving a single world system, both politically and economically. Men differ as to the quality of what was accomplished. And the moral foundation for the old imperialism has gone. But the political world system of the 19th century – that of the European balance of power and of European imperialism – did provide a reasonably stable framework for the internal and external lives of its constituent societies and nations. It was the framework within which the United States evolved and flourished. The European states-system kept the general peace, without substantial effort on our part. The United States, and many other non-aligned nations, were the beneficiaries of the system, without really understanding its methods, and without giving up, even for a moment, the right to complain about how badly the European nations were doing the job. I often recall that feature of American life when I read about American foreign policy in European newspapers.

At the turn of the century, the Concert of Europe had lost its sense of measure. By 1945, the old system vanished altogether, victim of its own follies, and of the conflict among the ideas and ideals to which it gave birth – antithetical ideas and ideals which have enriched and tormented our civilisation: peace among sovereign states, and the self-determination of peoples; freedom from the state, and freedom to fulfil a higher good prescribed by the state; socialism and individualism; reward in accordance with productivity; and equality.

For the last 29 years we have been struggling with the consequences both of the collapse of the old political system and of the conflict among its ideas and ideals. In that process, we have had to deal with the impact of four vast and interrelated flows of change in world affairs: first, the dissolution of most European empires, except for the Russian and the Portuguese, and the emergence all over the world of new states, often weak and ill-equipped for the tasks of modern government; second, the recovery and renewal of Western Europe, after the trauma of its experience with fascism, war, and withdrawal from empire; third, the outward thrust of Soviet and then of other Communist expansion, often addressed to the weakness of the new states, but addressed primarily, and above all, to Western Europe as well; and finally, the mutation in American foreign policy after a century of isolation, as the United States perceived the necessity for a protective response, and took the lead in organising coalitions, both in Europe and in Asia, which could contain hostile ambition and achieve something like an accepted equilibrium in world politics.

In the course of these efforts, to borrow a famous phrase, we have surely survived. But we have done more than survive. Europe and Japan are once again immense centres of power and influence, each separately allied with the United States with regard to security problems in its own area, and equal partners with the United States, and with each other, in the management of a worldwide economy on which all the nations in fact depend. By trial and painful error, we begin to understand what policies can assist in the development of third world countries, and those which do not work. And we have had a long experience in the difficult and often tragic effort to reach a condition of balance in the relationship among the nations, groups of nations, and competing social systems which now characterise world society.

We have rediscovered the truth which a famous English economist used to stress – that trees do not grow to the sky. Processes of imperial expansion do not necessarily go on for ever. Response and counter-response can bring them to a halt; in modern times, as in the past, imperial and even ideological dreams can be induced to fade.

For the last 29 years, this effort of dissuasion and persuasion has been the framework for all we have accomplished. It has preserved a realm of independence within which we could work together to advance the well-being of our own peoples, and contribute to the development of world society. That realm is by no means stable and secure. It may still be challenged, either from without or from within. But no one can deny that it was achieved during this period, and that it exists.

Clearly, the world that took shape during these 29 years was divided into two or perhaps three systems, in the sense of my topic here.

Some nations were ruled by Communist parties in a particular way. They were not hermetically sealed off from the rest of the world, as Tibet was once, or Japan, or the Yemen. But nonetheless, they were grouped into a system, one system at first, then a second, characterised by much closer and more intense relationships among the states within the system than those between that system and other nations or groups of nations.

A second grouping or system of nations consists of countries organised, generally speaking, as we are organised – as open and pluralist societies, built around one or another version of welfare capitalism. There is nearly complete freedom of economic activity among the states and groups of states within that system and indeed between them and those of the other systems. Those in exposed positions are linked to their neighbours, and to the stronger states, in a variety of security arrangements.

Finally, there is what we loosely call the third world, nations and societies of non-European culture, organised politically and socially in a variety of ways, but more and more dependent upon the United States, Japan and the industrialised nations of Europe for trade, investment and entrepreneurship, as well as for educational leadership and ultimate protection.

Do these three sets or groups of nations constitute a series of world systems, or a single world system? Nominally, they all accept the Charter of the United Nations. They participate in world trade, world transportation, and world communications, to varying degrees. There is some tourism, some exchange of students and teachers, some diplomacy as well among them.

Politically, of course there are walls of separation, and long-standing processes of rivalry. The phenomenon we call the cold war has been an important feature of the magnetic field of world politics for a long time. Some trace its origins to 1917, others its resumption, at least, to one or another date in the 1940s. There are as well other centres of intense rivalry, often exacerbated by

4

the intervention of the cold war. The conflicts of the Middle
East and of Southern and Eastern Asia are vivid instances of
this phenomenon.

Recently, several profound changes have taken place, or have
become visible, in the structure and dynamics of this set of
relationships. Those changes define the agenda for our governments as they seek to guide the adjustment of their policies to
the new condition of the world.

What are those changes, and how should they affect our conclusions about the future of our own relationships in the years
ahead?

The first, and perhaps the most important, is the
rapprochement between China and the United States. In many
ways, it is the most fundamental and most hopeful development
in the world political system since 1949. It is desirable to stress
the fact that the catalyst for the shift in Chinese policy was
China's perception of a Soviet threat, both from Siberia and from
South-East Asia. I emphasise the point not to disparage the
diplomacy of my own government, which I consider to have
been skilful and effective, but to bring out the essential nature
of this immensely significant event. China did not respond to
the inducement of American offers, put forward regularly for
many years, and pressed insistently during the last six. It did
respond, however, to the fear of a Soviet attack. The shift occurred
because the Chinese had finally reached the conclusion that the
mobilisation of some 50 Soviet divisions in Siberia, coupled with
the growing Soviet presence in South-East Asia, constituted a
danger to the régime, and to Chinese national autonomy, despite
their own formidable nuclear capability. The Soviet menace they
perceived is backed by huge military budgets and a political will
in the imperial mood. To such a danger at this point there was
only one possible response for the Chinese – association with the
United States.

The United States has wisely made it clear that while the hope
of deterring a Soviet attack on China is the heart of the new
relation between China and the United States, that relation
is not an alliance against the Soviet Union. The goal of American
policy is to achieve equally correct relations with both China
and the Soviet Union, based on reciprocal respect for the rules
of public order codified in the United Nations Charter. As China,
Japan, and the United States have now made abundantly clear,

they share a profound national interest in preventing Soviet hegemony in East Asia.

This new web of relationships involving China, the Soviet Union, the United States and Japan should, if well managed, assure restraint in Soviet as well as in Chinese policy. Indeed, we may be witnessing some consequences of these tensions both in the Middle East and in the negotiations with regard to European security and mutual and balanced force reductions. It is too soon to be confident, although it is perfectly legitimate to hope.

Some have written of this series of developments as if the world had become "multipolar". They seem to believe that the economic and political progress of China, of Japan, and of many other countries; the approaching formation of a political Europe; and the increasing strength of nations like Brazil and Mexico, and of Iran, Indonesia, Malaysia, and Taiwan, are bringing about a diffusion and dispersal of power in the world. They suggest that the day may be coming when nations would be assured against the risk of external attack simply by a natural law of harmonics or celestial gravitation. The large states would be the planets of the new system, each surrounded by its satellites. Each system would be kept in its proper orbit by fear of the responses of the others if it should stray, or break the rules. Some have spoken of a world of five autonomous centres of power – China, Japan, the Soviet Union, the European Community and the United States – in which the peace would be kept, hopefully, in the 18th century way, by the pure mechanics of the balance of power.

I do not read the lessons of recent history, nor those of the 18th century in this way. On the contrary, I perceive the world as becoming smaller, more tightly integrated, and more dangerous every day – so dangerous and so tightly integrated that it may soon have no alternative but genuine peace.

The reason why the balance of power worked better in the 19th than in the 18th century was the principle of the Concert of Europe to guide and control it. The Concert functioned diplomatically, and through occasional Congresses, to harmonise policy in the light of certain accepted principles. Politics are not governed by the laws of astronomy. We can hardly expect peace to come without sustained and well-conceived effort, especially on the part of the larger states.

The vision of autonomous regional blocs is not a genuinely viable alternative, at least for societies which wish to remain free and democratic in their internal life. The location of indispensable resources in the world, and the patterns of trade, do not readily permit a division of the world into blocs.

But there is an even deeper reason why I regard the notion of multipolarity as an illusion. In the context of world politics, the development of military technology, and particularly that of nuclear technology, makes the idea more and more obsolete. The geography of security no longer permits purely regional security arrangements. The case of China itself is a good illustration. Originally a Soviet ally, it became autonomous, and indeed a Soviet rival for the leadership of the world revolutionary impulse. But simple and primitive reasons of safety have forced it now into association with the United States, despite the ideological distaste, and guilt, this change must involve. As a result, the world is less multipolar, and far more decidedly bipolar, than it was before. This condition will continue, I should suppose, even when the Chinese acquire a firm second-strike capability, because it is nearly inconceivable that the nuclear weapon be used.

The logic of the Non-Proliferation Treaty implies wider pressures for ultimate political orientation in a similar sense. That Treaty does rest on assurances against nuclear blackmail. The import of those assurances work implacably against multipolarity, and towards interdependence.

The security problem for Western Europe and Japan is parallel to that of China, though far less dramatic for the moment. For the foreseeable future, even nuclear autonomy could not assure their security without the American nuclear guaranty.

It is this fact, instinctively understood, which requires the continued presence of American forces in Europe. If in 1949 anyone had predicted that 300,000 United States troops would be in or near Europe in 1974, he would have been committed to the nearest asylum. In 1949 the prevailing thought, both in Europe and in the United States, was that Europe would be rebuilt, a political Europe would be formed, and then the United States could withdraw its forces, leaving a strong, independent Europe to defend itself. That view has declined in importance on both sides of the Atlantic, although in both places there are still a few dreamers who cling to the vision of the prenuclear world. Both in European and in American eyes, however, the policy of maintaining American troops in Europe, not as a token but as a significant component of the military position of the Alliance, is unassailably correct, and is bound to remain so indefinitely, so long as Soviet policy is backed by its present military and para-military capacity, and remains in its present political posture.

The purpose of Western nuclear armament is to make certain that nuclear weapons will not be used, or brandished, in world politics. The territorial integrity and political independence of Western Europe are vital security interests of the United States, for manifest reasons. But the American nuclear umbrella over Europe has no plausibility without the continuing presence of substantial contingents of American conventional forces as well. Their presence is essential to give the Chiefs of Government viable non-nuclear choices in the event of new crises of the kind which have been so frequent since 1945 in Europe, and on the flanks of Europe. No one should responsibly propose forcing the Allies to choose between abandoning their vital interests and using the nuclear weapon in dealing with crisis situations of this order. In the nuclear world, deterrence must be effective at many levels of potential coercion.

It follows for both Europe and the United States that there is no possible alternative to the security policy of alliance. We share a common destiny, and should accept that fact as the first step in defining and organising our future relationships. As M. Michel Debré said recently, the alliance between Europe and the United States is based on "the nature of things", a phrase that draws its power not only from the influence of Lucretius, but from that of Montesquieu as well.

If M. Debré is right – and I should contend that he is – certain consequences follow.

First, we should deploy our military forces on the basis only of security considerations and completely neutralise their balance-of-payments implications. It is absurd to make security decisions on any but security grounds.

Secondly, if our security is indeed indivisible, we should do more to concert or at least to harmonise our foreign policies. We should have more influence on the course of events which affect our security if we could bring ourselves to address them together. This was the recommendation of the North Atlantic Council in the Harmel Resolution of 1967. But we have done far too little to carry out that Resolution, save on two or three of the most urgent questions. The greater burden of the security problem today genuinely requires a closer and more sustained concert of alliance policies on which all depend.

Third, we should approach all our common problems, economic and political alike, in the light of this over-arching fact, for none can be solved save through co-operative action. One weakness of our relationship in recent years has been a tendency to treat security problems on the one hand, and political and economic problems on the other, in isolation from each other. This is an approach which invites unilateralism, however self-defeating. There are many problems far too important to be left to the experts.

I fully realise that these conclusions are by no means universally popular or even palatable either in Europe or in the United States. Americans can readily understand the frustration of some Europeans who had hoped for complete autonomy once Europe was formed, but now realise that they must continue to work within the framework of interdependence with North America, as M. Jean Monnet has always steadfastly contended must be the case. For some Americans, too, there is a sense of frustration at the fading of their hopes that a united Europe could take care of its own defence, and allow us to withdraw once again into the isolationism of the happy past. That sense of frustration is compounded by the widespread American anguish, and anger, over the miseries we have endured in Korea and Vietnam. These parallel feelings of irritation are a great danger, far greater, in my opinion, than the risk of an American return to isolationism. I believe that fever has passed. But widespread American rage against the fate which has been thrust upon us is a fact, which could well express itself in a crude and destructive chauvinism, a positive preference for unilateral action. This attitude is the analogue of European political passivity, and equally dangerous. It should be the first task of statesmen, and of those who lead public opinion, to overcome these ailments of the spirit not only by faith, but by works.

Considerations of recent economic experience reinforce these conclusions about the future shape of world political systems. In this realm, too, we see not centrifugal processes of separation and multipolarity but centripetal trends towards closer and closer integration: in the first instance, integration among the economies of Western Europe, North America and Japan. We are witnessing as well an accelerating trend towards closer and more active relations between the integrated Western industrial economy as a whole and the economies both of developing and of Communist-controlled nations.

The fundamenal problem revealed by the events of the last few years is that the economies of the key industrial nations are now more completely and effectively integrated than their institutions for economic control, and particularly their institutions for monetary management. There have, of course, been errors of policy. But the primary cause of the recent cycle of recurrent economic crises is structural. The system is no longer governed by common rules. And, as presently organised, it can no longer handle the volume and complexity of international transfers required by the present and prospective volume of trade, investment, tourism, and security expenditure.

There is no blinking the fact that we have lost ground recently. But the cracks in the system must not be allowed to become chasms. We must not abandon the liberal economic policies of the last 25 years, and retreat into suicidal autarky, or retrogressive regionalism. Such steps would have more than economic costs. They would weaken the political foundation for our security relations.

For political as well as economic reasons, the effective consolidation of the monetary systems of the key industrial nations has now become indispensable. The current efforts at worldwide monetary reform through the IMF are promising, and should be supported and carried through promptly. But they may not, and probably cannot, accomplish the end I consider to be most urgently and immediately required – the development of a financial institution through which the main industrial nations could together manage their reserves, and harmonise their economic policies.

Stabilising the monetary system of the industrial nations is a condition precedent to success in every other realm of economic policy, and a condition precedent as well to the maintenance of our political cohesion. It is imprudent, to put it mildly, to expose our political and security relations to the stress of monetary chaos.

As a perceptive student of these problems has recently commented: "if the nuclear arrangements among [Europe, North America and Japan] break down, the result is likely to a dangerous political and economic fragmentation; equally, if the co-operative monetary and trade arrangements of the past quarter-century break down, the result is likely to be a dangerous political and military fragmentation."[1]

These pressures for closer and closer association are not confined to the circle of rich capitalist nations in the northern hemisphere.

[1] W. W. Rostow, "Leadership, Partnership and Disengagement", an address given in 1973.

As we have seen, China has sought to enter the circle, for funda-mental reasons of national security. And even the Soviet Union seems divided, as has happened several times in the past, between the advantages of economic and political co-operation with the West, and the appeal of its national and ideological ambitions.

Another phase of the same integrating process is taking place, a process with far-reaching implications for the shape of future world systems.

For the last 25 years, most industrial nations have suffered from a shortage of labour; during the same period, most of the developing nations have suffered from unemployment. In many of the developing nations, economic policy has been unable to mobilise either the capital or the entrepreneurship required to use its redundant labour force.

There are only two possible answers to this paradox: the industrialised nations which are short of labour can either import labour from the developing nations which have a labour surplus, or export capital, entrepreneurship, and management to them. On a large scale, the first course is socially untenable. The second, which has great promise, will require careful and co-operative control.

A large-scale new movement of private capital and manage-ment to the developing nations is already proceeding and pro-ceeding rapidly. Various proposals have been put forward in recent years for international agreements through which the developing countries – and indeed all countries – could be assured a larger and more regular flow of private capital and entrepreneurship. I regard the prompt negotiation and conclusion of a multilateral treaty that could assure this goal, on fair and agreed terms, as one of the most important tasks for world states-manship. The growth of most of the developing countries is inconceivable without it. So is the future of the industrial nations. I shall not pause here to discuss the economic and legal aspects of the process. From the point of view of my theme – future world systems – I call attention to the phenomemon as another factor making for the integration of supposedly distinct world systems.

In the end, then, I can offer no simple answer to the question put to me – What will be the shape of future world systems? Manifestly, a considerable part of the answer will depend on ourselves and on the governments who represent us.

If we allow the transitory irritations of the moment to erode our relationship, if our public opinion accepts hopes for realities, and if our governments adopt policies of weakness and division, in the field either of economic or of security policy, we shall deserve the catastrophes which follow.

If, on the contrary, we seek to make sure that public opinion keeps the real world steadily in focus, and that our governments pursue moderately rational policies in the future and carry them out about as well as they have carried out their policies in the past, then, I think, we can expect the world to continue to contract, under the pressures of technology, economic necessity, and fear, and at an accelerating pace.

The real question before us, I conclude, is not whether the future world system will be multipolar, or pentagonal, or even triangular, but whether the world is now becoming so dangerous, and so interdependent, as to require even the Soviet Union to accept the code of law and aspiration embodied in the Charter of the United Nations. The true acceptance and enforcement of that code, I am convinced, is necessary to the possibility of security and development in the long run, for our nations, and for the world society to which we inescapably belong.

But my crystal ball cannot tell me whether this result, devoutly to be sought, will actually be achieved in the near or not so near future. All I can conclude is that our policy must rest on the hope that this final shift from bipolarity to unity will come about, and the working assumption that it has not yet been achieved.

COMMENT by Sicco L. Mansholt

I agree that there will be a shift – let us hope there will be a shift – from multipolarity to unity, a united world. But in the world we are now living in we cannot transpose past bipolarity, especially in our defence systems, into a system for the future. We are living in a world of multipolarity. I believe that at this moment multipolarity is a necessary evil.

NATO, too, is a necessary evil: it is an organisation for defence that I prefer to national defence. After two world wars created by national defence, we have to learn. And so NATO, for me, is an organisation for preventing national outbursts. But let us not forget that there is a chance to strengthen polarisation without these organisations; and we have to see what is needed in the world to counterbalance this necessary evil of military alliances. We need a balance in military power at this very moment, but what we want is to create a situation where we can discuss disarmament, where we can discuss reduction of arms, and find a way for a lasting peace.

But more and more I am convinced that the real issues are not there. The real issues of today will be overwhelmingly influenced by two elements. One is the poor and the rich in the world; and the other is not less important, but overwhelmingly important, and it is the limit to growth.

We have to see our future organisation of mankind in the light of these two elements; and we all know that until now we have not succeeded.

There is very fast integration between the key industrialised countries including Japan, but from a human point of view we are dividing the poor part of the world from the rich part of the world. Anyone who has taken part in the conferences of Delhi and Santiago knows the great unrest in the world due to the fact that the rich are getting richer and the poor are getting poorer compared to the rich. Even the President of the World Bank, Robert MacNamara, has made it very clear that we are on the wrong road. We have no organisation and no system to solve the problem today. We are, in this field, very clumsy. The question is not only a question of bringing out capital and entrepreneurship to those countries: it is a question of the system of society. First of all, I ask myself, "Can we solve these problems, together with the developing countries, by means of our system, of our world system of production and consumption?" I think not. Can it be done by liberal trade? No. Can it be done by liberal capital flow? No. By liberal consumption and production? In my opinion, no. Is the increase of our gross national product really of interest to those countries in the process of development?

Of course, it is always said that we have to grow, and in our system we have to achieve the highest level of demand and production if we are to benefit the countries in the process of development. But reality is contrary to that: it can be proved.

Secondly, what we are doing in our world system, is to avoid other than more or less capitalistic systems in the developing world. Is it wise? No, in my opinion, no. With the limits of the growth in our world, the limits of the potential availability of material resources, in food, in ecological and biological balance, I cannot see that four-fifths of the world population can live in the same system as we are living in. We have to consider that. Is China an example how it should be done? I do not know: I have not been to China; but I am very much impressed by some world experts who have said there is a possibility of another society, living on less material welfare but happily living with a great population and not making a copy of our world system, in the less developed countries.

So we have to rethink our world systems. This is still more difficult when we know that in the coming 28 years, let us say until the year 2000, when with exponential speed there will be fundamental changes in the relation between demands and resources. The limits are unmistakable.

Take food. Already today the average food supply in the world since 1968 is going down. We cannot master the problem with the methods we are applying now. Take energy. Food is not a problem in America or Europe, but energy can be a problem, and for that reason we are dealing with the problem: but we should deal with food problems as well.

To seek to solve these problems still in alliances of Europe, America, and Japan is to evade the real difficulty. The real difficulty is in three-fifths of the world population, in the poor countries who have NO supply of oil. What will be the situation of India, of Pakistan, or of all African countries, with a supply that is, let us say, directed by an Atlantic, Japanese and OPEC treaty? What will happen now that prices are increased, and if they are increased still further? What will be the terrible situation for these poorer countries who need energy, who need basic material for their survival?

The unbalanced biological system will be a growing danger. As a farmer I have the greatest concern about what is happening in Western Europe, in the United States, in Africa, in Indonesia at this very moment, as far as the biological system is concerned; and yet what are we doing? What is there in our world system today that prevents the deterioration of the world ecological system of the future? Nothing. Everyone who was at the conference in Stockholm knows how clumsy and how poor are our methods. One hundred million dollars has been set aside – for studies. So if we are speaking of the new world systems, we have to have other horizons because these are the problems that are overwhelming. Of course, if we want an integrated world, we must be clear that it means sacrifices from us. It means a world of greater equality, not following the system that we have today. I think if we want to integrate the world, and come to the conclusion that what is available in the world has to be divided and distributed, then we must follow other policies than unlimited growth, look for other types of growth, and perhaps stop growth here in the west and north and other parts of the world. If not, in my opinion, then catastrophe will be upon us and perhaps we have not even to wait 30 years. To say this is not to panic; it is only seeing the situation and saying what can we do?

There is no possibility of action on a national basis, not even on a regional basis. Even when Europe is politically united, it cannot do so. Here, we have to work together, to develop programmes looking to the future of mankind. There is not any question in my opinion that the survival of mankind depends more on our success in mastering these great challenges of equality and living conditions in the world, than on balances of power. Otherwise, there will not be any balance of power in the future. We must accept a future world system that provides much greater cohesion; where a policy can be decided and executed in common; where, for instance, fair distribution of goods is normal; where discipline in respecting world resources is the basis of action; and where equality in general is the goal.

That means another system of organising the world. Perhaps we have a go by means of regional organisations: I very much welcome the prospects of European unification, political union, European government, a European parliament. In South America, Africa, the Far East, people are creating economic and social blocks, creating systems which correspond to a real necessity for preserving mankind – the organisation of decentralisation by means of regional blocks. But we also need some one organisation with decisive power and executing power, such for instance as Professor Berrigan has already many times proposed for the United Nations specialised organisations. That can be done in the food sector, at this very moment; but FAO is a very weak organisation. But if it were turned into a system of power, then I think that we could master a great deal of the problem. The same sort of thing has to be done to preserve nature, the ecological balance, the biological balance; to master the problems of material resources, to master inequality between poor and rich. I hope that we shall be forced to do all this; but it means perhaps other social systems. Personally, I do not believe that in a capitalistic world or in a capitalistic Europe or America, we can succeed. We have to adopt other systems of production and consumption. It is for that reason that I think there is a great chance of a unified world, provided that we do not come to that unified world along dead straight lines. If we do, I greatly fear that all efforts at balances of power will fail and the rich will get richer and the poor will get poorer.

Chapter XIX

New Openings in East–West Relations

JENS OTTO KRAG

A MILESTONE IN POST-WAR political relations between East and West was reached on 22 November 1972, when representatives of 34 European and North American nations met around the conference table in Finland's capital Helsinki. For the first time, since the war and the immediate post-war years had drawn a sharp dividing line through the middle of Europe, an assembly of all nations interested in the destiny of Europe could take steps to open a broad dialogue on some of the problems which are dividing Europe and which we have had to live with for so many years. To me, whose lot it has been to live through the period of the cold war and to have been active in politics during a large part of it, it was indeed a great satisfaction eventually to see the dawn of the day when a realistic East–West dialogue – and not merely exchanges of propaganda slogans – could get started in a multilateral forum created for that particular purpose.

A long process of political ripening and many years of painstaking diplomacy preceded the solemn but unceremonious opening of the consultations in Helsinki, the so-called Multilateral Preparatory Talks on a Conference on Security and Co-operation in Europe.

Outward manifestations of these developments since their modest start some ten years ago have been a great many contacts across what was once known as the Iron Curtain. And these contacts, which my country was among the first ones to establish, have been followed up by a number of agreements of varying scope in economic, cultural, industrial and other fields. The *Ostpolitik* generated with so much vigour and boldness by Federal Chancellor Brandt prepared the ground for a comprehensive set of agreements designed to normalise relations with the East including the German–Soviet and the German–Polish treaties of 1970, the Four-Power Berlin Agreement of September 1971 and, last but not least, the so-called *Grundvertrag* between

303

the two German states in an attempt to establish a *modus vivendi*, on the one hand recognising the political realities of the German situation, including the fact that the Federal Republic and the DDR are two states in one nation.

Equal in importance to these various treaties on the German problem – which also have had the important effect of making it possible for the countries of Western Europe to normalise their relations with the DDR – are the agreements between the United States and the Soviet Union resulting from the *rapprochement* of recent years, including the significant treaty on limitations of the nuclear arms race. And the preliminary high-water mark of these developments was the accord reached to start preparations for a conference on security and co-operation in Europe and to hold talks almost at the same time on mutual and balanced force reductions in Europe.

The past few years have thus seen many examples of openings in East–West relations; and there is no reason to believe that we are at the end of the road. The Conference on European Security will undoubtedly turn out to be merely one element, though a very important one, towards the gradual removal of the artificial barriers between East and West in Europe.

If we look at the new pattern of international relations which has emerged in the past few years we should bear in mind, however, that this is but an outward manifestation of something much more deep-seated – a growing recognition and understanding of the fact that in this age of nuclear stalemate co-existence and co-operation are the only keys to survival. But this understanding rests on one decisive factor: the existing East–West balance – politically and militarily – and the confidence it gives the individual countries, in East and West alike, that their security is reasonably safeguarded. This, in the final analysis, is not so much a question of greater understanding of the motives and intentions of the other side – although such understanding, of course, greatly facilitates co-existence and co-operation. Motives and intentions may vary or take on different shapes with changing leaders, and so they do not provide a sufficiently solid basis for safeguarding a country's security. The crux of the matter remains the balance, call it the balance of power or, by a term which I do not favour, the balance of terror – the awareness that neither party can alter the basic factors which determine the different political, economic and social systems of East and West. This is not to say that the balance is a static phenomenon; it can be created at higher or lower levels. And there is undoubtedly some tolerance, a range of variation within which the overall picture will remain unaffected. Also changes may occur, as seems to be the case at present, from a bipolar to a multipolar balance with all the uncertainties this entails.

However, it remains a fact that the chief elements of the current balance are the Soviet Union with its allies, the United States and Western Europe, of which Western Europe, taken in isolation, and speaking in purely military terms, is the weakest one, but in the midst of a transformation which definitely will give it progressively greater weight in world politics. In this context I should like to point to NATO as an element of fundamental importance to the balance and, in consequence, an indispensable factor in the conduct of a successful policy of *détente*. Peace is better off in a organised than in an unorganised world. This does not imply that the North Atlantic Alliance should be viewed as a static factor; NATO will also have to adapt itself to the new realities, and has in fact shown a remarkable ability to do so. But we must be careful to keep this adaptation within the tolerances of a reasonable East–West balance.

Other important factors to be taken into consideration are the United States' presence in Europe and the strengthening of Western European collaboration and cohesion. It cannot be denied that the events in Vietnam have generated a widespread and deep going animosity against the United States in Europe and consequently also against the United States as an ally of Western Europe. However, I cannot but warn strongly against placing exaggerated weight on one particular aspect of the foreign policy of the United States although I earnestly share the criticism of the United States' involvement in Vietnam.

On 1 January 1973, the European Community was enlarged by three countries: The United Kingdom, Ireland and Denmark. As a result, the Community will increasingly come to play a greater role in the world's economic development. It remains a fact that the EC and its enlargement has strengthened Western Europe. Nevertheless, the United States' presence in Europe will in the foreseeable future remain of undiminished importance to the East–West balance. However different Western Europe and the United States may be, they are nonetheless societies that are united by close ties, for historical, cultural and economic reasons, and by virtue of common political interests in a great many fields. A strengthening of the centrifugal forces which are making themselves slightly felt between Europe and the United States would, I think, be greatly detrimental not only to the direct relations across the Atlantic, but also by generating uncertainty in a world in which, as I just mentioned, the foundation of *détente* is the assurance of everybody that security is safeguarded.

After this review of various elements of the current stability I shall revert to the Conference on Security and Co-operation in Europe, the preparations for it, and the expectations we may reasonably place in it. We must realise that the Conference can only be a success if it leaves the East–West balance unaffected. This alone implies that the time has not yet come for a new and revolutionary system of relations between European states. The main task of the Conference will be on one hand to re-establish, amplify and secure the strict implementation of certain fundamental principles governing relations between states and, on the other, to give new impetus to co-operation and contact in human, cultural, environmental, economic, and other fields. And that is, in fact, the main content of the agenda being considered by the 34 countries in Helsinki. Thus, the short-term political goals of the Conference are actually rather modest, and I quite agree with those who warn against overplaying the importance of the Conference. And yet I strongly support the idea of holding a conference, primarily because I am convinced that the preparations for the Conference, the actual holding of the Conference and its continuation, in whatever form that might be, will assist in promoting the process of political ripening which could gradually consolidate and further develop the idea of co-existence and co-operation. Within the limits set by the desire to respect the political, economic and social structures of participating states there would unquestionably be room for closer contacts and increased mutual understanding. The Conference offers an opportunity of such developments, and we should grasp that opportunity.

Now it is a well-known fact that on the Western side it is considered essential that the Conference should provide a basis for increased human contacts and for increased dissemination of information. This viewpoint is a fundamental element of the Western ideals. I agree, therefore, that this item should be given considerable emphasis in the Western list of wishes. In fact the Danish Government, as you know, has proposed an outline for the discussion at the Conference of these questions. At the same time I must, however, caution against pushing these ideas too far or being over-optimistic as to how far they can be translated into practice at present. In that respect it is immaterial that it never was the intention of the Western countries that increased human contacts should undermine the Eastern systems. That would be contrary to the fundamental view that the prerequisites of *détente* are balance, stability and security within national boundaries. What is more important is that the Eastern countries seriously fear that such contacts would undermine their systems. It would be realistic to recognise that too much pressure on our part in this respect would have to be paid for by the peoples of Eastern Europe. Neither in the short nor in the long run would such developments be desirable.

What to me is the central aspect of the problem of increased human contacts is that we should strive at gradual developments in this field, in step with the increased understanding which I believe will develop little by little. Notwithstanding the great differences between East and West, the truth is, I think, that the two systems are not so far apart today as they used to be. "Capitalism" in the Western world is not what it used to be, nor are the societies in Eastern Europe static ones. Although I know that the "Theory of Convergence" in East–West relations is anathema in the East I nevertheless believe it to be basically a sound one.

The Security Conference will have before it a wide range of subjects, and its results will probably largely be in the form of compromises achieved by the weighing of many elements. That might open up possibilities which, if the elements were considered in isolation, would not be within reach. However, by and large I do not expect the Conference to lead to fundamental changes in East–West relations, at least in the shorter perspective. But in my view the Conference and the preparations for it are of importance also seen from another angle – namely that the Europeans have now for the first time been afforded the opportunity to speak with weight in a debate on the future of their own continent – a debate which to some extent was previously conducted over their heads, directly between the Soviet Union and the United States. This is no criticism of the United States. I have no reason to believe that European interests have been disregarded, and past procedures are very understandable if we recognise the realities of power politics and the fact that there does not so far exist any real European political identity. In this respect I think it is fair to say already at this stage of the preparatory talks that new vistas are opening up. First of all it is a remarkable feature how easily the nine countries of Western Europe who are members of the EC have been able to co-ordinate their positions at the MPT, thus in many respects showing the way ahead. It is, however, equally remarkable that this has in no way imposed strains on relations with the other partners in the North Atlantic Alliance nor with the other participants in the talks in Helsinki.

To sum up, let me say that I attach less importance to the immediate outcome of the Security Conference. Viewed in isolation, the results will probably be fairly modest although we should insist, in my view, on some concrete improvements of the present situation. The Conference itself, the preparations for it as well as the steps which will probably be taken to follow it up should rather be seen as essential factors in a lengthy process of gradually bringing East and West in Europe closer to each other. To use the words of Federal Chancellor Willy Brandt: "Über ein geregeltes Nebeneinander zu einem Miteinander zu kommen." The Conference idea is in itself a valuable opening in East–West relations. But the Conference will not – and should not – alter the balance which is the central political prerequisite for a durable *détente*.

An analysis of that element, of the currents that affect it and of the minor or major variations which these currents bring about or may be expected to bring about is therefore, I feel, more important than an analysis of the Conference itself.

COMMENT *by Sir Bernard Burrows*

A curious thing has happened to the discussion of the European security problem and East–West relations during the last couple of years. If one looks back even a few years at all the things that have been said, not only on the Western side but also on the Eastern side, about the problem of European security, up till fairly recently there was always the phrase about "the German problem being at the heart of the difficulties, the main cause of tension in Europe, and the need for German reunification being one of the prime reasons why new systems had to be found". Now, thanks to the agreements referred to above, while that problem in the very long run has not been solved, nevertheless a great deal of the tension has been taken out of it.

This has at least two results. One is that this fact and other developments have removed the main source of world tension and East–West tension from Europe to other areas outside. And one of the questions one asks oneself, if one accepts that, is this: Is it right that Western Europe should play so little part in what happens outside? Is it right that the competition for instance, should be left to the two or three superpowers, with Europe, except economically, playing very little part? Is there a danger of European isolationism, instead of, or in addition to, the fears of isolationism in another quarter that are so frequently mentioned? Secondly, if what has been so long described as the main source of tension in Europe, namely the German question, has been to a large extent and for some time defused, perhaps we should look more carefully at the question, what then does in fact divide us in Europe? What is the East–West question remaining in Europe? If we do not try to define this, we shall find many people, as they do now, and many more in the future, saying, "Well, now that seems settled, what is the point of having an alliance? Why do the Americans have to stay?", and so on.

So what is the remaining threat that makes us feel that some reassurance of this kind is necessary? I suppose, in very brief terms, the threat is that by the use of political pressure, based partly on superiority of conventional forces, the freedom of action of West European governments could be restricted, if they allowed this pressure to be successful – that is to say, if they allowed their defences to fall below a certain minimum level of efficiency. This is the tendency that can usefully be described in a way that some people find objectionable, as "Finlandisation" – the risk that the countries of Western Europe, if they were divided or if they allowed their defence position to be too weak, would have their freedom of decision in international affairs, and perhaps even in internal affairs, restricted – not by direct military invasion, which is less likely than perhaps once it was, but by this more subtle use of a preponderant military position for political pressure and blackmail.

We quite rightly defend the right to have differences between Western Europe and America, within a system which we broadly accept as being necessary: but the risk is that if we abandoned that system we should no longer have that right to have differences with the power that gave us the security reassurance. As has been pointed out, there is no need for a new and revolutionary system of security in Europe. This can be supported by noticing that the agreements which have been made, SALT, and the agreements following on the *Ostpolitik*, have been made across the alliance boundaries and without disturbing them. It used to be said that in order to make progress in these relationships it was necessary to have a new system of collective security in Europe. And there is still talk in some quarters of the disillusion of the blocs and joint guarantees of European security by the two superpowers. But it is significant that these very important agreements have been made without entering into any new system of that kind. Certainly a new system should be discussed, but it has not been proved that this is necessary in order to make very significant agreements reducing tension.

Thirdly, if we are to remain with the present system of security, safeguarded by the two alliances, obviously the main task is to reduce the level of confrontation between them. We have on the table MBFR. I think personally we shall find that extremely difficult, and I think we need to ask how important it is, in the context of American troop presence in Europe. How long will MBFR last as an argument that can be used in the internal American debate? If it is not going to last indefinitely, where does that leave us in that debate? Ought we really to be discussing force levels in a Western forum before we get into an East–West one – if it is not too late?

I think, however, that we should not be afraid of a continuing organisation for East–West contact arising from the conference. That indeed might be one of its more important results, with the condition only that this should not interfere with the development of greater unification on the Western side, in whatever form we want that to be.

Finally, if MBFR proves very long or very difficult, or in addition to it, we should also not be afraid to look at one other old idea, which was discredited at the time, of zones of limited armament, or controlled armament of some kind. In the form in which these used to be put forward, as nuclear-free zones, they made little sense because they gave advantage to the side which had the greater conventional forces; and nuclear weapons could affect them from outside. But perhaps in a more limited form, as narrower zones, through which no military movement should take place, on frontiers, as part of the measures to safeguard against surprise attack, they merit some further examination.

COMMENT *by Robert Pfaltzgraff*

The CSCE, as has been suggested, is increasingly concerned with the issue of co-operation rather than security *per se*. Yet what comes out of CSCE is going to be very important for European security. I believe that it is necessary to link CSCE to MBFR and also to SALT. It is also important to look at CSCE within the context of the general changes which are occurring in the international system.

First of all, the emergence of new potential centres of power in Europe and Asia, in particular Japan and China; and in particular the development of a tri-polar relationship among the United States, the Soviet Union and China. What does this mean for European security? We must also consider more particularly the structure of European or Atlantic security that we envisage for the next decade. And we also must look at the respective roles to be played by the United States and Western Europe in that security framework. And finally, in the context of the European security issue, we must examine the relationship between CSCE and other sets of negotiations which the United States and the West Europeans will be engaged in in the next few years.

My fear is that we are entering into a series of negotiations without having answered such questions. It seems to me that the danger we face is that the negotiations may become an end in themselves, rather than a means towards an end. I think that we must therefore give some greater thought specifically to the context within which we envisage the evolution of this European or Atlantic security environment.

The international environment of the 1970s has several very important characteristics, which are of relevance to East–West negotiations in Europe. There is the gradual transformation of the international system, and in particular the development of a new phase in Sino–American relationships in a period of continuing Sino–Soviet tensions. There is the emergence of strategic parity, however one wishes to define it, between the United States and the Soviet Union. What does this mean for the broad European security environment? And then there is the enunciation in the Nixon doctrine itself, of a framework calling for a partnership with other states, and especially with Western Europe, an area which might well assume a greater share of its own defence, and reduce over time the extent of the U.S. commitment.

These are some of the issue areas which I believe have direct relevance to European security and in particular to the question of the CSCE. For example, if we speak about the gradual transformation of the international system from bi-polarity to a form of tri-polarity, the question is what does the changing Sino–American relationship mean for the Soviet–American relationship? I would suggest that the changed Sino–American relationship has at least two specific implications for European security. First it may strengthen China in its dealings with the

Soviet Union, and increase the future security problems for the Soviet Union posed by China. This is an important problem which will enter into the European security framework of the next decade. Secondly, the heightening of Soviet concern with the problems of China by the end of this decade will probably lead the Soviet Union gradually to seek to diminish the problems posed by Western Europe. There is thus likely to be a Soviet interest in a gradual neutralisation of Western Europe, and conversely a Chinese interest in a strengthened Western Europe.

Where does this leave the Soviet policy *vis-à-vis* CSCE? CSCE, from the Soviet standpoint, then serves the purpose of increasing the neutralisation of Western Europe. At the same time in the Nixon doctrine, in American foreign policy, there should logically be a growing interest in the strengthening of a West European counterpart to the Soviet Union. Therefore American and Soviet interests in European security are likely to remain largely divergent. This makes the continuation of a U.S.–European security link vital, both to Europe and to the United States; we have not yet really faced the issue of updating our conception of European security. If we were to do so, we might find much broader support.

There is, moreover, another problem which I think needs to be brought out much more specifically in the context of European security: the problem of linking the MBFR, the CSCE and SALT 2. How do the various sets of interlinked negotiations in which we are about to be engaged relate to these broader European Atlantic security questions? This is something that I doubt that either the United States or Europe has done adequately. We need to develop a much clearer idea of the relationship between negotiations and the security concept appropriate for the 1970s. The negotiations in which we will be engaged in the next few years will be designed, I hope, to enable the United States and Western Europe to achieve several important goals; but the overriding goal must be the preservation of a strengthening Western Europe which is independent of any Soviet aspirations for Finlandisation or hegemony, however defined. In this context there are several very important considerations which should be kept in mind.

First of all, we have the problem of co-ordination among several sets of negotiations – even within the American foreign affairs establishment. This in itself is going to be a major problem. Secondly, how do we develop co-ordination simply among the sets of negotiations? How do we know which issue in one set has important implications for issues in another set of negotiations? SALT and MBFR are a particular case in point here. And then, how do we develop co-ordination as appropriate between the United States and Western Europe? Perhaps we need a new Atlantic mechanism, specifically for this purpose; at the very least we should subsume this within one of the Atlantic mechanisms which now exist. There has of course been some approach towards agreement among the West European states, in the Davignon Committee's work for example in CSCE. But this needs to be broadened into SALT and into MBFR. Here I see a series of very formidable problems arising. We are not agreed, for example, about the scope and the general nature of MBFR. Is MBFR to be limited to a token agreement? What is to be the ratio between indigenous station forces in an MBFR agreement? What is to be the linkage? What possible linkages exist between MBFR and CSCE? Between MBFR and SALT 2? Here are areas where we have just begun to address ourselves to important problems. How, finally, does one ensure that agreements are worked out in CSCE which are self-enforcing – in which violations can easily be spotted? From a Soviet perspective, CSCE is designed, as I see it, to change the European environment to one in which peaceful co-existence, Soviet style, can be developed. How is it to be ensured that we do not have a milieu which can easily be changed by the Soviet Union? Moreover, in SALT 2 we need to resist any efforts on the part of the Soviet Union to include nuclear-free zones; and here I would disagree slightly with the view expressed above. I believe that we must avoid, if at all possible, the forward-based system issue. I think we must avoid getting ourselves into a situation where we agree to "no first use" in a nuclear strategy for Europe; and finally, I think we must avoid a situation in which we agree to no transfer of technology. The difficulty is that we are entering negotiations before we have established the positions that we need to take in them, before we have looked at the goals that ought to be overriding in our security environment for the 1970s. But what we need most of all in the European–Atlantic security environment of the 1970s is a reaffirmation of the U.S. security guarantee under conditions of parity, however it is defined. We need, for example, agreement within NATO in advance of MBFR about the general force level that we are prepared to maintain in Europe over the next few years. And in return for such long-term agreements by the United States, we need to obtain agreement from the Europeans about burden-sharing. It is this, I believe, that should underwrite security arrangements, and of course negotiations, on the issues which we are discussing with the Soviet Union.

Chapter XX

The Global Triangle: The Changing Power Balance in Asia and its Consequences for the Foreign Policy of the Atlantic Nations

ZBIGNIEW BRZEZINSKI

THIS CHAPTER RESTS ON two premises, each of which will be developed more fully later on:

1. The post-World-War-II era of international politics, dominated by the primacy and centrality of American–Soviet conflicts has ended;

2. Asia has replaced Europe as the locale of conflicts potentially most dangerous to international order.

These two premises, in their turn, lead to our major policy conclusion, also to be developed more fully in the course of the argument:

That the promotion both of international stability and of social progress in Asia urgently requires the fostering of deliberate political consultation – and eventually of political co-operation – between the most advanced sectors of the emerging global community namely Japan, (West) Europe, and America.

It is, of course, extremely difficult to pinpoint the beginnings and ends of historical eras. History is like a river, an ever-changing and yet continuing process. Nonetheless, it is possible to identify historical watersheds, which delimit phases in international affairs dominated by a discernible pattern of relations. One such watershed occurred on 22 May 1947 with the signing by President Truman of a Congressional bill committing the United States to support Greece and Turkey against Soviet designs. The President took advantage of the occasion to proclaim it to be the American purpose "to support free peoples who are resisting attempted subjugation by armed minorities or by outside pressures". The post-war era, dominated by the primacy of the American–Soviet rivalry over all other aspects of international affairs, was on.

That era lasted until 1972. President Nixon's trip to China signalled U.S. reliance on the new and much more complex Soviet–Chinese–American triangular interplay as a major means for offsetting increased Soviet military power, while his subsequent visit to Moscow indicated that both he and his Soviet counterparts were now prepared both to codify their competitive relationship and to balance it by expanding co-operative ties. These new ties were to be both of a functional nature (e.g. arms control, scientific collaboration, expansion and trade) and of a regional character (e.g. European political and security talks). The willingness of the two rival powers to develop these ties marked the fading of the centrality of the American–Soviet competition.[1] Indeed, by a striking historical coincidence, President Nixon landed in Moscow exactly 25 years to the day after the promulgation of the Truman Doctrine, and this gave added symbolism to his 22 May 1972 statement that "we meet at a moment when we can make peaceful co-operation a reality".

Though it is highly probable that in the American–Soviet relationship competitive aspects will continue to outweigh the co-operative ones, it is already a fact that for each of the major powers other concerns now loom as large as earlier had been the case with their head-on rivalry. Thus the United States will remain the Soviet Union's principal rival, but China may now well be seen by Russia as the source of the greatest potential threat. The Soviet Union still remains America's principal rival but the problem of structuring stable and mutually beneficial relationships with Europe and with Japan is emerging as the central and most complicated preoccupation of American foreign policy-makers and of American economic leadership.

Indeed, the last few years have seen a basic revolution in the relations among all of the major powers of the world: the United States and the Soviet Union altered significantly the nature of their relations, so did the United States and China, the United States and Japan, Japan and China, the Soviet Union and West Germany, and – in some respects also – the United States and Western Europe. All of that reinforces the proposition that a

[1] This argument is developed more fully in this writer's "How The Cold War Was Played", *Foreign Affairs*, October 1972.

new phase has begun in international politics, a phase significantly and qualitatively different from the phase of bipolarity and bipolar hostility.

Perhaps the best way to conceptualise this new phase is to see it as involving two crucial triangular relationships, with each triangle involving a somewhat different mix of co-operative and competitive elements. The first triangle, involving a complex interplay between Washington, Moscow, and Peking, is the predominantly competitive one, though lately co-operative elements have been introduced into it as well. The principal stakes here are primarily political, and the crucial resources are still military, though both economic and ideological factors are also involved. In military power the U.S.A. and the U.S.S.R. find themselves in a bipolar checking relationship, while their political relations involve a very complex triangular interplay. The continuing need here is to make the competitive relationship more stable, less threatening to world peace, especially given the nature of nuclear weapons.

The other triangle involving Washington, Tokyo, and Brussels (or Europe) is fundamentally co-operative, though lately competitive factors have surfaced in it and have come to the fore in public and governmental discussions. The crucial stakes here are primarily economic, though political issues are not far beneath the surface; the resources involved are mainly financial, while ideological factors are by and large absent, with the three parties sharing a basic commitment to democratic processes. The obvious need here is to reduce the element of conflict, to fortify the reality of economic interdependence with a higher awareness of common political destiny, and thus to make this triangle the foundation stone of wider international co-operation.

These two triangles, as the chart overleaf indicates, are accompanied also by secondary triangular relationships, either already in the making or potentially significant for international affairs. There can be little doubt that the Soviet Union would like to promote a somewhat looser relationship between America and Europe, and that much of its diplomatic activity is still designed to attain that end.[2] Similarly, it is quite possible that in the years ahead conflicting American and Japanese views could

---

[2] Significant in this connection is a thoughtful paper by academician N. N. Inozemtsev, "Les Relations Internationales en Europe dans les années 70" (delivered in Varna, Bulgaria, October 1972) which subtly propagates a "pan-European" alternative to European–American relationships.

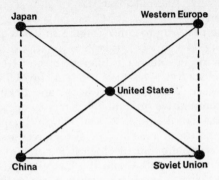

develop over such politically sensitive issues as Taiwan or Korea, and produce a more complicated interplay between Washington, Tokyo and Peking.

In any case, it is submitted here that a better insight into current global reality is conveyed through the use of the above two triangles than if one attempts to analyse it either in terms of the earlier primacy of the American–Soviet cold war, or – as lately suggested by President Nixon – in terms of a traditional balance of power among the major units, in which there are neither permanent allies nor permanent foes. So much, then, for the first major premise.

The struggle for European hegemony – a political extension by a quarter of a century of World War II – has so far been a stand-off. Each side has retained what it had gained in that war, though the respective relations between the two superpowers and their European associates have become in each case somewhat looser and more complex. On both sides, moreover, multilateral institutions have grown and there is no reason to expect that their role will decline. Both sides, finally, in spite of their conflict, have remained tacitly agreed that Germany should remain divided, with the Germans – at least for the time being – now formally acquiescing to this reality. The entry of the two German states into the U.N. will legitimate internationally the European *status quo*.

The situation in Asia is rather different. It is more fluid, more uncertain and complex. Unlike the two Germanies, neither Korea accepts its division and the Koreans, though still divided ideologically, desire reunification. They do so with a sense of passionate nationalism and a strong resentment against the arbitrary division of their country. The Japanese have yet to find their own sense of political direction and – in contrast to the European nations – they lack a larger framework for a positive political expression of their yearning for a larger role. The Chinese give every indication of fearing Soviet intervention, while their domestic stability is clouded by uncertainties associated with the problem of political succession. The ultimate disposition of Taiwan is still to be settled and conflicts in the Taiwanese straits could still occur. The future of South-East Asia remains ambiguous, and it will still take time – and probably more blood – finally to resolve the bitter Vietnamese civil war. India, having become the dominant South Asian power, sees itself as a political rival to China, though its internal social, economic and political weakness contain the seeds of major instabilities. Finally, the Soviet Union, concerned about the longer-range implications of Chinese power, is actively engaged in diplomatic efforts to contain China by fostering closer relations with India, and by cautiously cultivating the Japanese, while simultaneously striving to reduce the American presence in South-East Asia and the Far East.

It is thus premature to speak of a new balance of power in Asia. The situation is essentially in flux, and its eventual outcome simply cannot be predicted. The area is dominated by volatile nationalist passions and – with the notable exception of Japan – by intense efforts on the part of the states concerned to build up their military forces. This militarisation of the region (with its concomitant domestic political spin-off) tends to conflict with effective economic development, thereby sharpening underlying social tensions, and posing more generally the spectre of social fragmentation in some of the Asian countries.

Within this general context of Asian uncertainty, three major threats could challenge international order: first, an intensified Sino–Soviet conflict; secondly, a nuclear proliferation in Asia; and thirdly, a sudden change in the role of Japan.

Present Soviet policy seeks the grand objective of attaining a preponderant political position – though not domination – on the vast Eurasian continent. In the West, this means the deliberate promotion of the gradual neutralisation of Western Europe, while taking advantage of the *détente* to redress Soviet economic weaknesses. In the South, it means the consolidation of the Soviet presence in the Middle East and the expansion of Soviet influence in India. In the East it means the careful cultivation of Japan, and the containment and isolation of China, while perhaps also waiting for an opportune moment to influence the course of internal Chinese politics.

It is possible that Sino–Soviet differences may subside after the death of Mao Tse-Tung. The Soviet leaders appear to be counting on this. Nevertheless, existing differences have already prompted a massive build-up in the respective Soviet and Chinese forces poised on the Sino–Soviet frontier, while ideological and nationalist passions on both sides of the frontier serve further to inflame existing disagreements. It is no exaggeration to say that the major portion of the Chinese defence budget is at present devoted to preparations primarily directed at warding off a Soviet military intervention. On the Soviet side, the bulk of military expenditure with regard to conventional forces involves the Soviet Far Eastern Army, with the single largest concentration of the Soviet ground forces deployed in the Far East. It has grown from approximately 3 divisions a few years ago to some 49 divisions now. There is considerable evidence indicating that Soviet strategic forces have been partially redeployed against China.

Even short of direct Soviet intervention which would initiate a major war, such a concentration of forces creates tensions, which could become quite dangerous in the event of major political instability within one of the parties involved. The temptation to intervene indirectly, by tacit threats, by granting covert support to favoured rivals for power, even by economic bribery, is likely to be especially high once Mao has gone, and it could make the Far Eastern scene more unstable.

The quest for a viable international order in Asia may be further complicated in the years ahead by the other two potential threats already mentioned: the possibility of nuclear proliferation, and the uncertainty surrounding Japan's emerging international role. These two issues are, in part, interrelated. India and Japan are the potential Asian nuclear powers, though the mix between the political predisposition to obtain nuclear weapons and the actual technical and financial capacity to do so is quite different in each case.

Indian success in its war against Pakistan has stimulated a heady sense of power in New Delhi, and those Indian circles most closely and professionally concerned with foreign and security affairs do not hide their desire for India to become a nuclear power. A decision to that effect almost certainly would win widespread popular endorsement, in spite of India's poverty and backwardness. The Indians see themselves as the principal rivals in Asia to the Chinese, and many Indians (and also Japanese) comment ruefully on the fact that only the nuclear powers enjoy special status in the United Nations.

India has so far been held back by its awareness that any overt decision to acquire nuclear weapons would complicate its relations not only with the United States but perhaps even with the Soviet Union, and that it would also be likely to have an adverse impact on the international institutions and foreign states engaged in supporting India's economic development. Moreover, while India has the facility for the production of nuclear weapons, its capacity rapidly to develop an effective delivery system is very doubtful.

The situation is rather different in the case of Japan. There, both the economic means and the technical facility for the rapid acquisition of an effective nuclear deterrent do exist. What is still absent is the political desire, in spite of a favourable inclination among a narrower circle of defence specialists and some younger conservative politicians. The Japanese body politic would be severely split by a decision to go nuclear, and Japanese policy-makers are acutely aware of the adverse effect that any such decision would have on Japanese relations with China, the Soviet Union, and the United States. The present predisposition of the Japanese is thus against the acquisition of nuclear weapons.

This situation could change in the event of a precipitous American disengagement from the Far East, and it would certainly be affected by an Indian decision to go nuclear. Japanese national pride would be pricked by the appearance of yet another nuclear power, especially an Asian one, while Japanese insecurity would be heightened by the uncertainties produced by the appearance of a nuclear power that is visibly hostile to Japan's neighbour, China. The matter would be even made worse if India were to win some special international recognition as a consequence of its decision to go nuclear. More unsettling still for the Japanese, however, and even more likely to stimulate pressures on Japan to go nuclear, would be Japanese–American disagreements over security matters, especially if these disagreements were to precipitate an American disengagement from the security responsibilities which the United States at present exercise in the Far East.

Inadvertently, the Japanese themselves may stimulate such

disagreements. The present thrust of Japanese political development points towards the gradual emasculation of American–Japanese security arrangements, with the U.S. eventually being left alone with the problems of Taiwan and South Korea, though still committed to the defence of the Japanese islands proper. Given the probability that in the years ahead the American–Japanese relationship in any case is likely to remain burdened with economic tension, it appears unlikely that the American public would be prepared to assume such one-sided security obligations. American–Japanese disagreements over security matters would then be likely to stimulate in the Japanese an increasing inclination to seek security – and global status – in alternative ways.

Nuclear proliferation in the present fluid Asian international context inevitably would heighten international tensions. A nuclear India – not to mention the much less likely prospect of a nuclear Japan – would have a more unsettling effect on the international scene, with its current triangular configurations, than earlier has been the case with the nuclear U.K. or France. The French and British nuclear forces, whatever their leaders may have thought, were essentially appendages of U.S. power in an era of bipolar bloc confrontations. Accordingly, their international effect was less destabilising than would be the case with either India or Japan, especially given Sino–Indian rivalry and the recent history of armed conflicts between the two powers.

Some Major Asian Threats to International Peace

1. Sino–Soviet war – Soviet political intervention in China – the possibility of a major armed clash.

2. Indian nuclear development – an assertive policy – the heightened tension with China – unpredictable consequences of internal weaknesses.

3. Taiwanese straits – insecurity or political upheaval in Taiwan – armed clashes in the straits of Taiwan–American–Japanese disagreements.

4. Korean unification – strong impulses for unification since it seems rather unlikely that present reassociation will rapidly produce reunification – increasing temptation to resolve the

problem unilaterally as the U.S. military presence decreases.

5. Japanese military development – internal frustration and polarisation – increased tension with the United States – disagreements with its neighbours and widespread Asian anxiety.

The third major international uncertainty in the Far East – one closely related to those discussed above – pertains to Japan's political role. Japan is simply too powerful economically, too advanced in its social development, and potentially too powerful, to be fitted into a purely regional Asian role, where it has no real peers. It needs wider constructive outlets. This is not only an economic need, but also a political and even psychological requirement for an extremely energetic and industrially advanced people confined to three relatively small islands located far from the other advanced industrial societies. The need for a larger role, going beyond Asia, is complicated by the special cultural attraction of China,[3] and that makes for a Japanese mood full of ambiguity, especially now that Japan has emerged from the American tutelage it has had during the last quarter of a century.

The definition of Japan's international role is made all the more difficult by a similarly ambiguous attitude towards Japan on the part of the other Asian nations. On the one hand, they desire Japanese economic engagement in their own development, yet on the other hand they fear Japanese political predominance and resent Japan's physical presence. A consequence of this ambivalence has been the recent anti-Japanese boycott campaign in Thailand.[4] This further inhibits Japan from finding a con-

---

[3] In a thoughtful article on the Japanese relationship with China, a leading Japanese scholar has recently emphasised again the Japanese feeling of a shared destiny with the Chinese. In his article, he cited the writings of an earlier Japanese political writer, who more than 55 years ago argued that:

Looking at China as a politician, one of course perceives a border between Japan and China. But as a Japanese, one recognises no boundaries that separate our hearts. Japanese and Chinese are not strangers to each other. We are of the same flesh and blood ... Only the politicians treat Chinese coldly: the Chinese are not considered aliens by us Japanese people. This vast area consisting of the combined territories of China and the Japanese islands ought to be the arena for our activities; it is here we should breathe deeply the air of harmony.

Shinkichi Eto, "Japan and China – A New Stage?", *Problems of Communism*, Nov.-Dec. 1972, p. 6, quoting Aizan Yamaji, "Shina-ron" (A China Thesis), Tokyo, Minyusha 1916, pp. 3-5.

[4] The Japanese reacted to this boycott with great anxiety. The authoritative *Japan Economic Journal*, in its report of 5 December 1972, underlined its account with the words "Boycott campaign causes deep concern – efforts get actively under way to better relations with Thailand."

structive role for itself in Asian development, even though Japanese economic aid has already become a critical factor in the development of several Asian countries.

In the past, Japan has reacted to external challenge by withdrawing into prolonged self-imposed isolation (as after the initial shock of confronting the West), or by practising intense imitation of the West (as after the Meiji restoration), adopting even the practice and theory of European imperialism. The danger today is different. It is highly unlikely that Japan could again isolate itself or become militarily aggressive – though a nuclear Japan would be internationally unsettling, at least in its initial phase. Rather, the danger is that external ambiguity, the sense of political isolation, and the impact of increased economic tensions, could have a highly destabilising impact on the body politic, making for major internal tensions and even turmoil. Given the sensitive and politically fluid situation in Asia, any such development would further complicate the quest for international stability.

All three of these eventualities would adversely affect the Atlantic world. Sino–Soviet conflict, especially if protracted, would be a major threat to world peace, and would eventually probably force the Western powers into some form of indirect involvement, in the form of economic aid or political encouragement. A closer Sino–Soviet relationship, especially if achieved through some sort of Soviet political intervention in internal Chinese politics, would alter to the West's disadvantage the first of the two triangles discussed at the beginning of this chapter. The proliferation of nuclear weapons in the Far East would make the search for arms control even more difficult, not to mention more immediate hazards to peace. Moreover, a nuclear India would presumably be also intensely nationalistic and that would further complicate the South-East Asian political scene as well as introducing yet another factor into the already uncertain situation in the Indian Ocean. A nuclear Japan would be viewed as a threat by most of its neighbours, while Japanese political and social instability, reinforced by external frustration, would mean a sudden vacuum at one corner of the key co-operative triangle, thereby reducing the advanced world's capacity for responding effectively and imaginatively to global problems.

Atlantic–Pacific interaction in political-security matters is hence a fact of life, and it further underlines the emergence of a community of political interests spanning the two oceans. These common interests in the years ahead are likely to be reinforced by increasingly overlapping American, European, and Japanese economic investment in such places as Taiwan, Singapore, and Indonesia, thereby further enhancing the common stake of the Atlantic–Pacific worlds in Asian stability. Finally, the critical dependence of Europe and Japan, and also America, on Middle Eastern oil – a dependence that will grow further during this decade – creates still another pressure for the emergence of shared political perspectives with regard to international problems that ultimately are indivisible.[5]

Assuming that our argument so far has established some validity for our first two propositions, it becomes somewhat easier to develop further the third: that in the years ahead the three major units of the advanced non-Communist world will find it in their interests – as well as in the general interest of global stability and progress – to consult more closely.

Such consultation, eventually prompting closer co-operation, is needed also because each of the three units is suffering from a crisis of vision. America is still recovering from the trauma of Vietnam while seeking to define a new relationship for itself with the world, though lately it has been tempted to play a somewhat shortsighted game of economic brinkmanship, thus reinforcing the tendency of the major powers to view the world in narrowly selfish nationalist terms. Europe has still to define itself politically and to find a useful global role for its energy and genius, in keeping with its historical traditions. And Japan's attitude towards the rest of the world will have to move beyond self-centred economic motivations, especially now that the era of American political tutelage is past.

A closer interaction among the three would be healthy for each, and would also be a constructive response to the political problems already outlined. Global stability and progress – the twin requirements of peace in our age – cannot be regionally compartmentalised, especially in as volatile a context as Asia, in a time of overlapping power and economic interdependence.

To argue this proposition is not to postulate that Atlantic–Pacific relations should now begin to copy the patterns of co-operation and institution-building practised within the Atlantic world during the last 25 years. The situation is clearly not yet ripe for that. The first steps needed are more modest but no less urgent nor less important than they were a quarter of a century ago within the Atlantic world. They involve, in the first instance, the deliberate decision on the part of the leaders of the

[5] See also Chapter XI.

three units to develop more sustained political consultation among themselves on subjects of common concern, including that of Asian stability and progress. Such a decision would go a long way towards overcoming the uncertainties present today in America, the parochialism of the European vision, and the potentially conflicting ambiguities in the Japanese outlook.

The implementation of such a decision could take several forms, all of them initially modest and far short of anything resembling an alliance or a formal community.

First, in order to stimulate a greater degree of shared political perspective among the governmental bodies of the three units, to promote the practice of regular and increasingly formal political consultation, to develop common political planning with regard to problems or areas of mutual interest, it will be desirable:

- to adopt as a matter of regular practice the holding of annual trilateral cabinet meetings, somewhat on the model of the U.S.–Japanese cabinet meetings. In the trilateral setting, this could involve the EEC Council of Ministers as well as the Japanese and the American sides;

- to reinforce the above with a standing secretariat, particularly with a common policy-planning and review staff, in part as back-up for the above and in part as a stimulant to the emergence and crystallisation of common perspectives and policies;

- to promote consultation also in a larger framework, involving states outside the formal confines of the "co-operative triangle", it would be also useful to hold more frequent meetings of the OECD Foreign Ministers, so that common political problems can be frequently reviewed and also so that joint responses to the problems of development in the third world can be stimulated.

Secondly, in order to promote on a wider basis within the élites – political, economic, social, intellectual – of the three principal units a sense of common destiny and of shared responsibility in coping with the problems of political stability and social progress that beset the contemporary world; to develop within these élites more intimate personal contacts and franker exchanges of views; and to overcome the cultural and linguistic barriers, which particularly inhibit Japanese participation in world affairs, it will be desirable:

– to open up to Japanese participation some of the various informal Atlantic bodies, which have grown up over the last 25 years and which have contributed so much to the emergence of a mutual sense of trust and understanding. Political co-operation among democracies is impossible in the long run unless it is based on a solid foundation of open and sustained dialogue, and is reinforced by personal links among the respective élites. An example here might be the Bilderberg meetings: Japanese participation in them would be a foward step;

– to create, in addition to the above, special trilateral bodies for the purpose of promoting common programmes, studies and discussions. The very process of addressing a problem on a trilateral basis is an act of political significance. A desirable and important step in this direction is the Trilateral Commission now being formed by leading Americans, Europeans, and Japanese, for the purpose of developing joint policies on matters of common concern. It will deal with a broad range of issues in the political, security, economic, and social domains, both developing relevant policies and as an action group promoting their trilateral acceptance;

– to hold three-way meetings of the respective parliamentarians, on as wide a party basis as practicable.

Finally, the quest for a stable power balance in Asia will require new arrangements in Asia itself, though these too would involve, directly or indirectly, the Atlantic world. For example, closer Japanese–Australian–Indonesian consultations on political matters would seem desirable, since such a Pacific maritime triangle would not be a threat to the Asian mainland, while the extension of economic links between Indonesia and Australia and the other advanced countries is already fashioning a web of Pacific–Atlantic interdependence.[6]

Similarly, four-power consultations in Asia on Far Eastern stability, involving the U.S., the Soviet Union, Japan, and China, perhaps pointing to the adoption of a non-first-use-of-nuclear-weapons pledge and to the exploration of the feasibility of nuclear-free zones in Asia, might be timely before long. Last but not least, whenever economically feasible, joint rather than purely

---

[6] Bilateral high-level Australian–Japanese, Japanese–Indonesian, and Australian–Indonesian consultative talks have already been held.

solitary U.S., Japanese, and European ventures in Siberian or Chinese development would be helpful in spinning a web of larger co-operation in Asia between the major Communist and non-Communist states.

An agenda of this sort is obviously ambitious and it is not likely to be fulfilled rapidly. Deliberate movement along these lines, however, would be a creative response to the problems and dangers outlined. It would be in the interest of the parties concerned, and it would help to create a badly-needed inner core of stability and co-operation within the global system.

COMMENT by Roderick MacFarquhar

The foregoing analysis raises in my mind a number of questions. Its major starting proposition is the two triangle system, a very neat way of expressing certain important facts about the present world. But does the triangle formula express the most important facts relevant to Asia, and if it does is the co-operative triangle Japan, America, Europe the most relevant, or is it the combative triangle?

Secondly, it has been said that Asia is now more likely to be the seat of conflict endangering world peace than Europe. I certainly agree, but I am not sure that the issues mentioned are those that will really cause trouble in the future. A point which surely deserves more attention is the problem of social fragmentation in the countries of Asia.

Thirdly, although I am heartily in favour of all the policy suggestions mooted above, it seems to me that if one comes to them from a slightly different angle, one has to raise questions about their effectiveness in their present form.

Let me start with the proposition that Asia is the more likely scene of conflict than Europe in the future. In fact, of course there has been an enormous number of conflicts in Asia since the last world war, and there have been, I would say, three major causes for these conflicts. First, there were the end-of-empire wars, the Dutch in Indonesia, the French in Indo-China. These ended with the withdrawal of colonial power. Secondly, the Communist take-over, to use a shorthand phrase, or the wars, the uprisings, the insurgencies in Malaysia, the Philippines, Burma, in India in the late '40s, and most notably the Korean War, all of which ended in failure. The one exception, crossing both categories, is Vietnam, which now seems to have ended in a stalemate situation. The third major cause of war in Asia since the last world war has been the expansion of the new nations of Asia to their boundaries, seeking to establish their identities which the old colonial powers, being only temporarily there, were not always particularly concerned about. This has led to numerous clashes, and perhaps even wars on borders, and the expansion of countries into areas over which their hold hitherto was not very strong – China into Tibet, the Indo–China war or the Sino–Indian border-war, India's struggle against the Nagas, the India–Pakistan quarrel over Kashmir, and even indeed the Sino–Soviet border quarrel, though of course the origins of that were not the border itself.

By the mid-'sixties it was possible to suggest that all these major-causes of war, and particularly the last, were less likely to cause conflict in the future, if only because one power had come out as decisively superior. It is not likely in the foreseeable future that India would challenge China on the border or, if that was its intent, in the past, that China would challenge the Soviet Union. It has been possible for some time to argue that, Vietnam apart, the main source of conflict in the future is the likely instability in the large countries of Asia, leading possibly to the breakdown of central political apparatus – a breaking down for different reasons in different countries, but with a major ingredient of that breakdown being the sheer size of the nations and the difficulty of controlling them and ruling them in conditions of economic backwardness.

We have already in Asia two instances of this problem: Indonesia, which had this experience briefly in 1958, where there was, fortunately, minimal outside interference; and Pakistan, one of the major countries of Asia now split apart, internal dissension being exploited to some extent by external powers. In Japan there is less likelihood of regionalism, but as has been suggested, there is the possibility of domestic political instability, leading to confusion and perhaps exploitation from abroad. Finally of course, there are the two major countries in terms of size, India and China, where instability would be an irresistible magnet to outside interference. At the moment the problem looks less likely here, but it is quite possible that in both countries domestic instability could become extremely serious in the future; and what is more, once this instability develops as the example of Pakistan shows, it is an on-going process. Even in West Pakistan today, which might be thought to be a unit, there are still further centrifugal tendencies developing, and in Bangla Desh they still have to translate political authority into administrative viability.

If this is correct, then the problem raised is not likely to be controllable or even ameliorable by the greater development of the co-operative triangle of Japan, America and Europe. What is needed in the first instance, it seems to me, is a self-denying agreement, perhaps difficult to reach perhaps even more difficult to contain, regarding non-interference in internal affairs; an agreement essentially between the countries of the competitive triangle, i.e. the United States, the Soviet Union and China. This is the kind of agreement which China, I believe, would very much like to get. It is clear from Chinese policy statements in recent months and years that the examples of Czechoslovakia and Pakistan are regarded as a portent of what the Soviet Union would like to do in China. And it is conceivable that the Soviet Union could be brought into such a self-denying ordinance if it could be part of an agreement which would reassure the Soviet Union about its border relationship with China. If these three powers, the major powers of the competitive triangle, could be brought into agreement, then I should have thought that there would not be much difficulty in bringing in the minor powers which might want to exploit dissension elsewhere. For instance Pakistan, which might well welcome some kind of break-up in India, might be pressed into agreeing to a self-denying ordinance, if the major powers were to agree on it first.

But the number one international point of tension is of course the Sino–Soviet relationship. I do not think however that it is a threat to peace; but it is a threat to stability. China, having rid itself through its new American policy of the danger, as it saw it, of American attack or American encirclement, now faces not merely Soviet encirclement to the north and in India, but also the fear that the Soviet Union has the intention of moving into South-East Asia, even of barring the unification of Taiwan with the mainland, and most important of all of attempting to move into the Japanese orbit and to bring Japan into its influence.

It seems to me that we now have a situation in this competitive triangle which reeks of the old balance of power, in the sense that Japan is the country in the Pacific which the three nations of this competitive triangle are all out to get. China, indeed, has now adopted a major change of policy in order to prevent Russia getting hold of Japan. The Chinese have said to the Japanese that they do not object to the U.S.–Japan security treaty; and it is quite clear that this is because they are afraid that if any major breakdown occurs in the U.S.–Japanese relationship, then it can only, in the present state of Chinese development, be exploited by the Soviet Union to the disadvantage of China. So a balance of power situation is developing with Japan not quite clear where it is going. On the one hand it has made a breakthrough to China, and the indications now are that Premier Tanaka is anxious to make a breakthrough to the Soviet Union, perhaps even sacrificing the Japanese demand for the return of the islands occupied by Russia, in exchange for an agreement which will enable him to play off China and Russia against each other.

I am in agreement, as I have already stressed, with the highly imaginative proposals that Professor Brzezinski has put forward for trying to increase the attraction for Japan of coming towards the American end of the spectrum. But it seems to me that the involvement of Western Europe in this process is a highly artificial one – a necessary one, but a highly artificial one – because although there are many points of common interest in the relationship between Japan and Western Europe, and the relationship between the three powers of the co-operative triangle, it is very difficult, even at a superficial level, to make people in Western Europe understand that relationship. In the recent discussions on the dollar crisis, for example, the talks on both occasions were held between the Europeans, and the Japanese were brought in virtually to be told of the result at the end of it all. If we are to bring in Western Europe into this co-operative triangle, and make the imaginative leap that is necessary to develop the relationship between Western Europe, Japan and the United States, then I think we have to go even further and be even more ambitious. I believe that the only way in which Europe and Britain will be able to come to terms with the kind of relationship that is needed is if a major effort is made to bring not merely Japan but the whole of Asia into the consciousness of the people of Western Europe. I believe that this has to be done at the lowest possible level of participation: there has to be a conscious attempt to bring Asian history into the schools; the facts of contemporary Asian politics and economics should be at the fingertips of every European schoolboy – perhaps even, as a further step, one Asian language might be made compulsory, as Latin and Greek once were. There should also be exchanges at all levels, not just parliamentarians and intellectuals, but students, teachers, local government officials, and so on. All this has to be thought of now and to be built up, because otherwise we shall have a very insubstantial, literally upper-crust, kind of unity, and the situation is far too serious for something of that sort, which may turn out to be very fragile.

Chapter XXI

Regionalism versus Multilateralism

THEO SOMMER

THE MOMENT OF SLACK WATER in the tide of European affairs is obviously past. The Community of the Six has become, we hope, the permanent grouping of the Nine. At the 1972 summit, the leaders of the new Community took a number of important decisions about the internal structure of their association. They reconfirmed its "political finality", defined a long-term goal – European Union by 1980 – and set themselves a provisional timetable. Whatever procedural snags this renewed effort at pulling together may run into, and whatever vagueness may still becloud the ultimate objective, the *relance européenne* appears to be under way.

The range of choices has narrowed considerably since Herman Kahn sketched 88 possible Europes in the mid-'sixties, even since Alastair Buchan's ISS study of 1969 outlined six different models of thinkable European futures. There may not be a federated Western Europe by 1980, but there will be something rather close to it in a much more pragmatic fashion than the European idealists of the early post-war period were able to visualise.

There will not be an *American Europe*, the kind of U.S.–led Western Europe we had in 1949, divided into powerless, frightened states willingly submitting to American hegemony because it provided the only means of physical survival – although close links with the United States are no doubt going to be maintained. Nor will there be a *Gaullist Europe*, led by France in the basically anti-American spirit of Charles de Gaulle – although French influence will doubtlessly be significant and a rather more conflictual relationship between the European Community and the United States of America seems to be a likely prospect. A *fragmented Europe* – fragmented once more into its component parts, its Community organs and institutions having come unstuck again – can likewise be rated rather improbable. At the same time, a *pan-European evolution* leading to a Europe free from Brest to Brest does not, in view both of Soviet hegemonial rigidity and the still systematic inability of Communist régimes to co-operate with open societies, constitute a viable or attractive alternative to continued West European integration. Steadfast development of their Community to the point of full-fledged political union is the only option now open to the Nine.

In part, the European Community is already a palpable reality; in part it is still a dream, a hope, an aspiration.

The reality is made up of such dreary paper stuff as beef regulations and directives about barbed-wire fences, or shop-keepers' compromises about low-grade wines and cheap onions. But already it is more than that. Close to a hundred states main-tain accredited representatives at the Commission's headquarters in Brussels. The Community has established formalised relations with a number of international bodies like OECD, GATT, and UNCTAD, and concluded a score of trade and association agree-ments with as many different countries. National EEC Ministers travelling abroad have found to their surprise that their inter-locutors invariably regard them as European as much as Dutch, French or German ministers. True, only a small part of the reality encompasses Europe's external relations. These are still basically the prerogative of the member states. As Ralf Dahrendorf has pointed out in *The Round Table* (January 1973): "There is an almost absurd disproportion between the expectations of Europe's partners in the world, and the instruments which the European Community has at its disposal in order to respond to these expectations." But to do the West Europeans justice one must point out that during the past few years they have created habits of consultation, co-operation, and concertation in many more fields than would have been thought possible even three years ago. And if there was, for a long time, a pitiful shortage of ideas about what the Community's place and role ought to be in the world, Europe now stands at "the brink of a moment of creative tension", to borrow a phrase from Italian Commissioner Altiero Spinelli. Slowly the new European idea is taking root. The goals are being defined for tomorrow's Community. A sense of together-ness is growing despite all the workaday squabbles about nuts and bolts, chicken-feed and oranges.

Western Europe's approaches to Community-building have undergone very definite changes in the course of the past 20 years. In fact, there are three clearly distinguishable phases of develop-ment, each one characterised by a different approach.

Europe Mark I, originally conceived in the '50s, was con-nected with the name of Jean Monnet. Its propellant and policy executor was to be the Commission; its essence was supranational.

Europe Mark II, which France attempted to impose on its partners in the '60s is linked with the name of Charles de Gaulle. The driving force behind it was the General's hegemonial ambition for his country; its essence was national, even nationalistic.

Europe Mark III, as it has slowly been evolving, is a different kind of animal. It carries the name-tag of Belgian Ambassador Davignon; its main instrument is the systematic co-operation of governments leading to the negotiated, agreed extension of collective policies to a rapidly widening range of questions; its essence is, as it were, transnational.

This Europe Mark III is likely to be with us for some time to come. It will neither be dominated by a technocratic structure nor overwhelmed by one man's autocratic will. It will be a Europe of the Possible: pragmatic, without fanfare or panache. Joint action will emerge from negotiated communality rather than from agreed Commission plans. But as the nine members formulate collective policies affecting an ever-growing number of sectors, the sheer quantity of joint decisions is bound to change the basic quality of the Community. No doubt, its component parts will not disappear. National governments will not dwindle into insignificance: they are going to be the building-blocks of tomorrow's Europe as well. Yet in the eyes of the outside world the Community will more and more assume the character of one single entity, speaking, although in different tongues, with one voice, and implementing a collective will.

Contrary to earlier expectations, the Commission will not, or not for some time yet, become the main instrument of unity, the chief focus of political imagination and implementation. This may be a disheartening prospect for the Brussels apparatus, but it is not necessarily a disaster so long as the member governments themselves provide the impetus towards more unity. Recent history seems to suggest that this is precisely what is happening. There are limits to the technocratic approach. Real progress towards fusion must rest on the political consent of Europe's component parts; it can be inspired but not assured by the Commission. The main point is to "reduce each nation's capacity for making separate decisions without consulting the interests and wishes of its partners in the group". (Andrew Shonfield) If the frontiers of the nation-state are to be eroded, the nation-states themselves will have to take part in that process by voluntarily surrendering bits of national power. There is no way to get around them.

The new European commonwealth is already taking shape. The Summit Conference at The Hague (December 1969) and the subsequent Paris Summit Meeting (October 1972) started a pattern for progress through negotiated communality of action. At The Hague, the enlargement of the original EEC was finally agreed upon. In Paris, European sights were raised to the more distant goal of Union by 1980, but at the same time the summiteers laid down a detailed calendar for action. They agreed further to improve political co-operation on foreign policy matters. Foreign Ministers will in future meet four times a year instead of twice for this purpose. The aim, as the communiqué put it, is "to deal with problems of current interest and, where possible, to formulate common medium and long-term positions".

As a matter of fact, this kind of political co-operation has made considerable headway in recent years. Western Europe is indeed on the road to "establishing its position in world affairs as a distinct entity" (Paris communiqué) – slowly so, sometimes in a very fumbling fashion and all too frequently still by declarations rather than by actions. However, there is now an institutionalized process of comparing notes and agreeing on joint language as well as joint lines of approach that by no means stop short at regular conferences of department chiefs and meetings of their Political Directors, but reaches well down into the middle echelons of the nine Foreign Offices. On many issues, EEC ambassadors receive joint instructions. EEC ministers conducting talks abroad often personally inform the Community ambassadors about their conversations. This is what Chancellor Brandt referred to when he told the London *Times* recently: "Nowadays, in outside countries, in many cases our ambassadors meet. Not too much is said about this in public... Our ambassador saw Gromyko two days ago, and only a few hours after he had reported to his own government he reported to his colleagues from the Community." Beyond this, policy papers define the member states' attitude towards important questions such as the Near East or the Conference on Security and Co-operation in Europe. Recognition of the GDR, establishment of diplomatic relations with Hanoi, a joint reconstruction effort for Vietnam, provide further examples of policy co-ordination among the Nine.

In this context, the intensive joint preparations for the CSCE talks in Helsinki were particularly significant. Not only did the Community members harmonise their individual view on both substance and procedure: they also ensured the physical presence of the Commission at the talks and agreed that in all matters that legally fall within the competence of the Community organs, standard EEC procedures must be observed in the formulation of policy statements or decisions.

So Western Europe is on the way to a joint foreign policy. But its evolution is bound to be slow. Deeply engrained parochial attitudes will not vanish overnight. Furthermore, even imaginative European leaders find it difficult to visualise Europe's place in the world of the 1980s. The Community of the Nine is still in search of a role.

It is comparatively easy to define what Europe is not going to be like.

First, it is hard to imagine that the Community will want to become a superpower in the sense in which this term is currently used: a power with global aspirations to impose a certain kind of order, equipped with a worldwide intervention capacity. I do not envisage European gunboats patrolling the Straits of Malacca, or EEC paratroopers supporting wobbly régimes against rebellious populations. The Community will not try to export any particular way of life. It will neither substitute for nor compete with American or Russian efforts to avert or mitigate, by direct intervention, conflicts in the developing world. Its role could be assertive only where its immediate interests were impinged upon; for example, if its oil supplies were jeopardised.

Secondly, although the echoes of past glories still reverberate faintly in some quarters, the peoples of the Community at large will feel no temptation to resume a colonial role. Europe, whatever its special interests and relations with certain neighbouring areas, will not be a vehicle for the continuation of colonialism by collective means. The idea that the Community might develop into a regional power with its own satellites in the Mediterranean and in Africa is quite preposterous. It may appeal to the systematic ideologies of a pentagonal world order in which each of the five dominant powers possesses its private sphere of influence and dependence in the south, the United States in Latin America, Europe in Africa, the Soviet Union on the Indian subcontinent, China in South-East Asia, Japan in Oceania. But it has little to do with the real world. Europe cannot become a closed bloc, extending from the North Cape to the northern borders of South Africa. It must remain open to partnership with everyone: North America as well as Eastern Europe, Asian groupings as well as Latin American countries.

Thirdly, the Europe of 1980 will not simply be a Switzerland cast on a larger scale. To be sure, it is inevitably going to be a community of producers and traders, manufacturing, selling and buying. Yet for its own self-preservation it cannot but actively participate in the web of international organisations (from which Switzerland keeps largely aloof). It is not small enough not to be noticed but not big enough not to go unheard unless it speaks up, or not to be overlooked unless it makes its presence felt.

But if Europe is not going to be imperialist, colonialist, or helveticised what then is it going to be like?

It is difficult to answer this question in specific terms. Generally speaking, however, one might suggest three basic determinants.

First, the European Community has to see it that it cannot be pushed around. It must safeguard its existence, its prosperity, and its growth potential. On the one hand the EEC states must seek to prevent Finlandisation – being swallowed up, politically, if not militarily, by the Soviet Union, with only a semblance of autonomy left to them. On the other hand they have to ward off what might be called Canadisation – being pressed into economic subservience to the United States, their autonomy and their freedom of choice threatened by ruthless dollar diplomacy.

Secondly, beyond these fundamental requisites of self-preservation and self-respect, the Community must establish itself as a totally new type of entity: neither parochial nor imperial, neither unassuming nor overbearing – a building-block for a broader and more complex international order; a new intermediary between the nation states and the world system, to quote Andrew Shonfield once more; perhaps, as Jean Monnet has always seen it, the beginning of a "process of civilisation" whose repercussions extend well beyond its borders. Europe can serve as a model of how to achieve unity despite diversity. It is bound to be a force for openness and liberalism. And it can demonstrate, especially to the Third World, what Ralf Dahrendorf has termed "co-operation without dependence".

Thirdly, Europe has a moral role to play, and should unabashedly do so. This may irritate some as censorious, as in their time the Americans irritated others by their moralising. But as Peregrine Worsthorne has pointed out in *The Sunday Telegraph*, it is important that someone act as the conscience of humanity: "The world would be a much poorer place if there were no area which could be relied upon to preach a plausible sermon with some semblance of conviction from a posture of sufficient authority." America, Russia, China, the third world, Worsthorne suggested, could not fulfil this role. Europe could – for "the memory of how we ourselves used to behave badly in the past is too faint to be embarrassing and the likelihood of having to behave as badly in the future too remote to be worrying".

What does all this mean in practical terms for the European Community? By way of a very general answer I should like to list a number of points.

1. The Nine will continue their slow drift towards more and more integration. Their preparedness in principle to conduct a good-neighbour policy towards everyone will be subject to only the qualification *in dubio pro communitate*.

2. Their relationship with the United States is bound to grow more conflictual in the future. In particular, there will be a strong element of economic rivalry. This should not be permitted to overshadow the basic truth that close and good relations with the U.S.A. remain of highest importance to Western Europe. In the security field, there is no substitute for America's contribution to European defence. A breakdown of the Atlantic Alliance would force the West Europeans into an armaments effort which, if extended to the nuclear field, would be neither sensible nor credible. On the other hand, the gradual evolution of a European defence identity possibly crystallising around the Eurogroup, is a likely prospect for a more pronounced military profile of the Community against the background of a continuing U.S. Commitment to the security of Europe.

3. *Détente* with Eastern Europe will be continued, mainly as a multilateral effort – but not to the detriment of the Community. *Détente* cannot realistically include any measures which could hinder, decelerate or stop the transformation of the EEC into a political union. At the same time, West Europeans will be well advised to keep insuring against the possible miscarraige of the *détente* process.

4. *Vis-à-vis* the third world, Europe must adopt a posture of increasing openness. This does not preclude special attention to the Mediterranean littorals and to the French- and English-speaking states of Africa. Nor should it foil an aid policy concentrating on "threshold countries" about to reach the take-off stage rather than spreading the available funds far and thin. In the impending GATT round, Europe can best help the

developing countries by adopting a liberal stance on tariffs and non-tariff barriers.

The European Community is on the move again. It is not as monolithic as many might wish. Nor is it as amorphous as others seem to fear. At this particular juncture, Europe is perhaps less a precise prescription than a mood. But it is the mood of a new departure; and the mood is visibly hardening into a programme of action. Results are slow in coming, yet it would be wrong to be impatient. We are witnessing the first phases of a protracted historic process. What counts above all is the fact that it has begun – and that all the recent crises have not been able to weaken the new resolve towards unity, but have only served to reinforce it.

COMMENT *by André Fontaine*

Twice, de Gaulle's hegemonial views have been mentioned. I think this is a widespread feeling in several countries in Europe. But I don't think it's a very fair assumption. I remember having given a lecture in Munich some years ago, and I had been asked a question by one of the listeners precisely about de Gaulle's hegemonial views; and I had the opportunity of meeting Couve de Murville who was then Foreign Minister. I mentioned that, and he said "Well, that's silly. What we have proposed to the Germans is a common Franco–German *entente*." And I think there was some sense in it. If it had been otherwise, probably Adenauer would not have been such a follower of de Gaulle's policy.

Again, much is made of de Gaulle's anti-Americanism. It is a fact that de Gaulle very often resisted the United States, but it is also a fact that very often de Gaulle resisted either Germany, during the war years, or Russia, at the time of the Cold War. I think De Gaulle's foreign policy was aimed especially at trying to prevent the superpower from becoming too much of a superpower. So he resisted the leading superpower of the time. And I think he summarised his policy pretty well when he met Brezhnev in Moscow in 1966. "Mr Secretary-General," he said. "I must tell you something that will please you. We are so happy to have the Russians to help us resist the American pressure." A big smile came on Brezhnev's face. And de Gaulle added. "In the same way we are so happy to have the Americans to help us to resist the Russians." That, I think, was the core of de Gaulle's foreign policy. And I think that probably 99 per cent of the French supported de Gaulle in that.

Another point is called to my attention by the remark that the movement of the slack water in the tide of European affairs is obviously past, since the Community of the Six has finally grown into the wider grouping of the Nine. I do not myself think that the numerical growth of the Community means that it necessarily gains in strength, since very often the larger grouping is the loser; and it was one of the main objections of de Gaulle to the idea of Britain joining the Community, precisely that it would dissolve into a loose free-trade area. I think that something of that kind has still to be feared today.

This leads me to my main objection to the optimistic character of Theo Sommer's chapter. He says, for instance, that a fragmented Europe is very improbable. Well, I hope that it will not happen, but I should not call it very improbable. It may very well happen. In France, for example, there was the unrest of May 1968. If the Left – the students and the workers – had won, what would have been left of Europe? At the last French election, the Union of the Left had a long manifesto on Europe. It was the result of difficult discussion between the Socialists and the Communists – who of course are very much against Europe. There is a tendency to take for granted that the French Socialists are in favour of Europe. This may be true of Socialists over 40; it is less so of Socialists under 40. Among the young Socialists, who grow more and more Left-wing every year, there is a tendency to view Europe as simply an open field for the activities of multinational firms, and they do not like it at all. The general trend of the evolution of the Left is not, in my opinion, towards integrated Europe, but against it. Although the Left did not win the French election, they increased their figures and nobody can take for granted that in some future presidential election, the present majority will win. So from France there is a real danger that Europe will be fragmented. Nor is it certain that Britain will for ever remain in the Common Market, given the attitude of the British Labour Party. Even in Germany, which was the first in the class of Europe during a long period, we have seen the emergence of the so-called Juso movement, which does not seem to be very much in favour of Europe. In Italy, there are people who are looking more and more towards some bilateral relationship with the United States, which is not exactly the way in which the Europeans want to build Europe. These factors of fragmentation exist. I do not say that they will prevail: I hope they will not prevail; but I think we have to take them into consideration.

Again, it has been said that we are on the way to a joint foreign policy. I should very much like to discuss that point. I do not see clearly in which field we are about to have a joint foreign policy. I do not believe that many members of the European Community support the French policy towards the Middle East, for instance. True, in many fields the importance of the disagreement has diminished, because the conflicts themselves are watered down; but I find it hard to believe that we are moving towards a joint foreign policy. One sad token of this is the fact that when the European countries decided to recognise Bangla Desh, a year ago, they were not even able to make that move on the same day, because each wanted to draw some advantage from its recognition, *vis-à-vis* India or Soviet Russia. And if France had not been the place where the conference on Vietnam was taking place, I am fairly sure that we should have witnessed many disagreements on Vietnam between the various countries of Europe. I wonder if we are not moving towards a situation in which Europe will have no foreign policy, because there is such a lack of interest in the subject at least in France. I have been told that Henry Kissinger, when he visited Paris some months ago, complained about the fact that he had not met a single Frenchman really interested in foreign policy. This of course, is somewhat exaggerated, but there is not a major interest in France's foreign policy today; and I do not think that there could be an active foreign policy for a government without a minimum of support by the people.

It is said that the European Community is already a palpable reality, as witness the number of countries which have established diplomatic links with the EEC. That cannot be denied, and it is a striking fact that abroad much more attention is given to the Community than from within the Community. The Chinese, for instance, place very great hopes in a united Europe. They go so far as to call it the fourth superpower, or the third superpower, which is certainly rather preposterous. And the Japanese are very much interested in Europe; and the United States, of course, is very interested in Europe, whether they like it or not. But from within, it reminds me of my own experience as an editor; when I read my newspaper abroad I find it excellent; but at home I see all its failures, and I think it very far from our objectives. So Europe as seen from within is far from as consistent as it may look from outside. First we notice a deep measure of indifference, especially in France. Europe did not play the slightest role in the last electoral campaign, and when we had a referendum on Europe, the main Leftist party was the one of those which did not take part in the vote. A majority of French people reached the age of political consciousness at a time when Europe already existed, so they take it as a fact; and they are not specially interested in the fact. It exists and that is all. And when it is said that Europe is a dream, a hope, and an aspiration – well, I should be glad if it were true, but I am not sure. Europe has been a dream: this dream has been partly fulfilled, this aspiration has been partly fulfilled, this hope has been partly fulfilled. But do we still see it as a hope, as a dream, as an aspiration? I do not think one can keep a dream going for a quarter of a century. So I think it would be more appropriate to call Europe, as it exists today, a habit. And we do not dare to break it. Look at what took place in 1972 when President Pompidou threatened to postpone the European summit if some conditions were not fulfilled. Those conditions were not met, but we still had the summit. Why? Because he did not dare to break the machinery. Very often in the past we have had the same feeling: nobody dares to break it, because it is a habit. But it seems to me very, very dangerous to rely only on the force of habit, because some day people will question it. And the criticism proceeds, and some day the habit disappears. There is no reason to believe that something will last for ever, simply because it exists today.

Let us look at some examples of the present state of Europe. We have not been able to agree on a very minor issue, which is the creation of a European Secretariat – simply because we do not agree on where it should be located. The same difficulty appears with the European Monetary Fund. At the European Summit in Paris in October 1972, it was decided to proceed with some policy of mutual aid, but today this policy seems unlikely to be put in practice, at least for the time being. Each time a monetary crisis conference occurs – and it happens very often – we are usually divided. We have been able to build a front of some European powers, but the British and the Italians were left aside. So although we are agreed on a timetable, agreeing on a timetable doesn't mean that one will agree at every phase of that timetable on the steps which have to be taken.

So I think it is absolutely necessary to try to find new motives for Europe. To try to determine which targets can be ours, I think we have to refer to the reasons why the integration of Europe began. I think the creation of Europe was due to three main factors. One was awareness of the Soviet threat. Second was the fear of a new war in Western Europe, especially between France and Germany. We have had three, essentially, and we were at pains to find a way of avoiding a new war of this kind. And the third factor was the American pressure. Those three reasons have disappeared today. There is no awareness of a Soviet threat in Western Europe as such. There is fear of some kind of Soviet pressure among the ruling circles but not in public opinion; that is why military expenditure is so unpopular in our countries today. The fear of a Franco–German war has completely vanished; we are friends and allies, boys and girls on both sides of the border marry; we travel intensively and we are each others' best commercial partners. So in that way Europe has succeeded; there is no doubt about it. But we do not feel the necessity of Europe – simply because of that. And the third point is the American pressure. In the early '50s, America viewed the unification of Western Europe as the best way to resist Soviet threats; and at the same time, the American political belief was that each time people were to unite on a federal basis, they would be naturally led to adopt more or less the same political or economic standards as the United States itself. There was great faith on the American side, in the absolute value of the American ideal. This has changed. I think the U.S. still stick to the idea of federalism and they still think that Europe is probably better united than divided as far as security is concerned; but when it comes to commercial interests, which we have been told are now pre-dominant in the American thinking, the situation is quite different: the Americans view Western Europe as the direct challenge to their trade.

So, those reasons for uniting having disappeared, we must look for others. But do we have to look for reasons to unite Europe? After all, Europe is not an end in itself. The problem is to know whether there exist today problems of such magnitude that only Europe can provide the framework in which to try to solve them.

I think myself that the main problem in the part of the world in which we live is that more and more young people feel dis-abused, unconcerned by the ideals of the society they live in. So we have to try to reconcile them with our way of living – or to reconcile our way of living with their ideals. This is a difficult task, and on both sides we have to make some concessions. But there is no doubt that we have to look for a new pattern of civilisation. The crisis in urban life has seen the development, at least in France, of a very important class of immigrants who live in slum conditions, as in the third world. All this has to be cured: if we are not able to change it, the society in which we live will disappear sooner or later. And I think it is very difficult except in a European framework. It is difficult in an area dominated by one of the superpowers, because I deeply believe, like de Gaulle, that selfishness is the absolute rule of the superpowers. Only Europe can find the means of becoming a superpower without the inconvenience of a superpower. Only Europe can provide a device for securing a lasting peace in Europe, and for making sure that what has been during centuries a battlefield, does not continue to be, so to speak, a peaceful battlefield – a battlefield where American and Soviet ambitions meet every day. Only a Europe which can decide her fate by herself can avoid this.

And last but not least, there is another point which has been mentioned by Theo Sommer, which is the third world. As a Frenchman I find it hard to agree that Europe should make no distinction between the former colonial possessions of France, Britain, the Netherlands and Belgium, and the other parts of the third world. After all our resources are not unlimited, and we must give priority to those countries *vis-à-vis* which we have in the past assumed so many responsibilities. But it is no coincidence if, in our country, young people feel so much concern with the third world, because the present state of the third world is certainly the main evidence of our failure. We must do something; and probably the only way of trying to reconcile young people with our kind of society is to ask them to help us in improving, very quickly, conditions in Africa and in Asia.

Europe will live only if she is given new reasons for existing. Conservative reasons are not enough. Conservatism – to keep what you have – is a language which suits people over 40 or 50; it does not meet the aspirations of youth. And that is certainly what we have to do first, because in all our countries, one way or another, there is crisis among young people. Sometimes they simply don't work, don't participate; in other countries they criticise openly: but we have to meet their aspirations, and if we fail to meet their aspirations they will overthrow the present systems sooner or later.

COMMENT *by Isaiah Frank*

The dichotomy between regionalism and multilateralism is really quite a slippery one. Multilateralism in economic terms has at various times been defined narrowly to mean equal treatment of all foreign countries with respect to such economic matters as trade, finance, and investment. For example, in the field of trade, it is often regarded as equivalent to most-favoured-nation treatment. Regionalism, on the other hand, would comprehend any arrangement among a group of countries that departs from the principle of non-discrimination or equal treatment. I find myself very uncomfortable with this dichotomy because it carries the connotation that the two concepts are necessarily in opposition to each other: that multilateralism is good because it conforms to the Wilsonian conception of a universalist approach to world affairs in which the sovereign equality of nations is recognised and all get treated equally, whereas regionalism implies a system of self-serving and preferential blocks, pursuing their own interests without regard to the effect of their actions on the other countries.

In my view, however, there is no necessary conflict between a regional and a multilateral approach to international economic affairs. A multilateral economic system need not be one in which all foreign countries are necessarily treated alike, but rather is one that operates within a framework of internationally accepted rules and obligations, which define acceptable deviations from equal treatment in a way that furthers the common interest. Whether regional arrangements are consistent with or opposed to a multilateral system depends therefore on the nature of the arrangements. I should like to apply this theme to four very specific issues in U.S.–Western Europe relations.

First, the question of European monetary unification. Is the movement of the Community towards monetary unification consistent with the multilateral approach as I have defined it? Here, I think, we must differentiate the ultimate achievement of monetary unity from the process of moving towards that objective. One test would be, in my view, whether monetary unity contributes to, or detracts from, the smooth working of the international balance-of-payments adjustment process – which must include as an essential feature a substantial degree of exchange-rate flexibility, contrary to what we have seen under the Bretton Woods system for the past 25 years or so. It is not too significant whether exchange-rate flexibility is achieved through a system of floating rates, combined with rules for intervention – that is a managed system, with collectively established rules – or whether it is achieved through a system of par values combined with presumptive rules that would induce smaller and more frequent changes in rates. Either of these would avoid the kind of accumulative disequilibrium and crises that have marked our monetary experience of the past few years. I have no doubt that the ultimate achievement of monetary union would contribute to exchange-rate flexibility between a common European currency on the one hand and the currencies of the United States and Japan on the other. Whether the process of arriving at this goal inhibits or advances the sort of exchange-rate flexibility that is required remains to be seen. We are now going through a period in which an effort is being made, by those European countries that are locked in a joint float, to short-circuit the transitional period and operate substantially as if monetary union among them had been achieved. It remains to be seen, however, how the non-floating countries, Britain and Italy, will be accommodated within the system, and whether and how the joint float survives the strains that are bound to arise among countries which are locked in this way but which are as yet far from having achieved a common or even fully harmonised monetary policy.

Secondly, agriculture. I realise that in talking about agriculture one brings the cosmic discussion of Europe's long-run future and its role as the moral conscience of the world down to very mundane and almost niggardly things. But the stuff of life and much of the relations between Europe and the United States certainly do not consist of these cosmic matters. In agriculture, the problem does not arise from the fact that Europeans have adopted a common agricultural policy. The conflict between regionalism and multilateralism arises because of the nature of the common agricultural policy that has been adopted. I need not elaborate the essential features of Europe's common policy: the price supports for basic farm products, the import restrictions through variable levies, the export subsidies to get rid of surpluses and so on. I understand full well why these policies have been adopted. All of us, in all our countries, face the problem of how to reconcile the ultimate achievement of a rational and efficient domestic farm sector with the need to cushion the internal adjustments involved in reaching this goal, which can be very painful. Europe, the U.S., and Japan have all articulated similar objectives in this respect. The problem is whether the transitional cost of adjusting to a rational agricultural system is borne by the countries involved in adopting the system or whether it is transferred to other countries. I believe that it is fair to say that the burden, for the U.S., of the common agriculture policy is that much too large a share of the cost of the policy is borne not by the Europeans, but by others, including the United States. This is not to say that Europe does not bear a large cost: we are quite aware that the European consumer pays. But a large share of the cost is also borne by the U.S. in the form of restrictions on access for our farm products in the European market, and of subsidised competition in third markets. This is not the place to elaborate alternatives to this policy, which have been widely discussed; but there are alternatives which I hope in time the Western world can develop.

The third area where regionalism and multilateralism are an issue is that of trade. The big question under this heading is whether a trade arrangement which clearly discriminates against outsiders can be consistent with a multilateral trading world. Here, I think, the answer is simple. It can. We should remember that GATT, which is the charter of a multilateral trading world and which the U.S. had a very large hand in conceiving and drafting, recognised from the beginning that a customs union could be comprehended within a multilateral trading framework, provided certain principles were followed. These were designed basically to minimise the so-called trade-diverting effects of the arrangement and to maximise their trade-creating effects. In substance, GATT decreed that such arrangements, while eliminating trade barriers among their members, should avoid increasing such restrictions against outsiders. My own view is that, apart from agriculture, the trading arrangements of the Community have in fact evolved in a way that is broadly consistent with a multilateral approach far beyond the expectations of most people and at a much more rapid pace.

The main issue in the forthcoming negotiations will be how we jointly decide to deal with the internal adjustment problems that arise from rapid shifts in the international competitiveness of different industries, shifts which reflect today's high degree of international integration of markets not only for goods, but also for capital and technology, the mobility of which has been incredibly accelerated as a result of a variety of forces, of which the growth of the multilateral corporation is not the least. We all recognise today that on grounds of social policy, it is not fair that particular groups in society or particular industrial sectors should have to bear the full cost, the pain and trouble and dislocation, involved in changing comparative advantages, while the benefits of an open international trading system are enjoyed by society as a whole. The challenge that we face is to devise a way of relieving particular groups from having to bear the brunt of the burden whilst facilitating their shifts to other occupations.

A major subject of negotiation, far more important than further reductions in tariff barriers, is the extent to which so-called safeguard provisions should be employed to facilitate this internal adjustment process. By "safeguards" I mean import restrictions, often of a quantitative nature, whereby the burden of adjustment is shifted in part to the foreigner. The way to reconcile arrangements of this sort with a multilateral world economic system is to agree internationally on criteria for the imposition of such import restrictions and to ensure that the restrictions are degressive and are phased out within a defined period of time.

Lastly, there is the subject of north–south relationships. Is special treatment for the third world consistent with a multilateral world? In my view, indeed it is. On the contrary, equal treatment for the poor countries in economic matters would be equivalent to Anatole France's majestic equality of the law, according to which rich and poor alike have the right to sleep under bridges. The issue here is whether the particular form of preferential arrangements entered into between the Community and various developing countries contributes to a rational and orderly world system. Insofar as the Community's system of general preferences, the so-called GSP, is concerned, I think one can applaud the move as a step, though a very modest one, in the right direction. But the special preferential arrangements with various African and other countries, involving as they do reverse preferences in favour of the Community itself, are another matter. They are objectionable on several grounds. First, those arrangements, particularly with Mediterranean countries and African countries, impose a cost on the developing country granting the preference. Secondly, they discriminate against less developed countries in Asia and Latin America, which do not receive the same terms of access to the European market. Thirdly, they make it politically difficult for the U.S. to accord equal treatment to those countries which discriminate against the United States in favour of other rich countries. Fourthly, some of the arrangements at least tend to undermine the system of international economic law under which we attempt to operate, and create the impression in some quarters that anything goes. Once one starts flouting the law, and treating it as if it did not exist, the long-term consequences can be very serious indeed. Fifthly, although it is argued that the idea that the community might develop into a regional power with its own satellites in the Mediterranean and in Africa is quite preposterous, the arrangements that the Community has with the African countries do have a neo-colonial stigma. They tend to increase the degree of dependence of poor and weak countries on particular rich countries or groups of countries, rather than to encourage a widening of their international relationships which in most cases is a prerequisite to true independence. These arrangements are one of the points of tension in U.S.–European relations and I believe that they perpetuate a neo-colonialist relationship with the third world.

Post-war American policy has been somewhat schizophrenic on the issue of regionalism versus multilateralism. Both strands are apparent in U.S. policy. Multilateralism was the guiding principle of GATT, of Bretton Woods, of U.S. domestic legislation having to do with trade and finance and investment. At the same time, America was a strong supporter of a United Europe long before Europe itself, apart from the few isolated federalists in the early days, ever dreamed that such a thing could come into being. It was a strong supporter, before the Community, of the European Payments Union which was a regional arrangement, of intra-European trade liberalisation in OEEC, and it is still a strong supporter of the Community, provided it abides by rules of international comity which will reconcile what the Community does with world international order and equity. The U.S. supported these arrangements in part because it viewed them as consistent with, and in some cases as a step towards an open world economy and towards making Europe an independent force in world affairs which, far from fearing or discouraging, it wanted to encourage. In the restructuring of the international economic system that is now under way, the main challenge is how can we obtain the very great political and economic advantages that clearly flow from regional arrangements, without undermining the broader benefits that result from an open world economic system based on internationally accepted rules of conduct.

COMMENT by Peter C. Dobell

To a sympathetic Canadian, the Community represents a group of nations moving towards a modern form of federal structure, where the division of powers is horizontal as well as vertical and where the process seems, to me at least, to be marvellously pragmatic. Associated with this development, Europe is attempting to develop the basis for a common foreign policy. True, it is a long way from achieving this; but the Davignon type of consultation seems to me a valid arrangement: it has the potential for gradually and appropriately moving forward.

But there is a price to be paid for these arrangements in terms of the effects on others, and nowhere can this be better illustrated than by the multilateral preparatory talks that are taking place in Helsinki. There the Nine are meeting almost daily. This must be pretty heavy stuff for the Irish who have for so long been outside these regular and constant consultations. Naturally, after the amount of time and effort spent in Helsinki trying to find a consensus among the Nine, there is a reluctance afterwards to engage in a new round of consultations with the Fifteen, that is, within the NATO framework. Moreover, the Nine may find that they have little freedom of manoeuvre left, so sometimes the line of least resistance is adopted: that is, informal consultation with the United States, which is too big to be ignored. Other allies are left to adapt themselves to a practical *fait accompli*. The answer in these circumstances is not to give up the consultation, but rather to make sure that the diplomats are both sensitive to the problem and strong enough physically to endure the extra rounds of discussions which must be entailed. This is just an extra price which has to be paid, if the interests of the eight members of the Community who are also members of NATO are to be kept internally harmonious. The risk, if one fails to observe these requirements, will be some kind of disassociation and unhappiness on the part of those NATO countries for whom political consultation with the allies is important, particularly Norway and Canada.

This is, moreover, not only a problem with NATO; it will arise with increasing frequency in all international negotiating forums. If one gets used to the practice of negotiations with one's own allies, the force of habit is likely to help one to develop the same practices with countries which are not immediate allies — countries like Japan, whose responsibilities and policies in the world are such that they should not be ignored.

Finally, a brief word about mechanisms. I have to put this in terms of Canadian experience, because Canada in many ways is suffering from problems which are going to be experienced in Europe. Canada is actually physically larger than the enlarged Community and distance alone causes a substantial modification in political attitudes. Canada also differs from the United States, because its constitutional practice has not evolved in the centralist way in which it has in the United States and also because it has far fewer provinces than the Americans have states: indeed, it has only one more than there are states within the European Community. What has been happening in Canada in the post-war period is that increasingly activities have been taking place at an international level and are the subject of negotiation and agreement, and therefore the provinces are being forced into foreign affairs; and Canada is being obliged to innovate in order to find ways of accommodating to this new necessity. For example, it is being forced to develop techniques of consultation between the federal government and provincial governments in ways that were not only considered unnecessary but were more or less ruled out by the constitution; and this is really the development of techniques close to that of the Davignon type of consultation. Nowadays, delegations to international conferences include representatives of the federal government and of the provincial governments, and the problem arises of reconciling differences where these are based on divided powers between the federal and provincial governments. Canada is being forced to develop a new technique in order to give expression to this situation. One of the most interesting and complex is that of representation abroad. The provinces, because Canada was an amalgam of several colonies, had traditionally had representation in London, some of this going back before the Federation was established; so it is not strange to have the provinces represented abroad by their own officials who have not, in the legal sense, diplomatic status, but who are nevertheless quite clearly performing a function which is analogous to that of diplomatic representation. Traditionally the emphasis in these provincial offices has been on commerce and immigration, but as the range of involvement of the provinces has grown enormously so the range of interests of these offices is also growing. This is not the place to go in detail into this development, but I raise it because I think that within the Community Europe is going to have to accept the same ambiguous arrangements for representation abroad. It already has a few information offices abroad of which the most important is in Washington, but this is a process which has to be looked at extremely pragmatically. Canadian experience certainly suggests that one can proceed with two levels of representation, federal and provincial; and although this is complicating, and particularly complicating where each level of government is sovereign in its own field of activity, it works relatively effectively and can work even better. It is also worth noting that the United Nations has a broad system of representation through resident representatives abroad, who seem to be doing important and essential work. I suggest that the Community must be prepared to move in this direction, and that just as Canada has had to resist those purists who argue that sovereignty is indivisible and therefore the practice is impossible, so I think that the European Community must take up the same struggle.

Chapter XXII

Institutions for Interdependence

MAX KOHNSTAMM

MUTUAL COMPREHENSION AND UNDERSTANDING between Western Europe and the U.S. have been the basis of the post-war order. Today, the prevailing mood in the Atlantic world is one of growing unease and recrimination. The twin dangers of U.S. troop reductions, resulting in diminishing credibility of the U.S. nuclear guarantee, and of a monetary and trade free-for-all, threaten the very basis of Western European–American relations.

It comes naturally to us at times of political uncertainty to question the validity of our institutions, and to seek ways of improving them. Institutions, however, are not a panacea for political difficulties. They are at the same time the expression of a consensus on how a nation or a community of nations wants to manage its affairs, and a limited guarantee for the continuity of this consensus. If, however, such consensus breaks down, institutions become little more than forums for dramatising diverging views.

Institutions suited for the complex tasks of Atlantic political life in the coming decade and beyond, therefore, presuppose in the first place a consensus concerning the nature of the tasks ahead. Without this, no technical device for improving communications, for speeding up decision-making, etc., can give results.

When speaking about Atlantic affairs it is customary to give considerable space to the one institution which is exclusively Atlantic, namely NATO, and to give pride of place to the security community in which the U.S. and Western Europe have lived for three decades. Economic issues, from this perspective, are treated with a certain amount of impatience; they are seen as an irritating extraneous factor which impinges on the central and serious business of Atlantic solidarity, which is first of all a security solidarity. But in the present climate of relative *détente* between the U.S. and the Soviet Union, and as a result of the growing importance of *internal* social problems, demanding priority of attention of political leaders for *internal* problems, this way of looking at things does not help to solve our problems. On the contrary, a belief in the primacy of security politics leads to the ineffective advice to the policy-maker to practise moderation in economic matters, so as not to jeopardise for the sake of fractions of per cents of GNP a much more important security relationship. But management of bread and butter issues in European–American affairs may well assume a place akin to that which these issues have already in domestic and European Community affairs – on condition, of course, that the present stalemate *détente* on the northern half of our globe continues. Therefore, the security relationship is threatened more by economic difficulties than by problems arising out of the functioning of NATO. What is striking about the Atlantic Alliance is rather the continuing ability of its institutions to deal with current security problems. The greatest problem in the decade ahead, on both sides, will be to convince public opinion that good *détente* management implies the maintenance of a military capability strong enough to discourage on the Soviet side any brinkmanship, or any attempt to convert internal tensions into external pressures. The road from the present *status quo* to real security and co-operation between East and West will be long. Progress implies changes within Soviet society itself. We shall also see profound changes in our nations and societies! Our hope is that these changes will be gradual and peaceful. *Détente* management means giving these changes a chance, by joint Western diplomacy which knows when to be cautious and when to be generous, which grants successes to the constructive elements in the Soviet establishment, and denies successes to the maximalist. The conduct of a joint diplomacy – only partially institutionalised through NATO ministerial meetings and bi-weekly caucuses in Helsinki – is working well. As in military matters, the professionals are able to cope with the "high" politics of the Atlantic Alliance – as long as domestic politics do not intrude.

But the second precondition of *détente* management is that the strength of the Alliance must still be ensured. If in the past we understood this to mean ever-growing political and military integration of NATO, today, and in the new mood of Alliance politics, this simple prescription is as ineffective as it is unrealistic. The first condition of a sound political relationship in Atlantic security matters is a strong Europe; one that by its own efforts, through increased military efficiency and cohesion, becomes a valuable partner for the U.S., a partner who has something to offer; and a Europe which is not so internally divided and dependent on American goodwill that it tempts the U.S. to extort a high political and economic price for its security guarantee. Thus it is pointless to speak of improving Atlantic institutions unless and until this structural precondition for a sound political relationship has been created. Only a self-confident Europe and a U.S. whose power is not so absolute as to corrupt can form the basis of a sound Atlantic security relationship in the future.

Thanks to proven flexibility and basic strength of the present NATO structure, the institutional machinery to accompany such an increased "bi-polarity" should continue to evolve pragmatically rather than be submitted to a deliberate attempt to redesign it. The consensus on which such an enterprise would have to rest will remain fluid and uneven. Loose ends – France, Ireland, Scandinavia, non-EEC Southern Europe – will remain. The moment of truth – an integrated European defence and its relationship with the U.S. – is a long time off. In the meantime much can be done by "adhocery": the Eurogroup, naval co-operation in the Mediterranean, etc. But it is within Europe, in the speed with which a common defence commitment is given sufficiently concrete manifestation to create a bargaining situation where balance leads to restraint, and where strength attracts strength, that the true institutional development of the Atlantic Community must occur. In this last respect the task of restructuring the political framework for economic politics resembles that of security politics. In other respects the problems are more fundamental.

A first notion, implicit in many recent proposals for improving the Atlantic political machinery, must be discarded at the outset: that improved means of communication, a more intensive dialogue between Europe and America, would help to moderate the present crisis in economic relations. Dialogue there has been – between Commissioners and special U.S. representative for trade, between European and U.S. Heads of State, in GATT and the IMF, even in the comparatively intellectual context of the OECD's Rey Committee of wise men. The extensiveness of the dialogue has not prevented opposing views remaining unchanged – except for some movement on the monetary front. Perhaps a diagnosis of the present difficulties which goes beyond the enumeration of specific grievances may give some explanation for this failure. Before discussing institutional reform one must make sure that the problems which such institutions will have to deal with are understood.

Two factors seem to stand out as causes for the crisis of the post World War II economic order. One is a structural shift in the distribution of power, or rather in the role of the U.S. power in European–American relations. It is of course commonplace to point out that Western Europe has achieved near-parity with the U.S. in economic affairs. What is perhaps less commonly realised is that the shift of the U.S. position from being *primus inter pares* to being more nearly an equal among equals has robbed the post-war system of an essential prop, that of an arbiter and guardian of the rules. This means that the interpretation of rules is increasingly becoming a matter of national (or European Community) discretion. For a long time, U.S. leadership and the joint stake of Europe and the U.S. in the maintenance of order ensured widespread compliance with the rules. Today, consensus concerning the equity of these rules is being eroded, and freedom of national choice is given priority over compliance with international rules.

The erosion of consensus is as important a cause of the present crisis as the abdication of the U.S. as guarantor of the international economic system of which it was the main architect. But this erosion should not simply be laid at the door of national selfishness made possible through the more relaxed state of East–West relations. The more fundamental reason for the breaking and bending of international rules is the growing inadequacy of what has been an international night-watchman state to satisfy the social and political requirements of our day.

The contradiction between domestic economic policy, which involves both regulation of the economic activity and intervention by the state to temper the impact of market forces on weak sections of the population, branches of industry, or regions – the contradiction between this and an international economic system whose sole aim was to increase welfare through maximising market forces through an ever more perfect international division of labour, could only last as long as the impact of external market forces did not impinge too much on internal national policy objectives. Paradoxically, the last decade has seen at the same time a trend towards ever more far-reaching responsibility taken by each national government for the welfare of its citizens, and an equally pronounced trend towards a decreasing ability to cope with the effects of the extra-national environment.

The lessened role of the U.S. as guarantor of world order has magnified and precipitated the present crisis. However, it is important to realise that this crisis has objective causes, and that we have to face up to this very real cause for the decline of the post-war international economic order: the growing tension between national economic objectives and international *laissez-faire*. To be effective, institutional reform must enable us to cope with this tension.

Liberalisation has been achieved fairly recently – in the late '50s. Multinational business and multinational banking have seized the opportunities of this new liberalised world. They have not only increased the speed and magnitude of the exchanges of goods and capital, but also added a very important new element: namely the exchange of knowhow, speeding up the impact of local technological advances on the world economy.

The speed of change which is imposed on the structure of national economies through the impact of the international economy has altered both the economic and political context in which the existing institutions of the industrialised world have to work. Change brings with it real diseconomies – the cost of shifting factors of production, the premature write-off of capital goods, and the shift of the labour force away from activities declared uneconomic by the verdict of the international market.

Since in the short run the political costs to a government which sustains the liberal world system against the pleas of the victims of the market are often high, a growing number of exceptions is being made for this or that sector of economic activity. Increasingly, two much more formidable instruments of economic intervention than tariffs are distorting trade. The first instrument is quantitative restrictions: quotas, "voluntary" restrictions imposed on others, and safeguard clauses applied at national discretion. The second is domestic support policies: to shipbuilding, high technology industry, textiles and agriculture, etc. The implications of these phenomena are not always realised: the decision about who produces what is no longer left to the anonymous market, but for a growing number of products becomes a matter of discretion of public authorities.

The room for and effectiveness of such national discretion, however, depends on the degree to which the rest of the international community continues to play by the old rules. As soon as everyone intervenes, the international market becomes a place of direct or indirect inter-government competition and bargaining. To dramatise what is happening, one could say that for an

increasing number of products, the amount and direction of
international trade is beginning to be determined by methods
which begin to resemble those of Comecon. The new emphasis
on bilateral balancing of trade, and of balancing it with specific
commodities, proves this trend.

Comecon, whatever its shortcomings, has the advantage that it
knows what it is trying to do. Priority is given to internal planning goals; trade is the carefully controlled residual. In the West,
free trade rhetoric and night-watchman institutions co-exist with
the new reality of a politically bargained international division
of labour.

Within our domestic economies, the notion that the market
can be the sole arbiter of economic life is no longer accepted,
and intervention into economic life has become accepted practice. Leaving aside the theoretical debate as to whether the
market alone can assure an optimum allocation of wealth and
opportunity in the international economy, we must recognise that
the choice made in the preceding decades for domestic use has
destroyed the theoretical condition for a pure free trade
approach: that prices reflect real factor costs. That condition
has been strongly affected not only by specific intervention in
sectors of economic activity but also by distortions in the relationship between export and import prices as a result of badly
adjusted exchange rates. But even if prices were to assure the
welfare benefits of the international division of labour, the strains
on the free trade system would not disappear, because the diseconomies caused by accelerated change mentioned earlier
remain.

This situation should not lead to a rejection of international
interdependence but to a realisation that this interdependence
has to be given a political, and hence ultimately an institutional,
framework, which may well have to be as different from the
present one, as the modern administration of a state is from that
of the 19th century.

Rejecting the market as the only economic regulator and sole
distributor of wealth and opportunity must bring a whole range
of new and vital issues into the realm of international decision-
making. It demands joint international decisions on who produces what – taken deliberately, and not as the result of competitive dumping of each other's subsidised products with the
inevitable quantitative restrictions which are its results. It demands establishing common and accepted standards for making
exceptions (which means saddling others with their conse-

quences), standards which should distinguish between socially and purely mercantilistically motivated distortions. It involves accepting a *droit de regard* of others on internal policy-making, and the right of other nations to suggest alternative strategies to achieve national objectives; this being a reasonable requirement of those outside national borders who have to share the burden of policies taken within these borders. This is a far cry from the present practice of declaring one's internal policies to be non-negotiable. It may mean, eventually, positive steps of joint policy-making: indicative planning for investment threatened by overcapacity and an orderly transfer of capacity in certain industries to less developed countries. These tasks go far beyond those actually assumed by the international institutions designed to maintain economic order both between the industrialised countries of Europe and America, and in the world in general.

Institutional reform *must* come to grips with these new problems – at least if this diagnosis of our present troubles is correct. The institutions needed in the present situation will require more, not less, submission by "sovereign" decision-makers to a common discipline. However, today, the trend is in the opposite direction, towards more claims of sovereign determination concerning everyone's own affairs.

What is to induce governments to sit down together and to get to grips with this very difficult problem of managing the world economy? The odds that they will do so seem poor. But the risk of continuing the present trend towards competitive economic policy-making is very great. The claim for sovereign determination of each participant's own economic destiny will result in a dramatic shift towards autarky. For the enlarged Community with a trade/GNP ratio of below 10 per cent (and even lower if its preferential trading partners are taken into account), such a choice is theoretically not much less possible than for the U.S. But this choice would create very great tensions within the European Community and would furthermore seriously endanger the security interests of both the U.S. and Western Europe. Protectionism rapidly becomes a state of mind. And this state of mind is even more dangerous than the loss of efficiency resulting from protectionist measures. Furthermore, the impact of a hedgehog attitude of Europe and America on the third world would be disastrous: only a joint effort can lead to policies and measures mitigating the growing economic tension between north and south.

Governments will have to be made to realise the high price

of continuing the present trend, or else they will not devote the considerable energies needed to get to grips with the present rapidly deteriorating situation.

The first and crucial step has to be taken in the monetary field. Distortions caused by the dollar standard – never envisaged by the Bretton Woods system – must be eliminated. Better and speedier monetary adjustment, matching the speed of economic change, will do much to eliminate a major source of global price distortion which has prevented the market from contributing effectively to equilibrium. Furthermore, international liquidity, long talked about in terms of trade needs, must be treated in terms analogous to domestic liquidity: as a global co-determinant of inflation.

In matters of international trade the old system still provides us with an essential tool for international agreement: comparative advantage can and should remain the *measure of equity* in the international division of labour, the standard against which departures are measured, discussed, and agreed upon. This latter point is the crux of the matter, the precondition for a turning away from increasing unilateralism to a new system of rules. Exceptions are now decided upon unilaterally, one economic power trying to force its preferred solution on the others, including the third world. But this makes for a senseless zero-sum game, that may soon turn into a negative-sum game for all participants. Only a co-operative approach, attacking the problems that have arisen over the last decade by means of increasing joint management, and decreasing unilateral decisions can lead us towards a new positive-sum game.

As was pointed out in a joint report of a group of outstanding Americans, Europeans and Japanese,[1] the European Community has a very special responsibility in turning the tide. Jean Monnet has often pointed out that co-operation does not come naturally to human beings, or their collectives, but only as a result of necessity. Fortunately, the necessity produced by the cold war is diminishing in influence. *Vis-à-vis* Europe, the U.S. has behaved in the post-war quarter of a century with remarkable foresight, not to say generosity. But in the long run an equitable order cannot be maintained only on the basis of goodwill – it needs the basis of countervailing power. Even if its economic position is relatively reduced, the U.S. is still by far the strongest power in the world, and the one least affected by the economic actions of

---

[1] *Tripartite report: Reshaping the international economic order* (The Brookings Institution, Washington, December 1971).

others. Its monetary freedom is near absolute. It can live without international trade more easily than any of the others. Its military power gives it additional weight even in the economic field. It is therefore not unnatural that there seems to be a growing tendency in the U.S. to use the opportunities of the U.S. position to the full and in ways not conducive to establishing a new international economic order.

Under these circumstances, what should be done? As has been pointed out already, it is not lack of consultation on an official level that has led to the present situation. And there is little reason to think that institutional engineering such as fusing GATT and IMF would be helpful. Would a summit, be it European–American, or tripartite and including Japan, provide the solution? As *The Economist* has put it: "there is going to be a lot more whizzing about by all concerned. The question is whether there is the necessary leadership at the top, on both sides of the Atlantic, and particularly in Europe, to pull all the various whizzings together" (3 March 1973).

I should like to suggest that two conditions have to be fulfilled to make the "whizzing" fruitful. The first is a thoroughgoing analysis of the new problems that are upon us related to the clash between internal objectives, fixed independently by each nation, and the demands of international division of labour based on liberal principles. A correct analysis most certainly does not, by itself, solve a problem. But without a prior attempt to define anew common objectives, negotiations cannot succeed. And the objectives today are not simply free trade, but free trade combined with a socially acceptable rate of change.

The second condition, indicated by *The Economist*, can only be fulfilled by *European* action. A summit? Yes – but between whom? We have seen – and undoubtedly will see more of the same – U.S.-China and U.S.-S.U. summits. On the European side, however, who will climb to the summit? Nine heads of states, or prime ministers, and a representative of the European Commission to complete the party?

Even if on this particular mountaintop there would be room for so many mountaineers, will the members of the European team agree to make the difficult ascent on one and the same rope? In other words: will they speak with one voice? The tripartite report mentioned earlier rightly stated: "Unless Western European countries act in unity, the European Community will be a stultifying rather than a creative element in the reorganisation of the international economic order."

Unless Western Europe speaks with one voice, there will be no countervailing power to U.S. power, hence no real dialogue and no real summit. No change in the existing international organisations, no new transatlantic institution, will alter this basic fact.

Without a united Western Europe there is no necessity for the United States to submit to the discipline of jointly established rules. Without countervailing power no nation in the long run will refrain from imposing on others what it sees as its interest. If the nations of Western Europe do not unite, they should not be amazed to see this happen in their relations with the U.S. But solutions imposed by one side in default of the countervailing power of an equal partner are unlikely to keep the world economy reasonably open and may well destroy the U.S.–European security relationship, which will be just as essential for safe and constructive *détente* management in the next decade as it was for maintaining peace in the troubled and tense decade after World War II. Charity begins at home; institutions for interdependence require first of all the ability of Western Europe to organise itself.

There was a famous book written in America with the wonderful title *How to Stay in Business Without Delivering the Goods.* Well, Europe has been doing that for 25 years now, *vis-à-vis* the Americans who thought that we were going to unite and to be someone in the international discussion. In my view it has been a magnificent feat to stay in business for nearly 25 years without really delivering the goods, but I do not believe that this can be limitless.

We are therefore faced I think with a formidable choice over the next couple of years. Either we see, coming out of the three points I have mentioned, tensions which influence each of our countries in a different way, and the countries will fall apart; or, we shall see these tensions push us to something which is then much closer to political union than we seem to think possible now. Either we deliver the goods now, or we are going to go out of business. And on that depends the European–American relationship, much more than on a reshuffling or a reorganisation of the existing institutions. If there is not a centre with which America can talk, then we should not be surprised that the real talk will be with places where a man like Henry Kissinger can fly to and do business: it will not be on a summit which is so clouded that everyone is in danger of falling off.

COMMENT *by Mary T. W. Robinson*

Looking down from any typical conference platform, what one sees are grey hairs on those who still have hair, or a lot of bald heads and a lot of austere and grey suits. This, I think, illustrates the problem of the generation gap and involving young people. The language in which this problem is discussed is to a large extent language that is no longer relevant to the majority, the young. Very few citizens of either Europe or America at the moment, in their individual capacity, are interested in foreign policy. It has got a rather dirty name, and this has a good deal to do with problems such as Vietnam. It is not a matter of interest to the individual. Furthermore, there is no dream any more and very little idealism: Europe has become a habit – a habit not carved out by the younger people, but passed on to them; and either they are against it or it doesn't really interest them very much. We need, I think, very seriously and very quickly to rethink the whole problem and to reinvolve young people. I myself do not believe that that is necessarily impossible or very difficult. It would involve a different sort of emphasis.

The problem is that national governments have to cope with the individual demands and that individuals in the different countries are concerned about the bread-and-butter issues. I think that this is common to the countries of Europe and America. They are concerned with rising prices, inflation, employment, social welfare benefits, environment, pollution in the cities: these are what the problems really are, and therefore no government can talk in terms of increasing a defence budget as such or talk about security divorced from these issues. It is not a priority to the citizens: it is not something they are going to allow large sums of money to be directed towards; and there is no way of convincing public opinion except through what concerns public opinion. The difficulty is to redefine what the real scope of the whole world problem is, and how it can be approached in a way which is meaningful to the vast majority of the young people who are growing up in Europe and who are going to inherit and hopefully participate in this process. Given these facts, the only way in which dynamism and commitment can be got from young people is not in terms of Europe and America working out a better plan for themselves: it can only be in terms of a real commitment to the developing countries, a real understanding of the absolute necessity to think not in terms of east–west, or west–west, but in terms of north–south, in terms not of a patronising neo-colonial relationship, but of a real commitment.

There is one European spokesman at the moment who does appeal to youth, and he is Sicco Mansholt. He gets through to them: he can get a response from young people, and he could get a response from the average citizen who is not otherwise interested in foreign policy, because current foreign policy has been a cold and rather brutal exercise. The unifying force of the Second World War is now gone completely and we are a post-war generation, which did not live through it and is not interested in it and has not got the same fears and the same dynamism for creating the Europe that existed in the '50s. We need a new dynamism; we need the subject discussed in these terms and not in terms of ironing out the economic problems of the super-powers and creating a better international trade situation. This direction towards the third world, in a very real sense, in a sense which hurts America and hurts Europe and forces compromise, is the way to iron out the conflicts in a political framework. The motivation of superpowers is selfishness, but let the language that is used be an understanding of the selfish necessity to solve the ever-widening gap between the wealthy countries and the third world, and let the effect be a manageable world order giving justice and security. If governments and those speaking in the media began to talk, not about foreign policy, but about the necessity for this commitment in real terms, this would not be idealistic, but realistic. There is an enormous crisis, a personal crisis between people of a certain level who built up Europe, who had a certain understanding, and the majority of young people, who do not buy the system and who very badly need to be involved because they are very many and it is they who carry on the process. The only way to channel this into an inter-national framework is by creating a better structure for the third world countries, by bridging this enormous economic gap, and by involving the richer and more powerful countries, if necessary, in a painful way, in this dynamic process.

COMMENT *by Cyrus R. Vance*

At the present, the economic and monetary issues are at the fore and they raise real and important problems. We should recognise, however, that there also exist a number of political and security issues which can be divisive in European–American relations. Although these issues have received less press attention than the economic questions, they can be of major consequence in the period ahead. In focusing on these issues, I am not arguing for the primacy of security politics. Let me add that I applaud the progress which has been made in reaching a progressing *détente* between East and West and wholeheartedly support vigorous continuation of these efforts. With this background, let me turn to some of the political and security aspects of Atlantic relations which I suggest deserve further mention before commenting on the institutions required to deal with them. The first stage of SALT dealt almost exclusively with the Soviet–American strategic relationship, but the next round is likely to involve issues of more direct consequence to Western Europe. For example, it is doubtful that the question of forward based systems can be avoided. These, as you know, are aircraft and missiles based mainly in West Germany and on carriers in the Mediterranean. They are viewed by European governments as part of the common defence. Any negotiations with the Soviet Union on these forward systems will require the closest co-ordination with all Western Allies as the reduction or elimination of these systems in Europe would necessitate changes in the presently agreed NATO strategy. Another potentially difficult issue in SALT 2 is the Soviet proposal barring the transfer of nuclear technology to other nuclear powers. This could raise difficult questions for the continuation of the United States–U.K. atomic exchange agreement. A second sensitive area is the upcoming negotiations on mutual and balanced force reduction. These negotiations will be slow and complex. They involve the national forces and military doctrines of over a dozen nations. There is a question, however, whether these negotiations will produce sufficient results and early enough to continue to forestall the pressure in the United States Congress for major unilateral reductions. If the United States should be forced to make unilateral reductions, while the MBFR discussions are still under way, this could become a source of deep division between Western Europe and the United States. Then there is the conference on security and co-operation in Europe. The West is now committed to this conference which will discuss political, economic, cultural and military issues. I certainly welcome the fact that it is to take place. This will require an early determination of objectives, however, and much greater co-ordination than at present exists of Western policy towards Eastern Europe and the Soviet Union. Without this co-ordination the strains among the Europeans and the U.S. could become difficult.

If this analysis is at least partially correct, what can be done about it? I do not purport to have any magic prescription; but I do have a few suggestions as to how these issues might be dealt with from an institutional standpoint.

First, it almost goes without saying that there must be a proper view, within the alliance, of the European aspects of SALT 2. Moreover, as a continuing matter, these aspects of SALT will require improved co-ordination of Western policy. The past mechanism of consultations in NATO before and after every stage of negotiation worked quite well, but it is clear that that mechanism will not be adequate to deal with such questions as the forward based systems, and the non-transfer of nuclear technology.

Secondly, I would suggest that we must be increasingly sceptical as to whether we should rely upon the MBFR negotiations alone to deal with the question of future U.S. troop levels in Europe. Those discussions must of course, be pursued with vigour and earnestness. But we should begin now to discuss within the Alliance the level of U.S. troops in Europe over the next several years. We need an early NATO-wide review of force contributions, in a process which would permit some thinning down of American forces without the unravelling of the Alliance, an agreement for the longer term commitment by the U.S.

Thirdly, a more intensively co-ordinated, if not common, approach to future political relations, trade, technology and other policies towards Eastern Europe and the Soviet Union is important if we are to avoid divisions which could arise from the European Security Conference. The United States would strongly support the evolution of the European Economic Community and such other European institutions as the Eurogroup and the Davignon Committee. With respect to new or modified institutions, there has been some discussion of an Atlantic summit. It seems to me that such a proposal does present many problems, but perhaps if it were well prepared and held not more than once a year, it might be worthwhile. I think that at present NATO ministerial meetings are held twice a year. A possibility worth consideration would be a meeting of the foreign, defence, and treasury ministers of the Alliance countries every six months. One session might be primarily devoted to economic-monetary questions, and the next to political-security issues, with certain degrees of flexibility depending on the needs of the moment.

Whatever format is adopted, the essential point is that the inter-relationship between these questions must be more widely recognised than at present. There are undoubtedly other insti-tutional changes which will be required by the changing con-ditions, and these must develop by an evolutionary process. There is no reason for it to stop.

FINAL COMMENT *by Richard Mayne*

The debate continues; but there our symposium ends. Since it was completed, several of its participants have acquired new and greater responsibilities. A number of their prophecies have been dramatically fulfilled – notably in the field of energy. We are all now living in a still more dangerous world. Some land-marks have disappeared; some statesmen have left office; some policies have altered. But in the second half of the 1970s, the basic needs we face remain the same, although they have been highlighted. We still need to organise our world of interdepend-ence. We still need to turn our back on beggar-my-neighbour policies. We still need to meet the challenge of world poverty. And all these things we shall best do by pursuing the goals we long ago set ourselves: unity in Europe, Atlantic partnership, the unison of the West, and dialogue with the East. The truth is no less vital for being familiar.

Index

Printed in Great Britain by Northumberland Press Limited, Gateshead